Contents

Teaching
Generation
M

A HANDBOOK
FOR LIBRARIANS
AND EDUCATORS

Edited by

Vibiana Bowman Cvetkovic and Robert J. Lackie

Neal-Schuman Publishers, Inc.
New York   London

Published by Neal-Schuman Publishers, Inc.
100 William St., Suite 2004
New York, NY 10038

Printed and bound in the United States of America.

The paper used in this publication meets the minimum requirements of American National Standard for Information Sciences—Permanence of Paper for Printed Library Materials, ANSI Z39.48-1992.

Library of Congress Cataloging-in-Publication Data

Teaching Generation M : a handbook for librarians and educators / edited by Vibiana Bowman Cvetkovic and Robert J. Lackie.
        p. cm.
    Includes bibliographical references and index.
    ISBN 978-1-55570-667-8 (alk. paper)
    1. Young adults' libraries—Information technology. 2. Generation Y. 3. Technology and youth. 4. Libraries and teenagers. 5. Internet in young adults' libraries. 6. Education—Effect of technological innovations on. 7. Educational technology. 8. Information literacy.
I. Cvetkovic, Vibiana Bowman, 1953- II. Lackie, Robert J., 1966-

Z718.5.T43 2009
027.62'6—dc22

                                                          2009017658

Part II: The World of Gen M: A Culture of Technology

Chapter 14. Technology and Pedagogy: The Best of Both for Gen M Students 253

Chapter 15. Teaching Gen M Through Cooperative Learning 265

Chapter 16. Screencasting: Extending Your Educational Environment 277

Preface

MILLENNIALS AT THE MILLENNIUM

At the outset of this book, we feel obliged to play devil's advocate and to challenge the assumptions and generalizations upon which this work rests: first, that a new generational cohort exits—Gen M; and, second, that its members are computer-savvy technophiles whose lives are encompassed by gadgetry. Only by teasing out the myths and realities regarding a new generation of students can we thoughtfully adapt various media or technology for educational purposes. The key here, and the purpose of this book, is to facilitate thoughtful planning for teaching Gen M—planning which brings about new and powerful learning opportunities for student and teacher alike.

The *Oxford English Dictionary* has recently (September 2008) added as part of its definition for the term "millennial" its use as a noun to describe the "millennial generation." The *OED* credits the Strauss and Howe (1991) book, *Generations*, with the first use of the term (*OED*, accessed 2009). From the late 1990s onward, major business, political, and cultural writers in key media outlets such as *Business Week, Wall Street Journal, New York Times,* and *Rolling Stone* have all acknowledged the existence of this group as a unique cohort and have attempted to define who these young people are and how they are different from prior generations. The names for this group have varied from Net Gen to Gen Next to Gen Y, but now seem to have coalesced around Generation Media or Generation Millennial or Gen M; hence, the title of this book—*Teaching Generation M: A Handbook for Librarians and Educators.*

Gen M now (at the end of the first decade of the new millennium) ranges in age from adolescents entering (or soon to enter) high school (those born at the end of the era in the mid-to-late1990s) to young adults entering the work force (those born at the start of the era in the early 1980s). Members of Gen M are characterized as adept multitaskers, adroit with technology, and abysmal at sustaining long attention spans. Howe and Strauss state unequivocally that Gen M as a group exhibits a unique set of traits quite distinct from previous generations:

> As a group, Millennials are unlike any other youth generation in living memory. They are more numerous, more affluent, better educated and more ethnically diverse. More important, they are beginning to manifest a wide array of positive social habits that older Americans no longer associate with youth, including a new focus on teamwork, achievement, modesty and good conduct. Only a few years from now, this can-do youth revolution will overwhelm the cynics and pessimists. (Howe and Strauss, 2000: 4)

Howe and Strauss' words seem prescient in light of the 2004 and 2008 presidential election in the United States, where young voters (18–29) turned out in larger numbers than in any recent presidential election (Tankersley, 2008). Very recently, authors and political bloggers Michael Hais and Morley Winograd declared that Gen M represents "a new, large and dynamic generation and the realignment of American politics for the next 40 years . . . welcome to the Millennial Era" (Hais and Winograd, 2008).

Advertisers and marketers are paying close attention to the habits and personality traits of Gen M as well. One estimate puts the Gen M population at 64 million Americans with disposable income. *Women's Wear Daily* reports that from April 2007 through April 2008 Gen M women spent $33.7 billion on clothes—outspending Gen X and Baby Boomers (Tran, 2008). Retailers, like political strategists, are sitting up and taking notice of Gen M as a power bloc. Likewise, cultural critics, sociologists, and marketers all seem in agreement that Gen M represents a true generational cohort. Is it fair or accurate, then, to paint them in broad generalities as wired, multitasking, screenoriented, media-saturated youths?

The Trouble with Generational Generalities

In discussing any age cohort, be it the Greatest Generation (born between 1901 and 1924), Baby Boomers (1946–1965), or Gen M (1980–1999), it is customary to generalize that group's personality characteristics in broad strokes: members of the Greatest Generation are self-sacrificing, patriotic, and have a strong work ethic; Baby Boomers are idealistic, antiauthoritarian, and individualistic; Gen Ms are tech-savvy multitaskers with short attention spans (Lee, 2006). Critics of such sweeping generalizations are quick to point out that such descriptions seem closely akin to personality traits assigned to astrological signs.

This is not to say that members of an age cohort share no characteristics. Specific historical events, such as the attack on Pearl Harbor, the assassination of John F. Kennedy, and the acts of terrorism on September 11, serve as flashpoints of cultural change and have iconic and generation-defining meaning; but subgroups, as well as individuals within a generation, will have radically different interpretations and experiences of their cultural touchstones. George W. Bush and Al Gore, Cheech Marin and Rush Limbaugh, Sarah Palin and Janeane Garofalo—all are Baby Boomers. Based on this representative sampling, an interesting debate could be held regarding the shared generational values and vision of the Boomers. The point is to regard generational characteristics with healthy skepticism.

Net Natives and the Digital Divide

Although members of Gen M may indeed share a generational culture and characteristics, they are the most racially and ethnically diverse cohort in American history ("The Coming New Majority," 2008) and indications suggest deep differences among Gen M individuals regarding kind and degree of computer usage. While it is important for academic librarians and teaching faculty to be mindful that the "M" in Gen M does not stand for "monolith," it is also important to understand that many undergraduate students may not be members of Gen M at all. Giancola, Munz, and Trares in their recent study of adult college students found that approximately 73 percent of all postsecondary undergraduates are "nontraditional," i.e., are not full-time 18- to 22-year-old college students. Indeed, a full 30 percent of undergraduates are working adults (Giancola, Munz, and Trares, 2008). Thus assumptions that all college students are "Net-natives" and "grew up digital" may not be true in particular real-life applications. Diversity in undergraduate demographics calls for diversity in pedagogical style, tools, and approaches.

Given the fact that various generations coexist across our school and campus communities and within individual classrooms and libraries, it behooves us all to appreciate the unique perspectives of each other's generation and help each other learn and progress robustly through the twenty-first century. The editors and authors of *Teaching Generation M* fervently hope that the book offers some sociological grounding and understanding of Gen M and how to embrace new media and technologies to help meet our educational plans and goals.

ABOUT THIS BOOK

Teaching Generation M: A Handbook for Educators and Librarians is structured around three questions: Who are the members of Gen M? What is their culture? What educational practices best address their needs? Part I of this book answers the question of "whom." The book begins with the Introduction by Robert J. Lackie, John W. LeMasney, and Kathleen M. Pierce exploring various perspectives on Gen M and their relationship with new media and technology. Chapter 1 by Colleen S. Harris looks at the all-too-real digital divide that still exists despite the seeming ubiquitousness of the home computer. Patricia H. Dawson and Diane K. Campbell (Chapter 2) and Susan Avery (Chapter 3) examine the new literacies that are requisite for understanding, analyzing, and utilizing the flood of information that hits Gen M daily. In Chapter 4, Art Taylor discusses a longitudinal study focusing on the search process performed by Gen M students in a formal, academic setting. Finally, much controversy surrounds how constant-connectivity and multitasking between various media affects the members of Gen M. Michele D'Angelo (Chapter 5) reviews the current scholarly literature and provides some strategies and suggestions for educators based on this research.

Part II looks at the Culture of Technology that is one of the main signifiers of Gen M. A large part of that culture elicits debate over issues of privacy, security, and safety on the Web. These issues also represent areas in which generational differences are most pronounced. Karen J. Klapperstuck and Amy J. Kearns discuss Gen M and their perceptions of the public and private space on the Web in Chapter 6. The Internet tools, popular sites, and popular pastimes embraced by many within the Gen M community are detailed in Chapters 7 through 11. Laurie M. Bridges (Chapter 7) addresses social networking sites, such as Facebook, and their potential educational use. Katie Elson Anderson (Chapter 8) examines the history, uses, and abuses of YouTube. Jeffrey Knapp (Chapter 9) discusses Gen M's dependence on Wikipedia and Google and how that can serve as a springboard to more in-depth research. Nicholas Schiller and Carole Svensson (Chapter 10) discuss gamers and gaming culture. Tyler Rousseau (Chapter 11) looks at a new publishing medium for Gen M—Webcomics. This section closes with futurist Stephen Abram (Chapter 12) presenting an overview of the ecology of a new world that Gen M will inhabit in 2020–2025 and how libraries can be a part of it.

Part III specifically addresses educational theories, practical applications, and best practices. With regard to theory, Lauren Pressley (Chapter 14) discusses concerns regarding the implementation of new technology into the undergraduate curriculum. Chapters 13 and 15 through 19 present specific ideas for tools and technologies to engage Gen M and enhance their educational experience. These include: mobile technology (Boris Vilic and Robert J. Lackie, Chapter 13); cooperative learning strategies (Sharon L. Morrison and Susan L. Webb, Chapter 15); screencasting (Steve Garwood, Chapter 16); Google and Wikipedia (Mitch Fontenot, Chapter 17); the guided research paper (Joseph F. Joiner, Chapter 18); and the First-Year Experience (Beth Larkee, Chapter 19). The book concludes with a cautionary tale regarding teaching and technology and some thoughts for future planning and concerns (Laura B. Spencer and Vibiana Bowman Cvetkovic, Conclusion).

Strauss and Howe point out that at any given point America has extant four generations, a lineup that they refer to as "generational 'constellation'" with each phase constituting approximately 22 years. As the generations age, they shift up one life cycle notch at a time and replace the generation that came before. They further note, "*Whenever the constellation shifts up by one notch, the behavior and attitudes of each phase of life change character entirely* [authors' emphasis]" (Strauss and Howe, 1991: 31). If indeed we are all a part of a generational constellation, it is up to us as educators, librarians, trainers, and administrators, in particular, to provide the very best educational experience we can for our young adults. It is the intention of the editors and authors of this book to contribute in some small way to that effort by promoting understanding and providing some solutions.

REFERENCES

Giancola, Jennifer Kohler, David C. Munz, and Shawn Trares. 2008. "First- Versus Continuing-Generation Adult Students on College Perceptions: Are Differences Actually Because of Demographic Variance?" *Adult Education Quarterly* 58, no. 3 (May): 214–228.

Hais, Michael, and Morley Winograd. 2008. "It's Official: Millennials Realigned American Politics in 2008." *Huffington Post* (November 17). Available: www.huffingtonpost.com/michael-hais-and-morley-winograd/its-official-millennials_b_144357.html (accessed January 8, 2009).

Howe, Neil, and William Strauss. 2000. *Millennials Rising: The Next Great Generation*. New York: Vintage Books.

Lee, Jo Ann. 2006. "Generational Differences in the Workforce." Presentation at the Career-banding Implementation and HR Innovations Conference UNC-Charlotte, Charlotte, NC (November 8). Available: www.osp.state.nc.us/CareerBanding/NC%20HR%20JAL%20Presentation.ppt (accessed January 7, 2009).

OED (Oxford English Dictionary). "Millennial." Oxford University Press. Available through subscription: http://dictionary.oed.com (accessed January 8, 2009).

Strauss, William, and Neil Howe. 1991. *Generations: The History of America's Future, 1584 to 2069*. New York: Morrow.

Tankersley, Jim. 2008. "Youth Vote Finally Delivered, and Obama was Beneficiary." *Chicago Tribune* (November 5). Newspaper Source. EBSCOhost. Available through subscription: www.ebscohost.com (accessed January 6, 2009).

"The Coming New Majority." 2008. *America* 199, no. 10 (October 6): 4.

Tran, Khanh T. L. 2008. "Retailing's Sweet Spot: Stores Look to Lure Millennial Generation." *WWD: Women's Wear Daily* 196, no. 2 (July 2). Available through subscription: www.ebscohost.com (accessed January 7, 2009).

Acknowledgments

I (VBC) would like to thank John B. Gibson, friend and colleague from the Paul Robeson Library, for his technical help and assistance. I would also like to thank my husband, Nick, and my personal Gen M cohort (children, Elizabeth, Tatiana, Anna, Natasha, Michael, and David) for their love and support.

I (RJL) would like to thank the faculty and staff of Rider University Libraries—and some of their spouses and good friends—for all their help, advice, and support, with a very special tip of the hat to Julia Whitley, Alicia Jackson, and Walt Campbell. Love and enormous thanks to my wonderful wife Renee, our son Chris, and his wife Amber for giving me great Gen M material, and to all of my family members for putting up with me through the entire process of writing chapters and editing this book.

We, as editors, would also like to thank all the authors who contributed to this book for their hard work and diligence. And finally, we want to thank Sandy Wood, Project Development Editor at Neal-Schuman, for her patience, sage advice, and attention to detail in preparing our manuscript for publication.

PART I:

Defining Gen M

Introduction

The Myths, Realities, and Practicalities of Working with Gen M

Robert J. Lackie
John W. LeMasney
Kathleen M. Pierce

GEN M AS A DEMOGRAPHIC GROUP

"Generation M" ["M" for M(edia), M(illennials), M(obile), M(ultitaskers), M(ultisensory)] is the name applied to young adults born in the early 1980s through the mid-to-late 1990s. Many factors differentiate members of Gen M from their predecessors. One of the most significant is that they are the first generation raised in an era of personal and real-time global information sharing. Conventional wisdom has it that Gen M community members are constantly connected, early adopting, techno-savvy multi-taskers who enthusiastically embrace new technologies and weave them into the fabric of their daily lives. There are real reasons for the stereotype of a wired, techno-savvy high school student or college undergrad, yet we understand that the stereotype masks a more complicated reality. The authors in *Teaching Generation M: A Handbook for Librarians and Educators* respectively explore the complicated and various "realities" for members of Gen M, as well as for those who live and work with them.

Arguably, Gen M's connectivity has created a global youth culture that, as a community, has already impacted culture, politics, and economics. One example is music. Recently, this multibillion dollar industry began to radically change the way it markets, delivers, and promotes musical artists and their products in response to new technologies as well as the changing expectations and purchasing power of the Gen M population. Younger Gen M consumers want to purchase music in digital/downloadable format, and artists can self-promote and hit niche markets through MySpace and YouTube in addition to publishing their music within different mediums on the Web. Rather than relying on more traditional media outlets, Gen Ms worldwide seem to turn to the Web for news and trends while undeniably creating significant trends of their own. They may naturally begin turning to that same source for other kinds of information, such as formal education, scholarly research, and support for their ideas. Without the information and media literacy guidance of educators and librarians, for instance, they may find what appears to them to be legitimate source material and unquestionably accept it as truth (Larkee, Chapter 19).

The Simmons' National Consumer Study (re-named Experian Simmons in 2008), which "uses a patented, multi-frame sample design (U.S. Patent No. 7,246,035) to produce representative measures of consumer behavior and attitudes to products, brands and media among all American adults" (Experian Simmons, 2008), revealed some interesting data in its fall 2005 annual survey—data that may indicate a highly visible minority who represent prevailing assumptions about Gen M, at least Gen M adults. According to the 2005 survey, the Gen M adult population consisted of 18-to-24-year-olds born between 1981 and 1987 and represented 11.3 percent of the total adult group. Simmons reported that only 31.8 percent of Gen M adults had used instant messaging in the previous 30 days, and only 24.4 percent had used the computer to download music (Simmons, 2006). Obviously, then, not all of Gen M members have calloused thumbs and wires sprouting from their ears!

The Digital Youth Project even goes so far as to suggest that the strong relation between generational and technology identity is "an equation that is reinforced by telecommunications and digital media corporations that hope to capitalize on this close identification" (Ito et al., 2008: 4). So, who are the members of Gen M, really? Many myths, realities, and practicalities arise for educators, librarians, and technologists working with Gen M teenagers and young adults in educational and workplace settings. This book is an effort to acknowledge a generation, as well as to make bona fide strides in showing how to use new media and technology for potent learning.

TECHNOLOGY UNITES . . . AND ALSO DIVIDES GEN M

In the early 1960s, media critics, Marshall McLuhan chief among them, began using the term "the global village" (McLuhan, 1964; Wolfe, 2004) very much in reference to television that was seen as a common window into the world. However, with the Internet, the global villager has a mouth as well as eyes and ears because the medium allows for two-way communication and potentially a much more empowered voice in the village. In this global village perspective, humankind is united through technology, a unification that has the potential for good, when it allows intellectual freedom, or evil, when it allows the rise of totalitarian governments. The current globalization of popular culture among teens and young adults serves as evidence that the global village has truly arrived, and many of its inhabitants are Gen M. The long-term effects of the global village on personal and intellectual freedom are yet to be determined, but Gen M's immediate impact can be felt in the speed with which trends in music, fashion, and consumer goods circulate worldwide among the youth community. This cross-cultural impact happens through sharing and updates on personal blogs, social sites like Facebook, and in online discussions below news stories. This speed may be determined by the click of a mouse or the flick of a thumb on a cell phone keypad. There are many kinds of microphones and many kinds of speakers from which the village's voices can be heard.

The rise of a global youth culture is tied to the creation of the Internet and the rise of personal computers. However, it is important to acknowledge the existence of a digital divide between subcultures in the population—those who have easy access to information technology and those who do not. While worldwide personal computing and connectivity via the Web are increasingly the norm, some populations are excluded from thriving aspects of contemporary life like commerce, education, and politics because of their lower socioeconomic status. With the sudden economic realities that have changed our global financial outlook, we each may have entered a lower economic status. For some members of Gen M, access to technology and new media are limited by socioeconomic factors. Perhaps surprisingly, school does not always level that inequity of access. The National Center for Education Statistics

(NCES) reports that only 88 percent of students in inner-city schools can go online compared with 95 to 98 percent of classrooms in non-urban schools (Bausell, 2008). Access to new media and technology is just one factor in creating a digital divide for Gen M students. While contributors to this book embrace various technologies and pedagogical strategies and offer real and practical encouragement, it may be the case that many educators do not employ much new technology or media with curriculum and teaching. There is a rise in the popularity of $300 NetBooks, fairly inexpensive phones far more powerful than the supercomputers of the 1970s, free Open Source software, and cloud computing sites, where Web applications provide free-to-the user advertising supported services (Vilic and Lackie, Chapter 13; Pressley, Chapter 14). We see that, despite our financial outlook, we may still be able to meet Gen M's needs in terms of hardware and software.

With its capacity to unite, new technology can create other class divisions, including within Gen M itself. In *Here Comes Everybody*, Clay Shirky discusses a socioeconomic divide among teens' use of social networking and says ". . . technology doesn't free us from social preferences or prejudices" (2008: 224). Shirky cites the work of social network scholar danah boyd (who does not capitalize her name) demonstrating that Facebook and MySpace reflect divisions in the larger American class structure. Started as a site for college students, Facebook eventually allowed high school students to participate in its social network as college-bound students, while MySpace was a place for "kids who are socially ostracized at school because they are geeks, freaks, or queers," in boyd's words (Shirky, 2008: 225).

There is also a generational divide defined by use of technology that socially and educationally separates adults from younger people. This generational divide seems responsible for a phenomenon that creates what David Buckingham characterizes as a "'digital divide' between in-school and out-of-school use" (Ito et al., 2008: 4). Worrisome, as well, is the apparently increasing gap between children's everyday lives and the emphases of education systems (Ito et al., 2008; D'Angelo, Chapter 5).

Another concern here is that not everyone in Gen M embraces new media in the same way and, as a result, there may be another digital divide emerging, different from those defined by income, location, or generation. The new divide this creates may be one of choice, disinterest or neglect. However, the effect is the same—members of the generation falling outside the cultural or social expectations of that generation. In this case, the gap is between those members of Gen M who participate in social technologies, connectedness, and omnipresence and those who do not. Without participation in the most common activities of their generation (e.g., blogging, Facebook, or texting), some Gen M members may appear to be disconnected with their peers. Therefore, this new kind of digital divide could result, separating the "opt-ins" from the "opt-outs."

SEPARATING MYTH AND HYPE FROM THE REALITIES OF GEN M

The potential of many Gen Ms to use technology effectively so that they can easily and efficiently learn, inform, and share does seem phenomenal (Sweeney, 2006). From a very young age, Gen Ms have existed with technology and been exposed to the ideals of new technologies like social networking and the "Read/Write Web." They also have grown up in constant connection through texting, e-mail, and microblogging. Gen Ms might well regard using these technological tools much the same way that earlier generations thought about pencil and paper, chalkboards, and face-to-face conversation as the primary forms of exchanging information (Sweeney, 2006; Ellison, Steinfield, and Lampe, 2007). The chapters in this book, however, remind us that we cannot generalize or assume that all Gen Ms are uniformly information literate or media literate; nor can we assume that all Gen Ms will have the ability, desire, or interest in using new media and digital tools simply because of generational and cultural possibility (Harris, Chapter 1; Dawson and Campbell, Chapter 2; Avery, Chapter 3).

Because of their characteristic willingness to share their information with the world through new media, richer qualitative and more empirically sound quantitative data-based generational discoveries may be easier with Gen M than any generation that came before it (Ellison, Steinfield, and Lampe, 2007). While friending (digitally befriending) is often a prerequisite to admission, social networks allow digitally active Gen M authors to permit themselves to be discovered in wholly new and public ways, allowing their lives, or the parts of their lives they wish to openly share, to be more readily consumed (Ellison, Steinfield, and Lampe, 2007; Klapperstuck and Kearns, Chapter 6; Bridges, Chapter 7). Publication, in its variety of forms, is not so much a possibility as it is a probability (Klapperstuck and Kearns, Chapter 6; Rousseau, Chapter 11; Garwood, Chapter 16). As a result, research is apt to benefit greatly from the digital sharing so closely associated with Gen M. However, we are finding that despite the generalities about Gen M, like "impatient" and "technologically savvy" (Sweeney, 2006), those generalities are often contingent on the availability of technology as well as the willingness to use it. In addition, Gen M members are sometimes found to be no more or less impatient or technologically savvy than older adults (Thomas, 2008).

GEN M MYTHS

Probably the most common myth about Gen M is the pervading sense that all members are similarly technologically astute and connected. One widespread belief is that all Gen M students are technology aware, information literate, and Read/Write Web literate (Sweeney, 2006; Roberts, Foehr, and Rideout, 2005). Apparently, if you are a 20-year-old, you spend your days blogging, gaming, correcting Wikipedia articles, and updating your status on Facebook, LinkedIn, FriendFeed, and/or 20 other social networks (Bridges, Chapter 7; Knapp, Chapter 9; Roberts, Foehr, and Rideout, 2005; Ellison, Steinfield, and Lampe, 2007; Sweeney, 2006). Gen M members are often believed to have Internet-capable cell phones, omnipresent high-speed Internet access, and an innate sense of Netiquette in both the private and public realms in which they appear (Klapperstuck and Kearns, Chapter 6; Roberts, Foehr, and Rideout, 2005; D'Angelo, Chapter 5). That is, except when they do not have access, do not know what to do with their connectivity, or choose not to be connected (Avery, Chapter 3; Klapperstuck and Kearns, Chapter 6; Vaidhyanathan, 2008).

This kind of empirically controversial argument about the technical birthright of Gen M is no different than arguing that older people do not get technology or that YouTube or Facebook is more effective at entertaining people than it is at teaching people (Vaidhyanathan, 2008; Bridges, Chapter 7; Anderson, Chapter 8). For example, Gen M students may or may not be visual learners who are stimulated by the video-based content that they watch so much (Roberts, Foehr, and Rideout, 2005). They may or may not be driven by the kind of verbal learning that takes place in traditional classroom settings; instead, Gen Ms may be highly motivated by blogging or by social networks and information databases (Ellison, Steinfield, and Lampe, 2007; Taylor, Chapter 4; Avery, Chapter 3; Dawson and Campbell, Chapter 2). They may be most readily engaged by the boundless, navigable style of content and media that they have become accustomed to in the plastic, hyper-realistic gaming worlds that have exploded in popularity during their lifetime (Schiller and Svensson, Chapter 10). They may be more effective at learning in kinesthetic environments, in which case all of the online social network opportunities in the world will likely be ineffective in comparison to a pickup game or a traditional classroom with chairs in a circle. However, due to the assumed need for electronic stimulation (Wallis, 2006), they may believe that in order to belong to their generation they have to leave the circle of chairs behind.

GEN M REALITIES

Sweeney tells us that these impatient, experiential, digital natives are always connected, and need to stay that way (Sweeney, 2006). Thomas counters that technology can add to this perceived impatience and that Gen M is no more impatient than older adults (Thomas, 2008). The reality is that generalizations are flawed, and though there may be a stack of data saying that people of a certain age have certain dispositions, a sample of ten people of that age may render examples to the contrary. It is highly dangerous, as the controversy in the literature suggests, to predetermine the emotional affect, technological capability, or information literacy of a person based on when he or she was born (Thomas, 2008; Vaidhyanathan, 2008; Dawson and Campbell, Chapter 2).

Consider again the Simmons National Consumer Study. Simmons found that of all adults who reported libraries as their primary source for accessing the Internet, only 25.9 percent were from the Gen M population (Simmons, 2006). Gen M adults may or may not use technology beyond social networking sites or snapping photos with a smart phone, but the Simmons' study certainly indicates that they are in or are using libraries and so they can and must be reached there.

Simmons' National Consumer Study provides more hard numbers to pin down some realities. Almost one-third (31.8 percent) of Gen M adults use instant messaging. And the overall number of Gen M adults who had no online activity in the last month was about the same percentage as the other age groups surveyed: 12.1 percent for Gen M; 13.1 percent of adults aged 25 to 49, and 19.9 percent of adults over age 50. Statistically speaking, these percentages are surprising given what we have been told or assume about this generation. Perhaps this may lead educators and librarians to think that Gen M is average when compared with other generations. About one half of all Gen M users access the Internet in more than one place, like home, school, library, and work.

The Simmons Study also addresses Gen M's attitudes toward multitasking (of which they are often accused!). When asked if they agreed with the statement, "It is important to juggle various tasks," only 56 percent agreed with the statement, which gave them an Index of 89 (below average). Considering that the "M" in Gen M has been said to stand for "multitasking," it is interesting to see that only slightly more than half agree that it is an important skill, at least Gen M adults, anyway! Therefore, caution must be taken when speaking about this (and any other) cohort. Not all members of Gen M are technologically motivated and inspired. Some just like to text and socialize because it is fun and cool.

Because of the cultural norms of searching and owning what they find, modifying and mashing up what has come before, and readily making use of that which is available, Gen M's relative understanding of copyright, intellectual ownership, and economics of creativity will be interesting to compare with other generations (Anderson, Chapter 8; Sweeney, 2006; Avery, Chapter 3). The teaching, learning, and understanding that must take place to convey the importance of ethics in relation to information may be one of the largest tasks for librarians, teachers, and technologists working with Gen M (Joiner, Chapter 18). As an extension of their GoodWork Project, Howard Gardner and fellow researchers at Harvard University's Project Zero are delving into adolescents' sense of ethics and fairness related to their own and others' conduct on the Web, and preliminary findings suggest adolescents' ambivalence, even indifference, about what is fair and ethical use and conduct (Viadero, 2008). Another concern of researchers in the Good-Work Project is that students "often underestimate the size of the communities that have access to their personal information online, or they have difficulty mastering the controls on social networking sites that prevent unknown visitors from seeing that information" (Viadero, 2008: 12). The implication is that, despite Gen M's exposure to new media and technology, they might not be safe or savvy users. Working in smaller learning groups with digital components in a safe academic environment may also help to build this skill set, likely a life skill moving forward (Morrison and Webb, Chapter 15).

It is very clear that "M" for mobile also describes this generation who have a lot of exposure to media and often take it with them, where previous generations left it in the car or living room, which may breed a familiarity with media unknown to previous generations (Vilic and Lackie, Chapter 13; Roberts, Foehr, and Rideout, 2005). Because of the increased shorthand of Short Messaging Service (SMS) writing, the casualness of posting and pseudoblogging, and the relaxed writing styles associated with e-mail and other primary forms of writing today, it might be interesting to study those influences on Gen M writers in situations that traditionally call for more formal writing styles (D'Angelo, Chapter 5; Klapperstuck and Kearns, Chapter 6), for instance, the style of writing necessary for research papers or theses.

It is evident that the rigors of scholarship, both in writing and researching, are an acquired taste. No matter how many discussions, disclaimers, or pre-essay warnings are given about the use of non-peer-reviewed articles in their scholarly work, Gen M students may still go with what is most comfortable to them, resorting to Google and Wikipedia to begin their research journeys, even if the Google sites and Wikipedia articles themselves do not ultimately make it into the students' actual bibliographies (Fontenot, Chapter 17; Knapp, Chapter 9; Taylor, Chapter 4). As educators, librarians, and trainers, we must take all the potential realities into account when dealing with this user population.

GEN M PRACTICALITIES

Gen M is highly exposed and connected with media—even those who are less likely to work with computers or the Internet generally have access to media, such as television and movies (Roberts, Foehr, and Rideout, 2005). As a result, educators, librarians, and employers may be able to make a more solid reach for commonality with members of Gen M by focusing on media and media literacy first as a way of making a connection, and then building that out into a more holistic sense of information literacy (Abram, Chapter 12; Avery, Chapter 3; Dawson and Campbell, Chapter 2). However, as the realities of the potential to become an instant celebrity on sites like YouTube emerge, members of Gen M must struggle with issues that go far beyond information literacy into issues of copyright, privacy, and public restraint. In the case of creating original content, perhaps more pressing at the moment is the idea that participation in the media sites requires more than just a browser—it may require a camera, a microphone, a Webcam, and someone to help in the library or classroom to coordinate, train, facilitate, or assist in a student media event—is there still (or was there ever) a budget in your institution for such things? This may be the first question you will need to answer before using media to engage Gen M, or considering the macro issues of copyright, self-image, or digital social presence (Harris, Chapter 1; D'Angelo, Chapter 5; Klapperstuck and Kearns, Chapter 6; Bridges, Chapter 7; Rousseau, Chapter 11; Garwood, Chapter 16).

Despite the digital and generational divides between Gen Ms and their educators and librarians, there seems to be, more than ever, a need for parents, teachers, and librarians to help this younger generation explore new learning adventurously and smartly and to effectively build a strong foundation so that they can be successful in a world of too much information and stimulation, and ever-present technology and advertising (Abram, Chapter 12; D'Angelo, Chapter 5). The Digital Youth Project is deeply concerned about what it perceives as a lack of adult appreciation for youth participation in popular culture that "has created an additional barrier to access for kids who do not have Internet access at home" (Ito et al., 2008: 36). In some ways, Gen Ms have been abandoned by their elders at home and at school who are fearful, frustrated, or both about new media and technology and thus cling to teaching techniques and modalities that are culturally inappropriate and instructionally irrelevant.

Regarding educators' professional development around technology, it has been suggested that once educators can send e-mails and make electronic presentations, many school administrators consider their schools "technology-using" and no longer needing professional development in technology (Borthwick and Pierson, 2008: 20). Research supports the notion that educators who are more actively engaged with their own teaching and learning and integration of technology help their students to become more engaged in their learning, but many educators have yet to be compelled to change basic teaching and learning practices significantly to incorporate technology with curriculum, teaching, and learning (Borthwick and Pierson, 2008). As educators and librarians, the chapter authors describe their experiences connecting technology and pedagogy, especially in the later sections of this book. Their experiences serve as models of developing effective pedagogy first, and then adapting technology to its purposes—learning and accomplishment.

LEARNING AND ENGAGING DIFFERENTLY

Gen M is many things. Individual members of this cohort could be multitaskers, tech-savvy, disinterested in technology (except as a means to an end), impatient, or agents of social change. For those of us who work with these teens and young adults, we have every reason to be excited about the possibilities of what they bring to our educational settings.

What educators, librarians, and technologists must remember is that within the spaces where we learn and work with students and colleagues, there exists a constellation of generations. Designers of learning spaces must keep this at the forefront of their thinking when choosing lighting, furniture, and technology, as one size does not usually fit all, and this is just as true for online or distance learning spaces (Vilic and Lackie, Chapter 13). Emerging research and the work in this book suggest the profound potential for new media and technology to advance intragenerational and intergenerational learning and innovation. The authors in this book discuss and demonstrate how various modalities of teaching and learning address the needs of diverse learners—those who are tech-savvy, those who are not, and everyone in between, regardless of generation of birth.

Just as all educators have always done, we must learn who our students are so we can best help them learn. In order to continue to customize the experience for all those we serve and teach, we must challenge ourselves to work differently. Given the differences among generations and advancements in technology, this book's editors and chapter authors give us a glimpse of how we might begin to understand Gen M and work better—and differently—with them.

REFERENCES

Bausell, Carol Vinograd. 2008. "Tracking U.S. Trends: States Vary in Classroom Access to Computers and in Policies Concerning School Technology." *Education Week* 27, no. 30 (March 27): 39, 42. Available: www.edweek.org/ew/articles/2008/03/27/30trends.h27.html (accessed December 3, 2008).

Borthwick, Arlene, and Melissa Pierson, eds. 2008. *Transforming Classroom Practice: Professional Development Strategies in Educational Technology.* Eugene, OR: International Society for Technology in Education.

Ellison, Nicole B., Charles Steinfield, and Cliff Lampe. 2007. "The Benefits of Facebook 'Friends': Social Capital and College Students' Use of Online Social Network Sites." *Journal of Computer-Mediated Communication* 12, no.

4. Available: http://jcmc.indiana.edu/vol12/issue4/ellison.html (accessed November 29, 2008).

Experian Simmons. "The Experian Simmons National Consumer Study." Experian Marketing Solutions (2008). Available: http://smrb.com/aspx/content. aspx?pid=5&sid=21&page=Methodology_The_Simmons_Methodology (accessed November 17, 2008).

Ito, Mizuko, Heather A. Horst, Matteo Bittanti, danah boyd, Becky Herr-Stephenson, Patricia G. Lange, C. J. Pasco, and Laura Robinson. 2008. *Living and Learning with New Media: Summary of Findings from the Digital Youth Project: Final Report*. The John D. and Catherine T. MacArthur Foundation Reports on Digital Media and Learning (November). Available: http://digitalyouth. ischool.berkeley.edu/report (accessed December 7, 2008).

McLuhan, Marshall. 1964. *Understanding Media: The Extensions of Man*. Cambridge, MA: MIT Press.

Roberts, Donald F., Ulla G. Foehr, and Victoria Rideout. 2005. *Generation M: Media in the Lives of 8–18 Year Olds*. Menlo Park, CA: The Henry J. Kaiser Family Foundation (March 2005). Available: www.kff.org/entmedia/upload/ Generation-M-Media-in-the-Lives-of-8-18-Year-Olds-Report.pdf (accessed November 18, 2008).

Shirky, Clay. 2008. *Here Comes Everybody: The Power of Organizing without Organizations*. New York: Penguin.

Simmons Market Research Bureau. 2006. Simmons Choices 3 [Computer software: CD-ROM]. New York: Simmons Market Research Bureau.

Sweeney, Richard. 2006. "Millennial Behaviors & Demographics." Newark, NJ: New Jersey Institute of Technology (December 22). Available: http://library1. njit.edu/staff-folders/sweeney/Millennials/Article-Millennial-Behaviors. doc (accessed August 18, 2008).

Thomas. "Digital Immigrants Teaching the Net Generation: Much Ado about Nothing?" (September 22, 2008). Available: www.openeducation. net/2008/09/22/digital-immigrants-teaching-the-net-generation-much-ado-about-nothing/ (accessed November 23, 2008).

Vaidhyanathan, Siva. 2008. "Generational Myth: Not All Young People Are Tech-savvy." *Chronicle of Higher Education: The Chronicle Review* (September 19): B7. Available: http://chronicle.com/free/v55/i04/04b00701.htm?utm_ source=cr&utm_medium=en (accessed November 23, 2008).

Viadero, Debra. 2008. "Project Probes Digital Media's Effect on Ethics: Howard Gardner Leads Team Studying Youths' Web Norms." *Education Week* 28, no. 13 (November 19): 1, 12.

Wallis, Claudia. 2006. "The Multitasking Generation." *Time* 167, no. 16 (March 27): 48–55.

Wolfe, Tom. 2004. "McLuhan's New World." *Wilson Quarterly* 28, no. 2: 18–25.

Chapter 1

The Haves and the Have Nots: Class, Race, Gender, Access to Computers, and Academic Success

Colleen S. Harris

INTRODUCTION

It goes without saying that in the twenty-first century information technology literacy is a required component of a useful education that serves our students far beyond their days in the classroom. As educators, it behooves us to be aware of the inequities of access to and ability to use technology that may affect some of our students, a characteristic generally referred to as the "digital divide."

The digital divide as a concept encompasses not just ownership of computers, but disparities in access to the Internet and various information technologies, as well as inequalities in the ability and skills necessary to utilize those technologies effectively. Familiarity with computers and other technologies is increasingly essential to workforce skills, and those suffering from inadequate training, inadequate access, and other factors that suppress the development of computer and technology skills are at a severe disadvantage academically and economically. Those on the losing end of the digital divide are not just out of touch with what's new in cyberspace—they are at a disadvantage in the classroom among peers who come from more technologically privileged backgrounds, they have less experience with critical thinking assignments, and are less likely to compete successfully in the workforce.

In today's classrooms at all levels, educators are faced with students from diverse backgrounds who possess vastly differing skill sets when it comes to utilizing computers and the Internet. Some knowledge of the data behind the digital divide will be useful for those on the front lines dealing with these disparities in ability.

ACCESS

A number of demographic lines can be drawn to demonstrate who has access to computers and the Internet and who does not. When discussing the simple ownership of computers, the U.S. Department of Commerce 2004 report, A Nation Online, states that 61.8 percent of all homes in the United States have at least one personal computer, and 54.6 percent of U.S. households have access to the Internet. While these numbers are an increase from the 2001 data, the fact remains that nearly half of American households remain without computer and Internet access.

Ownership and access vary greatly, however, depending on factors such as race, age, geographic location, and a number of other factors. To counter the differences in home computer ownership, and recognizing the significance of the digital divide, a number of programs have been developed to introduce children to computers in schools at as early an age as possible. One attempted solution has been to simply ensure that computers and Internet connections are provided at as many schools as possible, in the hope that mere access to the machines and Internet will provide a way to overcome the digital divide at a young age for all students (Attewell, 2001; Warschauer, 2003). By 2002, more than 99 percent of U.S. schools both owned computers and had Internet access (National Center for Education Statistics, 2003), a development which helps shrink the digital divide starting with school-age children.

Unfortunately, studies show that mere technical access does not address the type of skill gaps that persist through all levels of education and follow people into their careers. Access to Internet technology, without proper training and education regarding efficiency, does not help those who suffer traditionally from the digital divide find various kinds of information that may be useful (Hargittai and Shafer 2006; Wilson, 2000). Thus we find it is not just access to computers and Internet technologies that matters; it also matters whether students are trained in the different types of information available, how to judge them for effectiveness, and how to develop effective navigation strategies through cyberspace.

It is now widely recognized that the digital divide is not a simple matter of access versus no access, but a differential access where certain groups are generally restricted to school computer labs or public libraries, and where people who have historically low access are relegated to instructional software that emphasizes low-level drills and practice, without access to the more sophisticated interactive programs that encourage the development of critical thinking and problem-solving skills (Brown, 2000; Bruce, 1999; Valadez and Duran, 2007). This emphasis on drills and basic maneuvering with the technology as opposed to higher-level interactivity and decision making puts these students at a disadvantage when they enter higher education with peers who have been utilizing computer technology to accomplish more complex tasks.

The concept of providing access to technology encompasses more than the simple measure of whether or not schools provide computers (or whether students have access to computers at home). It includes questions of what kinds of computers students are using (whether students have access to computers capable of handling large amounts of data and sophisticated communication, or are working with obsolete machines), whether teachers across school systems are receiving equal and adequate training on how to use technology effectively to enhance learning, and whether schools have the technical support required to maintain those machines. Viewed in this light, "access" becomes a catch-all term that encompasses the physical availability of technology, the knowledge structures required to make effective use of those technologies, and the support infrastructures required to maintain the physical machinery and effectively train educators.

Even when access is provided for all, equal access does not mean that there will be equal use of the technology (Jackson et al., 2001). There are other factors that come into play once physical and technical access have been equalized that contribute to the persistence of a gap in computer and Internet skills, including differences according to race, gender, age, income, and socioeconomic status that contribute to differential development of technology skills.

Race

Race remains a critical factor in measuring the digital divide as a predictor of technology skill development. A significant gap exists in computer ownership and Internet access between white and non-white households. A 2002 National Telecommunications and Information Administration (NTIA) study finds that whites and Asian Americans have higher computer and Internet use than blacks and Latinos, and a 2004 report demonstrates a significant difference in Internet usage: 65.1 percent for whites, compared to 45.6 percent for blacks and 37.2 percent for Hispanics (U.S. Department of Commerce, 2004). While all of these were an increase from 2001 access statistics, the persistent lag in access for minority users reflected in the Lenhart (2003) findings as well as the U.S. Department of Commerce (2004) data continues to be a cause for concern.

Most striking is that even when controlled for education and income, African Americans and Hispanics have significantly less access than whites (Mossberger, Tolbert, and Stansbury, 2001; Wasserman and Richmond-Abbott, 2005). The digital divide between the races cannot be explained simply by referring to differences in education attainment or socioeconomic status. The fact remains that students belonging to minority groups remain at a distinct disadvantage when it comes to not only access, but skill development in information technologies (Hoffman, Novak, and Schlosser, 2001).

This digital divide based upon race continues to be a cause for concern because it has remained so static, and because it has been demonstrated that less at-home access is related to both attitudes about technology and competence at using the technology efficiently (Novak and Hoffman, 1998; Messineo and DeOllos, 2005). Beyond the lack of access at home, students from minority backgrounds are often heavily dependent upon school systems to provide them with the training and access they need to be successful. However, race is also a factor when examining the efficacy of computer training in elementary, middle, and secondary schools. Schools with large numbers of students of color tend to offer less access to classroom technology (Brown, 2000), which contributes to students of color lagging behind other students in terms of access to and familiarity with using various technologies. Compounding the above issues, African Americans typically attend larger schools where the student-to-computer ratio is less favorable and where use is restricted to school hours only (Becker and Sterling, 1987), leaving most students without leisure-time access to develop skills and experience deeper social networking opportunities online.

In addition to access issues plaguing minority students, pedagogy issues also affect what skills students develop when they do have access to technology during instruction. Minority students are statistically more likely to attend high schools with fewer resources, and with teachers who may have access to computers but have not had the training on how to integrate computer technology into classroom learning. Students are often left with a drill and practice approach and basic approaches to technology as opposed to those approaches that encourage critical thinking and higher-level use of both software and hardware.

Due to differences in pedagogy and hands-on time in training with technology, where use is restricted to school hours and there is no computer at home, equal access within school between white and non-white students still does not lessen the digital divide. Minority students as a whole are left wanting when it comes to developing rigorous critical thinking skills as applied to technology programs and use, and their familiarity with computers and Internet technologies suffers (Brown, 2000).

In addition to statistically lower rates of access at home and problematic training and pedagogy at the school level, language often also serves as an additional barrier for minority students, particularly to Hispanic students (Wilhelm, 2000). Race has been one of the persistent fault lines of the digital divide, and though progress has been made both in the provision of access and in developing programs involving computer use in classrooms, educators should remain aware that students from different cultural backgrounds likely have vastly different experiences with information technology.

Gender

Over the past 20 years, a great deal of research has been conducted that demonstrates a considerable divide exists in computer use patterns of males and females. While the access gap between the genders has narrowed significantly (Goodson, McCormick, and Evans, 2001; Ono and Zavodny, 2003; Wasserman and Richmond-Abbott, 2005), gender-based differences remain in computer use and attitudes that affect performance in technology use. These differences exacerbate the digital divide that exists along gendered lines, often leaving women at a disadvantage when it comes to familiarity with Internet use and technologies geared toward entertainment and leisure-time purposes.

Historically, men have been more frequent Internet users and have more lifetime experience with technology than their female counterparts, making them more familiar with and more likely to use new technologies (Goulding and Spacey, 2003). Studies comparing men's and women's use of the Web have found women to be equally proficient (Cooper, 2006; Martin, 1998), creating the possibility that gender-specific differences in Internet use are likely more related to historical differences in regard to technology use than to any gender-specific innate ability. Women and men differ significantly in their attitudes toward their own technological abilities, though these attitudes are not always borne out in tests of actual ability. Women generally see men as being more able to comprehend the Internet and have a higher likelihood of computer anxiety. Research indicates that while men and women do not differ greatly in their capabilities, women's self-assessment of their skill in Internet use is significantly lower than that of men (Hargittai and Shafer, 2006), and their attitudes affect how willing they are to utilize technology both at work and especially during their leisure time.

There are also differences in how, and how often, men and women make use of the Internet. It has been demonstrated that males are more likely to utilize the Internet for entertainment (such as gaming, participating in discussion forums, gambling, and seeking information for personal use) whereas females are more likely to utilize the Internet to talk to family and friends, concentrating mostly on communication by using social networking sites, e-mail, and instant messaging (Goodson, McCormick, and Evans, 2001; Jackson et al., 2001; Shaw and Gant, 2002). The result is that even where equal access to computing technology exists, gender-based usage differences impact Web preferences and usage criteria. More recent literature suggests that the gender gap in Internet use has narrowed, but differences in Web preferences and usage remain. Men report notably higher preferences for sites with video and sound available, including higher instances of visiting sites involving humor, gaming, sports, and pornography, while women report a higher rate of visiting academic sites (Mitra et al., 2005). Even once access has been equalized, men remain more frequent and more intense users of the Internet (Ono and Zavodny, 2003).

Social context also plays a large role in the differential development of technology use skills along gender lines. In general, males and females have been socialized differently with respect to technology, and women are more likely to have developed attitudes and expectancies that attribute good performance with technology to luck or chance (Cooper, 2006; Cooper and Weaver, 2003; Hargittai and Shafer, 2006) and to continue to underestimate their abilities with technology compared to their male counterparts. Many of these misapprehensions become self-fulfilling prophecies, where women who underestimate their abilities tend to use technology less, and thus are more unfamiliar with emerging technologies, becoming more uncomfortable and performing less well when using those technologies.

For educators, it is important to note that gendered differences in computer use and preferences exist even at a young age. There are gender-based gaps in the appeal factor of certain computer program characteristics, which contribute to the digital divide. In particular, Cooper (2006) points to indications that school-age girls generally dislike computer games and learning software featuring sports, war, competition, and coordination, while these are exactly the features that boys prefer and that contribute to boys' learning success. Various researchers have demonstrated that designing learning software to mimic arcade and video games disenfranchises girls in the classroom, as such designs cater to the learning and computer use preferences of boys, forcing educators to question the efficacy of making learning programs for their classrooms adventure and action-based (Cooper and Weaver, 2003; Cooper, Hall, and Huff, 1990; Littleton et al., 1998). When educators were asked to design learning software, most of those involved in the study defaulted to developing arcade-like games involving conflict and competition (Cooper, 2006). For educators to become effective collaborators with students, they will have to recognize gender-based learning preferences and incorporate different strategies to implement them to provide an equitable learning experience in the classroom.

Economic Status

Aside from race, income is one of the most widely accurate indicators of the digital divide. When studies are controlled for age, race, education level, and various other factors, income remains one of the strongest predictors of both access to and use of technology.

According to U.S. Department of Commerce data, aside from education level, income is one of the best predictors of computer ownership and Internet access. Of households making $75,000 per year and above, 82.9 percent are Internet users, and the rate of broadband access for these households (45.4 percent) is nearly double that of any lower income bracket. On the other hand, of households with incomes of $25,000 to $34,999, only 62.1 percent are Internet users, and 19 percent have broadband access, and of the poorest bracket (less than $15,000 per year), 31.2 percent are Internet users and 7.5 percent have broadband access (U.S. Department of Commerce, 2004).

Nearly a quarter of the Americans who reported no home Internet connection cited "Too Expensive" as a reason, and another 22.5 percent reported "No or Inadequate Computer Available" (U.S. Department of Commerce, 2004), demonstrating the importance of income as a cause of lack of access. Given the data, it is obvious that people who rely on schools and libraries for computer and Internet access are those who already start with a distinct socioeconomic disadvantage, and inadequate access and higher-level training at public-use computers.

Even when computer ownership is not an issue, income still has a great deal of power over how people utilize their computers and Internet connections. Dial-up connections are cheaper but are far less able to accomplish complex tasks due to the speed of the connection, so dial-up users who technically have access to the Internet do not have access to myriad applications requiring speedy connections, such as certain online massively multiplayer online role-playing games (MMORPGs) like *World of Warcraft*, nor do they have the same capacity for downloading multimedia from services and sites such as iTunes and YouTube.

Though few educators receive information on the economic status of their students, it behooves those in the classroom to note that students do come from widely varying socioeconomic backgrounds, which means that they also come from extremely diverse points of comfort and familiarity with information technology.

Age

As undergraduate and more advanced degrees are required for more jobs, and distance-learning makes it easier for those already pursuing careers to come back and pursue higher education, educators will be faced with the prospect of tackling the digital divide as it occurs along the fault line of age, in addition to the various other social and economic differences. As educators deal with more nontraditional students, it becomes important for educators to be aware of the divisions in technological facility according to age.

Age and marital status are statistically related to access, with younger and married individuals having more access (Wasserman and Richmond-Abbott, 2005). Young people are far more likely to use the Internet than are older people: Internet use rates are highest between the ages of 12 and 50, and take a steady, sharp decline after age 55 (U.S. Department of Commerce, 2004). While only 22 percent of those 65 years and older utilize the Internet, as compared to 58 percent of Americans between the ages of 50 to 64 who claim to be Internet users, older adults are among the fastest-growing groups of Internet users. As baby boomers age and enter the senior bracket, they are likely to increase the usage statistics for older Americans, as this demographic does not tend to decrease their information technology use with age (Fox, 2004).

An additional concern regarding the digital divide as it relates to age of users has to do with the changing age structure of the labor force. Those 55 and older are projected to make up approximately 20 percent of the labor force by 2020, up from 13 percent in 2000 (Toossi, 2002). As information technology increasingly replaces older technologies in the workplace, seniors will be required to maintain and update their technology skills along with the younger population in order to maintain their employability, indicating the need for available training programs and sensitivity to the needs of older users.

Rural versus Urban Access

Information technology has the power to remedy some of the choice discrepancies between rural and urban households. While urban households often have more choice in service providers, retail outlets, education and jobs, computers and Internet access provide the means for rural households to order items online, participate in distance learning and telecommuting, and generally compete and stay active in events far beyond the borders of small towns. However, a consistent gap exists between home Internet use in metropolitan and non-metropolitan areas of the United States. Rural residents are limited with regard to quality of Internet providers (Bell, Reddy, and Rainie, 2004), and while the eastern and western United States generally have about equal levels of computer and Internet access, the states in the south have a much lower percentage of the population with home access to computers and the Internet (Spooner, 2003).

Data confirms that broadband connections at home are less prevalent in rural America than urban America (24.7 percent compared to 40.4 percent), and rural areas are significantly more dependent on dial-up access, which restricts users' activity due to the slow nature of the connection (U.S. Department of Commerce, 2004). Contrary to the common assumption that technology and infrastructure access explain this difference, household attributes such as education level and income account for nearly 63 percent of this divide (Mills and Whitacre, 2003). Because of this correlation, the urban/rural gap exists due to more factors than simply fewer lines and shoddier infrastructure. This, in turn, casts doubt on the idea that policies focusing solely on creating technical access will succeed in mediating the difference. Other studies have confirmed that rural-urban digital divide is more highly correlated with social indicators such as income, age, and education (Hindman, 2000).

Social indicators may be more important than focusing on the simple rural/urban divide, but additional data suggest that broadband connections are less prevalent in rural America, with nearly 75 percent of rural households dependent on dial-up access in 2003 (U.S. Department of Commerce, 2004). Because dial-up takes longer and has fewer capabilities with regard to downloading and utilizing multimedia files, this may create a significant difference in quality of experience with information technology for those in rural areas compared to those in more urban areas.

ACCESS REVISITED

Revisiting the concept of access, the importance of the digital divide is not merely in the provision of access to computers and the Internet. The skills students develop as early adopters of these technologies create differences in skill level and comfort levels related to technology use that persist throughout their careers as learners and then as working members of society.

Low-resource schools, where students already suffer from use restricted to school hours and practice-drill focused pedagogy, tend to suffer most from inadequate support networks to maintain the physical machines and support software upgrades. Teachers at these schools are often under pressure to address students learning English as a second language, as well as facing pressure to raise test scores. Even when school computers are made available, however, students without home computers never reach the comfort level with using technology of those students who do own computers (Warschauer, Knobel, and Stone, 2004), making those students more likely to be apprehensive and stressed when forced to utilize information technology for assignments and social networking.

Valadez and Duran (2007) emphasize that even when California's Digital High School Grants program (DHSGP) increased access to computers in resource-challenged schools, the hardware was not coupled with instruction on how to integrate technology into the teaching curriculum. In addition to physical access, training is a necessary component to make computer and Internet use in the classroom an effective tool. A study of a number of schools demonstrates that even when access is available, there are differences in the number of computers available, the number of Internet connections, and the age of the computers available even when there were no significant differences in physical access (Valdez and Duran, 2007; Warschauer, Knobel, and Stone, 2004).

There is a greater call to reconceptualize the digital divide as we understand it, not only as an access issue, but as a "use" divide (Cobb Payton, 2003, Jackson et al., 2001; Jackson et al., 2003; Brown, 2000). For educators, this should be read as a call to integrate various technologies—and the training to use those technologies—into coursework to provide a familiar and comfortable experience for students encountering these technologies either for the first time or as only sporadic users uncertain of their abilities.

IMPACT ON ACADEMIC ACHIEVEMENT

As students enjoy free Internet access 24 hours a day on most college campuses and as the Internet is increasingly required to make use of electronic library resources, technology skills are increasingly required for academic success. Virtual office hours (where students meet their faculty members in cyberspace), online course delivery systems (i.e., Blackboard), e-mail, and electronic delivery of class assignments via online tutorial or class Web sites in addition to myriad library databases required for research may easily overwhelm the underprepared student. Students are also avid users of instant messaging services and social networking sites such as Facebook, MySpace, and Flickr, meaning that students suffering from being on the wrong side of the digital divide are not just at a loss academically, but also socially, compared to some of their peers.

As discussed earlier in this chapter, experience engenders not just skill, but comfort with using information technologies. Lack of experience and skill increases student anxiety, likely reducing their sense of accomplishment and their academic success. Technophobia due to unfamiliarity is linked to academic success (or the lack thereof) (Bowers and Bowers, 1996; Di, Dunn, and Lee, 2000), making it clear that frequent, comfortable interactions with information technology are required to develop student comfort. Those students without a level of comfort and understanding are likely to become stressed under conditions involving newer applications and are likely to do poorly on assignments requiring computer use (Messineo and DeOllos, 2005).

School culture can shape the way technology is used. Those students coming to higher education from low-resource schools and schools in the inner city are already less skilled than their peers coming from higher-resource backgrounds (Brown, 2000; Warschauer, Knobel, and Stone, 2004), and are more likely to have trouble adapting to the high-tech life that encompasses many college campuses.

Minority students are often of lower socioeconomic status and have to work while in school, and do not have the leisure time to pursue information technology skill development in the same manner as those students who do not hold jobs. They also reported that due to work commitments, they were often unable to participate in certain aspects of group projects—such as data analysis—that those students with more time and familiarity with the software programs would address (Varma, 2006). In addition to technical training and practice, these students are also often in need of counseling and academic guidance in order to take full advantage of opportunities during their careers in higher education.

Assumptions made by educators as to their students' skills with technologies required for success in coursework, their ability to complete projects requiring data analysis or other special technology, and their lack of understanding of extracurricular commitments, such as family and work, may inadvertently jeopardize student success (Messineo and DeOllos, 2005). Preparedness to deal with differing skill levels and awareness of students' backgrounds can help faculty members prepare their students for success in the classroom.

As course management systems, podcasts, virtual office hours, and various other information technology-related education offerings become the norm across campuses, as more classes integrate information technologies and develop multimedia supplemental class materials, as more distance learners take advantage of online courses, those students suffering from the digital divide will become more and more disenfranchised and less likely to achieve success in higher education. Attention to student capabilities and training in the classroom, particularly in the early years of a student's academic career, has an incredible impact on academic progress.

A May 2008 College Board report finds that first-generation college students are less likely to complete degrees (Glenn, 2008), a phenomenon that has not improved since the National Center for Education Statistics report that revealed first-generation status is significantly negatively correlated with academic success and degree completion at the under-graduate level (Chen, 2005). Because being a first-generation college student is highly correlated with minority racial status, as well as lower income, it is highly likely that the failure of these students to complete their education is related to the digital divide, and in particular to their discomfort in experiencing not only the unfamiliar territory of higher education but unfamiliar technology skill requirements.

The effects of the digital divide on academic achievement also have an impact on students as they choose their specialties and then enter the workforce with their degrees. The National Science Board (2004) reported that in the year 2000, African Americans earned 3,497 computer science bachelor's degrees, Hispanics earned 2,155, Asians earned 5,401, and white students earned 21,719. This obvious disparity in minority representation in information technology undergraduate programs also feeds workforce disparities in those employed in information technology sectors.

Consequences for the Workforce

The repercussions of the digital divide and inequities in technology skills extend beyond the classroom. The digital divide has a significant impact on a number of groups, and this impact is reflected in the makeup of the workforce, particularly in those sectors where information technology is crucial to the job. According to the Bureau of Labor Statistics, women, minorities and older Americans will make up a larger part of the workforce than they have in the past (Toossi, 2002), making it imperative that these groups are well-equipped with the information technology skills they will need to succeed and flourish in nearly every sector of the economy.

Estimates suggest that 25 percent of all new jobs in both the public and private sectors will be technologically oriented by 2010 (AAUW, 2000). Those students who pass through the higher education system and remain unable to remedy their shortcomings in information technology skills will be left out of most of these new positions that rely heavily on such technology know-how. Being left out of jobs created in the new technology economy leads to fewer opportunities in the workforce, lower socioeconomic status, and reinforces the digital divide even further as lower socioeconomic status then feeds back into a loop of less access to information technology.

A 2003 study released by the Information Technology Association of America (ITAA) finds that between 1996 and 2002, the percentage of women and African Americans in the overall IT (Information Technology) workforce actually fell, though the presence of these groups rose when administrative positions are removed from the data. The report goes on to detail that women and minorities are significantly underrepresented in information technology work compared to their representation in the American workforce, except for Asian Americans, who are represented in the IT workforce three times over their presence in the U.S. labor force at large (ITAA, 2003). More recent data from the 2006 U.S. Census confirms that this underrepresentation of groups particularly impacted by the digital divide remains. Women, who make up 46.3 percent of the total American workforce, account for only 26.7 percent of computer occupations, and African Americans, 10.9 percent of the American work-force, are only represented at 7.3 percent in the IT sector. The disparity in representation of Hispanics is even greater, who only appear as 5 percent of the IT workforce and are 13.6 percent of the general population (U.S. Census Bureau, 2008).

The continued trend of low numbers of women, African Americans, and Hispanics in information technology positions reflects the data on the digital divide. Until efforts are made to lessen the impact of the digital divide, these groups will continue to be not only underrepresented in the growing information technology sector, but also disenfranchised in multiple other areas of life. As everything from professional conferences (now available in Second Life) to political discourse (where presidential candidates field questions from the public via YouTube) is now deeply integrated into information technology and particularly the Internet, the digital divide does not just present an obstacle to academic success, but creates barriers to full participation in the political process, in social networking opportunities, and avenues for personal fulfillment.

Given the differences in familiarity with the Internet, as well as dif-ferences in Web usage and site preferences, educators will be well served not to make sweeping assumptions about the skill levels, site preferences, and Web familiarity of their students. The digital divide is not a simple binary issue of have and have-not when it comes to computers and Internet access. It is highly unlikely that educators will be able to parse the digital divisions among their students simply along lines of gender, age, race, or socioeconomic status. Instead, educators will have to deal with a combination of factors at work within each student. The complexities of the issue make their way into the classroom in the form of gender, age, and race, and geographic and socioeconomic differences, which can conflate or confound the effects of the skill and access divides. While educators would be well-served to keep the data on the digital divide in mind, the best route to counteract the effects of the divide is to integrate technology effectively into their classes, emphasize critical thinking skills in conjunction with technology use, and to create an atmosphere where students can learn without undue anxiety.

Rigorous development of information and technology literacy has become the key to overcome various barriers to learning in higher education, and will serve students throughout their lives. Harnessing technologies available in the classroom, educators have the opportunity to level the professional playing field and to bring members of every socioeconomic, racial, and age group to a more equal social and educational footing. Until these persistent gaps in training and education are rectified, people will remain unable to fulfill their potential. This area is where educators can have their greatest impact.

REFERENCES

AAUW Commission on Technology Gender and Teacher Education. 2000. *Tech-Savvy: Educating Girls in the New Computer Age.* Washington, DC: American Association of University Women.

Attewell, Paul. 2001. "The First and Second Digital Divides." Sociology of Education 74, no. 3: 252–259.

Becker, Henry J., and Carleton W. Sterling. 1987. "Equity in School Computer Use: National Data and Neglected Considerations." *Journal of Educational Computing Research* 3, no. 3: 289–311.

Bell, Peter, Pavani Reddy, and Lee Rainie. 2004. *Rural Areas and the Internet.* Washington, DC: Pew Internet and American Life Project.

Bowers, David A., and Vickie M. Bowers. 1996. "Assessing and Coping with Computer Anxiety in the Social Science Classroom." *Social Science Computer Review 14*, no. 4: 439–443.

Brown, Monica R. 2000. "Access, Instruction, and Barriers: Technology Issues Facing Students at Risk." *Remedial and Special Education* 21, no. 3: 182–192.

Bruce, Bertram C. 1999. "Speaking the Unspeakable About 21st Century Technologies." In *Passions, Pedagogies, and 21st Century Technologies* (pp. 221–228), edited by Gail E. Hawisher and Cynthia. L. Selfe. Logan: Utah State University Press.

Chen, Xianglei. 2005. *First Generation Students in Post-Secondary Education: A Look at Their College Transcripts*. Washington, DC: National Center for Education Statistics.

Cobb Payton, Fay. 2003. "Rethinking the Digital Divide." *Communications of the ACM* 46, no.6: 89–91.

Cooper, Joel. 2006. "The Digital Divide: The Special Case of Gender." *Journal of Computer-Assisted Learning* 22, no. 5: 320–334.

Cooper, Joel, Joan Hall, and Charles Huff. 1990. "Situational Stress as a Consequence of Sex-Stereotyped Software." *Personality and Social Psychology Bulletin* 16, no. 3: 419–429.

Cooper, Joel, and Kimberlee Weaver. 2003. *Gender and Computers: Understanding the Digital Divide*. Mahwah, NJ: Lawrence Erlbaum Associates.

Di, Xu, Denise Dunn, and S. J. Lee. 2000. "An Integrated Approach to Instructional Technology." *Action in Teacher Education* 22, no. 2A: 1–13.

Fox, Susannah. 2004. *Older Americans and the Internet*. Washington, DC: Pew Internet and American Life Project.

Glenn, David. 2008. "Study Finds Graduation Gap for First-Generation Students, Regardless of Preparation." *Chronicle of Higher Education* (May 28).

Goodson, Patricia, Deborah McCormick, and Alexandra Evans. 2001. "Searching for Sexually Explicit Materials on the Internet: An Exploratory Study of College Students." *Archives of Sexual Behavior* 30, no. 2: 101–118.

Goulding, Anne, and Rachel Spacey. 2003. "Women and the Information Society: Barriers and Participation." *IFLA Journal* 29: 33–40.

Hargittai, Eszter, and Steven Shafer. 2006. "Differences in Actual and Perceived Online Skills: The Role of Gender." *Social Science Quarterly* 87, no. 2: 432–448.

Hindman, Douglas B. 2000. "The Rural-Urban Digital Divide." *Journalism and Mass Communication Quarterly* 77, no. 3: 549–560.

Hoffman, Donna L., Thomas P. Novak, and Ann E. Schlosser. 2001. "The Evolution of the Digital Divide: Examining the Relationship of Race to Internet Access and Usage Over Time." In *The Digital Divide: Facing a Crisis or Creating a Myth* (pp. 47–97), edited by Benjamin M. Compaine. Cambridge, MA: MIT Press.

Information Technology Association of America. "Report of the ITAA Blue Ribbon Panel on IT Diversity." Paper presented at the annual National IT Workforce Convocation, Arlington, VA (May 5, 2003). Available: www.itaa.org/workforce/docs/03divreport.pdf (accessed May 14, 2008).

Jackson, Linda A., Gretchen Barbatsis, Alexander von Eye, Frank Biocca, Yong Zhao, and Hiram Fitzgerald. 2003. "Internet Use in Low-Income Families: Implications for the Digital Divide." *IT & Society* 1, no. 5: 141–165.

Jackson, Linda A., Kelly S. Ervin, Philip D. Gardner, and Neal Schmitt. 2001. "Gender and the Internet: Women Communicating and Men Searching." *Sex Roles* 44, no. 5/6: 363–379.

Lenhart, Amanda. 2003. *The Ever-Shifting Internet Population: A New Look at Access and the Digital Divide.* Washington, DC: Pew Internet and American Life Project.

Littleton, Karen, Paul Light, Richard Joiner, David Messer, and Peter Barnes. 1998. "Gender, Task Scenarios and Children's Computer-Based Problem Solving." *Educational Psychology* 18, no. 3: 327–340.

Martin, Shelley. 1998. "Internet Use in the Classroom: The Impact of Gender." *Social Science Computer Review* 16, no. 4: 411–418.

Messineo, Melinda, and Ione Y. DeOllos. 2005. "Are We Assuming Too Much? Exploring Students' Perceptions of Their Computer Competence." *College Teaching* 53, no. 2: 50–55.

Mills, Bradford F., and Brian E. Whitacre. 2003. "Understanding the Non-Metropolitan/Metropolitan Digital Divide." *Growth and Change* 34, no. 2: 219–243.

Mitra, Ananda, Jennifer Willyard, Carrie Ann Platt, and Michael Parsons. 2005. "Exploring Web Usage and Selection Criteria Among Male and Female Students." *Journal of Computer-Mediated Communication* 10, no. 3 (June 23). Available: http://jcmc.indiana.edu/vol10/issue3/mitra.html (accessed July 23, 2008).

Mossberger, Karen, Caroline J. Tolbert, and Mary Stansbury. 2001. *Virtual Inequality: Beyond the Digital Divide.* Washington, DC: Georgetown University Press.

National Center for Education Statistics. 2003. *Internet Access in U.S. Public Schools and Classrooms: 1994–2002.* Washington, DC: U.S. Department of Education.

National Science Board. 2004. *Science and Engineering Indicators 2004.* Arlington, VA: National Science Foundation.

Novak, Thomas P., and Donna L. Hoffman. 1998. "Bridging the Racial Divide on the Internet." *Science* (April 17): 390-391.

Ono, Hiroshi, and Madeline Zavodny. 2003. "Gender and the Internet." *Social Science Quarterly* 84, no. 1: 111–121.

Shaw, Lindsay H., and Larry M. Gant. 2002. "Users Divided? Exploring the Gender Gap in Internet Use." *Cyberpsychology & Behavior* 5, no. 6: 517–527.

Spooner, Tom. 2003. *Internet Use by Region in the United States.* Washington, DC: Pew Internet and American Life Project.

Toossi, Mitra. 2002. "A Century of Change: U.S. Labor Force from 1950 to 2050." *Monthly Labor Review* 125, no. 5: 15–28.

U.S. Census Bureau. 2008. Table 598: Employed Civilians by Occupation, Sex, Race and Hispanic Origin 2006 in *Statistical Abstract of the United States 2008.* Washington, DC: U.S. Census Bureau.

U.S. Department of Commerce. 2004. *A Nation Online: Entering the Broadband Age.* Washington, DC: U.S. Department of Commerce.

Valadez, James R., and Richard Duran. 2007. "Redefining the Digital Divide: Beyond Access to Computers and the Internet." *High School Journal* 90, no. 3: 31–44.

Varma, Roli. 2006. "Making Computer Science Minority-Friendly: Computer

Science Programs Neglect Diverse Student Needs." *Communications of the ACM* 49, no. 2: 129–134.

Warschauer, Mark. 2003. *Technology and Social Inclusion: Rethinking the Digital Divide*. Cambridge, MA: MIT Press.

Warschauer, Mark, Michele Knobel, and Leeann Stone. 2004. "Technology and Equity in Schooling: Deconstructing the Digital Divide." *Educational Policy* 18, no. 4: 562–588.

Wasserman, Ira M., and Marie Richmond-Abbott. 2005. "Gender and the Internet: Causes of Variation in Access, Level, and Scope of Use." *Social Science Quarterly* 86, no. 1: 252–270.

Wilhelm, Anthony G. 2000. *Democracy in the Digital Age: Challenges to Political Life in Cyberspace*. New York: Routledge.

Wilson, Ernest J. 2000. *Closing the Digital Divide: An Initial Review: Briefing the President*. Washington, DC: Internet Policy Institute.

Chapter 2

Driving Fast to Nowhere on the Information Highway: A Look at Shifting Paradigms of Literacy in the Twenty-First Century

Patricia H. Dawson

Diane K. Campbell

INTRODUCTION

Gen M (aka the Millennial Generation) has started arriving on campus, and one can spot them a mile away: iPod plugged into one ear, Bluetooth headset in the other, hunched over a laptop while they pound out instant messages to their friends, update their Facebook page, and work on their latest project. This chapter will attempt to illuminate their information-seeking habits, learning styles, and abilities. Also discussed will be the assumptions made by adults, including librarians, who believe that these students are tech savvy and information literate. Contrary to this impression, these students are generally not sufficiently computer literate and definitely not information literate when it comes to scholarly or business communication. The phrases "computer literacy" and "information literacy" have meanings that have changed over time. These changes result in confusion and conflation of ideas, making it difficult to teach and to measure these types of literacy. The final sections address what impact this has on library instruction and how librarians can adjust to meet the needs of Gen M for better learning outcomes.

A way of thinking about all of this is to use the metaphor of a driver's license. Getting a driver's license is a milestone of freedom in the life of many Americans. Tired of depending on adults and public transit, adolescents dream of independence and autonomy. The open road beckons, or at least the road to the mall. When adolescents think of driving, they understand that knowing where the gas pedal is and how to turn on the windshield wipers is not enough information to get them to the "indie" film being shown three towns over. They can also easily understand that just finding a route to that film will not guarantee them the easiest trip or the least traffic. They also understand that being able to find the movie theater will not help them plan a cross-country trip.

When they sit down to a computer, the mechanical steps such as turning it on, clicking on icons, and saving text or links are so well known that they are as automatic as driving is for many adults. Also familiar is searching for the information they use every day, such as the Web page for the newest band. They think that being able to find this kind of information means they are ready to go anywhere. They consider themselves quite expert in finding any information because they can "Google" anything and "get lots of hits." Yet, many cannot find information easily on a scholarly topic or evaluate the information they do uncover. Frequently when they cannot find information, they assume that the information does not exist. They may be traveling quickly on the information highway, but they are not arriving where they need to be.

This attitude also extends to computer skills. Many Gen M students feel very confident that because they have been using computers "forever," they know everything they need to know about them. In a recent study of first-year business students, Ballantine, Larres, and Oyelere found "a significant self-assessment leniency bias in respect of computer competence among entry-level undergraduate business students. Furthermore, contrary to a significant body of earlier research, the tendency toward self-assessment leniency was no less pronounced among more experienced students than among their less experienced colleagues" (Ballantine, Larres, and Oyelere, 2007: 987). This research looked at computer use for word processing and applications such as spreadsheets, but it also included e-mail and database use.

When the students' self-confidence is coupled with some adults' lingering self-doubt about keeping up with the newest applications, it is easy to see a developing problem. Observing someone who casually opens four windows to IM his friends, check out a favorite blog, pull up the paper that is half-finished, and check Facebook, a librarian or teacher may be hesitant to question his/her assurance that he/she can find what is needed. Both the Gen M and the observer have an inflated idea of what he/she can achieve. This excessive confidence in their perceived ability means that instruction is not offered or requested, and another learning opportunity escapes them.

This discussion is about Gen M students who are from a background with access to home computers and broadband Internet service. The digital divide still exists. Measuring this divide is complicated because even if a student answers "yes" to questions such as "Do you have a home computer?" and "Do you have Internet access?" the computer may be an older generation machine and the access could be dial-up, or the only access obtainable is at the public library (Hawkins and Oblinger, 2006). The number of members of Gen M who have home access to broadband is greater than ever before, but it is still not 100 percent. This topic is addressed elsewhere in this volume.

COMPUTER LITERACY "DEFINED," INCLUDING BACKGROUND AND HISTORY OF CONCEPT

When computer use began to spread throughout the working world, there was a call to educators to determine what a student needed to know to use computers and to be prepared for the future. It was obvious that the world was changing, but it was not obvious what everyone needed to know. In 1985, Kenneth M. King wrote "Evolution of the Concept of Computer Literacy," in which he compared the arguments for computer literacy through three decades and projected what they might be in 1995. His look back to 1965 included "students who lack the ability to use a computer language are as illiterate as students unable to use mathematics" (King, 1985: 18). Notice that it was not the *use* of computers but the use of computer *language* that was highlighted. At that time, the only way to use computers was to speak to them in their language. Therefore, a natural component of computer literacy was computer *language* literacy.

Jumping forward to 1975, King notes that, "a working knowledge of applications packages appropriate to one's discipline became as important as the knowledge of a computer language in defining computer literacy" (1985: 19). In 1985, a major question was, "Should every student be required to buy a micro?" Finally, he projects that by 1995, "everyone will have the ability to use quite a broad spectrum of computer tools for accessing and processing information of necessity because that's the way they'll bank and shop" (1985: 21). This pocket history of computer literacy illustrates the evolution of computers and computer literacy. A significant shift happened when desktop models and software stepped in and eliminated the need for most users to truly understand computers. The computer could now be a "black box" and still be a vital functioning tool. Where does that leave the idea of computer literacy?

Is "literacy" the correct term to be using at all? Literacy implies a fundamental skill in reading and writing and is critical to participation in our world. Literacy is also linked to the idea of some sort of baseline, unchanging skill set. The difference between literate and illiterate says nothing about what is being read but says something only about the skill level in reading. If this term is to be applied to computers and information, it is important to have clear definitions.

The problem with defining a baseline skill set that marks a clear divide in computer literacy is that the skills themselves keep changing. Continuing on with the perhaps abused metaphor, computer use evolved somewhat like automobiles. The first automobile drivers needed to know how to fix the engine as well as change a tire. Roadside assistance was nearly nonexistent. The driver had to be competent and confident to a much greater degree than today. In the same way, early computer users were programmers, and the idea that a novice could just click and go was unimaginable.

When it was necessary to learn a computer language to work with computers, learning the language was a natural part of the basic skill set. Along came graphical interfaces and off-the-shelf applications, and it was no longer necessary to use programming language at all. There came to be a natural divide between using computers and software applications to perform specific tasks and using computer programming skills to actually design computers and applications. On one side were computer users and on the other, computer scientists. The computer scientists would open the black box, create new functions, analyze them, evaluate the new program, and improve it.

If everyone did not need to be a computer scientist to use computers for education and work, then what did everyone need to know? One response to this question was Scott Childers' chart of computer proficien-

cies in his article "Computer Literacy: Necessity or Buzzword?" (2003).
He amplified the chart first developed by the Technology Committee of
The Library Network, a public library cooperative in southeast Michigan.
It has three levels of proficiencies: Level 1: Baseline; Level 2: Desired;
and Level 3: Target.

The basic level includes starting and operating a standard work-
station, being able to load paper into printers, being able to send and
manipulate e-mail, and being able to search the Internet. Searching is only
mentioned as a basic skill; however, when moving to a higher level of
proficiency, there is no mention of developing the searching skill further.
The higher level Internet skills include awareness of computer viruses
and cookies, but not advanced searching techniques.

This chart was created in 2003, and six years might as well be forever in technology. For instance, Level 1 consists of a baseline skill for
knowing how to navigate without a mouse. It could be argued today
that operating without a mouse or mouse equivalent would be a desired,
perhaps even optional, rather than a basic skill. Level 2 describes a desired
level of proficiency with a browser including the knowledge of dealing
with frames when printing e-mail, which is no longer much of an issue.
The Level 2 skills with printers involve changing a toner cartridge and
clearing a paper jam. It is entirely possible that future printers will be
configured so that these are antique skills. This once again illustrates that
the details of computer literacy change as technology changes.

Today, computers are not the only technology that is important.
Defining computer literacy is no longer enough to address technological
competence. *Computer literacy* is not sufficient to encompass the multimedia world in which we live and work. The phrase *technologically
literate* is now considered more accurate. What is the definition of this
new phrase? This definition is no easier to pin down than the earlier
one, since it incorporates so much more. The No Child Left Behind Act
had a goal of technological literacy for every student by eighth grade.
However, the question of what that means was neatly sidestepped by
allowing the definition of technological literacy to be determined by each
state (OSPI, 2005). For the purposes of this chapter, the phrase *computer
literacy* will be used.

Comparing and contrasting information literacy and computer
literacy makes a useful definition of the latter easier to understand.
Computer literacy should encompass basic skills such as turning the
device on and off, being able to save and distribute information, and

being able to activate applications. Intermediate skills would be demonstrated in the ability to choose applications or appropriate devices for a
given task. Higher-level skills then become the domain of the computer
scientist, programmer, or electronic engineer. The higher-level skills
that are often described in technological literacy properly belong to
information literacy.

DEFINING INFORMATION LITERACY, INCLUDING BACKGROUND AND HISTORY OF CONCEPT

What is information literacy and how did this phrase originate? This
section will answer those questions and will address the background
and history of the concept of information literacy. In addition, alternative names and some controversies surrounding this terminology will be
discussed. Paul Zurkowski is credited for coining the phrase "Information Literacy" in 1974 as president of the now defunct U.S. Information
Industry Association (Garrett, 2001; Lee, 2002). "People trained in the
application of information resources to their work can be called information literates. They have learned techniques and skills for using the wide
range of information tools as well as primary sources in molding information solutions to their problems" (Garrett, 2001: 2). Other definitions
have evolved since then, and the dominant definition used now is from
the American Library Association Presidential Committee on Information
Literacy, Final Report: "To be information literate, a person must be able
to recognize when information is needed and have the ability to locate,
evaluate, and use effectively the needed information" (Lee, 2002; Garrett,
2001: 1). However, over the years additional meanings for this phrase
have proliferated. Information fluency, competency, facility (Lorenzo and
Dziuban, 2006), lifelong learning, resource-based learning, and critical
thinking (Garrett, 2001) are some examples of synonyms for information
literacy. These alternatives indicate some confusion and disagreement
about the terminology for information literacy. Some object to using the
phrase "information literacy" because of the connotation for "literacy"
in general: "The trouble is that the word 'literacy' is a magic word, which
conjures up a very strong metaphor" (Harvey, 1983: 1). Literacy is the
ability to read and write, "the learning and mastery of symbols and how
to interpret them" (Childers, 2003: 102). Diane Lee (2002) describes objections by Stephen Foster, who questions how one can measure a student's
level of mastery of information literacy, and he suggests that it is just

public relations. Lee also mentions Lawrence McCrank's observation that information literacy is just repackaged bibliographic instruction, and he maintains that librarians have no control over aspects of information literacy that delve into content area.

Is this terminology and concept really new or is it just the repackaging of an old concept as stated by Lawrence McCrank (Lee, 2002)? A paradigm shift in the development of library instruction is discussed in this section. Societal changes in the United States have had parallel impacts on both libraries and public education since the founding of the Republic. The next few paragraphs describe these changes and how the concept of information literacy evolved as a result.

Librarians have been concerned about teaching people how to access and use library collections since the 1800s, as noted in Hannelore Rader's extensive literature review of information literacy (2002). Donna Gilton (2004) has written a lengthy history of information literacy instruction by drawing parallels between libraries, public education, and changes in society. She begins this story prior to the 1860s when the United States was mostly an agricultural society. Only the wealthy could afford to buy books, to have their own personal libraries, and to have their children taught at home by tutors. Other children were sent to one-room schools with all ages taught by one teacher. When the Industrial Revolution began in the United States following the Civil War, a mass movement of people left the farms and entered the cities, and the advent of assembly-line factories began to influence the manner in which students were taught in the public schools. In addition, public libraries came into being, and developed into centralized, standardized places for information, just like public schools.

Interestingly, Gilton reports that library research skills were taught in the universities between the Civil War and the 1920s. However, between the 1920s and 1960s, few colleges with academic libraries offered library instruction because of the emphasis of research and graduate education during this period. She credits B. Lamar Johnson for laying the foundation of bibliographic instruction at Stephens College between 1931 and 1950. He offered tours of the library, "instruction in the use of basic reference tools, point-of-use instruction, individualized instruction, course-related instruction and full courses" during this era (Gilton, 2004: 10). Evan Farber's library instruction program at Earlham College, similar to Johnson's, was presented at the ALA conference in 1969 and had a huge impact on other librarians at this meeting.

During this time, young librarians were not beholden to the old way of doing things in libraries, and rebellious students on many campuses were demanding "relevance" in their courses and programs. A greater number and more diverse mix of students began attending colleges, requiring more services in the libraries. Gilton calls the start of bibliographic instruction in the academic libraries a "bottom-up grass-roots" movement stimulated by all of the social upheavals taking place in American society at this time (2004: 13). The Library Orientation Exchange began during the 1970s along with the Instruction Section of the Association of College and Research Libraries (ACRL), which stimulated new ways of teaching library instruction. Apparently, librarians taught college students like they were taught in their own reference courses in library school: long laundry lists of resources in the absence of the context of class assignments. Changes began by integrating library instruction with class assignments, making the experience for the students more relevant. With the arrival of computers and the "information society," library instruction shifted to finding information inside the building to virtual online databases. The influence of the computer and the Internet has transformed the older model of an industrialized society from assembly-line efficiency, top-down hierarchy to a more fluid state. This has had impacts on the workplace, education, and libraries. For instance, distance education has had tremendous impacts on serving students from afar. Electronic databases and resources mean that students can access information 24/7 and never step inside a physical library.

The electronic age resulted in changing bibliographic instruction to the information literacy movement, a "top-down movement led by education, library, and other leaders, including accrediting agencies and state legislatures" (2004: 19). The Middle States Commission on Higher Education, the American Chemical Society, the American Psychology Association, and other professional organizations involved in accrediting programs now include information literacy standards (Lorenzo and Dziuban, 2006). This involves integrating information literacy into various disciplines and curricula. Gilton (2004) mentions the report *A Nation at Risk*, published in 1983, which promoted information literacy because of the perceived need to acquire skills in managing electronic information. She also mentions a paper, "Educating Students to Think," published by the National Commission on Libraries and Information Science that defines information skills. In 1987, the ALA Presidential Committee on Information Literacy was established, confirming the shift from bibliographic instruction to information literacy. Two organizations formed during the early 1990s, the National Forum on Information Literacy and ACRL's Institute of Information Literacy, have been influential in promoting information literacy teaching skills to librarians and non-librarians, as well as in developing techniques for assessment of those skills (Gilton, 2004; ALA, 2000).

RESEARCH ON GEN M'S SKILLS IN COMPUTER AND INFORMATION LITERACY

Despite all of the news about Gen M's computer skills and constant connectivity to social networks, there have been rumblings in the academic arena and some complaints by employers regarding the lack of basic writing, communicating, and higher order information skills such as analyzing and evaluating content. Gen M students have been stereotyped as computer wizards since they have grown up with the technology. Do the statistics and reports support this image? If they are indeed tech savvy, does this skill translate into expertise in areas such as the ability to find, evaluate, and appropriately use information for formal, academic research papers as defined in the previous section? This next section will examine the data that is accumulating about this generation of students, which suggests that Gen Ms are not necessarily sophisticated in using all of this technology, and that they are deficient in their information literacy skills requiring critical evaluation of the found materials.

As early as 1962, Fritz Machlup coined the phrase "Knowledge Industry." He was the first to publish about the rapid and deep changes taking place in the U.S. economy (Miller, 1988). George Miller reports that the trends predicted by Machlup have been on target, with "a 1980 survey of workers reflecting a cross section of occupations found that nearly 99 percent participate in some form of reading every day, with a daily average of nearly 2 hours of reading" (Miller, 1988: 1293). Purposeful literacy involves "comprehending print, including the appreciation of tables, maps, diagrams, or mathematical symbols and formulas" (Miller, 1988: 1293). In 1985, the National Assessment of Educational Progress (NAEP) tested literacy skills of 21 to 25-year-olds, and found that only 37 percent scored at college level reading skills (Miller, 1988). This is almost a decade before the advent of the graphical Web and the ubiquitous use of computers. By 2001, Julie Oman (2001) reports that employees spend even more time dealing with information, averaging 9.5 hours per week. The need for more advanced information literacy skills is evident as stated by Anthony Comper, president of the Bank of

Montreal, in his address to University of Toronto graduates: "You need to acquire a high level of information literacy. What we need in the knowledge industries are people who know how to absorb and analyze and integrate and create and effectively convey information and who know how to use information to bring real value to everything they undertake" (Julien, 2007: 1).

Jill Jenson (2004) reports that a study conducted in the fall of 2000 showed that 78.5 percent of entering freshmen at UCLA used computers regularly. The article also states that 66 percent of freshmen at the University of North Carolina failed their post test in information literacy skills, but two-thirds of these students were confident in their library skills, indicating that many thought their skills were good! This over-confidence in library and information skills was noted in the first section of this chapter. Another article (Lorenzo and Dziuban, 2006) indicates broad usage of word processing programs with Gen M students (100 percent); however, only 65 percent use presentation software, 63 percent use spreadsheets, 49 percent use graphics software, and only 25 percent have Web creation abilities. Although they use computers for writing, they are not competent in other low technology applications, according to this report.

OCLC, Inc. (Online Computer Literacy Center) conducted a survey on college students' perceptions of libraries and resources, and 89 percent of college students stated that they begin researching topics with Internet search engines (2005). Only 2 percent indicated they would start with an online database or library Web site. The Pew Internet and American Life Project (Estabrook, Witt, and Rainie, 2007) confirmed this high reliance on the Internet for information, and found that 91 percent of Gen M students had access to the Internet. The study found that 79 percent of these students had access to broadband Internet at home. The OCLC study reported that Google was the favored search engine (68 percent), with Yahoo favored by 45 percent (these answers are more than 100 percent because they could check more than one box). Students discover new electronic resources primarily through friends (67 percent), other Web site links (61 percent), teachers (50 percent), and librarians (33 percent) (OCLC, 2005). These results confirm the observation that Gen M students are not using the best resources, just the fastest means to find resources for their research.

The Educational Testing Service (ETS) has created a standardized test called the iSkills Assessment. Students are presented with scenarios to read and, based on the information presented, they choose the best sources and search terms. This assessment has been tested with cut-off scores determined for core (high school and college freshmen) and advanced iSkills (for upper classmen). A pilot was conducted at 63 institutions and involved about 6,400 students composed of 1,016 high school students, 753 community college students, and 4,585 college and university students. The sample of students was not random and cannot be extrapolated to students in general, but the results indicate some disturbing trends (Tannenbaum and Katz, 2008; Katz, 2007):

- Only 49 percent identified a unique Web site that was objective, authoritative, timely
- 44 percent identified correctly the research question related to the class assignment
- 35 percent were able to narrow search terms with appropriate query statements
- 40 percent were able to enter multiple search terms to narrow results from a Web search
- 12 percent used relevant points in constructing a presentation slide designed to persuade
- Few test takers were capable of using material for a new purpose

Irvin Katz, at a recent Princeton-Trenton SLA meeting (2008), mentioned that approximately 27 percent of college seniors were deemed information literate from these results. In summary, these results confirm the observations noted by faculty and employers that Gen M students may be great with using the newest recreational technology, but they are not competent in managing information or using critical thinking skills for analyzing and using the information for academic or business purposes. Obviously, librarians and faculty need to work together to address these shortcomings and determine what needs to be taught and what methods to use to engage Gen M students. The concluding section of this chapter addresses these concerns.

COMPARISON AND CONTRAST BETWEEN TWO CONCEPTS

Previously, we have discussed the definitions for literacy, computer literacy, and information literacy. There is confusion and overlap in the usage of these terms and phrases, and as questioned earlier, one of the problems is the term *literacy*, the ability to read and write. Computer literacy and information literacy require the ability to read, but these types of literacy are more complicated, and are harder to pin down. To help illustrate these issues, Table 2.1 "Comparison of Different Types of Literacy" lists the concepts and their attributes as cited by others or discussed in the previous sections. Bloom's Taxonomy is used because it clarifies the attributes needed for critical and creative thinking. Each type of literacy is compared in columns, with increasing levels of complexity as one reads down the columns. Reading the table from left to right can lead to false equivalencies that are not being asserted.

However, those information literacy skills at the lowest skill level on Bloom's scale, *knowledge*, assume that the knowledge-level skills for literacy and computer literacy are already mastered. Therefore, information literacy competency at the *knowledge* level depends upon the knowledge level of literacy and computer literacy. At the higher order levels in Bloom's Taxonomy (analysis, synthesis, and evaluation), the computer literacy column is blank because using those skills with technology more properly belongs to the programmer or computer scientist, not the average user of computers. Using the car analogy, a designer or even a mechanic would more likely be applying the cognitive skills of analysis and synthesis to the car itself. Referring to our driving analogy, using a map successfully is also distinct from putting together all the information needed to discern the best route for a scenic drive or to avoid the latest construction project. Likewise, a person may be able to find information for academic or business purposes (the location), but may not be able to discern biases, timeliness, and the suitability of the information to complete the task (the best route).

Many librarians, educators, and others may be intimidated by the technological skills of Gen M students. However, they must realize that these are not the same as skills needed to accomplish more complex, critical thinking tasks for academic research or the reports and memos expected in the business world. The table compares these concepts and helps visualize the differences with the objective of making clear the distinction between computer literacy and information literacy. While common, this blending of computer and information literacy concepts can lead to missing learning opportunities and problems with assessment. Clearly marking the divide helps focus instruction and assessment of competencies.

Table 2.1. Comparison of Different Types of Literacy

Bloom's Taxonomy	Literacy*	Computer Literacy	Information Literacy**
Knowledge	Decodes symbols and letters	Turns on machine; controls mouse; recognizes icons	Determines nature and extent of information needed by identifying key concepts and terms
Comprehension	Constructs meaning from written text	Manipulates simple text applications	Identifies variety of types and formats of potential sources for information
Application	Makes inferences from text; expresses understanding of text in written responses	Manipulates standard search engine, spreadsheet, and presentation applications	Accesses needed information efficiently by constructing effectively designed search strategies
Analysis	Synthesizes, analyzes, and extends meaning of text		Examines and compares information from various sources to evaluate reliability, validity, accuracy, authority, timeliness, point of view, and bias
Synthesis	Makes connections in order to generate new ideas		Uses information effectively to accomplish a specific purpose
Evaluation	Judges and evaluates value of knowledge		Judges information for reliability, validity, accuracy, authority, timeliness, point of view, or bias. Observes laws, regulations, and institutional policies concerning copyright; cites resources used

* The Literacy column contains terminology from the State of New Jersey (Department of Education, 2006).

** The Information Literacy column contains terminology from the American Library Association (ALA, 2000).

IMPACT ON LIBRARY INSTRUCTION AND NEW WAYS TO TEACH INFORMATION LITERACY SKILLS

In a recent presentation, Lynn Silipigni Connaway and Marie L. Radford shared their research on virtual reference. They found that Gen M students are striking in their preference for "figuring it out for myself" (Connaway and Radford, 2008: slide 28). Their preferred method of learning to drive would be to get in the car and go. They enjoy pushing every button to see what it can do and trying every gear. This is the way they have learned since childhood and new machines hold no fear for them. The online environment also holds no fear despite the number of times they become lost. How do we convince them that information literacy is valuable? Why use a map when exploring is such fun?

One major change should be letting go of the idea that we need to tell them exactly the way to go when they start their journey. After all, a map shows the territory, but it does not dictate the path the car must travel. When a student is first assigned a research paper, we often attempt to teach them all the tools they will need to do all research in that discipline, if not all disciplines. Conscious of how little time the student will spend with us, we try to force all our treasure into their hands. We try to make them remember where all the roads are closed, where all the traffic ties up, and where the short-cuts lead. However, research indicates that a better model would be for librarians to be "guides on the side" and more passive. Librarians can construct guides and maps that students can use in their own way. The challenge, then, will be to make guides and maps in Gen M's perspective so they will be useful to the self-guided seeker.

Despite growing up with computers and the Internet, Gen M students cause concerns among librarians, faculty, and employers with their lack of skills in critical thinking and analysis of information. As pointed out in previous sections of this chapter, there is quantitative evidence that Gen M is not as sophisticated with computer and information tasks as everyone assumes, and they have the mistaken view that "everything they need to conduct and complete an assignment can be found online through the freely available Internet resources" (Lorenzo and Dziuban, 2006: 8). With their multitasking, split attention between their work, the Internet, and their friends, how can librarians and faculty grab their attention long enough so that these students may become proficient and literate information users and communicators?

Devin Zimmerman suggests "focused multitasking or metatasking" as one means of teaching research skills (Zimmerman, 2007: 60). Instead of discouraging or disparaging multitasking, the author shows students how to open other windows for information management software, such as RefWorks while searching a database and a Word document to write notes while searching and reading articles from a database. This "focused multitasking" saves time because the information is being gathered and saved in different formats for later use in writing the research paper. Nicoletti and Merriman report on Gen Ms' learning styles and recommend tailoring teaching methods to match these traits (2007). Some of the ways these students learn include collaborative and team environments, with projects and assignments that are goal-oriented and directed toward their future careers; flexible programs ("let me do it my way"); and the use of technology that "enables them to be more productive and connected" (Nicoletti and Merriman, 2007: 29). They suggest teaching strategies that are visual and interactive. Internet resources provided by textbook publishers or simulations are resources for these activities. Group work projects and cooperative learning opportunities involving real-life problems and activities appeal to this age group.

It is not a new idea that active learning engages these students instead of passive lectures. Teachers have been urged to become "guides on the side" instead of being "sages on the stage" for quite some time. Faust, Ginno, Laherty, and Manuel at the California State University in Hayward, California, presented a poster at the ACRL 10th National Conference in 2001 outlining strategies for teaching information literacy to Gen M students, and the information is posted on the college's Web site (Faust et al., 2001). This Web site compares the traditional library instruction methods with newer approaches to teaching these students, and includes data showing improvements in skills with the newer techniques. One example compares the use of a traditional worksheet with the use of a concept map to visualize a broad topic and narrower subtopics. There was a 22.2 percent decline in totally non-focused topics, and a 34-44 percent increase in fully focused projects. Handouts and fill-in-the-blank sheets to locate various parts and services in a library do not work well with these students. A crossword puzzle used instead increased post-test scores by 10 percent when asked to recall names of the library's catalog, types of reference services, and so on. Traditional worksheets do not work as well as using activity cards with questions to answer like those used in Trivial Pursuit. This more "active and kinesthetic learning" increased post-test scores by 28 percent. Handouts with screen shots that show how to use the catalog in a more visual and graphic way created higher scores on post-tests. A new Web search assignment with search engine basics and using specialized search engines produced an increase in student scores, and a decrease of 10–16 percent of students refusing to do the assignment. These librarians found different ways to present information literacy skills with better learning outcomes for this group of students.

The University of San Francisco Library uses podcasts for online tutorials, blogs for literature searching, and a Web site to help students with searching skills. The technology used is familiar to the students, and they can access these instructions at their convenience (Tan, 2008). As pointed out by Nicoletti and Merriman (2007: 31), "if teaching is an exchange of ideas, then the way people convey their thoughts in this day and age—text messages, podcasts, the Internet, instant messaging—must find a place in the modern classroom." This technology has many implications for librarians and educators. One of the major changes involves reading text, which is not Gen M's preferred way of learning. According to Nicoletti and Merriman (2007), students retain 10 percent of what they read, but 30 percent of what they see, because they tend to scan rather than read. By knowing and understanding the learning styles of Gen M, librarians and educators can modify their instruction to accommodate them with better learning outcomes. The data shows that these students are not as Net savvy as they and everyone else thinks they are, and to really engage them one needs to alter the traditional lecture and demonstration way of teaching to more creative forms of instruction. By using the social networking services such as blogs, wikis, and podcasts, more creative and meaningful assignments can be used to teach the needed skills to these students.

CONCLUSION

For many decades, we have been discussing the librarian's role in creating the lifelong learner, and this generation may be the first where being a self-directed "scientific" learner is the norm. In *The Academic Library and the Net Gen Student*, Susan Gibbons quotes James Gee's research on video games and learning (2007). Gee describes the process of learning a video game as being identical to the basis for scientific inquiry. The player forms a hypothesis, tests it with various actions, considers the results, re-forms the hypothesis, re-tests, and so on, until success is achieved (Gibbons, 2007). If we can deliver information literacy instruction in such a way as to take advantage of this hypothesis testing, we can make it as integral to Gen M as the rest of their world. The key to our relationship with Gen M may be the recognition that we are made for each other, the mapmakers and the lifelong travelers on the information highway.

REFERENCES

ALA. "Information Literacy Competency Standards for Higher Education." Chicago: American Library Association (2000). Available: www.ala.org/ala/acrl/acrlstandards/standards.pdf (accessed May 17, 2008).

Ballantine, Joan A., Patricia McCourt Larres, and Peter Oyelere. 2007. "Computer Usage and the Validity of Self-Assessed Computer Competence Among First-Year Business Students." *Computers & Education* 49, no. 4 (December): 976–990.

Childers, Scott. 2003. "Computer Literacy: Necessity or Buzzword?" *Information Technology and Libraries* 22, no. 2 (September): 100–104.

Connaway, Lynn, and Marie Radford. "Smiling Online: Applying Face-to-Face Reference Skills in a Virtual Environment: A Special Presentation from OCLC Research." Dublin, OH: OCLC (April 16, 2008). Available: www5.oclc.org/downloads/research/webinars/smilingonline.pdf (accessed June 30, 2008).

Department of Education. 2006. Performance Level Descriptors. Trenton: State of New Jersey. Available: www.state.nj.us/education/assessment/descriptors/es/lal3.htm (accessed September 23, 2008).

Estabrook, Leigh, Evans Witt, and Lee Ranie. *Pew Internet: Libraries Report*. Washington, DC: Pew Internet and American Life Project. (December 30, 2007). Available: www.pewinternet.org/PPF/r/231/report_display.asp (accessed May 25, 2008).

Faust, Judith, Elizabeth A. Ginno, Jennifer Laherty, and Kate Manuel. "Generation Y Demographics." Hayward: California State University East Bay Library (Spring 2001). Available: www.library.csuhayward.edu/staff/ginno/ACRL/demograp.htm (accessed May 2, 2008).

Garrett, Marie. "What Is Information Literacy?" Knoxville: University of Tennessee Libraries. (September 2001). Available: www.lib.utk.edu/instruction/infolit/infolit.html (accessed May 23, 2008).

Gibbons, Susan. 2007. *The Academic Library and the Net Gen Student*. Washington, DC: American Library Association.

Gilton, Donna. "History of Information Literacy Instruction." Kingston: University of Rhode Island (2004). Available: www.uri.edu/artsci/lsc/Faculty/gilton/InformationLiteracyInstruction-AHistoryinContext.htm (accessed May 23, 2008).

Harvey, Brian. 1983. "Stop Saying 'Computer Literacy'!" *Classroom Computer News* 3, no. 6 (May-June): 56–57.

Hawkins, Brian L., and Diana G. Oblinger. 2006. "The Myth about the Digital Divide: We Have Overcome the Digital Divide." *EDUCAUSE Review* 41, no. 4 (July-August): 12–13. Available: http://connect.educause.edu/Library/

EDUCAUSE+Review/TheMythabouttheDigitalDiv/40646 (accessed July 24, 2008).

Jenson, Jill. 2004. "It's the Information Age, So Where's the Information? Why Our Students Can't Find It and What We Can Do to Help." *College Teaching* 52, no. 3 (Summer): 107–112.

Julien, Heidi. "CAIS–Paper Calls–Journal–Special Issue." Canadian Association for Information Science (2007). Available: www.cais-acsi.ca/journal/special. htm (accessed May 27, 2008).

Katz, Irvin. 2007. "Testing Information Literacy in Digital Environments: ETS's iSkills Assessment." *Information Technology and Libraries* 26, no. 3 (September): 3–12.

Katz, Irvin. 2008. "Are You Information Literate–RU Sure?" Lecture presented at a chapter meeting of the Princeton-Trenton Special Library Association, Princeton, NJ (March 17).

King, Kenneth M. 1985. "Evolution of the Concept of Computer Literacy." *EDUCOM Bulletin* 20, no. 3 (Fall): 18–21.

Lee, Diane. "Information Literacy: Definitions." Vancouver: School of Library, Archival and Information Studies, University of British Columbia (April 12, 2002). Available: www.slais.ubc.ca/COURSES/libr500/01-02-wt2/www/ d_lee/definitions.htm (accessed May 23, 2008).

Lorenzo, George, and Charles Dziuban. 2006. "Ensuring the Net Generation Is Net Savvy." *Educause Learning Initiative* ELI Paper 2 (September): 1–19. Available: net.educause.edu/ir/library/pdf/ELI3006.pdf (accessed July 20, 2008).

Miller, George. 1988. "The Challenge of Universal Literacy." *Science* 241, no. 4871 (September 9): 1293–1299.

Nicoletti, Augustine, and William Merriman. 2007. "Teaching Millennial Generation Students." *Momentum* 38, no. 2 (April–May): 28–31.

OCLC. "Part 1. Libraries and Information Sources-Use, Familiarity and Favorability." *College Students' Perceptions of Libraries and Information Resources.* Dublin, OH: Online Computer Literacy Center (2005). Available: www.oclc. org/reports/perceptionscollege.htm (accessed May 25, 2008).

Oman, Julie. 2001. "Information Literacy in the Workplace." *Information Outlook* 5, no. 6 (June). Available: www.sla.org/content/Shop/Information/infoonline/2001/jun01/oman.cfm (accessed July 18, 2008).

OSPI. "Implementing Technology Literacy & Integration Reporting Requirements." Olympia, WA: Office of Superintendent of Public Instruction (2005). Available: www.k12.wa.us/EdTech/TechRequirements.aspx (accessed June 16, 2008).

Rader, Hannelore. 2002. "Information Literacy 1973–2002: A Selected Literature Review." *Library Trends* 51, no. 2 (Fall): 242.

Tan, Josephine. 2008. "How Online Tutorials, Podcasts, and Blogs Transformed Librarians into Virtual Teachers." Paper presented at the annual meeting of the Medical Library Association, Chicago, IL (May 20).

Tannenbaum, Richard, and Irvin Katz. "Research Memorandum: Setting Standards on the Core and Advanced iSkills Assessments." Princeton, NJ: Educational Testing Service (February 2008). Available: www.ets.org/ Media/Research/pdf/RM-08-04.pdf (accessed May 25, 2008).

Zimmerman, Devin. 2007. "Metatasking vs. Multitasking." *Library Journal* 132, no. 7 (April 15): 60.

Chapter 3

Expanding Our Literacy Toolbox: The Case for Media Literacy

Susan Avery

INTRODUCTION

Does Gen M really experience and use media differently than past generations? What is the impact of media on the social and academic lives of Gen M students? Answering questions such as these is critical to addressing the importance of media literacy in the education of Gen M students. This generation has grown up with the Internet and technologies such as instant messaging, blogs, and online video. These students "see little difference in credibility or entertainment value between print and media formats" (Abram and Luther, 2004: 34). Numerous reports from projects, such as the Pew Internet and American Life Project, have shared information about these students and their media usage. These reports reveal information about Gen M students that is particularly relevant when examining the importance of media literacy. The studies indicate:

- 70 percent of 18 to 29 year olds visit video-sharing Web sites (Rainie, 2008).
- When dealing with a personal problem, 76 percent turn to the Internet for help with the problem (Estabrook, Witt, and Rainie, 2007).

- Significantly higher numbers of Gen Ms use their cell phones to text message, access the Internet, view videos, and get directions than any other age group (Horrigan, 2008).
- 76 percent watch or download online video and 67 percent send video links to others (Madden, 2007).

These numbers provide compelling arguments for librarians and educators to move beyond a dependence on text-based resources in their interactions with Gen M students. Many instructional approaches that have been successful with past generations of students are unlikely to be effective with a generation for whom media has become a ubiquitous part of their lives. Understanding the role of media literacy in our culture is an important step in helping students both understand and use media effectively.

WHAT IS MEDIA LITERACY?

Defining Media Literacy

Finding one clear, concise definition of media literacy is a difficult task, as numerous definitions exist. The most succinct definition, the result of the 1992 Aspen Institute National Leadership Conference on Media Literacy, defines media literacy as "the ability of a citizen to access, analyze, and produce information for specific outcomes" (Firestone, accessed 2008: 1). The National Association for Media Literacy Education expands on this definition to state: "Media literacy is the ability to encode and decode the symbols transmitted via media and the ability to synthesize, analyze and produce mediated messages" (National Association, accessed 2008, under "Variety of Terminology"). The Center for Media Literacy further expands the definition to say: "Media Literacy is a 21st century approach to education. It provides a framework to access, analyze, evaluate and create messages in a variety of forms—from print to video to the Internet. Media literacy builds an understanding of the role of media in society as well as essential skills of inquiry and self-expression necessary for citizens of a democracy" (CML, 2007: 1). In a society that embraces information in numerous formats, an informed citizenry must be able to evaluate and interpret the messages they receive, regardless of their format.
Media literacy is built upon ideas from numerous disciplines, includ-

ing communication, literacy theory, cultural and media studies, and semiotics. The core concepts of media literacy include:

- All messages are constructions, created by authors for specific purposes.
- People use their knowledge, skills, beliefs, and experiences to construct meaning from messages.
- Different forms and genres of communication use specific codes, conventions, and symbolic forms.
- Values and ideologies are conveyed in media messages in ways that represent certain worldviews, shaping perceptions of reality.
- Media messages, media industries, and technologies of communication exist within a larger aesthetic, cultural, historical, political, economic, and regulatory framework. (Hobbs, Jaszi, and Aufderheide, 2007: 4)

William G. Covington notes that in the teaching of media literacy, students "are taught the way media operate and influence behavior for all members of society" (Covington, 2004: 123). The packaging of the message is just as important as its content, as it is often the packaging that most strongly influences the perception of the message. In an evolving information landscape, the structure of information is continually changing, especially with regard to format and production. Students are increasingly spending time in social networks, creating and sharing information. They may not always fully understand the implications of the messages they create, send, and receive. Media literate students are able to interpret media messages, regardless of format, and integrate them into their knowledge base.

In order to examine media literacy more closely, it is important to differentiate between media literacy and visual literacy. Visual literacy is associated with images; media literacy is associated with media and its messages, many of them visual. Maricopa Community College, an institution actively engaged in the digital video literacy movement, defines visual literacy as "the ability to understand and produce visual messages" (Bleed, 2005: 5). Additional definitions of visual literacy indicate it is "a group of competencies that an individual can develop by seeing and at the same time having and integrating other sensory experiences" or "the ability to interpret messages as well as generate images for communicating ideas and concepts" (5). Visual literacy is clearly an essential skill for the media literate person.

A Brief Background of Media Literacy Education

In 1964, Marshall McLuhan proclaimed, "the medium is the message" in his book, *Understanding Media: The Extensions of Man* (McLuhan, 1964: 7). McLuhan observed that the medium of a given message strongly influences the message itself, and the medium has the ability to impact directly how someone perceives the message content. John Culkin, a former Jesuit priest and colleague of McLuhan, is often credited with the beginning of media literacy education. In 1969, Culkin founded the Center for Understanding Media at the New School for Social Research. Among its work, the center engaged in projects to bring media education into schools. Culkin's programs strove to help teachers feel more comfortable introducing media and new formats in the classroom. In spite of the efforts of McLuhan, Culkin, and others, the United States has lagged behind other countries in the inclusion of media education in its schools. Media literacy education has had a much more significant role in the education of students in other countries, particularly Canada, Australia, the United Kingdom, and South Africa. Media literacy has been mandated in schools in these countries for many years.

In 2005, Robert Kubey noted that "formal media education in the United States lags behind every other major English speaking country in the world" (Kubey, 2005: 1). Countries with more centralized governance of educational systems can much more easily include media literacy in the school curricula (Brown, 1998). The decentralized nature of the public school system in the United States often places the impetus for inclusion of media literacy programs on the local district. Given the large degree of autonomy of local school districts and the educational mandates of the No Child Left Behind Act, the inclusion of media literacy education remains difficult for many districts. Renee Hobbs observes, "media literacy is on the books at the state curriculum level in 49 states" (Barack, 2007: 22). Critical thinking and communication skills are among those reflected in the standards for media literacy. However, Hobbs goes on to say: ". . . we estimate only 10 to 15 percent of children are getting exposure to those ideas" (22).

David Buckingham, Director of Centre for the Study of Children, Youth and Media at the University of London, defines media education as "the process of teaching and learning about media; media literacy is the outcome—the knowledge and skills learners acquire" (Buckingham, 2003: 4). His arguments for the inclusion of media education in schools stress the need for a curriculum that relates to the lives of students outside of school. The ability to make sense of and interpret the messages students receive on a daily basis is crucial to their success in a media-saturated world.

There are many that argue for the inclusion of media literacy in the education of students. Perhaps Patricia H. Hinchey provides one of the strongest arguments for its inclusion:

> The primary concern of media literacy education is not the transmission of information, though certainly there is a world of information worth sharing. Instead the goal is to offer students practice in becoming critical readers of the world around them—of the ads on buses and in magazines; of the movies that they swarm to on weekends and that fill the shelves of their DVD libraries; of the music videos that play nonstop on their televisions; of the advice of talk show hosts and gurus; of the newscasts and newspapers sponsored and routinely censored by a handful of corporate giants. (Hinchey, 2003: 269)

Given the difficulty of incorporating media literacy into the education of K–12 students in the United States, its introduction in higher education is increasingly more critical.

An examination of courses with a focus on media literacy in higher education reveals most are connected to communication or journalism departments. Everette E. Dennis observes that they are often associated with introductory media courses, and "only a tiny proportion of other university students choose to take this course as an elective" (Dennis, 2004: 205). Given the ubiquitous nature of media in the lives of college students and their increasing reliance on media resources in their academic research, placing some responsibility for media literacy education within the library is entirely appropriate. Academic libraries pride themselves on creating lifelong learners, encouraging students to become self-sufficient information users for their lives beyond academia. James A. Brown's observations of media literacy education reveal a similar objective. He states: "a major goal of media education is to help recipients of mass communication become active, free participants in the process rather than static, passive, and subservient to the images and values communicated in a one-way flow from media sources" (Brown, 1998: 47).

WHY MEDIA LITERACY?

Media in Society

As noted in the introduction, numerous studies demonstrate the growing role of media in the lives of Gen M students. How do students deconstruct and differentiate the messages they receive from news outlets with varied perspectives, reality television, blogs, user-generated video, and advertisements in print, online, and via television? The omnipresence of media can make it difficult to separate that which is real from that which is not. The messages students receive do matter, regardless of their format, and students must be able to interpret these messages to make informed decisions. Media literacy skills empower students to filter the information around them, allowing them to incorporate the best of it into their academic and social lives, and reject that which is inaccurate, inappropriate, or manipulated.

An examination of the changing role of media in society strengthens the argument for the inclusion of media literacy in our educational systems. A better understanding of this role helps both educators and their students successfully access, analyze, and interpret information in multiple formats. Without question, the role of media in society is being transformed in the twenty-first century. Mark Glaser, a journalist and new media expert, suggests seven "New Rules of Media." The rules he provides further illustrate the ways in which media usage and production are changing (Glaser, 2008, under "New Rules of Media"):

1. "The Audience Knows More Than the Journalist (News Is a Conversation and Not a Lecture)." Collectively, audiences possess a great deal of knowledge; news has become an ongoing conversation, moving from the broadcast or stage to online.
2. "People Are in Control of Their Media Experience." Digital recorders and on-demand viewing allows users to control what they watch and when they watch it.
3. "Anyone Can Be a Media Creator or Mixer." The affordability of devices and software allows users to both create media and post it online.
4. "Traditional Media Must Evolve or Die." Innovation and change in the technology industry is reaching the media industry.
5. "Despite Censorship, The Story Will Get Out." Digital video and the Web make it possible to share information in real time.

6. "Amateur and Professional Journalists Should Work Together." Bloggers often have valuable contributions to share with journalists.
7. "Journalists Need to Be Multi-Platform." Journalists need more than one skill to reach audiences in multiple spaces.

An examination of these "rules" serves to emphasize the changes that are occurring. Media literacy creates a community that can better filter the messages received through varying media platforms, integrate the messages into their lives, and participate in their culture as knowledgeable, informed citizens.

A Culture of Many Literacies

Numerous authors discuss the growing need for an educated population to become fluent in multiple literacies. Often the word "literacy" itself takes on an all-purpose nature that "seems hopelessly anachronistic, tainted with the nostalgic ghost of a fleeting industrial age" (Tyner, 1998: 63). Kathleen Tyner makes a case for multiliteracies including computer literacy, information literacy, technology literacy, visual literacy, and media literacy. The intersections between these literacies can make it difficult to isolate aspects of one without converging on another. Tyner's categorization of multiliteracies can help educators better connect the varying literacies. Her categories include the following:

Tool Literacies:

• Computer literacy: a general understanding of how computers work.
• Network literacy: knowledge, awareness, and understanding of the world of networked information and skills to retrieve and use this information.
• Technology literacy: analyzing, evaluating, and managing solutions to technology problems.

Literacies of Representation:

• Information literacy: the ability to find, to evaluate, and use information effectively.
• Media literacy: understanding mass media and how its messages are constructed and organized, and the ability to create media products.

- Visual literacy: the ability to comprehend and create media in order to communicate effectively and to use and understand images. (Tyner, 1998: 94–95).

Tyner's categorization of literacies illustrates the close relationships that exist among them and the complexities present in clarifying their differences, particularly when delineating media literacy and visual literacy.

The MacArthur Foundation's 2006 occasional paper, *Confronting the Challenges of Participatory Culture: Media Education for the 21st Century* (often referred to as the Jenkins Report), provides some compelling arguments for the inclusion of multiple literacies in our educational systems. A participatory culture encourages individuals to increase their sense of civic engagement and their willingness to share knowledge and information with one another. The paper does note three concerns in need of pedagogical interventions. These include the "participation gap" that recognizes the unequal access to opportunity, skills, experiences, and knowledge; the "transparency problem" that focuses on the difficulties students face in learning to examine how media can change our perceptions; and the "ethics challenge" that focuses on how traditional education is failing to prepare students to become active participants in the growing role of media in their lives (Jenkins et al., 2006).

Supporting the growth of a participatory culture requires the development of multiple literacies including basic research skills and technical skills. Further bolstering the need for media literacy in a participatory culture, the Jenkins Report stresses "students also must acquire a basic understanding of the ways media representations structure our perceptions of the world; the economic and cultural contexts within which mass media is produced and circulated; the motives and goals that shape the media they consume; and alternative practices that operate outside the commercial mainstream" (Jenkins et al., 2006: 20).

Acquiring media literacy skills is a responsibility that must be shared across the academic arena. A media literate person possesses not only the ability to access and evaluate media, but also the skills necessary to produce media. Production skills can be quite specialized, and acquiring the necessary competencies to teach media production is a growing focus in teacher education programs. Because media literacy, like information literacy, is not "owned" by any particular discipline, aspects of it can be successfully incorporated into many classes. Addressing aspects of media literacy that focus on the production of media can cause concerns within libraries, as such skills generally do not fall within the scope of the support provided by the library. Individual libraries and educational institutions must determine where the specific expertise necessary to teach students the technical aspects of video production, photography, or Web page development lies on their campuses. It is essential to keep in mind that, "at its best media literacy education is nonpartisan and includes production (i.e., the ability to 'write') as well as analysis (the ability to 'read')" (Rogow, 2004: 32).

MEDIA LITERACY AND INFORMATION LITERACY

As the literacies essential for Gen M students to become informed citizens continue to expand, it is important that libraries begin to examine closely the linkages between information literacy and media literacy. Jeremy H. Lipschultz asks, "Why do media and information literacy matter? They matter because people in all walks of life across the globe need to be able to deconstruct media messages and critique the quality of information sources" (Lipschultz and Hilt, 2005: 2). Although the two literacies may sometimes focus on different formats, their ultimate goals are quite similar: producing users capable of accessing, analyzing, and effectively utilizing resources for an information need, whether academic or social. Lipschultz continues to argue the importance of both of these twenty-first-century skills because media viewers ". . . armed with media and information literacy knowledge and skills would immediately recognize what is happening and why" (Lipschultz and Hilt, 2005: 2).

Much of the library profession continues to be grounded in print and text-based information and, as a collective population, must begin to recognize that its users participate in a culture that has become increasingly more visual. Barbara MacAdam urges librarians to take on a new set of assumptions "about how students think, what they value, and how external incentives shape their behavior in the information environment" (MacAdam, 2000: 77). She compels librarians to examine closely undergraduate behavior to better understand how these students think and work with the information, letting those observations provide the impetus for redefining our roles.

A review of the competencies information-literate students demonstrate helps to further establish correlations between information literacy and media literacy. The Association of College and Research Libraries (ACRL) *Information Literacy Competency Standards for Higher*

Education, approved in 2000, are "a set of abilities requiring individuals to 'recognize when information is needed and have the ability to locate, evaluate, and use effectively the needed information'" (ACRL, 2007, under "Information Literacy Defined"). The document goes on to state that information literacy "is an intellectual framework for understanding, finding, evaluating, and using information . . . " that "extends lifelong learning through abilities which may use technologies but are ultimately independent of them" (ACRL, 2007, under "Information Literacy and Information Technology"). Just as possessing information literacy skills increases a student's ability to work independently, so, too, do media literacy skills. The successful incorporation of either literacy into the academic life of an institution "requires the collaborative efforts of faculty, librarians, and administrators" as is stated in the ACRL Information Literacy Standards document (ACRL, 2007, under "Information Literacy and Higher Education"). In the case of information literacy, this often includes the identification of increasingly higher order skills that are scaled throughout the curriculum, moving from general introductions of information literacy in first-year courses to more specific applications of information literacy in upper-division courses within the disciplines.

It is unfortunate that no prescribed standards for media literacy currently exist. Although not media literacy standards, per se, Joshua Meyrowitz identifies three separate types of media literacy. The first of these is *media content literacy*, which focuses on the ability to "access, interpret, and evaluate content from a variety of media" (Meyrowitz, 1998: 99). A direct correlation can be found between this type of media literacy and information literacy. Of utmost importance to media content literacy is the ability to critically evaluate and analyze media.

The second type of media literacy Meyrowitz identifies is *media grammar literacy*, which focuses on the production aspects of various types of media and "unlike media content literacy, media grammar literacy demands some understanding of the specific workings of individual media" (Meyrowitz, 1998: 100). Examples of media grammar literacy include the ability to recognize how varying techniques are employed in the production of different media types, often with the intent of manipulating the media message. For example, knowing how various type sizes, fonts, and spacing impact print media; understanding the impact of shot lengths, dissolves, focus, and camera angles in television and film; or the influence of framing, angles, shutter speed, lenses, and filters in photographs.

As Meyrowitz notes, in its entirety, media literacy involves more than simply accessing and evaluating sources; it includes the ability to produce media. This does not necessarily mean the library profession must become fluent in media production. It does mean, however, that librarians must make connections with those on their campuses who can address these issues. In many cases, it is simply a matter of recognizing the expertise of colleagues, and encouraging students to take advantage of those best prepared to provide assistance with the various components of media literacy skills. Those who provide library instruction must be realistic in acknowledging the research practices and resources of current students and provide them with criteria that will allow them to evaluate critically all of the resources they utilize, regardless of format.

Meyrowitz's third type of media literacy is *medium literacy*. This type of media literacy is identified most closely with the theories of Marshall McLuhan and examines the characteristics inherent in each individual medium. Medium literacy analyzes how specific mediums influence the impact of a message. For example, the same message received via e-mail and telephone may be perceived very differently through each medium; a political debate may have an entirely different impact when heard on the radio than it does on the television; and a news story may be perceived quite differently through a newspaper article than it would be on a television broadcast. This particular aspect of media literacy "involves explicit or implicit comparison of one medium of communication with another medium of communication" (Meyrowitz, 1998: 106).

MEDIA LITERACY IN THE LIBRARY

To remain relevant to Gen M students, it is essential that libraries recognize and address the changing needs of a media-savvy student population. Librarians must begin to rethink their roles to accommodate both new materials and literacies. Examining elements of the ACRL Information Literacy Standards alongside Meyrowitz's media literacies and the multiliteracies defined by Tyner can provide guidance as librarians begin to discuss the incorporation of media literacy into course-integrated library instructions in the classroom, one-on-one help sessions with a librarian at the Reference Desk, and the individualized learning that occurs via instructional pages on library Web sites. College writing courses are increasingly encouraging and permitting students to utilize other formats as alternatives to the traditional research paper for assignments in their writing classes. These may include formats such as photo essays, videos, or Web pages. Just as students are accustomed to relying on sources in a variety of mediums in the research for their assignments, they may now use these same formats as the medium for their "writing."

Two examples of universities that make extensive use of media as the medium for the creation of student work are the University of Southern California (USC) and the University of Illinois. USC's Institute for Multimedia Literacy was established in 1998 and is "dedicated to developing educational programs and conducting research on the changing nature of literacy in a networked culture" (Institute, accessed 2008a). A growing number of programs and courses utilize multimedia tools in the classroom, allowing students numerous alternatives to the traditional written paper. Such courses are important in their efforts to acknowledge "that to be literate in the 21st century requires not only effective skills in reading and writing, but also the ability to use and interpret media effectively" (Institute, accessed 2008b). Through an extensive training program, faculty members develop courses in which students utilize video documentaries and digital essays as the medium for assignments in a wide variety of disciplines. At the University of Illinois, the School of Art and Design offers "Writing with Video," a course that fulfills the general education advanced composition requirement in which video is the medium for all of the students' writing assignments. In the fall of 2008, students in first-year rhetoric classes were provided with the option of using a multimodal medium for one of their assignments, rather than the traditional written paper. The number of universities offering options such as those at USC and Illinois will only continue to grow, and libraries must be prepared to support students in these courses.

How can librarians begin to participate in the media literacy dialogues on their campuses? First, they must immediately begin to address the changing student dynamics and student reliance on information from a wide variety of resources. Student media usage continues to grow as they "use media to achieve goals that are intimately connected to their identity and their social interaction" (Maness, 2004: 47). Media literacy requires the same critical thinking skills inherent in information literacy that focus on perception, reflection, reasoning, and evaluation. Just as exemplary information literacy instruction focuses on teaching the concepts necessary for successfully finding and evaluating information, rather than teaching how to use specific search tools, care must be taken to assure media literacy instruction is not focused on "discrete skills such as programming, Internet access, or presentation skills" (Tierney, Bond, and Bressler, 2006: 360).

Librarians must keep their eyes and ears open as they strive to stay current with curricular changes on their campuses. Doing so allows librarians to become proactive in addressing the inclusion of library instruction in courses that focus on media literacy. Advocating for the inclusion of media literacy in the teacher education curriculum is one way to assure that new teachers entering the profession understand its importance. Courses that focus on instructional technology, commonplace in most teacher education programs, are a good place to include an introduction to media literacy. Librarians can further work with faculty in education departments on introducing various aspects of media literacy. Of course, media literacy in higher education is of importance beyond the teacher education curriculum. David L. Martinson notes, "If budget and other academic or curriculum restraints make it impossible to develop and establish a specific media literacy course, then media literacy instruction must be built consciously, and specifically into existing curriculums" (Martinson, 2004: 158). Librarians who have been involved in the integration of information literacy instruction into courses on their campuses can be instrumental in accomplishing a similar objective with media literacy. Introductions to media literacy should sit side-by-side with information literacy in first-year writing courses. More detailed aspects of these literacies can then be scaled throughout the curriculum in upper-division courses focusing on higher-level skills and more advanced critical thinking skills.

Libraries can put specific practices into place immediately to address the importance of media literacy. "How do I" type pages on library Web sites should address multiple resource formats. Guides can be created that assist students in locating videos, digital sources, and images. Such pages can steer students to reputable resources already vetted by librarians and indicate how they may be able to locate similar information in specific library databases. Similarly, pages that focus on evaluation must move beyond the "Is it a magazine or a journal?" models to include media and visual resources. Many commonalities exist when evaluating resources, such as authorship and credibility, the purpose of the source, and the presence of bias or propaganda, that are applicable to all sources, regardless of format. Teaching students to look for such elements, rather than focusing on scholarly vs. popular periodicals, is crucial for a population of students who rely on such a multiplicity of resources in their research.

Obviously including more detailed information about elements specific to each particular type of resource should be included as well.

In many cases, media messages are not packaged in customary ways and the packaging of the message strongly influences the perception of the message itself. It can be generalized that, given the recognizable visual cues present in print formats, the ability to distinguish between a tabloid publication, a magazine, and a scholarly journal is not difficult. However, inaccurate and biased information on the Web can easily imitate credible information through formatting techniques, and video messages can likewise be impacted by the employment of varying camera techniques. The visual cues that are present when examining print sources are not always present in other formats, and a new set of evaluative guidelines must be applied. An awareness of such cues and the ability to read them is at the heart of media literacy.

Providing facilities and physical space that can be used for the production aspects of media literacy is another option for libraries that wish to further demonstrate their support for media literacy on their campuses. Growing numbers of libraries are providing productivity software on computers in their libraries in an attempt to serve more completely the research needs of their students. As space is often at a premium in libraries, dedicating specific spaces for media production may not be a realistic option. However, libraries with computer labs may be able to dedicate a small number of machines to digital and video production. Technical support for these programs can be a challenge, and it might be the case that this kind of support cannot be provided during all of the hours a library is open.

Librarians and educators, in spite of their best efforts, may not always be successful in reaching students. "[B]ecause people always interpret what they see, hear, and read through the lens of their own experience, we also must allow for the distinct possibility that students, when provided with the skills to analyze for themselves, will come to conclusions that differ from our own" (Rogow, 2004: 31). At the very least, libraries must begin to think more holistically about their students and their research practices. Libraries that truly examine the whole picture will quickly realize the need to change and/or revise many of their past practices and look for new ways to accommodate Gen M students on multiple levels.

MEDIA LITERACY, COPYRIGHT, AND CITATION ISSUES

Copyright Issues

Effective use of media materials in the classroom and in the completion of student assignments is at the core of media literacy education. The use of information from mass media is critical in many classes. Media literacy and its dependence on information from multiple technologies is undeniably impacted by copyright law and this, in turn, affects teachers, librarians, and students. An awareness of copyright law, fair use, and its bearing on the media used by instructors in the classroom is increasingly important. As students continue both to use and create media for their academic and social lives, educating them on appropriate use of media, particularly as it relates to class assignments, is also crucial. However, finding common interpretations of the law is difficult and varies from institution to institution.

In 2007, the Center for Social Media at American University's School of Communication published "The Cost of Copyright Confusion for Media Literacy" to gain a better understanding of the beliefs and interpretations of copyright and its impact on media literacy education. Led by investigators Renee Hobbs, Peter Jaszi, and Pat Aufderheide, interviews were conducted with "63 educators, educational media producers, and organization leaders in media literacy" (Hobbs, Jaszi, and Aufderheide, 2007: 2). Participating were high school teachers, college professors, authors, editors, and filmmakers. Among the group of 63, it was found that "[w]hile they respect the rights of owners of intellectual property, they also believe that it is necessary to use copyrighted works for the purpose of strengthening students' critical thinking and communication skills" (Hobbs, Jaszi, and Aufderheide, 2007: 4). However, finding common ground in the understanding of copyright was simply not possible.

It is the fair use provision of the copyright law that is employed when media is used in the classroom and library. Fair use "is intended to balance the rights of users with the rights of owners, by encouraging the widespread and flexible use of cultural products" (Hobbs, Jaszi, and Aufderheide, 2007: 6). There are four considerations that need to be taken into account when determining fair use. These are "the purpose and character of the use; the nature of the copyrighted work; the amount and substantiality of the portion used; and the effect on the potential market for or value of the copyrighted work" (Aufderheide and Jaszi,

2008: 3). This Center for Social Media study found that, as a group, the educators were not familiar with and misunderstood fair use (Aufderheide and Jaszi, 2008). Its interpretation varied greatly, from broad to very restrictive. The purpose of this chapter is certainly not to make specific recommendations with regard to the use of media materials and copyright law. However, this author would like to note the difficulties inherent in the interpretation of copyright law and the impact it creates for effectively utilizing media when teaching media literacy. Additionally, this author encourages dialog with those on an individual's campus who are responsible for addressing copyright concerns.

Citing Media Sources

Citing sources used in the creation of student projects that utilize various media in lieu of the traditional research paper can also present difficulties. The fluid nature of information and continually changing formats are often reflected in citation styles that seem to change relatively frequently. Citations of media resources such as transcripts of news programs can be relatively straightforward, but the creation of a video mash-up that utilizes digital content and video from numerous sources can be much more challenging. Current practices regarding the proper citation style are often best addressed through Web sites for specific publication styles (APA, MLA, etc.). As with any type of resource, it is best to encourage students to get the most complete information possible when incorporating a media source into their papers or projects. Unfortunately, much of the information that exists in online citation guides created by individual institutions is for the citation of electronic resources such as online periodicals, database sources, and Web pages. Turning to a resource such as Google can be useful in locating pages developed by universities, libraries, organizations, and schools that address citation styles for media resources.

CONCLUSION

The importance of addressing media literacy in libraries and classrooms cannot be denied. Media literacy education is crucial in a society where the "explosion of technology and media has led to a culture in which we are constantly exposed or, one might argue, oversaturated with both" (Kenner and Rivera, 2007: 59). Higher education and libraries have a responsibility and, some might argue, an obligation to bring media literacy to the forefront for all students, not simply the small number of students in the few communication, journalism, or education classes that introduce media literacy. If our ultimate goal is "to help students ask newly critical questions of media policies and messages, encouraging them to become not only far more savvy consumers but also more self-determined human beings and more active and reflective democratic citizens" (Thoman and Jolls, 2004: 21), then it is essential that media literacy be included among the growing number of tools that enable us to reach a new generation of students.

REFERENCES

Abram, Stephen, and Judy Luther. 2004. "Born with the Chip." *Library Journal* 129, no. 8 (May 1): 34–37. Available: www.libraryjournal.com/Article/CA411572. html (accessed July 8, 2008).

ACRL. *Information Literacy Competency Standards for Higher Education.* American Library Association (May 21, 2007). Available: www.ala.org/Ala/Acrl/Acrl-standards/informationliteracycompetency.cfm (accessed May 18, 2008).

Aufderheide, Pat, and Peter Jaszi. "Recut, Reframe, Recycle: Quoting Copyrighted Material in User-Generated Video." Center for Social Media (2008). Available: www.centerforsocialmedia.org/files/pdf/CSM_Recut_Reframe_Recycle_report.pdf (accessed April 26, 2008).

Barack, Lauren. 2007. "Concern Over Copyright: Unfamiliarity with Fair Use Hampers Media Literacy." *School Library Journal* 53, no. 11 (November): 22–23.

Bleed, Ron. 2005. "Visual Literacy in Higher Education." *ELI Explorations* (August): 1–11. Available: http://net.educause.edu/ir/library/pdf/ELI4001. pdf (accessed June 5, 2008).

Brown, James A. 1998. "Media Literacy Perspectives." *Journal of Communication* 48: 44–57.

Buckingham, David. 2003. *Media Education: Literacy, Learning and Contemporary Culture.* Cambridge, MA: Polity Press.

CML. "Media Literacy: A Definition . . . and More." Center for Media Literacy (2007). Available: www.medialit.org/reading_room/rr2def.php (accessed May 14, 2008).

Covington, William G. 2004. "Creativity in Teaching Media Literacy." *International Journal of Instructional Media* 31, no. 2: 119–124.

Dennis, Everette E. 2004. "Out of Sight and Out of Mind: The Media Literacy Needs of Grown-Ups." *American Behavioral Scientist* 48, no. 2: 202–211.

Estabrook, Leigh, Evans Witt, and Lee Rainie. "Information Searches that Solve Problems." Washington, DC: Pew Internet and American Life Project

(December 30, 2007). Available: www.pewinternet.org/PPF/r/231/report_display.asp (accessed July 8, 2008).

Firestone, Charles M. "Aspen Institute National Leadership Conference on Media Literacy: Foreword." Aspen Institute Communications and Society Program. Available: www.medialit.org/reading_room/pdf/358_AspenFrwd_Firestone.pdf (accessed July 8, 2008).

Glaser, Mark. "Arkansas State Talk: The New Rules of Media." MediaShift Blog (March 31, 2008). Available: www.pbs.org/mediashift/2008/03/Arkansas_state_talkthe_new_rul.html (accessed June 5, 2008).

Hinchey, Patricia H. 2003. "Teaching Media Literacy: Not If, But Why and How." *The Clearing House* 76, no. 6: 268–270.

Hobbs, Renee, Peter Jaszi, and Pat Aufderheide. "The Cost of Copyright Confusion for Media Literacy." Center for Social Media (September 2007). Available: www.centerforsocialmedia.org/files/pdf/Final_CSM_copyright_report.pdf (accessed July 7, 2008).

Horrigan, John. "Mobile Access to Data and Information." Washington, DC: Pew Internet and American Life Project (March 5, 2008). Available: www.pewinternet.org/PPF/r/244/report_display.asp (accessed July 7, 2008).

Institute for Multimedia Literacy. "About IML." University of Southern California. Available: http://iml.usc.edu/?page_id=2 (accessed July 12, 2008a).

Institute for Multimedia Literacy. "Multimedia in the Core." University of Southern California. Available: http://iml.usc.edu/?page_id=15 (accessed July 12, 2008b).

Jenkins, Henry, Katie Clinton, Ravi Purushotma, Alice J. Robison, and Margaret Weigel. 2006. *Confronting the Challenges of Participatory Culture: Media Education for the 21st Century*. Chicago: MacArthur Foundation.

Kenner, Adam, and Sheryl Rivera. 2007. "Media Literacy: Good News." *Knowledge Quest* 35, no. 4: 59–60.

Kubey, Robert. 2005. "Commentary: How Media Education Can Promote Democracy, Critical Thinking, Health Awareness, and Aesthetic Appreciation in Young People." *Simile* 5, no. 1: 1–6.

Lipschultz, Jeremy H., and Michael L. Hilt. 2005. "Research Note: International Issues in Media and Information Literacy." *Simile* 5, no. 4: 1–4.

MacAdam, Barbara. 2000. "From the Other Side of the River: Re-Conceptualizing the Educational Mission of Libraries." *College and Undergraduate Libraries* 6, no. 2: 77–93.

Madden, Mary. "Online Video." Washington, DC: Pew Internet and American Life Project (July 25, 2007). Available: www.pewinternet.org/PPF/r/219/report_display.asp (accessed July 7, 2008).

Maness, Kevin. 2004. "Teaching Media-Savvy Students about the Popular Media." *English Journal* 93, no. 3: 46–51.

Martinson, David L. 2004. "Media Literacy Education: No Longer a Curriculum Option." *Educational Forum* 68, no. 2: 154–160.

McLuhan, Marshall. 1964. *Understanding Media: The Extensions of Man*. New York: McGraw-Hill.

Meyrowitz, Joshua. 1998. "Multiple Media Literacies." *Journal of Communication* 48, no. 1: 96–108.

National Association for Media Literacy Education. "Definitions." Available: www.amlainfo.org/what-is-media-literacy (accessed May 14, 2008).

Rainie, Lee. "Pew Internet Project Data Memo: Video Sharing Web Site." Washington, DC: Pew Internet and American Life Project (January 9, 2008). Available: www.pewinternet.org/pdfs/Pew_Videosharing_memo_Jan08.pdf (accessed July 7, 2008).

Rogow, Faith. 2004. "Shifting from Media to Literacy." *American Behavioral Scientist* 48, no. 1: 30–34.

Thoman, Elizabeth, and Tessa Jolls. 2004. "Media Literacy: A National Priority for a Changing World." *American Behavioral Scientist* 48, no. 1: 18–29.

Tierney, Robert J., Ernest Bond, and Jane Bresler. 2006. "Examining Literate Lives as Students Engage with Multiple Literacies." *Theory into Practice* 45, no. 4: 359–367.

Tyner, Kathleen. 1998. *Literacy in a Digital World*. Mahwah, NJ: Lawrence Erlbaum Associates.

Chapter 4

Gen M and the Information Search Process

Art Taylor

INTRODUCTION

Gen M has come of age in a digital world with expansive and widely available information resources. The computer and the global network used to access these resources has become a constant in the lives of Gen M community members. These digital resources are used for a broad spectrum of social interaction, entertainment, and easy access to global information resources. Research has suggested that Gen M has distinctly different expectations for information gathering. They search, gather, and evaluate information using techniques and strategies that are different from those used prior to the World Wide Web. Existing information behavior models may require modification to reflect these changes.

The longitudinal study detailed here involved Gen M students searching and evaluating documents in a naturalistic environment to fill a need for information. Participants provided detailed information on their search choices and judgments of document relevance constantly over a five-week period. The empirical results provide information on how Gen M are progressing through a Web-based search process, and suggests that the information behavior of Gen M using the Web may differ from that identified in previous search process models.

LITERATURE REVIEW

Gen M is a generation raised with technology. They are only familiar with a world with personal computers and easy access to the body of information that is the Internet. This generation comprises individuals who have distinct expectations concerning technology, communication, and access to information. These expectations are having a profound effect on academic libraries and are pertinent to any current discussion of information behavior. Stephen Abram (2006) notes that Gen M students expect instant access to information (cell phones, portable computers, Internet), and tend to procrastinate with research and the choices it requires. They tend to be considered multitaskers, because they are often seen doing several tasks at once (including use of the ubiquitous cell phone). They exist in a noisy, media-driven world, a condition that may lead to issues with filtering out what is valid and important to their task. Constant socializing in a connected world also provides distractions (Essinger, 2006).

The postmodern condition is a rejection of the objective, scientific evaluation of knowledge, and the general acceptance of an open, subjective, uncritical view of knowledge. This view can result in a piecework composition and fragmentation of an epistemology. The hypertext interface that is the foundation of the Web encourages this fragmentation (Harley, Dreger, and Knobloch, 2001). The young adults of Gen M are comfortable with this environment, and often do not recognize incomplete fragments as such. They have a tendency to regard each fragment as valid as any other. Some researchers have found that critical evaluation of Web content by Gen M subjects appears to be lacking. These subjects are concerned about the time it takes to find and evaluate content (and thus may avoid a particular research track if it seems too time consuming), they prefer a comfortable work environment when seeking information, and they generally prefer visual information to textual (Harley, Dreger, and Knobloch, 2001; Weiler, 2004; Vondracek, 2007).

The constant barrage of media information is considered by some researchers to be the harbinger of a *consumerist* society within which Gen M exists. In Harley, Dreger, and Knobloch (2001), the postmodern condition, as applied to the dissemination of information, is considered a disruptive force in the growth and distribution of knowledge in our culture, specifically as it applies to the administration of academic libraries. Consumerism, superficiality, and knowledge fragmentation are a result. In the "information economy," information is just another commodity that is consumed at the lowest cost. The cost, in this context, is *effort*, and the Gen M seeking information often perceives the lowest cost as the most convenient, readily available information with limited consideration for quality (Young and Von Seggern, 2001; Thompson, 2003; Buczynski, 2005).

INFORMATION BEHAVIOR

Examining the information behavior of Gen M subjects requires a context or framework within which to examine their actions. The search process and how Gen M searchers work to fill their information need can be examined within the framework of a search process model. Two commonly referenced search process models are Kuhlthau's (1991) information search process and Ellis's (1989) search patterns. Kuhlthau (1991; 1993) modeled information-seeking as a series of stages. Her model was built on personal construct theory, Taylor's (1968) stages of need formation, Belkin's, Oddy's, and Brooks' (1982) anomalous states of knowledge, and theories and models of expression and mood. Ellis (1989; 1997) identified several *search patterns* used for gathering information to fulfill an information need. His model emphasized the subjective, iterative nature of the search process and avoids suggesting that a consistent sequential process is taking place. Wilson (1999) provided a synthesis and comparison of Ellis's and Kuhlthau's models, which maps Ellis's behaviors into Kuhlthau's stages.

These models were developed prior to the widespread use of the Internet as an information resource. Ellis's subjects were adult professionals, not Gen M students. Kuhlthau's subjects were from a variety of age groups and may have included some young Gen M subjects, but the research was done before the availability of the Internet. Research has provided little insight into how information behavior differs on the Internet, specifically with Gen M, and whether or not previously identified models are appropriate. Gen M subjects are more likely to search for information on the Internet using commercial search engines (Oblinger, 2003; Abram, 2006). Research on how these searches are conducted could inform us on the current information behavior of Gen M. Capturing information on the criteria used by subjects to evaluate documents, the types of Web sites searchers visited, and the progression through the search process can deepen our understanding of this behavior.

RESEARCH QUESTIONS

In order to better understand the information behavior of Gen M, this research tracked Gen M subjects as they progressed through a five-week research project. The goal was to gather information to answer the broad question of how pragmatic Gen M information seekers are in filling an information need. Specifically, do they proceed through an orderly search process, or is their behavior somewhat erratic and symptomatic of procrastination? Do Gen M information seekers make some effort to discern the quality of documents reviewed on the Web and, if so, are they discerning throughout the search process? In general, is the search process used similar to previously identified search process models, or are there indications that their search behavior has changed? These broad questions lead to the following specific research questions:

1. Do Gen M information seekers progress through a search process similar to that of Wilson's (Wilson, 1999) consolidated model, or is their search behavior different?
2. Do Gen M information seekers evaluate the quality of Web resources? Are they discerning about quality related attributes of the sources retrieved from the Web?
3. How do Gen M information seekers make use of general information Web sites such as Wikipedia? At what stage(s) in the search process are these pages used?

RESEARCH DESIGN

The study examined the search behavior of subjects through a user interface that interacted with a commercial search engine (Yahoo!). The interface executed the subject's search similar to the manner of the commercial search engine, and then inserted a series of relevant survey questions into the process of evaluating search results. Subjects were able to access this search engine interface over the Internet, thus allowing them to work in a naturalistic environment at their own pace. Approximately 80 subjects were drawn from a convenience sample of junior and senior undergraduate students at an American university. Data was collected in 2007 and subjects were, on average, 19 through 22 years of age, and were, therefore, born between 1985 and 1988, members of Gen M.

Subjects were allowed to choose a research topic from a list:

Computer Security: Making Computer Technology Accessible
and Secure
Computer Security: Making Desktop Systems Secure
Computer Security: Preventing Computer Fraud
E-Commerce: After the Internet Bubble
E-Commerce: How to Put Your Company on the Web
Internet Business Models
ERP Systems: The Future
Customer Resource Management (CRM) Systems: Current Status
Does IT Matter: What Role Will IT Take in the Future?
New Technologies: Can Linux be Mainstream?
New Technologies: The Future of WiFi
Microsoft: Dealing with the 500-Pound Gorilla
Ethics and the Information Age: Is It Really Stealing If It's Digital?
Distributed Computing
Grid Computing
Group Collaboration with Computers
Computer Aided Design (CAD) Systems
Supply Chain Management with Computers
Privacy and Computers
Decision Support Systems
Implementing Enterprise Resource Planning (ERP) Systems
Alternatives to ERP Systems
The Current State of Artificial Intelligence and Expert Systems
Systems Design and Development
Enterprise Portals and Application Integration
Open Source Software on the Desktop: Current Status
ERP: Implementation Issues

Topics were all of the same approximate level of difficulty and were
related to course content. Subjects were given several weeks to complete
their research assignment and were required to complete specific interim
assignments during that time period. A project abstract was due the first
week, a detailed outline was due the next week, a rough draft of the presentation slides was due the following week, and the final presentation
slides were due the final week.

Project data was collected anonymously using survey instruments
integrated into the Web search engine interface (see Figure 4.1). Subjects
examined the documents returned from the search engine (see Figure 4.2),
indicated the relevance for the documents they examined (relevant, not

Figure 4.1.   Search Engine Interface

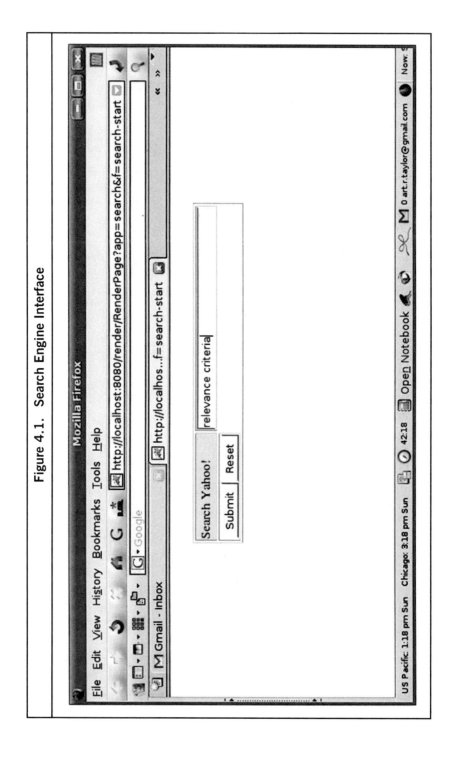

Figure 4.2. Search Results Page

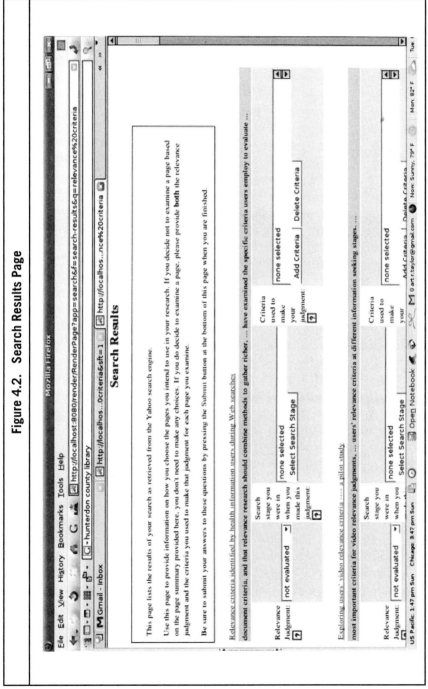

* Note: Relevance judgment choices are presented in a drop-down list that presents a mutually exclusive choice of *relevant, not relevant,* and *partially relevant/unsure about relevance.*

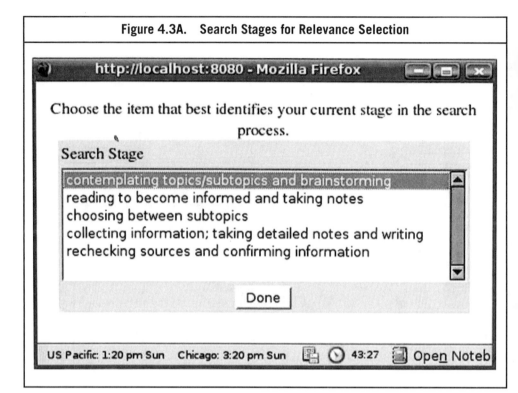

Figure 4.3A.   Search Stages for Relevance Selection

relevant, partially relevant/not sure about relevance), identified a stage in the search process by selecting from a predetermined list of search stages (see Figure 4.3A), and indicated the criteria used to make that relevance judgment by selecting from a predetermined list of relevance criteria (see Figure 4.3B).

The Web site used for data collection contained detailed instructions on the use of the site and how to record information about their searches and relevance judgments. Help pages were also available to explain the search stage choices (see Figure 4.4), relevance judgment choices (see Figure 4.5), and criteria for relevance judgment choices (see Figure 4.6) to be used by the subjects. The Web site captured data by subject (using an anonymous user ID) for the search stage choices, the document selected (as a URL and associated ID code), and the relevance judgment.

Data collected on search stage provided an indication of how subjects were progressing through the information search process and provided data for evaluation of research question one. The quality-related criteria identified by subjects (accuracy, source quality, etc.) provided informa-

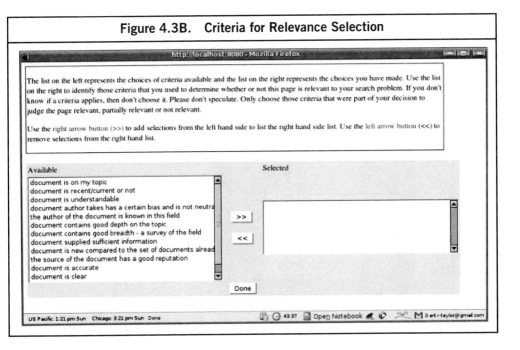

Figure 4.3B.   Criteria for Relevance Selection

tion for evaluation of research question two, and also provided some indication of how and when subjects were evaluating documents, data relevant to question one. Data collected on Web sites visited (URLs) provided information for research question three. When these Web sites were being visited and the criteria being used during each search stage also provided information about how subjects were progressing through the search process, data relevant to research question one.

(Continued on p. 83)

Figure 4.4.   Relevance Judgment Help

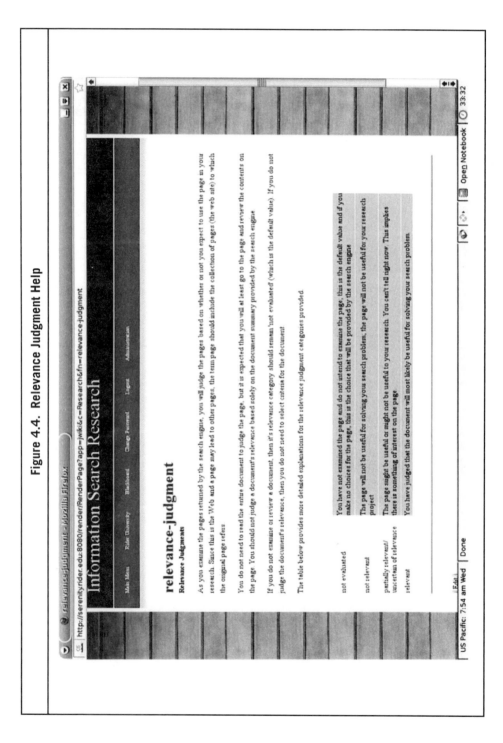

relevance-judgment

Relevance Judgments

As you examine the pages returned by the search engine, you will judge the pages based on whether or not you expect to use the page in your research. Since this is the Web and a page may lead to other pages, the term page should include the collection of pages (the web site) to which the original page refers.

You do not need to read the entire document to judge the page, but it is expected that you will at least go to the page and review the contents on the page. You should not judge a document's relevance based solely on the document summary provided by the search engine.

If you do not examine or review a document, then it's relevance category should remain 'not evaluated' (which is the default value). If you do not judge the document's relevance, then you do not need to select criteria for the document.

The table below provides more detailed explanations for the relevance judgment categories provided.

not evaluated	You have not examined the page and do not intend to examine the page, this is the default value and if you make no choices for the page, this is the choice that will be provided by the search engine
not relevant	The page will not be useful for solving your search problem, the page will not be useful for your research project
partially relevant/ uncertain of relevance	The page might be useful or might not be useful to your research. You can't tell right now. This implies there is something of interest on the page
relevant	You have judged that the document will most likely be useful for solving your search problem

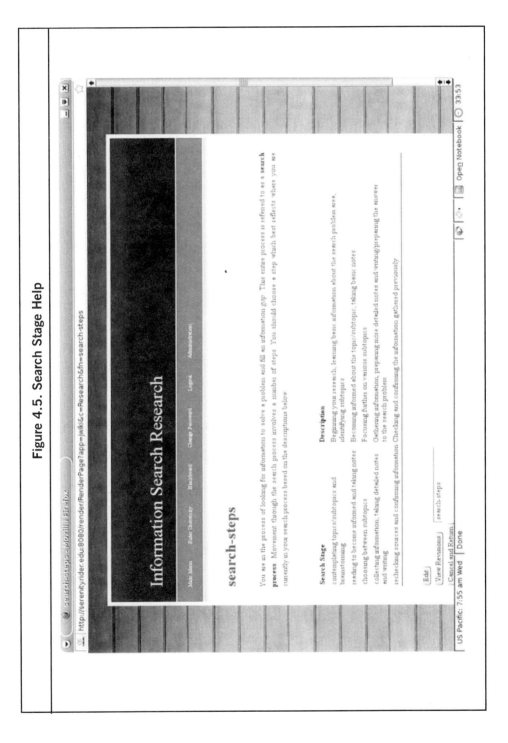

Figure 4.5. Search Stage Help

Figure 4.6. Criteria for Relevance Judgment Help

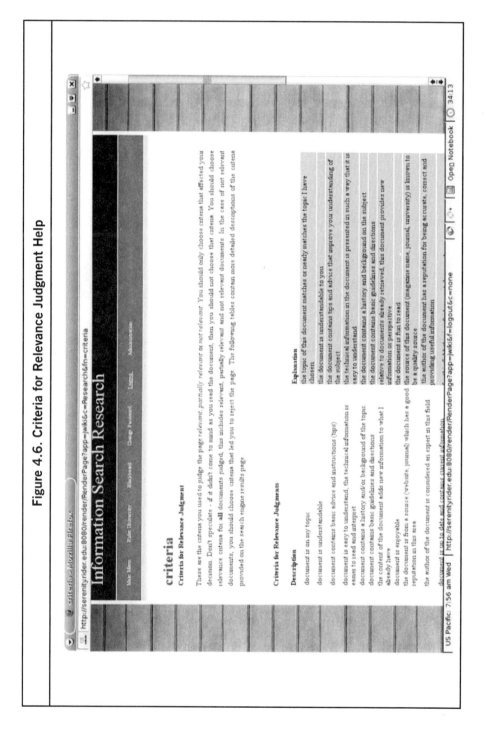

Search Process, Stage in Task Completion, and Relevance Criteria Choices

The search stage model used for this research (see Table 4.1) was developed from the phases suggested by Wilson (1999), which synthesized the information behaviors of Ellis (1997) with the search process of Kuhlthau (1993). The list presented to the subject is shown in "Description Displayed to Subject" column in Table 4.2. The term "initiation" was selected because it was considered clearer than "beginning" or "starting." The term "browsing" was avoided because this term is now commonly used for all Web-related searching and would potentially be confusing to subjects. Instead, the term "exploration" was used to describe the process of scanning and gathering information. The remaining terms, "differentiating," "extracting," and "verifying" are from Ellis (1997), and were used in lieu of Kuhlthau's terminology because they were considered more precise. The process of "ending" the search was considered implied by the submission of the final deliverable, would not have generated activity relevant to the research questions, and was, therefore, not presented as a choice to the subjects.

Table 4.3 contains the criteria identified by subjects as having some bearing on their relevance decision (relevant, not relevant, don't know / partially relevant), the decision whether or not the document (or Web site) is relevant to their information need. The relevance criteria are those factors that contribute to their relevance decision. Prior research by Barry (1994), Barry and Schamber (1998), and Cool, Belkin, Frieder, and Kantor (Cool et al., 1993) identified the criteria listed in Table 4.3. A number of studies have acknowledged these criteria and have provided some

Table 4.1. Search Stage Model

Ellis's (1997) Information Behavior	Kuhlthau's (1993) Search Stage
starting	initiation
browsing/chaining/monitoring	selection/exploration
differentiating	selection/exploration
extracting	formulation/re-formulation
verifying	formulation/re-formulation

Source: Adapted from Wilson, 1999.

Table 4.2. Search Stage Choices Presented to Subject

Search Stage Choice	Description Displayed to Subject
initiation	initial search; start of search process
exploration	scanning for information
differentiating	choosing between different areas of focus
extracting	extracting information
verifying	verifying information that has been gathered previously

confirmation as to their consistency across information retrieval tasks (Xu, 2007; Xu and Chen, 2006; Park, 1993; Schamber, 1991; Schamber and Bateman, 1996). A subset of these criteria was presented to subjects not as specific criteria, but by using the contents of the "Description Displayed to the Subject" column in Table 4.3. Subjects were allowed to choose one or more criteria that they felt contributed to their relevance decision.

The criteria selected for this research are a subset of those identified in Table 4.3. The reasons for these selections are as follows. The "source" column in Table 4.3 identifies the source of the relevance criteria: Barry (1994), or Schamber (1991), both Barry and Schamber (1998), or Cool et al. (1993). To reduce the potential for confusion and survey exhaustion on the part of the subject, the number of relevance criteria presented to the subject was limited to 15. Criteria common to both Barry (1994), and Barry and Schamber (1998) were used. Excluded are those criteria that are specific only to Schamber's (1991) earlier study and relate to document qualities that were peculiar to her topic (weather reports) and did not apply to the computer-related technical topics used in this study.

Deliverables required of the subject and the month/day they were due are identified in Table 4.4. Some feedback was provided upon submission of the abstract and detailed outline deliverables to encourage the students to produce a thorough and well-researched presentation. Feedback concerned only the technical aspects of the topic and the scope of their final presentation. Feedback did not concern choice of Web sites, search stage choices, or relevance criteria choices made by the subjects.

The final deliverable was a 10- to 30-slide PowerPoint presentation. Subjects were encouraged to go beyond general information sites (such

Table 4.3. Relevance Criteria

Criteria	Type	Source*	Used	Description Displayed for Subject
depth/scope/ specificity	document	Barry; Cool	Yes	document contains good depth on the topic
accuracy/validity	document	Barry; Cool	Yes	document appears to be accurate
currency (recency)	document	Barry; Cool	Yes	information is current, recent, up-to-date
tangibility	document	Barry; Cool	Yes	information relates to real, tangible issues; not esoteric or theoretical
quality of sources (source quality)	document	Barry; Cool	Yes	source is reputable, trusted, considered expert
availability of information	situation	Barry; Cool	Yes	the extent to which the information is available
verification	document	Barry; Cool	Yes	the information is consistent with the body of knowledge the field; the information supports the user's point of view
affectiveness	document	Barry; Cool	Yes	the user's emotional response to the information; pleasure, enjoyment, entertainment
effectiveness of proposed approach	document	Barry	Yes	how effective is the approach proposed
consensus within the field	document	Barry	Yes	how much consensus there is in the field for what is proposed in the document
time constraints	situation	Barry	Yes	how much time is allowed for the task to be completed
background/ experience/ ability to understand	situation	Barry	Yes	expression of concern over the ability to understand a document (same as "understandability")
novelty/content novelty/source novelty	document	Barry	Yes	the source or content of the document is new to the subject
geographic proximity	document	Schamber	No	refers to weather information in a geographic location

Table Continued

Table 4.3. Relevance Criteria *(Continued)*

Criteria	Type	Source*	Used	Description Displayed for Subject
dynamism	document	Schamber	No	refers to the ability to dynamically manipulate the information in a document
presentation quality	document	Schamber	No	indication that the source of the information could be manipulated in some way
structure	document	Cool	Yes	the structure of the document; how the information is presented/organized
amount of information	document	Cool	Yes	document provides sufficient information
depth	document	Cool	Yes	document covers the topic in good depth
timeliness (age of document)	document	Cool	Yes	is the time frame of the document appropriate? (current where recent information is required; written in a certain time period for historical significance)
understandability	document	Cool	Yes	the document is understandable by the subject (ability to understand)
bias	document	Cool	Yes	the document is written with a particular viewpoint
authority	document	Cool	Yes	the author or publication has a good reputation in this field

Source: Adapted from Barry, 1994: 154; Barry and Schamber, 1998: 226; and Cool et al., 1993: 3.

as Wikipedia), and to use *quality sources* such as trade journals whenever possible (computer trade journal content is widely available on the Internet). Subjects were also encouraged to use between 10 and 20 sources to prepare their presentation.

Table 4.4. Deliverables Required

Deliverable	Description	Due Date
Abstract	Several paragraphs explaining what will be covered in the presentation	11/2
Detailed outline	One or more pages of outline text that explain the topic and subtopics to be presented and the flow of the presentation	11/10
Rough draft of presentation slides	PowerPoint slides containing the rough draft of the presentation	11/20
Final presentation slides	PowerPoint slides containing the final presentation	12/7

RESULTS

A total of 82 subjects participated in the study and examined and provided 758 distinct Web page evaluations. Table 4.5 identifies the number of documents evaluated by subjects for each project deliverable. This table shows that the number of documents evaluated varied significantly for each deliverable ($\chi^2 = 98.9$, df = 3, p-value < .001). Subjects evaluated 81 documents for the "abstract" project deliverable, but evaluated 225 documents for the "detailed project outline." This finding is not unexpected considering that instructions for the abstract were to create a brief explanation of the project and thus did not require a detailed knowledge of the topic. Table 4.5 also shows that the majority of the documents

Table 4.5. Document Count by Deliverable Due

Project Deliverable	Count	% of Total
Abstract	81	10.69
Detailed Outline	225	29.68
Rough Draft	187	24.67
Final Presentation	265	34.96
Total	758	100.00

Table 4.6. Search Stages Reported by Subjects

Stages Reported	Users Reporting
5	5
4	22
3	21
2	21
1	13
Total	82

were identified in preparation for the "detailed outline." suggesting that subjects gathered information early in the search process.

Table 4.6 lists the number of search stages reported by subjects. As this table indicates, only five subjects reported having progressed through all search stages, and a significant number of subjects (67 percent) reported utilizing fewer than four ($\chi^2 = 9.6$, df = 1, p-value < 0.001).

Tables 4.7 and 4.8 identify the percentage of documents evaluated in each search stage. Table 4.7 lists percentages within search stage, and Table 4.8 lists percentages within project deliverable. This data provides some indication how subjects proceed through the information search process. As subjects evaluated documents, they indicated which search stage they were in based on a list of search stage explanations (Table 4.2). Expectations were that research done for preparation of the first deliverable, the "abstract," would be the "initiation" stage (identified as the "initial search; start of the search process"). As Table 4.7 indicates, slightly less than half of the subjects indicated that they were in the "initiation" stage while preparing the project abstract. This finding indicates that over half the subjects reporting for the "abstract," the first deliverable, reported being in a search stage other than the "initiation" stage.

Table 4.8 provides another perspective on the "initiation" stage and the relationship between search stage and deliverable. As a percentage of documents evaluated within a search stage, during the preparation of the detailed outline, approximately 50 percent of the subjects reported being in the initiation stage, and they reported this after completing the "abstract," the first deliverable. In addition, 13 percent reported being in the initiation stage during the preparation of the rough draft, and 11

Table 4.7. Percent of Documents Evaluated by Search Stage within Deliverable

Search Stage	Abstract (%)	Detailed Outline (%)	Rough Draft (%)	Final Presentation (%)
initiation	47.08	25.32	16.25	8.89
exploration	22.81	25.67	9.96	12.72
differentiating	7.48	10.57	2.85	9.22
extracting	20.62	35.69	65.84	53.18
verifying	2.01	2.75	5.10	15.99
Total	100.00	100.00	100.00	100.00

percent reported being in the initiation stage during the preparation of the final presentation. This indicates a non-serial progression through the information search process in relation to project deliverables.

As Table 4.7 indicates, only 16 percent of the subjects reported being in the "verifying" stage while preparing the "final presentation" deliverable. Subjects were more likely to identify "extracting" as their current search stage (defined as "extracting information to answer the question") during this time frame. This indicates that these subjects were not concluding the search process in a manner consistent with Kuhlthau's (1993) information search process, which has an expectation that the subject will perform some verification or evaluation of the research collected in the final stage.

The selection of general information sites (defined in this study as the Wikipedia site) varied significantly in relation to project deliverable due ($\chi^2 = 12, n=80, df = 3, P < 0.01$) as shown in Table 4.9. This site selection was 10 percent of the total documents chosen overall (80 out of 818). Subjects were instructed to search beyond basic informational sites, and numerous sites were available for their assigned topics. As Table 4.9 indicates, these sites were used consistently during the preparation of the abstract and rough draft, ranging between approximately 6 and 10 percent of the total sites chosen. A significant increase was found in the usage of these sites during the preparation of the final presentation. Table 4.10 provides additional insights into the use of these sites, showing a statistically

Table 4.8. Percent of Documents Evaluated by Deliverable within Search Stage

Search Stage	Abstract (%)	Detailed Outline (%)	Rough Draft (%)	Final	Total (%)
initiation	25.75	49.70	13.67	10.88	100.00
exploration	14.37	58.05	9.66	17.93	100.00
differentiating	10.62	53.89	6.22	29.27	100.00
extracting	5.59	34.72	27.45	32.25	100.00
verifying	3.62	17.76	14.14	64.47	100.00

significant relationship between the search stage and the selection of Wikipedia Web sites ($\chi^2 = 15.7$, df = 3, p-value = 0.001306). These results indicate that Wikipedia sites represent approximately 40 percent of the sites evaluated when subjects reported being in the "extracting" stage (identified as "extracting information to answer the question").

An examination of the criteria that subjects reported in selecting pages provides some indication of their reasons for selecting or rejecting pages as they progress through the search process. Since there were a large number of criteria examined by the subjects, Table 4.11 is simplified to identify those criteria that changed most in terms of their selection as the subject moved through the search process. As this table indicates, subjects were more likely to select "amount of information" and "depth"

Table 4.9. Wikipedia Pages Reviewed by Deliverable Due

Deliverable Due	Count	% of Total *
Abstract	8	9.30
Detailed Outline	29	9.90
Rough Draft	15	5.84
Final Presentation	28	14.97
Total	80	40.01

* Percentage of all pages evaluated for the deliverable due.

Table 4.10. Wikipedia Pages Reviewed by Search Stage

Stage Code	Count	% of Total
initiation	20	25.97
exploration	17	22.08
differentiating	6	7.79
extracting	31	40.26
verifying	3	3.90
Total*	77	100.00

* Three subjects did not report a search stage, and were counted in Table 4.9, but were not counted in Table 4.10.

as criteria in the earlier search stages (initiation and differentiating) than in later stages (initiation and verifying). The criteria of "novelty" of sources, the "structure of the document," and "time constraints" of the subject were selected more in later stages. This may indicate the subjects are looking for new sources of information and possibly documents of different structure, providing a different approach and new information for their subject area. The criterion of "time constraints" is also more likely to be selected later in the process as deadlines loom. The criteria of "amount of information" and "depth" are selected less frequently later in the search process, when other criteria such as "authority" and "structure" are more likely to be selected. Though "authority" is selected more in later stages, the criterion of "source quality" is selected less, suggesting that based on the subjects' selections; subjects may not apply equal weight to "authority" and "source quality" as criteria.

An examination of results grouped by deliverable required provides a slightly different perspective on the progress of the subjects, as shown in Table 4.12. This table examines criteria selected based on the date the subject made the evaluation. The date was then correlated with the deliverable due in that time frame. Based on this evaluation, subjects working on the final presentation, who were approaching the end of their research effort, were more likely to select "amount of information" and "understandability" as criteria in their document choice. However, the "accuracy" and "source quality," "depth," and "breadth" were less likely to be selected by these subjects.

Table 4.11. Stage/Criteria Percentages*

Relevance Criteria	Initiation (%)	Differentiating (%)	Extracting (%)	Verifying (%)
affectiveness	0.57	4.37	2.77	3.52
amount of information	8.92	12.23	10.77	7.42
authority	1.90	3.49	2.65	3.91
bias	1.90	1.75	1.94	3.13
depth	8.92	12.23	9.03	7.42
novelty	1.14	3.93	2.06	2.73
recency	8.35	7.86	6.97	6.25
source quality	4.93	3.49	4.06	3.13
structure	6.26	5.68	7.55	8.20
time constraints	0.57	1.31	1.29	2.34

* Reported as a percentage of the total choices within a search stage

Table 4.12. Comparison of Criteria Codes for Rough Draft
and Final Presentation

Criteria Code	Rough Draft (%)	Final Presentation (%)
accuracy	14.66	11.71
affectiveness	3.02	5.43
amount of information	12.07	14.00
authority	3.23	4.29
bias	3.23	2.14
breadth	7.76	6.71
depth	13.36	10.29
novelty	1.94	3.14
recency	8.84	9.14
source quality	5.17	4.00
structure	8.41	9.14
time constraints	2.80	2.43
understandability	15.52	17.57

DISCUSSION

These empirical results suggest that the search behavior of Gen M subjects does not proceed in an orderly fashion through an information search process. Though models such as Kuhlthau's (1993) did not predict a strictly linear progression through the information search process, it was assumed that subjects would complete all of the steps in the process. Subjects in this sample gathered almost half of their source documents (45 percent) for the detailed outline project deliverable in the second week of the five-week project, and, therefore, had completed a significant portion of their research (in terms of sources selected) within two weeks. A significant portion of subjects (67 percent) reported being in fewer than four search stages (Table 4.6).

If subjects had made an orderly, pragmatic progression through the information search process, it would be expected for them to report they were "verifying information gathered previously" during the preparation of the final project deliverable. This search progression would be based on the expectation that subjects had gathered research previously, and were now examining and verifying that research as part of the completion of the final deliverable. The empirical evidence gathered with this subject pool suggests otherwise. The majority of subjects (53 percent) evaluating documents for the final presentation identified themselves as being in the "extracting" stage, described as "extracting information to answer the question." Only 16 percent of subjects preparing the final deliverable identified themselves as being in the "verifying" stage. A closer examination of the "verifying" stage indicates that the selection of this stage as a percentage of the stages reported for a particular deliverable never exceeded 15 percent of the total (see Table 4.7), an indication that subjects were not "verifying information that has been gathered previously." Most of the documents evaluated by the subjects (approximately 70 percent) were evaluated in the final two stages, the latter portion of the project's duration. This statistically significant amount ($\chi^2 = 28.1214$, df = 1, p-value < .001) suggests that subjects may be procrastinating, or "backfilling."

The finding was that over half the subjects reporting for the first deliverable reported being in a stage other than the "initiation" stage. This result could be an indication that in this time frame, subjects found several documents and reported being in the initiation stage. Then, after absorbing the initial set of documents, subjects considered themselves out of the "initiation" stage and in some other stage. Subjects may have performed some significant portion of their research in this early stage, quickly moving beyond the "initiation" stage.

Examination of the results concerning subjects' evaluation of the quality of Web resources provides some indication that subjects were not concerned with the quality or validity of the documents selected. Subjects did not select "verifying" (presented as "verifying information that has been gathered previously") for any particular deliverable at a rate higher than 16 percent (Table 4.7), suggesting that subjects generally found that some other search stage category provided a better description of their behavior. Based on these results, subjects did not attempt to verify their sources, and it can be assumed they considered the information valid or were not concerned that it was invalid.

Subjects did appear to make use of general information sites such as Wikipedia, but they did not select these sites the majority of the time. The instructions presented to subjects on the use of general information sites are obviously an intervening factor to be considered in the evaluation of this statistic. However, the timing of the selection and use of these sites by the subjects suggest that they were likely to select these sites in the "extracting" stage. Also, approximately 15 percent of the sites selected for the final deliverable were Wikipedia, suggesting that, for some subjects, these sites were useful in the later stages of the research project. However, the difference between the selections of these sites in early stages versus late stages is not statistically significant. For this sample, subjects appeared just as likely to use these sites in early stages (initiation, exploration) as in later stages (differentiating, extracting, verifying).

LIMITATIONS

The subjects in this study were from a U.S. university. The articles referenced in the literature review also cited studies performed on subjects in U.S. schools. It is not clear that search behavior, or more broadly the behavior of Gen M subjects, will be the same in other cultures. Subjects were also undergraduate students with a mixed scholastic background (below average, average, above average). Graduate students or professionals may perform differently.

The tasks assigned to students provided specific instructions to encourage students to perform research. Students were told that they were being graded partially on the quality of their research, and this meant that more quality sources cited would result in a higher grade.

This intervening factor may have encouraged students to evaluate more documents, and perform the research done in the latter stages of the project. Specific instructions also addressed limiting research to using general information sites such as Wikipedia. In the absence of these instructions, it is possible Wikipedia sites may have represented a larger portion of the sites selected and referenced.

ACKNOWLEDGMENTS

The author would like to thank Dr. Marie L. Radford, Associate Professor at the School of Communication, Information and Library Studies, Rutgers University, for her input concerning the topic and scope of this chapter, as well as Rutgers University Libraries' faculty and staff for their help and support in conducting this research.

REFERENCES

Abram, Stephen. 2006. "Millennials: Deal with Them." *Texas Library Journal* 82, no. 3: 100–103.

Barry, Carol L., and Linda Schamber. 1998. "Users' Criteria for Relevance Evaluation: A Cross-situational Comparison." *Information Processing and Management* 34, no. 2–3: 219–236.

Barry, Carol L. 1994. "User-defined Relevance Criteria: An Exploratory Study." *Journal of the American Society for Information Science* 45, no. 3: 149–159.

Belkin, Nicholas, Robert N. Oddy, and Helen M. Brooks. 1982. "ASK for Information Retrieval Part I." *Journal of Documentation* 38, no. 2: 61–71.

Buczynski, James A. 2005. "Satisficing Digital Library Users." *Internet Reference Services Quarterly* 10, no. 1: 99–102.

Cool, Colleen, Nicholas J. Belkin, Ophir Frieder, and Paul Kantor. 1993. "Characteristics of Texts Affecting Relevance Judgments." In *Proceedings of the Fourteenth National Online Meeting* (pp. 77–83), edited by M. E. Williams. Medford, NJ: Learned Information.

Ellis, David. 1997. "Modeling the Information Seeking Patterns of Engineers and Research Scientists in an Industrial Environment." *Journal of Documentation* 53, no. 4: 384–403.

Ellis, David. 1989. "A Behavioural Approach to Information Science Retrieval Design." *Journal of Documentation* 45, no. 3: 171–212.

Essinger, Catherine. 2006. "X/Y: Managing the Millennial Generation." *Texas Library Journal* 82, no. 3: 104–107.

Harley, Bruce, Megan Dreger, and Patricia Knobloch. 2001. "The Postmodern Condition: Students, the Web, and Academic Library Services." *Reference Services Review* 29, no. 1: 23–32.

Kuhlthau, Carol. 1993. *Seeking Meaning: A Process Approach to Library and Information Services*. Norwood, NJ: Ablex.

Kuhlthau, Carol C. 1991. "Inside the Search Process: Information Seeking from the User's Perspective." *Journal of the American Society for Information Science* 42, no. 5: 361–371.

Oblinger, Diana. 2003. "Boomers, Gen-Xers, Millennials: Understanding the New Students." *EDUCAUSE Review* 38, no. 4: 37–47.

Park, Taemin Kim. 1993. "The nature of Relevance in Information Retrieval: An Empirical Study." *Library Quarterly* 63, no. 3 (July): 318–351.

Schamber, Linda. 1991. "Users' Criteria for Evaluation in a Multimedia Environment." In *Proceedings of the 54th Annual Meeting of the American Society for Information Science* (pp. 126–133), edited by Jose-Marie Griffiths. Medford, NJ: Learned Information.

Schamber, Linda, and Judy Bateman. 1996. "User Criteria in Relevance Evaluation: Toward Development of a Measurement Scale." *Proceedings of the 59th Annual Meeting of the American Society for Information Science* (pp. 218–225), edited by Steve Hardin. Medford, NJ: Information Today.

Taylor, Robert S. 1968. "Question-Negotiation and Information Seeking in Libraries."*College & Research Libraries* 29, no. 3: 178–194.

Thompson, Christen. 2003. "Information Illiterate or Lazy: How College Students Use the Web for Research." *Libraries and the Academy* 3: 259–267.

Vondracek, Ruth. 2007. "Comfort and Convenience?: Why Students Choose Alternatives to the Library." *Libraries and the Academy* 7, no. 3: 277–293.

Weiler, Angela. 2004. "Information-seeking Behavior in Generation Y Students: Motivation, Critical Thinking, and Learning Theory." *Journal of Academic Librarianship* 31, no. 1: 4653.

Wilson, Thomas D. 1999. "Models in Information Behavior Research." *Journal of Documentation* 55, no. 3: 249–270.

Xu, Yunjie. 2007. "Relevance Judgment in Epistemic and Hedonic Information Sciences." *Journal of the American Society for Information Science and Technology* 58, no. 2: 179–189.

Xu, Yunjie, and Zhiwei Chen. 2006. "Relevance Judgment: What Do Information Consumers Consider Beyond Topicality?" *Journal of the American Society for Information Science and Technology* 57, no. 7: 961–973.

Young, Nancy J., and Marilyn Von Seggern. 2001. "General Information Seeking in Changing Times: A Focus Group Study." *Reference and User Services Quarterly* 41, no. 2: 159–169.

Chapter 5

Gen M: Whose Kids Are They Anyway?

Michele Kathleen D'Angelo

WHO ARE THEY?

As Lee Rainie indicates in his speech given to the Public Library Association in 2006, Generation M is the most racially and ethnically diverse group of students to call themselves middle class in the history of our country (Howe and Strauss, 2000). Based much on the Howe and Strauss book, *Millennials Rising*, Rainie represents that Gen M students believe they are special, and they are the products of "play dates, No Child Left Behind, and SAT prep courses" (Rainie, 2006: 2). They have led a sheltered life, as parents have created rules to live in a so-called unsafe world. They were the first to be legislated into wearing bicycle helmets, and the first to have metal detectors in their schools. They are confident like no generation before them, and they believe they have a right to high self-esteem. They are team players and put much stock in the group. They are used to acting instantly on information. They are less concerned with their own privacy, hence MySpace, Twitter, and other social networking sites, and they are likely to survey what others are doing—a kind of voyeurism that present technology allows. Boundaries have shifted and the idea of proprietary information no longer means to Generation M (those born between the early 1980s and mid-to-late 1990s) what it once meant to generations before them (Rainie, 2006; Howe and Strauss, 2000).

Gen M students achieve, feel pressured to achieve, and are, in fact, rather conventional. They chronicle their self-absorption on digital cameras, smart phones, and social networking sites, and for the first time in history, project their own personal adolescent angst to an entire world. They are natural followers. Everyone's doing it, and, in fact, they have co-opted many of their parents into their technology maze. They have become what their Baby Boomer parents wanted, and yet those same parents wonder why their children are so complacent.

Marketing people love Generation M. Gen M thinking and buying patterns influence their parents more so than any other generation before them, and since they live with their parents longer than most generations, they are often largely supported by their well-off parents. Today's Gen M students will be a powerful source of influence in future trends. They are great consumers, mostly because their parents want them to be. They are good information manipulators; they are socially conscious followers; and they are skilled at analyzing visual data and images.

Interestingly, Gen M students spend less time with friends and family and more time interacting electronically. Unlike previous generations who had a war or a great social movement to define them, they are not defined by a world cause and are looking for something that says that they matter. Although the war in Iraq has been going on for years, they have not embraced it as their own. While technology offers many advantages for both students and families, it also presents challenges and even risks to our students. This author would like to examine issues that affect a Gen M adolescent in school and at home, doing homework, and interacting with parents and friends as well as unknown persons/entities online. Let's see what their world looks like.

WHAT IS GOING ON IN SCHOOL?

How can teachers better teach Gen M? Is there more involved than employing digital content and developing visual literacy? Teachers have always known that incorporating real world problems—or making their subjects relevant—encourages student interaction. Even if we encourage digital production and give students access to cameras and software at home, where does that leave us? Certainly students who learn how to do podcasting and make digital storytelling a part of their learning process will be more engaged. Enter into that mix peer teaching/tutoring, and we have a fairly successful formula for not only learning but for retaining information.

These are good methods, but this author disagrees with George Lucas who says, "If students aren't taught the language of sound and images, shouldn't they be considered as illiterate as if they left college without being able to read or write?" (Daly, 2004: under "When People Talk to Me about the Digital Divide"). Much of the language of sound and images are intrinsic to our understanding and, Marshall McLuhan notwithstanding, there appears to be much more than that to the education of our students. McLuhan was a Canadian professor of English Literature whose contributions mark the cornerstone of media theory. He coined the phrases "the medium is the message" and the "global village" (McLuhan, 1964; Wolfe, 2004: 21–23).

Just what education programs have been teaching for a generation has finally shown up in our students. The type of students that educators have been wanting for years has been created, and now many K–12 and college educators and administrators seem to be confused as to why the students act the way they do. For instance, collaborative teaching and differentiated instruction, as well as peer coaching, have been heralded for years in teacher education programs and teachers have taught students how to learn collaboratively. Now, however, after decades of collaborative learning, some students have difficulty reading and writing on their own. Gen M is particularly good at teamwork, experiential activities, and incorporating technology into their learning. While the jury is still out on whether they are efficient multitaskers, researchers state that Gen M students are goal-oriented and collaborative and display positive attitudes (Oblinger, 2003). They have learned to learn in groups.

Moreover, students will often express dissatisfaction at their teachers' use of technology and rate it uninspiring or worse. Many students complain about PowerPoint presentations—that there are too many words or too much time is spent viewing them in class. Many students want the PowerPoints just e-mailed to them because taking notes is getting in the way of other activities, such as texting while in class. The same teacher education programs that taught displaying content visually as well as auditorily are getting low marks by Gen M students. According to Levin and Arafeh (2002), students are using up-to-date technology outside of school, but not in school.

So what do students think about technology? First of all, to the Gen M crowd, the desktop computer is not really viewed as technology, just like the older generations now do not view the television as technology. Gen M students see computers as essential pieces of their landscapes. The Web provides students with interactivity and is their preferred method of socializing. In addition, students have their perceptions of reality constantly challenged online. Errors occur, intentionally or through carelessness, that can make a huge impact on friendships, work products, and the general state of angst in adolescence. All of these technological changes have changed the way Gen M students view productivity. They are less interested in accumulating knowledge and facts and are more results-oriented. If they can put together a report with online sources that boast a collaboration of four other students and put it in a format that is pleasing to the eye, they believe they have accomplished much. They place less value on knowledge for knowledge's sake and engage in trial and error programming. Students, who were raised on game playing, where losing was the catalyst for learning, view trial and error as an appropriate methodology. They are less inclined to be rule-based problem solvers and actually resemble the learners of Skinner's Skinner Box. Students getting Cs and Ds and lower grades spend approximately three-quarters of an hour more engaged in media each day (9 hours, 15 minutes) than students achieving higher grades, according to a widely cited 2005 Kaiser Foundation study report. "Grades appear to be negatively related to video game exposure" (Roberts, Foehr, and Rideout, 2005: 47). Furthermore, high sensation-seeking students report more time listening to music than lower sensation-seeking students. This same 2005 Kaiser Foundation study report tells us that students who engage in video game use tend to read less.

SOCIAL PROGRAMMING: WHO'S WATCHING THE KIDS?

Albert Bandura has said, "much of the social construction of reality and shaping of public consciousness occurs through electronic acculturation" (Bandura, 2001: 271). Media Cultivation Effects Theory (Gerbner, 1969, 1972; Gerbner et al., 1994) suggests that students will adopt media messages with repeated exposure. It becomes a "socializing agent," which initially seems small, but will become important over time. Gerbner et al. (1994) found that people who viewed a lot of television found the world to be more violent than it really is and negative portrayals of race and gender became reality to viewers (Ziegler, 2007). What about the disrespect component that seems to be mandatory in the media industry? According to Raessens and Goldstein (2005), games on the 2005 list of the National Institute on Media and Family were 46 percent more violent, contained 800 percent more sexual content, and were 30 times more likely to use profane language than games from ten years ago. Buchanan et al. (2002) claim that viewing media violence increases physical and relational aggression. Anderson (2004) found increases in aggressive behavior and thoughts and a decrease in helping behaviors. Desensitization to violence occurs in children, and they tend to believe the world is like what they witness in their video games.

So what is the role of video games in all of this? Video games have been successful in the teaching of health skills, physical movements, attention skills, and conflict resolution skills (Gee, 2003). Gee found 36 principles of learning and suggested that learning theory might connect with game theory in teaching higher-order thinking skills. So, there are good things happening with video games if the content of the game is not overwhelmingly destructive. Another problem, of course, is that gaming sessions often lack the necessary debriefing sessions that connect the learning and allow generalization.

In addition to increases in disrespectful behavior in school and at home, students often have sleep problems and may develop anxiety concerns as a result of extensive video game playing. Like the horror movie of yesteryear gave nightmares, explicit video game content has the same effect on children today. This phenomenon pertains to music as well; that is, song lyrics and aggressive behaviors are linked, according to Anderson et al. (2003). Although this may seem inconclusive to some—arguing whether it is the chicken or the egg—aggressive music does seem to become a self-fulfilling prophecy, in that students imitate profanity and derisive language in everyday use.

According to the Kaiser Foundation study, students seem to be using technology more for social programming than academic endeavors. It appears to be an indispensable social tool on college campuses. Cell phones, texting, and IM personas tell the other connector who Gen M is. Something as simple as their "away" message, their icon, or list of "favorites" sends a loud outgoing message. Do students have an online identity? Yes. Students use media to become socialized, but it is the household environment that will determine where and when that socialization takes place.

Who is watching the kids? No one is watching the kids according to the Kaiser Foundation survey. Only 23 percent of households have rules about computer usage; 17 percent have restrictions on video-game time (Roberts, Foehr, and Rideout, 2005). A student's access to personal media and household rules about the use of that technology comprise the formula for student usage. Patricia Wallace directs the Johns Hopkins

Center for Talented Youth program. She says that the students experience "intermittent, variable reinforcement" through e-mail and other pursuits (Wallis, 2006: 55). Some people check their e-mail 20 times a day, trying to keep up and trying to stay connected to other people (Wallis, 2006). Teens, as well as adults, are lonely. What to do about this? Experts have been recommending old-fashioned family meals as a way of connecting and checking in with the family. New England psychiatrist Edward Hallowell (author of *CrazyBusy: Overstretched, Overbooked, and About to Snap! Strategies for Coping in a World Gone ADD*) states, "it is not what we are doing that is necessarily so destructive. It is what we are not doing that is going to be the downfall of the family and its children" (Wallis, 2006).

What's the bottom line? Parents need to intervene, turn things off, and sit face-to-face with their children as painful as that may be for everyone. They need to begin conversations, maybe even establish some rapport, so future conversations will develop. Going to the movies, taking a trip—even that dreaded shopping trip—all allow opportunities to talk and argue and find the boundaries kids are searching for. Parents need to take back their homes and put limits on the use of technology in their homes because the use of that technology has created a wedge in the American family. As far as families are concerned, technology should be a tool, not a destination.

WHAT'S GOING ON AT HOME?

In addition, many Baby Boomer parents have worked through their child-rearing years and in their absence left their children on their own more than any other previous generation of middle-class parents. Baby Boomer parents are very good providers, but they are not always very good at providing boundaries. Some parents take children to "R"-rated movies, allow their elementary school-age daughters to wear makeup and color their hair, and allow both their sons and daughters to get tattooed and pierced at a young age. According to Ziegler, students today outfit themselves in clothing and electronics that typify brand names (2007). Even television shows watched and music that is listened to are considered palpable extensions of oneself. Jay Dover, former program director of the Center for Media Literacy claims, "media is no longer looked at as part of culture, it is culture" (Conover, 1996: 10). It is not a surprise to students of communications that media today acts as a socializing instrument. Many parents who grew up at the lower end of the socioeconomic scale, who can now afford to, often lavish material items on their children to demonstrate their own success, as well as attempt to provide a better life for their children. Some parents who struggled with self-esteem feel that a reversal of that phenomenon for their children will somehow save the day for their kids. Ultimately, technology-engaged students allowed parents to work longer, attend to household chores, or just relax.

Almost 75 percent of American homes have three or more television sets. Of course, media accessibility is largely a function of parental income. Factors such as age, race, ethnicity, and parental education also influence students' access to media. Generally, more educated parents will have more media in their homes, often in excess of three computers with instant messaging capabilities (Roberts, Foehr, and Rideout, 2005). Boys tend to have more personal media accessible in their bedrooms than girls, and they are also more likely to have their own TV, VCR/DVD player, computer, and Internet connection.

Students who have their own television, video game console, and/or computer in their bedrooms spend about two hours longer each day engaged in media than students who use centrally located family media. Furthermore, students with bedroom televisions average 16 fewer minutes daily of leisure reading. A similar phenomenon exists for students with bedroom gaming consoles. The one exception to this is the personal computer. Students with their own bedroom computer spend about eight more minutes a day reading (Roberts, Foehr, and Rideout, 2005). Students with computers in their bedrooms may be more academically minded than those who only have televisions and gaming systems in their bedrooms.

Unfortunately, "media used in the presence of parents was more the exception than the rule" (Roberts, Foehr, and Rideout, 2005: 3). For instance, pornography enters a child's life through the Internet at about the age of 11, according to the Internet Filter Review. Their report estimates that 80 percent of 15–17 year olds have repeatedly seen hardcore pornography via the Internet (Ropelato, 2003–2008: under "Children Internet Pornography Statistics"). The general assumption here is that parents have had little actual influence on their teenagers, and, instead, students' peer groups have influenced them the most. However, what we have now is a virtual or online world, created often by unnamed or unknown persons, constantly interacting with Gen M students. Parents and in-person peers seem to be influencing students even less today.

Moreover, according to current research, parents and children are not reuniting at the end of the day (Wallis, 2006). Technology has changed the face of the American home in that children are often isolated in their bedrooms, multitasking and monitoring their electronic universes. Parents seem to respect their children's engagement, much like they would if the kids were doing homework—afraid to disturb them. Another thought is that everyone is sufficiently alienated from each other—living in parallel universes. Technology in the home seems to be another form of anesthesia—much like television was/is. It has become an addiction to ward off social anxiety, and, conversely, it has become a crutch, blocking the establishment of intimacy with one's self—a necessary tool for intrapersonal growth. Where is the time for introspection if students are spending roughly six and a half hours a day connected?

And what is all of this about multitasking? According to Jordan Grafman, chief of the Cognitive Neuroscience section at the National Institute of Neurological Disorder and Stroke (NINDS), "Kids that are instant messaging while doing homework, playing games online and watching TV, I predict aren't going to do well in the long run" (Wallis, 2006: 52). Decades of research point out that an individual's output and critical thinking abilities dissipate as more tasks are engaged. Technology has not created super students but more like *diluted* students because the human brain cannot handle true multitasking. The brain actually orders the tasks and switches back and forth between them. It cannot simultaneously process separate tasks. For instance, one can have a conversation and drive and chew gum at the same time because two of these actions are automatic actions, according to Hal Pashler, psychology professor at the University of California-San Francisco. While these tasks may be sequential, they are "highly practiced" and involve planning that takes place naturally, and so do not require extensive thinking before performance (Wallis, 2006). Doing math homework while singing and answering a mother's question about what happened in school that day actually requires three separate and distinct thought processes that really cannot effectively compete with one another if a student is going to perform his or her best. Tasks that require movement while speaking, for instance, can be planned for and executed seemingly simultaneously when it comes to our multitasking Gen Ms. What needs to be learned as parents and educators is that activity should not be mistaken for achievement. Multitasking and print use are not relative, as students would be hard-pressed to read and process that reading while engaging in another activity. For instance, students generally use their computer and watch TV or use a computer and listen to music or switch between media on the same computer.

Ultimately, we confuse "multitasking" with sequential processing according to Grafman. Interestingly, young children and adults over 60 do not multitask well because the prefrontal cortex is the last place in the brain to develop and the first to decline. Students who suffer with attention-deficit/hyperactivity disorder demonstrate this phenomenon as well. However, young adults are better at tuning out background noise and music, for instance. It appears that they are listening and working, but actually they are *ignoring* and working. According to David E. Meyer, director of the Brain, Cognition, and Action Laboratory at the University of Michigan, students performing two or more related tasks simultaneously or in rapid sequence commit more errors or take much longer to complete the tasks. Meyer claims that it is a "myth" that a person can write an essay while reviewing for a math test; he equates this to a person running a one-minute mile. It is just not probable (Wallis, 2006). Earl Miller, a Picower Professor of Neuroscience at MIT, reinforces this idea as well. He explains that, "You cannot focus on one while doing the other. That's because of what's called interference between the two tasks. They both involve communicating via speech or the written word, and so there's a lot of conflict between the two of them" (Hamilton, 2008).

What about the stimulation conundrum? It appears a little stimulation/stress is good for the brain, but too much will render it less efficient. Human brains need down time to process and order thoughts so that they can be accessed at a later time. Constant stimulation short-circuits that process. Concentration is a learned behavior and one that should be practiced. Constantly being connected leaves little time for processing—an essential element in learning. Claudia Koonz, a history professor at Duke University, has expressed concerns that students coming to Duke are unwilling to read entire books, and that they are not investing the time for critical thinking that university learning requires (Wallis, 2006). Most people know that Web sites like SparkNotes.com do not really tell the whole story and are no substitute for actually engaging with a text.

CONCLUSION: A SUMMARY AND SOME SUGGESTIONS

Students who engaged in media while their parents were present are unusual according to the previously mentioned 2005 Kaiser Family Foundation study. We also know that students who reported being bored watched television more than those who did not report being bored. Students who report lower overall satisfaction had higher exposure to all types of media except print media. Instant messaging is one of the most fashionable computer actions among youngsters and carries social weight. The types of media available in the home, access to personal media, and household attitudes toward time spent with media create the formula for students' media usage. There is also a tendency for media usage to be highest among students with the lowest grades. The exception to this is a positive relationship between using print media and higher grades. The higher the grades, the more time spent reading. And while race is not often correlated with most functions of media use, race is an indicator of music listened to. African-American students listen to Rap/Hip Hop, Rhythm & Blues/Soul, Reggae, and Gospel/Christian music more than whites or Hispanics (Roberts, Foehr, and Rideout, 2005). Researchers' claims that music with aggressive lyrics turns into the executed behavior of youth should resonate for all people. A serious look should be taken at the impact of aggressive music to determine whether it might be best to set standards as was done for smoking and drug use.

Although staying connected is part of the game of socializing, the American Academy of Pediatrics recommends that parents limit the use of media, make positive media choices, select creative alternatives to media consumption, develop critical thinking and viewing skills, and understand the political, social, economic, and emotional implications of all forms of media (Committee on Public Education, 1999).

Educators should also teach students to evaluate media sources by having them answer the following questions:

- Who created the media message and why?
- Who is the target audience?
- What is the text of the message?
- What is the subtext?
- What kind of lifestyle is presented and is it glamorized?
- What values are expressed?
- What tools or techniques of persuasion are used and what part of the story is not being told?

It occurs to the author that all college-educated persons learn how to answer these questions during their university studies, but that most teenagers have not been exposed to these critical questions. Educators are in search of critical thinking skills and the requisite analysis that goes with it. Access to information is not enough. Evaluation is key.

Educators need to tell students that media has not replaced parents and teachers. While parents, teachers, and peers continue to influence Gen M students in person, it is the online person or social networking organization online that is spending the most time with kids. Someone else is socializing Gen M.

REFERENCES

Anderson, Craig. 2004. "An Update on the Effects of Violent Video Games." *Journal of Adolescence 27*, no. 1: 113–122.

Anderson, Craig, Nicholas Carnagey, and Janie Eubanks. 2003. "Exposure to Violent Media: The Effects of Songs with Violent Lyrics on Aggressive Thoughts and Feelings." *Journal of Personality and Social Psychology 84*, no. 5: 960–971.

Bandura, Albert. 2001. "Social Cognitive Theory of Mass Communication." *Media Psychology 3*, no. 3: 265–299.

Buchanan, Audrey, Douglas Gentile, David Nelson, David Walsh, and Julia Hensel. 2002. "What Goes in Must Come Out: Children's Media Violence Consumption at Home and Aggressive Behaviors." Paper presented at the International Society for the Study of Behavioral Development Conference, Ottawa, Ontario, Canada (August). Available: www.mediafamily. org/research/report_issbd_2002.shtml (accessed July 28, 2008).

Committee on Public Education. 1999. "Media Education." *Pediatrics 104*, no. 2: 341–343.

Conover, Kirsten A. 1996. "Decoding the Media: A Growing Trend Teaches Children How to Analyze and Critique Today's Media Messages." *Christian Science Monitor 88*, no. 96 (April 12): 10.

Daly, John. 2004. "Life on the Screen: Visual Literacy in Education." *Edutopia: What Works in Public Education* (September). Available: www.edutopica. org/life-screen (accessed August 30, 2008).

Gee, James. 2003. *What Video Games Have to Teach Us About Learning and Literacy*. New York: Palgrave Macmillan.

Gerbner, George. 1969. *The Analysis of Communication Content: Developments in Scientific Theories and Computer Techniques*. New York: Wiley.

Gerbner, George. 1972. "Violence and Television Drama: Trends and Symbolic Functions." In *Content and Control: Television and Social Behavior, Volume 1* (pp. 128–187), edited by George Comstock and Eli Rubinstein. Washington, DC: U.S. Government Printing Office.

Gerbner, George, Larry Gross, Michael Morgan, and Nancy Signorielli. 1994. "Growing Up with Television: The Cultivation Perspective." In *Media Effects: Advances in Theory and Research* (pp. 17–41), edited by Jennings Bryant and Dolf Zillmann. Hillsdale, NJ: Erlbaum.

Hamilton, Jon. 2008. "Think You're Multitasking? Think Again." *National Public Radio*. Available: www.npr.org/templates/story/story. php?storyId=95256794 (accessed October 9, 2008).

Howe, Neil, and William Strauss. 2000. *Millennials Rising: The Next Great Generation*. New York: Vintage.

Levin, Douglass, and Sousan Arafeh. "The Digital Disconnect: The Widening Gap between Internet Savvy Students and Their Schools." Washington, DC: Pew Internet and American Life Project (August 14, 2002). Available: www.pewInternet.org/pdfs/PIP_Schools_Internet_Report.pdf (accessed June 18, 2008).

McLuhan, Marshall. 1964. *Understanding Media: The Extensions of Man*. Cambridge, MA: MIT Press.

Oblinger, Diana. 2003. "Boomers & Gen-Xers, and Millennials: Understanding the New Students." *EDUCAUSE Review* 38, no. 4: 37–47.

Raessens, Joost, and Jeffrey Goldstein. 2005. *Handbook of Computer Game Studies*. Cambridge, MA: MIT Press.

Rainie, Lee. "Life Online: Teens and Technology and the World to Come." Speech to the Annual Conference of the Public Library Association, Boston (March 23, 2006). Available: www.pewinternet.org/ppt/Teenspercent20andpercent20technology.pdf (accessed July 25, 2008).

Roberts, Donald F., Ulla G. Foehr, and Victoria Rideout. 2005. *Generation M: Media in the Lives of 8–18 Year Olds*. Menlo Park, CA: The Henry J. Kaiser Family Foundation (March 2005). Available: www.kff.org/entmedia/upload/Generation-M-Media-in-the-Lives-of-8–18-Year-olds-Report.pdf (accessed August 2, 2008).

Ropelato, Jerry. "Internet Filter Review: Internet Pornography Statistics." TopTenREVIEWS (2003–2008). Available: http://Internet-filter-review.toptenreviews.com/Internet-pornography-statistics.html (accessed July 30, 2008).

Wallis, Claudia. 2006. "The Multitasking Generation." *Time* 167, no. 16 (March 27): 48–55.

Wolfe, Tom. 2004. "McLuhan's New World." *Wilson Quarterly* 28, no. 2: 18–25.

Ziegler, Susan G. 2007. "The (mis)education of Generation M." *Learning, Media and Technology* 32, no. 1: 69–81.

PART II:

The World of Gen M: A Culture of Technology

Chapter 6

The Wired Life: The Public and Private Spheres of the Gen M Community

Karen J. Klapperstuck

Amy J. Kearns

INTRODUCTION

Generation M spends much of their time interacting with multiple types of media and has not known a life that isn't completely "wired," or perhaps more accurately, "wire-less." Reports, such as the Kaiser Family Foundation's widely read *Generation M: Media in the Lives of 8–18 Year Olds* report, published in 2005, updating a similar 1999 study, *Kids & the Media,* state that Gen M students spend an average of 6–8 hours a day in multitasking mode with their media (Roberts, Foehr, and Rideout, 2005).

They are not just media users; they are considered by many to be multitasking, mobile media users. According to Foehr, "81 percent of young people spend their time using more than one medium at a time" (Foehr, 2006, under "Media Multitasking"). They are plugged-in for most of their waking hours and are often plugged-in through more than one source at a time. This is how they have managed to increase their use of new media (i.e., text messaging with their cell phones and live voice chat via free Web sites), while continuing to use older forms of media, such as television and music broadcasts and landline telephones. They have not totally replaced older formats with a new one; they have added the new formats to the old ones and use them in combination.

Gen M still watches TV, but now they do it while texting their friends on their cell phones, at the same time they are doing their homework on the computer, using the Internet. As the new technologies result in smaller and more mobile ways of staying connected, Gen M takes their multitasking media with them everywhere. While on their cell phones they can text, instant message, listen to music, watch videos, and talk to their friends from anywhere. This, in essence, means that they are never alone. They do not interact with their media; they *are* their media. The media they use are an extension of them and serve to keep them connected to their peers and the world at large at all times of the day and night.

Computers, MP3 players, cell phones, videos, and other technology have changed the way this generation thinks and communicates (Simpson, 2006). New technology has changed the way information is disseminated and how people interact with one another. The online context changes the way public and private are defined. "When asked, all youth know that anyone could access their profiles online. Yet, the most common response I receive is '. . . but why would they?'" (boyd, 2007a: 4).

"While being totally wired doesn't change the fundamental reality of being a teenager, it does raise new issues for our society around privacy, safety, and parenting" (Goodstein, 2007: 14–15). What does this mean for the way this generation thinks about privacy and the self? How does this generation see the public self versus the private self? In a world where one can be connected to one or more people no matter where one is, no one ever has to be alone. In a world where there are multiple points of access to many different kinds of media, what relationship does one have with the content there? When one can be just as easily a creator as a consumer of content, what does this mean for the individual?

A REMINDER

Although this discussion will focus on the members of Gen M that are tech savvy, it should be remembered that these are generalizations. Not all of Gen M is interested or skilled in technology. To not at least acknowledge this is to ignore "the needs and perspectives of those young people who are not socially or financially privileged. It presumes a level playing field and equal access to time, knowledge, skills, and technologies" that do not truly exist (Vaidhyanathan, 2008: B7). Conflicting data exist regarding the levels of skills, especially as compared with adults. Some research is showing that Gen M is no more impatient or tech savvy than adults (Thomas, 2008: under: "Conflicting Data").

An important thought to keep in mind is that even though Gen M is not all digitally connected or tech savvy, they do approach things in different ways to previous generations. Stephen Abram and Judy Luther identify nine factors providing insight into this generation. Their discussion focuses on the technology but can be applied to other behaviors and practices. Included in the nine factors are multitasking, collaboration, and being direct. These and the other factors have further-reaching implications than just where they apply to technology (Abram and Luther, 2004).

IN PHYSICAL SPACE

It is not uncommon to see more than one member of Gen M together in the same physical space, yet also connected virtually to other people or to other media sources. Two students sitting together in the library while also texting their other friends and listening to their MP3 players are not ignoring each other or violating any rules of etiquette. In this super-connected world, it is not rude to divide one's attention among different people and various tasks because others do it all the time as well.

To those outside of Gen M this may seem either rude or unnecessary. If with friends at the mall, why is there a need to be talking to or connected to other people who aren't even there? Being out in public with friends, Gen M is often updating their "status" to the rest of the world via sites such as Facebook, MySpace, or Twitter. If they are at the mall, they can post a message about where they are, whom they are with, and what they are doing. This is really no different from teens of other generations who also felt that they were the center of the universe and that everyone was looking at them, paying attention to them, or otherwise interested in everything they are doing. Having multiple forms of mobile media at one's fingertips means that everything one is thinking, doing, and feeling can be publicized at a moment's notice to one's network. The network may be small and personal or large and impersonal, but where one is and what one is doing is as important to Gen M as it ever was to any other generation. Gen M just has more ways of communicating who they are to the world.

ON SOCIAL NETWORKING SITES

Having a public profile on sites such as Facebook and MySpace allows Gen Ms to experiment with who they are. They communicate to the rest of the world: this is what I like, this is the kind of person I am, and these are my friends. They can see their peers and how they are trying on different identities. "What teens are doing with this networked public is akin to what they have done in every other type of public they have access to: they hang out, jockey for social status, work through how to present themselves, and take risks that will help them to assess the boundaries of the social world" (boyd, 2007b: 21). Since those at this age are prone to thinking that there is nothing outside of themselves and their own spheres, these public profiles seem private to them in a way that is difficult to understand.

Individuals select online networks. Users "friend" those they want to include and reject those who want to add them to their network if they do not want to be a part of their group. This gives the users a sense of having great control over whom they are providing with access to their lives. Once the network is selected, individuals feel that they are simply communicating with friends, just as anyone would. There is a sense of urgency and privacy when updating these networks. It is no different than calling up a best friend to tell him that one just said "hi" to a crush. However, instead of telling one person, it is like "telling" many people all at once, from one update point.

While there is not as much control over their information, in reality, as those in Gen M may think, they feel that they have established their own group and, therefore, there is no need for censoring themselves. It is just as if a group of friends has retreated to the bedroom and this group does not expect information expressed within the confines of those four walls to escape to the rest of the world. Of course, sometimes this happens, in real life and in virtual life, but it is this sense of security in their self-selected group that creates a different sense of what is public and what is private when using media.

Celebrity and Public-ness

The exponential creation of new technologies that enables mobile multitasking access to many forms of media has given this generation a different sense of public and private. The Internet is ubiquitous in their lives and they have 24/7-access to friends, entertainment, news, and more information sources than ever previously available. On a daily basis they experience a world of constant input in a variety of formats. Everything moves at a very fast pace, and their expectations of what they can consume or create differ from those of generations before them. Their expectations have been shaped by their constant access and exposure to multimedia. Now, new, instant, customizable, re-mixable, constantly updateable, and consumable information surrounds them. Everyone around them operates in this 24/7 plugged-in way. Their idols and heroes have instantly knowable lives. They see celebrities with completely consumable public lives. Celebrity and public-ness have almost become synonymous and it is difficult to tell, in some cases, which comes first: the celebrity or the public access to one's entire life.

Multiple formats of mobile media provide them with access to a world of celebrities (who may be almost anyone for any reason) whose lives are for public consumption 24/7. Even previously "serious" famous people who would not normally qualify as celebrities are turned into such figures through media access to their lives, that is, politicians and media-makers themselves. Gen M experiences less and less distinction between online life and real life. In fact, Gen Ms with the most online participation seem to be the most involved in real life; however, they may make less and less of a distinction between a public and a private life.

They watch reality TV and "don't really see the value of privacy or are a little cynical about it and see a world where everything is made public and that that's okay," according to Candice Kelsey, author of the book *Generation MySpace* (Dretzin, 2008, under "Candice Kelsey"). danah boyd further asserts: "Privacy is not about just me. Privacy is about control of audience. It's about being able to say, 'I want to hang out with these people. These are the people that I trust; this is the audience to hear my speech that I care about, the audience that I trust to tell secrets to.' That's what privacy is. And so even though they're in public in some sense, they want this privacy. They want a control over their audience" (Dretzin, 2008, under "danah boyd").

Making a Profile Private

Gen Ms can access their social networks via the Internet on a computer or laptop, cell phone, or PDA. Most online sites provide a certain measure of control over what is public and what is private. "If you're on MySpace, you have an opportunity to be private. What is private? Private means friends only. It's very simple: Those you've accepted as friends are the only people who can see things," says danah boyd of Berkman Center for Internet and Society at Harvard University (Dretzin, 2008, under "danah boyd").

Tom Anderson, co-founder of MySpace, notes the differing perspective on privacy of Gen M and that of older generations, especially as seen in reactions to marketing. He explains that Gen M's attitudes about privacy are not the same as previous generations' attitudes. Unlike their parents, Gen M is less concerned about being targeted by advertising. They don't feel that ad targeting is an invasion of privacy. According to Anderson, "…younger people say, 'I want ads that speak to me.' It's a totally different divide when you see people responding to how their information is used online and what they reveal online" (Dretzin, 2008, under "Tom Anderson and Chris DeWolfe").

All of the social networks on the Web have some way to make profiles private to varying degrees. Gen M does take advantage of this. Many of them have extensive networks with friends that are not necessarily real-life friends. There has been an effort to educate and increase awareness of the privacy features and control that are available on these Web sites. However, Gen M seems content to continue to share bits and pieces of their private lives via their profiles in these public spaces.

GEN M AS CREATORS

Multiple forms of media also allow Gen Ms to become creators and not just consumers of content. They not only publicize things for themselves and their friends, but they become authors of new content for everyone. According to "Teen Content Creators and Users," Pew Internet and American Life Project, "57 percent of online teens create content for the Internet. That amounts to half of all teens ages 12-17, or about 12 million youth" (Lenhart and Madden, 2005: i).

Amanda Lenhart, senior research specialist, and Mary Madden, research specialist for Pew Internet and American Life Project, say that,

"Today's online teens live in a world filled with self-authored, customized, and on-demand content, much of which is easily replicated, manipulated, and redistributable. (They have) the tools to create, remix, and share content on a scale that had previously only been available to the professional gatekeepers of broadcast, print and recorded media outlets" (Lenhart and Madden, 2005: 1).

In such a world, creator and consumer have equal legitimacy in terms of control over content. Furthermore, as a result of the speed and ease of using new media to create such content, it takes only a moment now to record a video and upload it. Gen Ms are, once again, in the position of feeling that what they create is for them and their networks alone. Considering the consequences of creating and sharing such content, and its long-lasting nature, are not part of their creation process. New media and Web 2.0 tools make access to others' lives, as well as access to their own, simpler, quicker, and more pervasive. The advancements in technologies for audio and video provide the tools to continue to put oneself out into the public in even more voyeuristic ways than ever before.

As with most situations, there are consequences and rewards to this. Their increased ability to multitask may result in their need for time management skills; however, they seem to accomplish about the same amount as they did in the past. The increased ability to create content allows some Gen Ms to be "super communicators," according to the Pew Internet report on Teens and Social Media. They blog, build Web sites, create video, and remix audio and other content to make new content. And, their expectations, as a result, include their right to be involved, engaged, and in control of the creation and consumption of content whether that content be video, audio, text, or print.

Blogs: The New Diaries

Teens have always kept diaries or journals. Gen M is no different, except that their journals are being kept digitally instead of under lock and key. More than half of all blogs are published by teens (Goodstein, 2007). "Blogs have transformed what used to be the solitary act of teens writing their personal thoughts and feelings in a diary into a strange intersection of private and public" (Goodstein, 2007: 30). Teens are using blogs to get their feelings out and to work through their real life experiences. It is also a way for them to develop their own identities and a sense of voice.

Blogs provide a context where teens can write about their private feelings and communicate those feelings to their friends and the larger network or world. There is a concern, however, as to when blogging becomes over-sharing. Parents and educators alike are worried about the safety of teens online. Experts think that the public sense of blogging is lost on some teens. "'During those years, we share in order to figure out how we fit into culture, online or offline. The difference is that online, the possible scope of audience is much larger and teens are not always aware of what it means to be public online,' says boyd" (Goodstein, 2007: 37).

Gen M is largely creating and sharing their lives online. Blogs are a prime example of the blurring line between what this generation deems private and public. However, research from the Pew Internet and American Life Project shows that teens are mostly creating their blogs for their personal networks to read and, in turn, mostly read the blogs of those they already know. "About 62 percent of blog-reading teens say they only read the blogs of people they know. The remaining group (36 percent) reports reading the blogs of both people they know and people they have never met. A mere 2 percent report only reading the blogs of people they do not know" (Lenhart and Madden, 2005: 8). These teen bloggers are also more likely to create and mash-up content than their non-blogging counterparts.

Although teens are keeping their journals as blogs, they intend that much of what they write remains somewhat private. Given the generation to which they belong, their definition of private now includes a larger network.

Social Activism

The extended networks that Gen M members create online help them become more involved in the global community. Technology provides a way for them to be more active in the issues they believe in, as they gain more information about social causes from the Internet than from any other source. "Social networking sites have also ignited teen activism as a viral way to spread the word about an issue" (Goodstein, 2007: 152–154). Through Web sites, e-mail, text, and IM, Gen M can contact their friends, business people, and government officials about their views, empowering them to believe that they can make a difference.

Technology can help to connect teens to one another both locally and on a larger scale. "We began to see the power of social networking when thousands of Latino teens poured into the streets to protest proposed immigration legislation after hearing about the protests on MySpace.

. . . Even politicians have started taking their message directly to young people on sites like MySpace and YouTube" (Goodstein, 2006). MySpace has a Web page for groups and individuals to register to be part of the IMPACT directory, and MySpace even provides incentives to register and get involved by seeking nominations each month of its members who are using their profiles to make a difference. The winning organizations are then given $10,000 donations called Impact Awards (MySpace.com, accessed 2008).

The social activism is just one example of Gen M moving from the local to the global. Online multimedia tools provide a way for teens to be involved in causes that may not be based locally. The implications of local versus global in many ways mirror those of public versus private.

In a guest post on the YPulse blog, Alex Steed writes about using social media for good: "Feeling concerned and doing the right thing is as ingrained into the psyche of some of us as the importance of owning Dolce & Gabbana glasses is in others" (Steed, 2008). A large part of this generation is actively working to overcome the apathetic and rude labels that have been placed on them.

GROWING UP IN THE MEDIA

All of these experiences result in a very different concept of privacy from those older than Gen M. According to a 2007 OCLC report, *Sharing, Privacy and Trust in Our Networked World*, "youth are less likely to feel that online activities are extremely or very private" (De Rosa et al., 2007: 3–10). This report also found that "the longer they use a site, the more they trust a site" (De Rosa et al., 2007: 3–40).

In a PBS FRONTLINE report, "Growing Up Online," C. J. Pascoe, PhD, Digital Youth Research, University of California, Berkeley says, "What is public realm for them . . . is much more expansive than what adults think belong in the public." Talking about recording and posting life Pascoe says, ". . . it's all part of that identity work, where they're reflecting back to themselves who they think they are . . . digital media has . . . given them a more intense way to do this" (Dretzin, 2008, under "C. J. Pascoe, PhD").

According to this report, the resultant extensive use of video has led to new varying degrees of "publicness." One new type of publicness is "publicly private" behavior, in which a content creator's identity is revealed, but the content itself remains relatively private because it is not made widely accessible. Another new type of publicness is "privately public." This behavior involves the sharing of widely accessible content with many viewers, while keeping access to detailed information about the creator's identity less accessible (Lange, 2007).

This generation also has not missed the fact that people sometimes become celebrities after posting something publicly online. In addition, they seem to believe that if it is for commercial purposes it is okay. Candice Kelsey states in the FRONTLINE report that "many of the kids today believe that if it makes money, it's okay. So a corporate mindset has really been instilled in a lot of our teenagers [. . .] the fact that a corporation would be . . . harvesting personal information from teenagers so that they can further their product or their profit—I may find unethical. Teenagers today would say, 'Hey, good for them, that's great business'" (Dretzin, 2008, under "Candice Kelsey").

FURTHER IMPLICATIONS

"Millennials have a special relationship to technology. They are not all tech-savvy . . . in the sense that they all know what's going on 'under the hood' of their gadgets . . . but they have a unique attachment to the communications power of these new technology tools" (Rainie, 2006: 3). Gen M recognizes the control this provides over what they can create and share in a multimedia environment. "This is the first generation to have grown up with interactive media. They want to manipulate, remix, and share content. If you add up all the possible ways that teens might have created and shared content online, some 57 percent of all teen Internet users have contributed a creation of theirs to the online 'commons'" (Rainie, 2006: 9). And this content is not limited to blogs; it also includes artwork, photos, music, video, podcasts, creative writing, and so on.

Linda Stone, a former Microsoft executive has another perspective. She believes that Gen M lives in a state of "continuous partial attention." She notes: "Continuous partial attention is not the same as multitasking; that's about trying to accomplish several things at once. With continuous partial attention, we're scanning incoming alerts for the one best thing to seize upon: 'How can I tune in in a way that helps me sync up with the most interesting or important opportunity?'" (Maxwell, 2002: under "The Always-On Society"). This characterization of continuous partial attention lends itself to the perception that Gen M is never fully engaged or that they never provide undivided attention to anything.

Marketing

Always of interest to marketers, Gen M now has a new, unique draw. Their unique relationship with multiple forms of media, along with their multitasking skills make them new marketers and makes them targets and tools of business. A new concept, the viral video, refers to video clip content which "gains widespread popularity through the process of Internet sharing, typically through e-mail or instant messages, blogs and other media sharing Web sites" (Wikipedia.com, accessed 2008, under "Viral Video").

The availability of mobile video recording devices, such as camera phones, has resulted in many amateur videos being made by Gen Ms. Easy access to free or low-cost video and audio editing and publishing tools allows for video to be edited and distributed on the fly, instantly and virally by e-mail, Web site, or between phones.

Viral video is one implement in the marketers' toolbox of viral marketing. As described by Wikipedia, viral marketing refers to "techniques that use pre-existing social networks to produce increased brand awareness or to achieve other marketing objectives through self-replicating viral processes, analogous to the spread of actual or computer viruses" (Wikipedia.com, accessed 2008, under "Viral Marketing"). This can be accomplished in a variety of ways, for instance, via word-of-mouth or via the Internet.

Viral marketing is a "phenomenon that facilitates and encourages people to pass along a marketing message voluntarily" (Wikipedia.com, accessed 2008, under "Viral Marketing"). This sort of advertising may take the form of video clips, images, or even text messages. In order for a viral marketing campaign to be successful, marketers need to find individuals with high social networking potential and create messages that target them. This increases the likelihood that these messages will be passed along. Gen Ms who have constant connections to the Internet and multitask with mobile media are especially positioned to carry out this process of viral spreading.

Public and Private

Gen Ms have a different idea of what it means to own content created and shared via multiple media formats. According to *Teen Content Creators and Consumers*, "teens currently outpace adults in video downloading by two to one. Nearly one-third (31 percent) of online teens say they download video files to their computer so they can play them at any time" (Lenhart and Madden, 2005: 15). Their impression of being able to easily download audio and video is that it wouldn't be rational or logical to attempt to prevent such downloads. Their experience of and relationship to online content is such that it is easy to acquire, manipulate, and re-share content, so who is really the "owner"? This has consequences for the issues of copyright and digital rights management, because the sense of ownership has changed. Gen M is "often uncaring about their own privacy and they enjoy 'soft surveillance' of others. This creates a world in which the line between what's public and what's private is less clear; where boundaries of taste and etiquette are shifting; and where the notion of property is in flux" (Rainie, 2006: 13). All one has to do is look at controversies over the illegal download of videos and music to see that the consequences can be damaging to the content owners and Gen M downloaders alike.

Susan B. Barnes has written in *A Privacy Paradox: Social Networking in the United States*: "In America, we live in a paradoxical world of privacy. On one hand, teenagers reveal their intimate thoughts and behaviors online and, on the other hand, government agencies and marketers are collecting personal data about us" (Barnes, 2006: under "A Privacy Paradox"). Retail and grocery stores, credit card and insurance companies, and a variety of government agencies all collect information about consumers on a daily basis. Much of this data, which many people would assume is private, and would want it to remain so, is readily available in some form on the Internet. Gen M may be the most cognizant of the melding between what is public and what is private. Maybe in their approach to privacy and their public private lives, Gen M is living more accurately and authentically in the world of today.

CONCLUSION

"Adults tend to use the Web as a supplement to real-world activities while teenagers tend to ignore the difference between life online and offline" (Barnes, 2006: under "Public versus Private Boundaries"). To teens, their online life is an extension of their real life. Ultimately it is Gen Ms who may be the most realistic about the differences between the public and private life. They are aware of the way content and information can be replicated and spread. Although they may not be fully aware of all technology and about privacy and control, they are taking steps to be part of their local and increasingly global networks.

Every generation feels a certain disconnect with other generations. A large part of Gen M's disconnect is due to the fact that they are digital natives and all previous generations are digital immigrants. However, teens are teens and there are more similarities than differences in the teen experience. "What's different about today's totally wired teens is that the viral and public nature of these new technologies has magnified and publicized, though not changed, what it means to be a teen" (Goodstein, 2007: 12).

REFERENCES

Abram, Stephen, and Judy Luther. 2004. "Born with the Chip." *Library Journal* 129, no. 8 (May 1): 34–37. Available: www.libraryjournal.com/Article/CA411572. html (accessed November 22, 2008).

Barnes, Susan B. 2006. "A Privacy Paradox: Social Networking in the United States." *First Monday* 11, no. 9 (September). Available: www.firstmonday. org/issues/issue11_9/barnes/index.html (accessed October 30, 2008).

boyd, danah. 2007a. "Social Network Sites: Public, Private, or What?" *Knowledge Tree* 13 (May). Available: http://kt.flexiblelearning.net.au/tkt2007/?page_id=28 (accessed November 2, 2008).

boyd, danah. 2007b. "Why Youth (Heart) Social Network Sites: The Role of Networked Publics in Teenage Social Life." In *MacArthur Foundation Series on Digital Learning–Youth, Identity, and Digital Media Volume*, edited by David Buckingham. Cambridge, MA: MIT Press. Available: www.danah. org/papers/WhyYouthHeart.pdf (accessed November 1, 2008).

De Rosa, Cathy, Joanne Cantrell, Andy Havens, Janet Hawk, and Lillie Jenkins. 2007. *Sharing Privacy and Trust in Our Networked World*. Dublin, OH: OCLC (September 11). Available: www.oclc.org/reports/pdfs/sharing.pdf (accessed October 31, 2008).

Dretzin, Rachel. "PBS FRONTLINE: Growing Up Online: Their Very Public Private Lives." WGBH Educational Foundation (January 22, 2008). Available: www.pbs.org/wgbh/pages/frontline/kidsonline/inside/publicprivate. html (accessed November 1, 2008).

Foehr, Ulla G. 2006. "Media Multitasking Among American Youth: Prevalence, Predictors and Pairings." Menlo Park, CA: Kaiser Family Foundation (December). Available: www.kff.org/entmedia/upload/7592.pdf (accessed November 1, 2008).

Goodstein, Anastasia. "Activism 2.0." YPulse (November 14, 2006). Available: http://totallywired.ypulse.com/Archives/2006/11/Activism_20_1.php (accessed October 31, 2008).

Goodstein, Anastasia. 2007. Totally Wired: What Teens and Tweens are REALLY Doing Online. New York: St. Martins Press.

Lange, Patricia G. 2007. "Publicly Private and Privately Public: Social Networking on YouTube." *Journal of Computer-Mediated Communication*, 13, no. 1: Article

18. Available: http://jcmc.indiana.edu/vol13/issue1/lange.html (accessed October 15, 2008).

Lenhart, Amanda, and Mary Madden. "Teen Content Creators and Consumers." Washington, DC: Pew Internet and American Life Project (November 2, 2005). Available: www.pewinternet.org/pdfs/PIP_Teens_Content_Creation.pdf (accessed November 1, 2008).

Maxwell, Jill Hecht. "Stop the Net, I Want to Get Off." Inc.com (January 2002). Available: www.inc.com/magazine/20020101/23805.html (accessed November 1, 2008).

MySpace.com. "MySpace IMPACT: A Place for Impact: The Official Guide for Non-profits, Campaigns, Organizers, and Advocates." Available: www.myspace.com/Aplaceforimpact (accessed November 11, 2008).

Rainie, Lee. "Life Online: Teens and Technology and the World to Come." Speech to the Annual Conference of the Public Library Association, Boston (March 23, 2006). Available: www.pewinternet.org/ppt/Teenspercent20andpercent20technology.pdf (accessed July 25, 2008).

Roberts, Donald F., Ulla G. Foehr, and Victoria Rideout. 2005. *Generation M: Media in the Lives of 8–18 Year Olds*. Menlo Park, CA: The Henry J. Kaiser Family Foundation (March 2005). Available: www.kff.org/entmedia/upload/Generation-M-Media-in-the-Lives-of-8-18-Year-olds-Report.pdf (accessed October 15, 2008).

Simpson, Steven W. 2006. "Can Generation M Learn Its ABCs?" *T.H.E. Journal: Technology Horizons in Education Journal* (March): 48–50. Available: www.thejournal.com/Articles/18043 (accessed October 14, 2008).

Steed, Alexander. "We (Millennials) Care A Lot!" YPulse (October 13, 2008). Available: www.ypulse.com/ypulse-guest-post-we-millennials-care-a-lot/ (accessed October 15, 2008).

Thomas. "Digital Immigrants Teaching the Net Generation: Much Ado about Nothing?" (September 22, 2008). Available: www.openeducation.net/2008/09/22/digital-immigrants-teaching-the-net-generation-much-ado-about-nothing/ (accessed November 23, 2008).

Vaidhyanathan, Siva. 2008. "Generational Myth: Not All Young People are Tech-savvy." *Chronicle of Higher Education: The Chronicle Review* (September 19): B7. Available: http://chronicle.com/free/v55/i04/04b00701.htm?utm_source=cr&utm_medium=en (accessed November 23, 2008).

Wikipedia. "Viral Marketing." (Last updated November 23, 2008). Available: http://en.wikipedia.org/wiki/Viral_marketing (accessed November 23, 2008).

Wikipedia. "Viral Video." (Last updated November 23, 2008). Available: http://en.wikipedia.org/wiki/Viral_video (accessed November 23, 2008).

Chapter 7

Face-to-Face on Facebook: Students Are There . . . Should We Be?

Laurie M. Bridges

SOCIAL NETWORKING SITES: AN INTRODUCTION

In the past seven years, social network sites (SNSs) have moved from relative online obscurity to become the most trafficked Web sites in the United States and internationally. As of November 2008, two SNSs ranked in the top ten Web sites globally: Facebook (5th) and MySpace (7th). The same two ranked in the top five in the United States: MySpace (3rd) and Facebook (5th) (Alexa.com, accessed 2008). Social network sites have several key elements that, when combined, make them unique compared to other Web sites; according to boyd [*sic*] and Ellison, SNSs are "web-based services that allow individuals to (1) construct a public or semi-public profile within a bounded system, (2) articulate a list of other users with whom they share a connection, and (3) view and traverse their list of connections and those made by others within the system" (boyd and Ellison, 2007: 211). As SNSs have grown in popularity, librarians, professors, and teachers have decided (on various levels) if and how to use them; in particular, Facebook has become part of the educational discourse on many college and university campuses due to its widespread use among students. In this chapter, I will examine current scholarly research on social networking sites; discuss the treatment of SNSs in popular media; and investigate the educational uses of SNSs, specifically Facebook, by educators and librarians.

The Demographics

SNSs are extremely popular with Generation M. More than half of online teens, ages 12–17, use SNSs, and 85 percent of college students have an account with Facebook (Lenhart and Madden, 2007; Facebook, accessed 2008a). It is important to note that Generation M is not the only age group using social network sites. The fastest growing demographic on Facebook is users age 25 years and older (Facebook, accessed 2008a). According to Rapleaf, a research company, 63 percent of the users on Facebook are female and 36 percent are male (2007).

A Brief History

Social network sites arrived on the Internet scene in 1997 with the establishment of SixDegrees.com, the first Web site to combine the three elements of a social network site as mentioned in the Introduction (boyd and Ellison, 2007). Although SixDegrees folded in 2000, other social network sites soon followed. Many of the first sites were (and still are) popular with various U.S. subcultures. Friendster, Asian Avenue, and BlackPlanet all started in the late 1990s/early 2000s and still maintain a loyal user base.

MySpace started in Los Angeles in 2003 when two friends, Tom Anderson and Chris DeWolfe, had an idea to create a Web site connecting local L.A. bands, club owners, and friends (Sellers, 2006). Bands quickly began using MySpace to self-promote events to their fans, and by promoting their bands they brought more users to MySpace, and those users invited their friends, and those friends invited their friends, etc. Reaching out to local bands was pivotal in MySpace's quick success. At the same time, rival SNS, Friendster, began to flounder because of imposed restrictions on user profiles (bands, dogs, and buildings, for example, were not allowed to have profiles) and slow loading times (rapid growth slowed their servers to a crawl); Anderson and DeWolfe took notice and benefited by allowing users to have more control over their profiles and by providing quicker loading times (Sellers, 2006). Many Friendster users quickly migrated to MySpace.

As MySpace continued its rise in popularity, Facebook emerged in 2004 when several university students, Mark Zuckerberg and three of his friends, Dustin Moskovitz, Chris Hughes, and Eduardo Saverin, began the SNS in their Harvard dorm rooms (Facebook, 2008b). For the first month access to Facebook was limited to Harvard students, but Zuckerberg et al. opened the site to three additional universities within one month. Word quickly spread about Facebook, and students around the country were requesting their university be added to the Facebook network. Originally, Facebook was only open to higher education institutions; every member had to have an ".edu" e-mail address to register and access the site. Within one year, the site had reached more than one million college and university students, faculty, and staff (Facebook, 2008b). Today, anyone can join Facebook and it still remains the most popular Web site among college and university students, even more popular than Google (Anderson Analytics, 2007).

As of June 2008, MySpace maintained the highest overall popularity in the United States, but Facebook dominated as the most widely used SNS among college and university students (Alexa.com, accessed 2008; Anderson Analytics, 2007). Although MySpace is the most popular SNS among high school students overall, students who aspire to attend a university or college generally connect online through Facebook, since it is widely acknowledged as the place where university and college students go (boyd, 2007a).

THE RISE OF FACEBOOK

I joined Facebook in late 2004 when I was employed as the marketing coordinator for Housing and Dining Services at Oregon State University (in 2007, I became the Business & Economics librarian at the same institution). I had some student "friends," but overall I found most staff and faculty were not interested in joining and, as a result, my network of friends was relatively small and uninteresting. That all changed in the summer of 2007. It was then that Facebook experienced a meteoric rise in popularity. Within one week, I had ten Facebook "friend" requests in my e-mail inbox from staff and faculty at Oregon State University. As the invitations continued to pile up, I quickly turned to the media to find out, "What is going on with Facebook?"

On May 24, 2007, Facebook launched the "Facebook Platform," which allowed any third party to develop applications for Facebook; and on that day 85 new applications were added (Kirkpatrick, 2007). Facebook applications are small programs that work on the Facebook Web site.

There are all types of applications including games, news aggregators, political opinion sharing, quizzes, sports affiliation, daily quotes, and book reviews; by adding an application to a profile, the user adds the ability to interact with that small program. So, from a user's Facebook page she can play games with other people, get the latest news, and read a funny quote sent from a friend—all for free. By opening up the development of applications to third-party developers, Facebook quickly set themselves apart from other major social network sites. Sites like MySpace closely guarded the development of applications and typically shut down third-party applications or acquired them for a small sum (Arrington, 2007). As of June 2, 2008, developers had added 24,000 applications, roughly 140 applications per day, to Facebook since the Facebook Platform was launched (Vora, 2008).

Although most applications do not have an educational component, many educational institutions and enterprises are now engaged in creating applications with the hopes that students will connect with their service or product through Facebook. Libraries, such as the Harvard University Library System, Hennepin County Library, and UCLA, have created online catalog applications for students to embed into their profiles. Library database providers, like JSTOR and Worldcat.org, have also created search engine applications for their services. While these different library and database applications do get some use, social applications where users interact with one-another, such as Library Gifts created by Michael Porter of the OCLC Online Computer Library Center, are considerably more popular; as of November 2008 Library Gifts had 20 times more monthly users (2,005) than the top ranked library catalog application from Ryerson University (77 monthly users). This is understandable since socializing is the primary objective of Facebook.

Another educational use for Facebook applications is the creation of the applications themselves. Instructors BJ Fogg and David McClure at Stanford developed a hands-on learning opportunity for university students using applications. In the fall of 2007, Fogg and McLure taught the computer science course, "Creating Engaging Facebook Apps" (Stanford University, accessed 2008). In this class, 80 students created more than 50 applications that were installed over 20 million times (Ammirati, 2008).

ACADEMIC RESEARCH INTO FACEBOOK

danah boyd, a sociologist, PhD student, and pioneering researcher in the field of SNSs, keeps an online bibliography of all known academic publications, conference papers, trade publications, works in progress, and theses on the subject of SNSs (boyd, accessed 2008). A review of the academic publications listed on her site as of May 29, 2008, revealed there was one publication about social network sites in 2003, three in 2004, 11 in 2005, 20 in 2006, 24 in 2007, and 12 for the first half of 2008. A search using the term "social networking site*" in Academic Search Premier revealed 71 scholarly articles; five were published in 2006, 19 in 2007, and 66 in 2008 (as of November). The same search in Web of Science uncovered 35 articles; 1 in 2005, 3 in 2006, 9 in 2007, 22 in 2008 (as of November). It is obvious from these numbers that interest in SNSs is slowly growing in academia.

Popular media often focuses on the negative aspects of emerging technologies and its effect on youth and young adults, but published academic research into Facebook reveals many positive correlations between Facebook use and student life. A study conducted at two large public universities in Texas showed a positive relationship between intensity of Facebook use and students' life satisfaction, social trust, civic participation, and political engagement (Valenzuela, Park, and Kee, 2008). Similar research at Michigan State University (MSU) found Facebook plays an important role in which students form and maintain social capital (Ellison, Steinfield, and Lampe, 2007). French sociologist Pierre Bourdieu first analyzed social capital in the 1980s when he linked social connections and resources with economics (Portes, 1998). MSU Professors Ellison, Steinfield, and Lampe define social economics as "the resources accumulated through the relationships among people" (2007). Three types of social capital are discussed in the MSU findings: bridging social capital, bonding social capital, and maintained social capital. Bridging social capital is defined as a weak tie or loose connection that may prove useful, but does not typically provide emotional support. Bonding social capital is described as emotionally supportive connections, like relationships with close friends and family. Maintained social capital is the ability to maintain valuable connections as a person moves through life. According to the researchers, "Facebook appears to play an important role in the process by which students form and maintain social capital, with usage associated with all three kinds of social capital included in our instrument" (Ellison, Steinfield, and Lampe, 2007).

Interest in SNSs is high among librarians and as of November 20, 2008, the Facebook Group "Librarians and Facebook" boasted 7,395 members. The largest educators' Group "Educators Using Facebook" had 533 members. In 2006, Charnigo and Barnett-Ellis (2007) conducted a study about academic librarians and their perspectives toward Facebook. Out of the 126 librarians who participated in the study, 114 had heard of Facebook. When given a list of possible effects Facebook has had on their library, 10 percent of the participants indicated computer use had gone up due to student use of Facebook. Fifty-one participants indicated that librarians needed to keep up with Internet trends like Facebook. Fifty-four percent of the librarians indicated Facebook might serve an academic purpose, whereas 34 percent said they were unsure. Nineteen percent of the librarians expressed concern over privacy issues related to Facebook. Because the research conducted by Charnigo and Barnett-Ellis is over two years old, and in that time the popularity of Facebook has quickly spread beyond colleges and universities, it would be interesting and enlightening to replicate the study and compare results.

EDUCATIONAL ASPECTS OF FACEBOOK

When I discuss Facebook and other SNSs with faculty and staff members of universities and colleges and teachers at high schools, many questions pop up but are generally centered around one focal question: "Should we (I) be there?" These worries are what I've come to refer to as "Facebook anxiety"; they include concerns about generational differences, technological expertise, appropriateness and professionalism, privacy, and legality. Researcher Alice Marwick calls anxieties such as these "technopanic" (2008). As outlined by Marwick, technopanic has three defining characteristics: a focus on new media such as computer technologies; widespread negative media attention of young people's use of the technology; and cultural anxiety that results in parents, educators, or lawmakers curtailing or controlling young people's use of the new technology or the producers of the new technology.

Popular media has sensationalized the supposed threat of online predators and privacy concerns. Most of the hype centers on only a handful of incidents. In June 2008, Facebook had 80 million active users. It is only fair to assume the online community will mirror the social ills of the larger offline society; however, it is important that educators and librarians recognize the benefits of online social networking. As Marwick points out, "While new discoveries almost always have both benefits and disadvantages, breathless negative coverage of technology frightens parents, prevents teenagers from learning responsible use, and fuels panics . . . teenagers should be encouraged in their use of technology. Technological skills are advantageous both in terms of social capital and job prospects, and we should promote technological knowledge among young people rather than discourage it" (2008).

When librarians and educators are on Facebook, what is the impact? Does the time, energy, and learning curve necessary for a SNS presence by educational institutions merit such a presence? A review of the available literature holds some surprising findings. A study by Mazer, Murphy, and Simonds examined what students would expect of classroom climate, learning, and motivation based on an instructor's Facebook profile (2007). In this study, 133 undergraduate students at a large university were shown one of three instructor profiles; the same instructor was used, but each profile had a different level of self-disclosure (low, medium, and high). The low disclosure profile featured only a head shot and no comments on the "Wall," the medium disclosure profile included photos of the instructor at home with her family but no comments on the "Wall," and the high disclosure profile included photos of the instructor in various social situations with friends and family in public locations and many comments (not related to teaching) were featured on the "Wall." Over 80 percent of students who viewed the high and medium disclosure profiles made comments emphasizing what they believed the teacher's strengths would be based on her use of Facebook and a small group of students made negative comments. Sixty-one percent of the students who viewed the low self-disclosure profile indicated they could not determine the effectiveness of the instructor based on the profile. The majority of all the participants in the study viewed the teacher's use of Facebook positively.

Another quantitative study by Hewitt and Forte (2006) found contact between professors and students on Facebook had "no impact on students' ratings of professors" when compared with students who had not had contact with the same professors through Facebook. However, in the qualitative section of the survey, several students indicated Facebook contact had a positive impact on their perceptions of the professor and no students indicated it had a negative effect. Gender did seem to be a factor in the qualitative section, with males being twice as likely to say faculty should be on Facebook.

In 2006, two librarians, Chu and Meulemans, did an investigation into the problems and potential of MySpace and Facebook in academic libraries (2008). They administered a survey at California State University San Marcos to four sections of a general election course for first-year students. Of the 89 students who participated in the survey, 45 percent felt it would be useful if professors had a MySpace/Facebook profile page and 29 percent didn't know if it would be useful.

Professorial presence and activity in Facebook is a somewhat new phenomenon. As mentioned earlier, while an ".edu" account was originally required to join Facebook, most librarians and educators were not active in the site and students viewed the site as their exclusive community. However, it is possible students will become more open and interested in having educators and librarians on Facebook, especially now that Facebook is open to the general public and the largest growing group in Facebook is persons over age 25. In the not-so-distant future, students will no longer remember a time when Facebook was only open to university students, faculty, and staff, because all of the students who had Facebook accounts in 2004 and 2005, when Facebook was an exclusive community for universities and colleges, will have graduated and moved into the workforce.

CREATING A PROFILE, ADVERTISEMENTS, AND A "FACEBOOK FAN PAGE"

As mentioned in the previous section, many students have favorable views of professors and librarians who have Facebook profiles. Creating a profile is simple:

1. Visit Facebook.com.
2. Fill in your name, e-mail, birth date, gender, and password.
3. Confirm your e-mail.
4. Fill in some basic profile information.
5. Done. You now have a simple profile from which you can connect with students and colleagues, add photos and Facebook applications, create advertisements and "Facebook Fan Pages," etc.

When creating a personal profile in Facebook you should consider the following hints:

- Include photos. Keep it professional, but remember that adding several photos of yourself makes your profile more interesting and approachable. In Facebook the third most popular activity is browsing pictures, after browsing profiles and interacting with applications (Freiert, 2007).

- Don't search out your students, instead, wait for them to invite you to be their "friend" in Facebook.
- Once you have student "friends," don't invite them to add applications to their profile, as this may be considered annoying and "spammy"; this also goes for coworkers unless the application relates directly to their jobs.
- Invite friends and colleagues already in Facebook to "friend" you.
- Join Facebook Groups and Facebook Fan Pages that interest you or are related to your field, for example, "Librarians and Facebook" or "Arts Education is Absolutely Necessary."
- Consider discussing Facebook and other SNSs in your classes. Students may become more engaged in the conversation if they know you have a profile and are truly interested in their opinions about these popular communities. Possible conversation topics include: privacy, usage, media-coverage, employer and instructor presence, relationships, and information sharing.

Once you have set up a profile you can begin promoting your school, library, and services through advertising and/or a Facebook Fan Page. Advertisements are displayed in the right hand side of Facebook profiles, Fan Pages, or directly in the News Feed. The ads are small blocks of space that are available for purchase by anyone including libraries, schools, and private companies and can be targeted to specific audiences (for example undergraduates at your university or students at your local high school). You can purchase ads by the number of times users click on your ads (CPC) or by the number of views (CPM). Visit www.facebook.com/Business/?socialads for more information.

Another way to advertise, without the cost, is through a Facebook Fan Page where students can "fan" your school or library, write on your Wall, upload photos, talk with other fans on the discussion board, view your hours, and interact with applications. When your Fan Page is updated, fans are notified in their personal News Feed. Usage stats, including the number of visitors to your page every day, can provide valuable information about the popularity of your Fan Page. Visit www.facebook.com/home.php#/Business/?pages for more information on setting up a Fan Page. A keyword search in Facebook for the term "library" in Facebook Fan Pages uncovered more than 500 pages; the most popular pages were (1) NASA Glenn Technical Library with more than 3,000 fans, (2) The British Library with more than 2,200 fans, and (3) the Seattle Public Library System with more than 1,600 fans (accessed November 20, 2008).

As a final note, before creating an advertisement or a Facebook Fan Page, consider contacting the media or marketing specialists at your institution to inquire about any guidelines regarding the creation of an online presence in social networking sites.

CONCLUSION

In the past ten years, social network sites have gone from relative obscurity to the most highly trafficked Web sites in the world. Most recently, Facebook has emerged as the most popular Web site among college and university students in the United States. While not every librarian or educator needs to have a Facebook profile, all should know what effect SNSs are having on students, how they're being used, why they are so popular, and how students share information with one another on the sites. Librarians and educators should not be discouraged from creating profiles and participating in the Facebook community. Rather, they need not only to be where the students are, but also explore ways to effectively serve them in their online communities.

REFERENCES

"Alexa: The Web Information Company." Alexa.com. Available: www.alexa.com/ (accessed June 2, 2008).

Ammirati, Sean. "What Stanford Learned Building Facebook Apps." ReadWriteWeb (March 3, 2008). Available: www.readwriteweb.com/Archives/what_stanford_learned_building_facebook_apps.php (accessed June 2, 2008).

Arrington, Michael. "Facebook Launches Facebook Platform: They are the Anti-MySpace." TechCrunch (May 24, 2007). Available: www.techcrunch.com/2007/05/24/facebook-launches-facebook-platform-they-are-the-anti-myspace/ (accessed June 23, 2008).

boyd, danah. "Research on Social Network Sites." danah.org. Available: www.danah.org/SNSResearch.html (accessed May 29, 2008).

boyd, danah. "Viewing American Class Divisions through Facebook and MySpace." Apophenia Blog Essay (June 24, 2007a). Available: www.danah.org/papers/essays/ClassDivisions.html (accessed June 2, 2008).

boyd, danah. 2007b. "Social Network Sites: Public, Private, or What?" *Knowledge*

Tree 13 (May). Available: http://kt.flexiblelearning.net.au/tkt2007/edition-13/social-network-sites-public-private-or-what/ (accessed May 29, 2008).

boyd, danah m., and Nicole B. Ellison. 2007. "Social Network Sites: Definition, History, and Scholarship." *Journal of Computer-Mediated Communication* 13, no. 1: 210–230. Available: http://jcmc.indiana.edu/vol13/issue1/Boyd.ellison.html (accessed May 29, 2008).

Charnigo, Laurie, and Paula Barnett-Ellis. 2007. "Checking Out Facebook.com: The Impact of a Digital Trend on Academic Libraries." *Information Technology and Libraries* 26, no. 2: 23–34.

Chu, Melanie, and Yvone Nalani Meulemans. 2008. "The Problems and Potential of MySpace and Facebook Usage in Academic Libraries." *Internet Reference Services Quarterly* 13, no. 1: 69–85.

"College Students: Facebook Top Site, Social Networking Really Hot." Stamford, CT: Anderson Analytics (October 5, 2007). Available: www.marketingcharts.com/interactive/college-students-facebook-top-site-social-networking-really-hot-1914/ (accessed June 23, 2008).

"Creating and Connecting // Research and Guidelines on Online Social—and Educational—Networking." Alexandria, VA: National School Boards Association (July 2007). Available: www.nsba.org/SecondaryMenu/TLN/CreatingandConnecting.aspx (accessed June 20, 2008).

Ellison, Nicole B., Charles Steinfield, and Cliff Lampe. 2007. "The Benefits of Facebook "Friends:" Social Capital and College Students' Use of Online Social Network Sites." *Journal of Computer-Mediated Communication* 12, no. 4. Available: http://jcmc.indiana.edu/vol12/issue4/ellison.html (accessed May 29, 2008).

"Facebook Company Timeline." Facebook. Available: www.facebook.com/press/info.php?statistics=#/press/info.php?timeline= (accessed June 20, 2008b).

"Facebook Statistics." Facebook. Available: www.facebook.com/press/info.php?statistics (accessed June 20, 2008a).

Freiert, Max. "14 Million People Interacted with Facebook Applications in August." Compete.com (September 14, 2007). Available: http://Blog.compete.com/2007/09/14/ (accessed June 25, 2008).

Hewitt, Anne, and Andrea Forte. "Crossing Boundaries: Identity Management and Student/Faculty Relationships on the Facebook." Poster presented at Computer Supported Cooperative Work, Banff, Alberta, Canada, 2006. Available: www-static.cc.gatech.edu/~aforte/HewittForteCSCWPoster2006.pdf (accessed May 29, 2008).

Kirkpatrick, David. 2007. "Exclusive: Facebook's New Face." Fortune (May 25). Available: http://money.cnn.com/2007/05/24/technology/fastforward_facebook.fortune/ (accessed June 5, 2008).

Lenhart, Amanda, and Mary Madden. "Social Networking Websites and Teens: An Overview." Pew Internet and American Life Project (January 3, 2007). Available: www.pewinternet.org/pdfs/PIP_SNS_Data_Memo_Jan_2007.pdf (accessed June 6, 2008).

Marwick, Alice. 2008. "To Catch a Predator? The MySpace Moral Panic." First Monday 13, no. 6 (June). Available: www.uic.edu/htbin/cgiwrap/Bin/ojs/index.php/fm/Article/view/2152/1966 (accessed June 20, 2008).

Mazer, Joseph P., Richard E. Murphy, and Cheri J. Simonds. 2007. "I'll See You on "Facebook": The Effects of Computer-Mediated Teacher Self-Disclosure on Student Motivation, Affective Learning, and Classroom Climate." *Communication Education* 56, no. 1 (January): 1–17.

Portes, Alejandro. 1998. "Social Capital: Its Origins and Applications in Modern Sociology." *Annual Review of Sociology* 24, no. 1: 1–24.

Sellers, Patricia. 2006. "MySpace Cowboys." *Fortune* (September 4): Available: http://money.cnn.com/magazines/fortune/fortune_archive/2006/09/04/8384727/index.htm (accessed June 16, 2008).

Stanford University. "The Stanford Facebook Class: Persuasive Apps & Metrics." Stanford, CA: Stanford University (October 28, 2007). Available: http://credibilityserver.stanford.edu/captology/facebook/ (accessed June 16, 2008).

"Statistics on Google's Open Social Platform End Users and Facebook Users." Rapleaf. (November 12, 2007) Available: http://Business.rapleaf.com/company_press_2007_11_12.html (accessed November 21, 2008).

Valenzuela, Sebastian, Namsu Park, and Kerk F. Kee. 2008. "Lessons from Facebook: The Effect of Social Network Sites on College Students' Social Capital." Paper presented at the 9th International Symposium on Online Journalism, Austin, Texas, April 4-5, 2008. Available: http://online.journalism.utexas.edu/2008/papers/Valenzuela.pdf (accessed May 29, 2008).

Vora, Ami. "Happy Anniversary (and Facebook Open Platform)." Facebook (June 2, 2008). Available: http://developers.facebook.com/news.php?blog=1&story=117 (accessed June 4, 2008).

Chapter 8

YouTube and YouTube-iness: Educating Gen M Through the Use of Online Video

Katie Elson Anderson

INTRODUCTION

The Discovery Channel created a commercial by taking an old camp tune and customizing it to market their programming. When my infant son first saw it, he couldn't help but dance. Wanting to be able to see him dance again, I went to Google and typed in "YouTube and Boom-De-Yada" and the first hit brought me to a streaming video of the commercial, which I bookmarked. Now, with one mouse click it plays and he immediately stops crying and starts dancing. As he jumps up and down on my lap drooling on my keyboard, I think: "This is one of the greatest inventions of modern times!"

The admittedly hyped-up judgment of a sleep-deprived mother aside, YouTube is widely recognized as a serious influencer of popular culture. It was cited by *Time Magazine* as the 2006 Invention of the Year (Grossman, 2006a) and is mentioned again in 2006 as a tool for user-generated content that led to the naming of "You" as *Time*'s Person of the Year (Grossman, 2006b). With its content showing up in daily conversations and nightly newscasts, this video-sharing Web site is an innovation that simply cannot be overlooked.

YouTube has shown itself to be an immensely popular Web site for entertainment such as catchy commercials, "lonely girl" diaries, and Lego figurines acting out Shakespeare's plays. There is no question that the site is being used heavily with reports of 91 million users viewing five billion videos in the United States during the month of July 2008 (comScore, 2008). The question then arises: what are people watching and how are they using what they watch? Many educators are tempted to dismiss YouTube as a popular site filled with amateur home videos that are mildly entertaining at best, a waste of valuable time at worst. However, it is a mistake to overlook what is available on YouTube alongside the questionable and sometimes inane offerings. The social and culture impact alone of the site is an important component to discovering ways to engage and excite Gen M. Conversation on the educational aspects of YouTube and other video streaming and sharing sites has been getting louder as more and more educators are realizing the potential for enhancing their teaching of the Millennial Generation.

SEEK AND YOU SHALL FIND

It is difficult at this point to not have heard of YouTube, with its burgeoning popularity in the last two years. Hearing about it, however, does not necessarily mean knowing where to go and how to use it. In fact, with the increased media attention due to Google's purchase of YouTube, many people who heard about it were unsure of the domain name and the spelling. This uncertainty actually caused difficulties for an Ohio company, Universal Tube and Rollerform Equipment Corp, whose Web site, utube.com was knocked offline due to millions of hits from people trying to locate the site (Zappone, 2006).

Once the correct Web site is located (youtube.com) users will find a place where videos can be viewed, uploaded, and shared. Anyone may view the videos, while only registered users may upload videos, respond to videos by uploading their own videos, and comment on the videos. A simple search box can be expanded into an advanced search, and videos can also be found under specific categories such as "featured," "rising videos," "most discussed," and "most viewed." When a video is selected, related videos appear, allowing for more browsing of videos with similar subjects or keywords. Along with watching a video, any user can share the video by posting it to a variety of social networking sites such as Facebook, MySpace, StumbleUpon and Digg. Registered users can mark videos as Favorites, create playlists of videos, and flag other videos for inappropriate content. Uploaded videos can be marked as private and shared with specific e-mails. Videos not marked private (there are many out there that probably should be marked private) will be available to anyone who goes to the site. Registered users may create channels, which are individualized YouTube pages containing detailed information and the videos created by the user. A registered user can subscribe to a channel and receive alerts when items are added to that channel. Channels are searchable by user name and by subject. Users can also connect via the "Community" tab that includes contests, a blog, and forums. YouTube's organization and options encourage users to go beyond simple viewing of the video and engage in conversation, both textual and video. The site is in constant development, with new and enhanced features appearing on a regular basis.

A VERY BRIEF HISTORY OF YOUTUBE

Steve Chen, Chad Hurley, and Jawed Karim founded YouTube in February 2005. Already working in the technology sector for the online payment company PayPal, these three friends were seeking a place to view videos of current events and share videos on the Web, similar to the photo sharing Web sites that already existed. Unable to find a site that allowed for the easy creation and sharing of videos, they began working on creating their own site (Hopkins, 2006; Yadav, 2006). Registered under the domain name, youtube.com, the site was released as a public beta site in May 2005. In order to entice users, the site offered free iPods for random users who either signed up, invited friends to sign up, and/or uploaded videos. This contest, along with YouTube's ease of use and social networking capabilities led to the swift growth of registered users and site views, with millions of video views per day (Yadav, 2006).

The rise in popularity and use of YouTube brought a need for more capital to support the growth. Fortunately it also brought the attention of an investor, another former PayPal employee, Roelof Botha, who convinced his company, Sequoia Capital, to invest in the startup. With $3.5 million in funding, the founders were able to officially launch the site to the public in December 2005, opening it up to even more users and site views per day (Yadav, 2006). The number of users and views increased at a remarkable pace, hitting an average of 100 million video streams per day, worldwide in July 2006 (comScore, 2006). The popularity of the site caught the eye of Google who purchased it in November 2006, for

$1.65 billion in stock (Google, 2006). As Google continues to find ways to profit from YouTube, the site grows at an excellent pace with 122 million unique users in the United States in October 2008 (Nielsen, 2008) up from 91 million in July 2008 (comScore, 2008).

YouTube's impressive growth in such a short time can be attributed to many factors ranging from timing to formula. Before YouTube, there was not a well-known simple way for everyday users to easily upload, share, and view videos. Little evidence exists of video-sharing sites existing before YouTube's creation, and those that did exist were not simple or easy to use. The creation of YouTube unlocked a whole new area of Web 2.0, expanding the user created-content of blogs, wikis, and photos to the realm of video. The creation of YouTube coincided with the emergence of inexpensive video technology, from reasonably priced digital camcorders and webcams to cameras and phones with video capabilities. The videos were already being made; YouTube's usability provided the creators with an outlet to share them.

The social networking aspect of YouTube played a part in its quick rise in popularity. In the beta period, users were encouraged (by the iPod contest) to get their friends to join and to share the site and the videos. Users complied, sharing the site and the videos not only via e-mail and physical word of mouth, but also on their social networking sites such as blogs, MySpace, and Facebook. With YouTube's comment feature and the ability to find specific users, a YouTube community emerged and users who were already savvy with social networking tools simply added YouTube to their repertoire of Web 2.0 tools.

A discussion of the history of YouTube would be incomplete without mentioning that there is a YouTube video on the history of YouTube. An anthropology class at Kansas State University created and posted a brief history of YouTube called *The History of YouTube* (Hinderliter, 2007). Several related videos appear next to this video, including the highlighted videos from the history, in case you missed them the first time. Another interesting way to learn more about the history of YouTube is to read the archives of the YouTube Blog, www.youtube.com/Blog. While many of the posts are just detailed instructions to users, it is interesting to see the development play out through time.

IS IT LEGAL?

During its brief history, YouTube has consistently been plagued with questions of copyright. With billions of videos available on YouTube, it is expected that not all of these are original material. A part of YouTube's early allure was the ability to locate, view, and, in some cases, modify copywritten material. A sense of gaining the system and guerilla-like creativity was accompanied with each trip to the site. As YouTube's popularity rose it grabbed the attention of the owners of the copyright material. Media moguls were not happy to find that users were actually uploading entire television episodes, splitting them into parts in order to work around the ten-minute limitation on uploaded videos. Users of course were thrilled to find their favorite television shows available albeit the video quality was usually poor and shows were typically sliced into multiple parts. Before Google's purchase of YouTube, the copyright issues were often overlooked since YouTube's low-level player status did not warrant large monetary lawsuits. When a copyright owner notified YouTube of a problem, YouTube would remove the item with little fanfare. Users searching for the item would find the link with a message indicating that the owner had requested that the item be removed. In YouTube's eyes, it is up to the user to be responsible and to not upload copyrighted material as per the registration agreement; if you uploaded material you do not own, your account would be deleted. By providing this Copyright Infringement Notification to users, YouTube is acting in accordance with the Digital Millennium Compliance Act, which protects copyright holders and Internet service providers from their users' copyright violations (Christensen, 2007).

When discussions of Google's purchase of YouTube began, many users correctly believed that copyright would become a much bigger deal. Although YouTube was not a large enough target for a lawsuit, Google was. Google's ownership of YouTube would put YouTube at risk for legal action. As was expected, shortly after Google's purchase of YouTube, the media conglomerate Viacom filed a $1 billion lawsuit against YouTube in March 2007 (Peters, 2007). As the owner of popular shows like *South Park*, *The Daily Show*, and *The Colbert Report*, Viacom claimed to have found more than 150,000 of their clips on YouTube that had been viewed billions of times. In its lawsuit, Viacom further claimed that YouTube created and supports technology that willfully infringed copyrights and allowed YouTube to profit from others' illegal activities (FindLaw, 2007). This lawsuit is still pending. The most recent action occurred in July 2008; Google was ordered to turn over records of what users were watching (Helft, 2008). This action has been met with a large outcry regarding user privacy. Google and Viacom have responded by promising to make the information anonymous. There remain concerns however as to how effective this process will be and how much privacy is really being protected.

In order to deal with copyright issues, YouTube has several initiatives. They have recently released a beta version of Video ID, the details of which are found on its Web site. Video ID is a technology that helps copyright holders to identify their works. Once an item has been identified, the copyright owners then have the choice of having the clip taken down or leaving it there and placing ads on the page and collecting half of the revenue. This option is proving very popular—about 90 percent of identified content is now maintained on YouTube with advertisements (Stelter, 2008). YouTube has also been working to create partnerships with copyright owners in order to have better relationships with the media companies. An example of such a partnership is with CBS, who has created a channel that offers clips from its shows as well as entire episodes. They have even created a Web Original Series, with episodes averaging about 20,000 views.

The emergence of YouTube has reshaped media companies' thinking on how and where their material should be made available. There is obviously a huge amount of exposure for a company when its clip is available on YouTube. While Viacom was busily having its material removed, companies like the NHL were embracing the exposure and sponsoring channels like "NHL Hockey Fights," which features the more popular portions of some hockey games. In a response to pirated movie trailers, movie companies such as Lionsgate offer the official trailers, on their own YouTube channel. Many other companies are waiting in the background to see what the outcome of the Viacom lawsuit is before going forward with YouTube, preferring to offer their content on their official sites or on other video streaming sites.

The fact that entire episodes of popular television shows and even entire feature-length films are available for online viewing is due in large part to YouTube. It became evident that the American public was very interested in watching video on small grainy screens for free. If they were willing to watch the YouTube clips, it would follow that they would be even more willing to watch a higher quality video with ads. This realization led to the creation of other video streaming sites, such as Hulu and Veoh, along with the presence of streaming video on major network sites such as Time Warner and Walt Disney. The questions of copyright on YouTube forced the hand of many big media companies to provide what the users demand.

Despite all of the warnings and the identification technology, copyrighted material continues to make its way to YouTube. YouTube's guidelines suggest that the best way to avoid copyright issues is to only upload original material since the fine points of affair use and copyright violations are often hard to discern. Even with the uploading of original content it provokes questions such as image permissions for individuals, utilizing corporate logos, and proper dissemination of the video. Later in this chapter, there will be discussion of how to use these tools with regard to copyright. The issue of copyright continues to be an important discussion, not only with YouTube but also with all digital media. It is important to be aware of the copyright issues and the impact that they have on the tools for video sharing and video streaming. Avenues do exist for limited copyright protection. Creative Commons (CreativeCommons.org, 2008) "provides free licenses and other legal tools to mark creative work with the freedom the creator wants it to carry, so others can share, remix, use commercially, or any combination thereof." Users may select the copyright conditions of their works and license them with a Creative Commons license. Enforcement of these licenses is usually up to the individual as Creative Commons is open-source software maintained by donations and volunteers and not a law firm or legal enforcement team.

IS IT USEFUL?

The cultural impact of YouTube is enormous. The fact that millions of people worldwide are gathering to share, view, comment on, and respond to the billions of videos is a social phenomenon. From the mundane to the hysterical to the profound, the videos run the gamut of the human experience. As educators it is important to recognize the value and cultural, historical, and emotional significance of these videos.. It is also important to recognize that students can become part of this experience by creating their own original material and taking part in the worldwide conversation.

Gen M has embraced the creation and collaboration that distinguish the tools of Web 2.0 from the more static tools that existed before the rise of Web 2.0. This creation and collaboration is taking place both informally and formally. Examples of informal venues include blogs, video sharing sites such as YouTube, and social networking sites like MySpace and Facebook. Formal creation and collaboration often takes place in the classroom as more and more educators are realizing the importance of engaging Gen M with the tools that make up their daily life. Creation with the expectation of sharing is an integral part of this generation and thus educators need to respond with appropriate tools. Already there is evidence of video sharing and video streaming being used in educational forums.

In order to realize the potential of using YouTube and other video streaming sites in the classroom, educators need to become familiar with the characteristics of Gen M students. As this generation travels through the educational system, more studies and discussions regarding their unique learning styles are being written, including chapters of this book. In addition, on a discussion regarding YouTube and Gen M it is appropriate to use the tool to learn about the target.

In the YouTube video "A Vision of Students Today" (Wesch, 2007), the spring 2007 Cultural Anthropology Class from Kansas State University, presents information on Gen M. According to the video's accompanying blog (http://mediatedcultures.net), the class attempted to "summarize the most important characteristics of students today, how they learn, what they need to learn, their goals, hopes, dreams, what their lives will be like, and what kinds of changes they will experience in their lifetime." The class created a survey for themselves and compiled the answers in order to "create a visual representation of the characteristics of the students of today." Recorded in the classroom during one class period, the students hold up pieces of paper with the statistics from the survey. These statistics, found on the blog, reveal some interesting points about this select group of Gen M students who spend an average of three and a half hours online per day, writing 500 pages of e-mail, reading 2,300 Web sites and 1,281 Facebook profiles within a semester, which is in contrast to the eight books read and the 42 pages written during the same time. According to the count on YouTube, this video had been viewed 2,828,234 times as of November 21, 2008, obviously making an impact on educators and students. A less viewed, but no less informative video is "A Vision of K–12 Students today" that addresses the younger generation of digital natives (available www.youtube.com/watch?v=_A-ZVCjfWf8). Videos such as these are excellent representatives of the power of a short video. Haunting music fills the background as poker-faced students hold up what at times are surprising statistics on how they learn, how they are being taught, and how they see their future. Arguably, these four minutes can make as great an impact as a four-page article—if not greater.

In the past two years, educators have begun to take more notice of the pedagogical potential in YouTube. A class was taught in the fall of 2007 at Pitzer College in Claremont, California, on YouTube about YouTube. The professor developed the course in order to attempt to understand the site's value. Classes were filmed and posted to YouTube and student assignments included having to comment on and respond to existing videos by creating their own videos (Bigham, 2007). Paul Robeson Library, Rutgers—Camden, has several tutorials available on YouTube on topics that include plagiarism and Wikipedia. University of California, Berkeley and other universities have begun to post full-length lectures on YouTube, allowing anyone with access to YouTube to take part in their educational offerings. Several colleges and universities have created channels for their institutions, posting lectures, promotional materials, and other sanctioned videos. The power to reach a wider audience is an incentive for educational institutions to have a presence on YouTube, as well as the understanding and embracing of this social and far-reaching technology. By using YouTube, both as a viewing tool and a teaching tool, educators of Gen M are acknowledging its cultural significance. As mentioned previously, Professor Wesch of Kansas State consistently finds creative ways to use YouTube to teach anthropology, including "An Anthropological Introduction to YouTube" (www.you-tube.com/watch?v=TPAO-lZ4_hU&feature=channel), which provides an excellent description of the social impact of this technology and why the educational community should be paying attention.

As a creative classroom tool, YouTube is revolutionary. The simplicity of creating a video log or filming a presentation and then sharing it with the class and the world has allowed this generation to learn and present in ways that previous generations could not and it has also allowed both educators and students to reach out to each other in ways that have not been possible. Tutorials and instructional videos that are created for local audiences are being shared with and viewed by thousands more than the intended audience. Educators and students are creating, finding, viewing and sharing videos in a community that is larger than any known by previous generations. The exercise of creating the video engages students in formal creation and collaboration. For this chapter I did a search on YouTube using the term "student project." This search yielded more than 30,000 hits. The results included a variety of disciplines including art, film, and engineering. Many countries were represented as well as a wide range of age groups. The number of views ranged from double digits to thousands. This simple search illustrates that educators and students are currently using the creative aspect of YouTube in their teaching and learning.

Politicians and news media also have been working to engage users and gain audiences and voters using YouTube. In 2007, CNN and You-Tube worked together to host both Democratic and Republican primary debates in which voters were able to submit videos of questions for the candidates (TimeWarner, 2007). As the campaigns continued, the major candidates created their own channels, which included campaign ads and clips from speeches, debates, and rallies. During the 2008 Election, PBS partnered with YouTube to encourage participants to "Video Your Vote," asking for interesting stories and possible problems to be videotaped and shared. Indeed, at that time, according to YouTube, President Obama plans to continue to use YouTube during his presidency with weekly addresses and interviews (available www.youtube.com/watch?v=TPAO-lZ4_hU&feature=channel). Obama's use of You-Tube to address the nation is being compared to FDR's use of the radio to conduct his Fireside Chats. What is amazing about YouTube is that both Obama's and FDR's addresses can be found quickly and easily. Mixing the past with the present, YouTube provides an immense catalog of material. With copyright controversies aside, YouTube's catalog is filled with historical clips, ranging from bootleg songs to presidential speeches to public service announcements. Current events appear on YouTube as they are happening; there is an expectation that an important cultural or historical event will be available virtually real-time on YouTube—an expectation frequently realized.

YouTube's ease-of-use contributes to making it a valuable resource for educators. With more and more students watching hours and hours of online videos, the video creation and streaming part of curriculum is likely to garner more attention than a simple lecture. The content on YouTube is relevant to a variety of disciplines including media literacy, cultural studies, advertising, political science, communications, journalism, technology, anthropology, sociology, history, and the sciences. Interviews with students and a quick survey of blogs and articles provide evidence that educators are enhancing their course content with viewings of relevant YouTube videos and subsequent conversations regarding the clip. As with new teaching tools, there are concerns regarding the use of YouTube. A major concern is, again, the issue of copyright. Other concerns are privacy, slander (the comments can be abrasive to say the least), and appropriateness. It seems that for every educationally appropriate video there are probably no less than twenty inappropriate ones. Users have also criticized the search algorithms, rating system, and tagging conventions utilized by YouTube. While many of these concerns are valid, some can be addressed by familiarity with the site as well as being aware of video sharing alternatives (which will be discussed later in this chapter).

HOW TO USE YOUTUBE

A good way for educators to become familiar with YouTube is to watch YouTube. People who are successfully using it in the classroom have uploaded instructional videos on how to maximize its potential. There are videos that discuss copyright, Creative Commons, how to embed, how to stream, and even how to use YouTube videos in your school even if the site itself has been blocked (Tarrant, 2008). The most popular utilization of YouTube by educators at this time is the streaming of videos into the classroom. Choosing relevant videos enhances the class and the social nature of YouTube promotes conversation. YouTube is different from simply showing a clip or movie in class as it is always available to the students, even after class viewing and the comments and discussions can be used for further educational purposes.

The easiest way to share YouTube videos with a class is to watch the video either directly from the Web site, or to embed it into a document. This live streaming is also the only allowed sharing use of YouTube (Tarrant, 2008). In the case of a school administration blocking YouTube, there are ways to work around this, especially if the video is not also available on non-blocked alternative sites. Part of the reluctance to use YouTube is because of copyright and legal issues. It is unfortunate to think that tools will not be used because of a lack of understanding on the part of educators or a lack of clarity on the rules. Fortunately, there is help on the topic of copyright and fair use for educators. The Center for Social Media at American University publishes "The Code of Best Practices in Fair Use for Media Literacy Education" (Center for Social Media, 2008) and the Media Education Lab at Temple University (Media Education Lab, accessed 2008) provides assistance on ways to reduce confusion with copyright.

Finding the videos on YouTube that are relevant to curriculum is not always easy, though the actual searching of YouTube is. Search results are often based on popularity and user ratings, so something that is useful but not necessarily popular will be more difficult to locate. The "related" videos feature is at times helpful in developing a serendipitous finding of material, however, it can also include unrelated and even inappropriate items. When searching it is important to remember that the most popular items appear in the results more often than the best items. There are also several alternatives to YouTube that will be discussed later in this chapter. Each of these sites has different search algorithms, target audiences, and search capabilities. With each of these sites, it takes some time to become familiar with the searching and the results. Those who have experience with finding videos are sharing their findings through blogs and articles, including a nice overview of searching on YouTube by the editor of the Media Literacy department of the University of North Carolina at Chapel Hill. Suggestions by James Trier include focus on a username of a person who has uploaded videos that you have located and paying attention to the tags placed by the users (Trier, 2007). The community nature of YouTube adds an interesting element to searching, as it is possible to find items based on favorites and reviews by users who share similar interests.

Along with finding videos by searching, it is possible to have the videos delivered by subscribing to particular users videos or to specific channels. When a YouTube user logs in, any new videos uploaded by these chosen users appears on the user's homepage. Once videos have been selected, registered users may save these and rate them for other uses. These saved items appear on user's homepage along with suggested items related to previous searches. Other customizable options allow a user to personalize his/her YouTube experience. These timesaving features allow educators to easily monitor new developments, creations and applications.

Many educators and librarians take the time to share their knowledge with the community. Offering information and opinion on blogs encourages conversation and sharing information among the educational community. Rather than focusing on individual bogs, since they are plentiful and constantly changing, this discussion will focus on how to find useful blogs to read them. The nature of a blog is such that an author can choose to share information quickly or speak in length on a subject. Some blog entries are simply a link to a story while other entries are several paragraphs of musings on a recent incident in the classroom. The most time-consuming part of reading blogs is initially identifying those that are most useful. This could mean reading several for a few days and determining if the content is helpful while continuously searching for different ones. Most communities have several bloggers that have established reputations and finding out what they are reading is also a good way to locate related blogs.

The easiest way to read several blogs is through an aggregator, or RSS (Real Simple Syndication) feed. Most blogs provide these feeds, which allow a user to compile all of his/her subscribed-to blogs into one customizable location. These aggregators allow users to skim the headlines and determine if an entry is worth reading and save or mark it for later. Examples of aggregators are Bloglines and Google Reader, both of which also provide a way for users to search for blogs on specific topics, such as library, education, and technology. Aggregators are useful for following the on-line conversations of current topics. Another way to keep up to date is through an alert service like Google Alerts. This is a simple request for information to be mailed to you based on standard keyword searches. News stories and blogs are searched for the chosen keywords and the links are sent to an e-mail address. For example, a Google Alert on YouTube and education consistently alerted me to news stories and blog entries relevant to this chapter. Social bookmarking sites are also good places to find information and advice on using video technology in the classroom. As other users identify links, they post them and tag or label them, making it easy to locate with simple keyword searching. Examples of social bookmarking sites are de.li.cious, StumbleUpon, and Diigo.

In reading current news and blogs on the topic of YouTube and education, it is clear that alternatives are available and being used and discussed. While YouTube revolutionized video sharing and continues to be the best known and popular site, it is by no means the only or even the best site for video uploading and sharing.

BEYOND YOUTUBE

Imitation may not necessarily be the sincerest form of flattery—it may just be profitable. The fact that many competitors to YouTube have recently emerged gives credence to this suggestion. Most of the alternative sites follow YouTube's organization and structure. For example, they highlight the most popular, highest-rated and discussed videos. Some of these sites are dedicated to entertainment while others specialize in education and educational topics. Not all of these sites allow upload of user-created content, but most allow posting comments and taking part in discussions. It is clear that the newly created Web sites are searching for a specialization to distinguish themselves from the others. These specialties range from offering high-definition quality to marketing to independent filmmakers. Many of these Web sites address some of the concerns with YouTube such as copyright and privacy, creating specialized content with tighter controls and smaller communities. The best example of this type of site is TeacherTube, which was developed by educators wishing to use YouTube but concerned with content, copyright, and privacy. As educators it is important to be aware of the many different alternatives to YouTube that exist, from the teacher-oriented sites to those marketed toward consumers. Some of these sites are getting greater attention as more people utilize video sharing and video streaming technology. Listed below are some of the sites that I have reviewed and recommend as YouTube alternatives. The blog, "Free Technology for Teachers" lists some other sites that are also worth exploring (Byrne, 2008).

Big Think (www.bigthink.com)

Big Think (bigthink.com) presents discussions on a variety of topics divided into the meta such as faith, beliefs, love, and happiness and the physical, which includes arts, culture, science, and technology. According to the Web site, its mission is "to move the discussion away from talking heads and talking points, and give it back to you" and its motto is "We are what you think" (Big Think, accessed 2008). The site is made up of interviews on the specific topics given by specialists, authors, politicians, educators, and other leaders. The site allows a user to respond to an interview or express an idea. The site can be browsed by idea or by expert with a friendly user interface and clear organization. The interviews are professionally directed, making them more refined than most videos found on YouTube. Big Think does have a channel on YouTube and interestingly enough more users have commented on the ideas and interviews on YouTube than on the actual Big Think Web site.

Hulu (Hulu.com)

Hulu's tagline states, "Watch your favorites. Anytime. For free." Founded in March 2007 by NBC Universal and News Corp, it features clips, full episodes, and even full-length movies. This site is Hollywood's answer to copyrighted material appearing on YouTube. Recognizing the demand for video streaming, several networks including Fox and Viacom have partnered with NBC and Hulu to provide high-definition viewing of legal material with advertisements. As with YouTube, material can be viewed without registering, but registering provides a user with a heartier experience, including the ability to resume playing a video, something useful when watching a full-length feature film. Hulu does not contain user-created content, though commenting and rating is available for registered users. Videos can be found using keyword searching or through browsing the available channels. Similar to YouTube, videos are organized by most popular and highest rated. Hulu provides the user with free legal access to a large catalog of content and easy links for sharing and embedding of the material.

Internet Archive (www.archive.org)

The Internet Archive holds more than 130,000 movies, films, and videos in its Moving Image section. Divided into sub-collections, anything from animation to vlogs (video logs) can be accessed and used for free by anyone. The goal in organizing this collection is "to encourage widespread use of moving images in new contexts by people who might not have used them before" (Moving Image Archive, accessed 2008). One of the many sub-collections that can be used for educational purposes is the Prelinger Archives, which contains more than 60,000 ephemeral videos. According to the Web site, Prelinger was founded in 1983, its goal being to "collect, preserve, and facilitate access to films of historic significance that haven't been collected elsewhere" (Prelinger Archives, accessed 2008). The material on the site is public domain and free for downloading and reuse. Users are encouraged to reproduce, share, exchange, and redistribute any of the material. While some of the content that is available on Internet Archive has been redistributed to YouTube (The Nixon/Kennedy debates, for example), there is certainly part of the collection unique to the archives and the video quality is better than YouTube. Use of the site is similar to the others with the ability to comment and easy links for embedding. What distinguishes this site from some of the others are more advanced searching tools and a more academic organization providing the user with a less chaotic experience in locating what is needed.

TeacherTube (www.teachertube.com)

TeacherTube was launched in March 2007 and according to the Web site "sets out to provide an online community for sharing instructional videos . . . and to fill a need for a more educationally focused, safe venue for teachers, schools, and home learners."(TeacherTube, accessed 2008).

Quite simply it is YouTube for, by, and about teachers and teaching. The content is vetted by educators and is intended to provide professional development for teachers as well as be a place for teachers to create and share videos that teach concepts and skills to students. As with YouTube, TeacherTube encourages its users to play an active part in the community, not just viewing and uploading, but also commenting, rating, and flagging the content. TeacherTube has a YouTube channel that directs users to the main site. There are several TeacherTube videos on YouTube, but in no way near the full inventory available on the TeacherTube site. With teachers doing the vetting, commenting, rating, and flagging, many of the concerns with YouTube are addressed, providing teachers with access to the videos without having to wade through the extraneous content on YouTube.

UStream (www.ustream.tv)

Featured recently in EDUCAUSE's "7 Things You Should Know About" series, (EDUCAUSE, 2008), UStream is unique in that it provides live streaming video. Users may chat during the video streaming and then save and archive the event. This kind of technology is especially useful for distance education, as streaming video and chat comes closer to creating a classroom environment than either element alone. YouTube has recently added a "Live" feature that is similar to Ustream.

"V Sites": Vimeo, Viddler, and Veoh

Vimeo (www.vimeo.com)

Vimeo offers high-definition video, and if video quality is important, this is the place to be. In looking at the available videos, it appears to have mostly original content. Much of that original content seems to be more refined than the original content on YouTube. It appears that this site is where the artistic crowd is sharing videos, with independent films, higher quality home video, and more sophisticated conversation. It is interesting to note that according to the Web site, Vimeo was founded in 2004, before YouTube.

Viddler (www.viddler.com)

Viddler does not seem to be much different from YouTube, other than the fact that it has less chaotic feel. On the Web site viddler.com, Viddler is described as a platform for video publishers. Viddler does not have the same open community feel as other video-sharing sites. The organization of the content is not unlike other sites, but it struck me as difficult to find videos unless I already knew they existed. Viddler has a more private, businesslike feel to it despite the public nature of its videos.

Veoh (www.veoh.com)

Unlike the previous sites that are more focused on user created content, Veoh markets itself as an Internet TV service. Available for viewing on the site are television clips and shows from CBS, ABC, WB, ESPN, and Comedy Central. Veoh also provides users access to Hulu and YouTube content. The viewing quality is better than YouTube while the organization and options, such as commenting, are similar to all other video sharing sites. A feature that appears to be unique to this site is the Family Filter, which defaults to "on," limiting the search content. The only way to expand a search and turn Family Filter off is to register as a user.

BACK TO THE FUTURE

In 1996, while working for the Olin School of Business Library at Washington University in St. Louis as the technology person in the library, my boss asked me to attend a lecture by someone from Microsoft. Begrudgingly, I went, thinking that it would be all about business and a waste of time. I do not remember the exact words spoken (and could not locate the speech on YouTube), but I vividly remember the speaker announcing that in the future, people would be able to select the television shows they wanted to watch whenever they wanted and view them on their computers. He spoke of a future without a need for television, as all content would come to users online. I scoffed at this idea of unstructured viewing of my favorite shows. How could anyone watch television without channel flipping? Why would I even want to watch television this way? And even more perplexing was how that would be possible when at the time of the speech most Web sites I was viewing were only textual. As I write this, I am still amazed at the prescience of his words.

This predicted ability to view television on a computer is only a small part of the technology of today. Along with the viewing of available media, there is conversation and creation, merging the professional with the amateur. While some are appalled at this rise in popularity of the amateur, others look to embrace this new player on the field as a whole new game is being created. The opportunity to use both the viewing and creating technology in education is especially important to the Millennial Generation who has grown up with the new rules. It is important, too, that educators do not assume that all Gen M students are familiar or even comfortable with video-sharing technology. It is wise to proceed with some caution and take the opportunity as educators to help students not only learn by this technology but also about this technology. The opportunity to teach students about technology, copyright, and correct searching arises with all of the mentioned sites. As our culture embraces these new technologies and changes because of them, more pedagogical challenges emerge, forcing educators into determining what is and what isn't useful.

It is difficult to say if the reviewed sites will still remain in a few years or if even more will exist. Part of the challenges of teaching in today's world is keeping up with the tools and determining how much time to dedicate to learning and employing these tools. It is not out of the realm of possibility to imagine a time when students will submit a paper that contains only a link to the video version of their class project (Skiba, 2007). Video streaming is not a fad that will fade in the future. It is obvious that video is going to continue to rise as a much more predominant part of daily communication. Video chat enhances Instant Messaging, Web cams are being used in place of telephones, and YouTube continues to be an extremely popular way to express ideas, instruct, and entertain.

With this in mind, it is obvious that educators need to explore the ways in which video can be employed, from viewing historical and recent events to creating and presenting projects for class. In the review of some of the different Web sites available for video streaming it is clear that there is a place for both the professional and the amateur as is true for copyright issues, with those places yet to be determined. Wherever the material exists, it is certain that there will be many places for both original and copyrighted content as more and more people are attempting to attract attention and gain viewers.

In writing this chapter, I discovered that one of the best ways to understand video sharing is to actually join the conversation and become part of the growing community. The professional benefits of this are obvious. There are personal benefits as well, which include being able to watch a video of 100 people smiling on "YouTube Smiles!" (available: www.youtube.com/watch?v=IGU_SHufUBk). Even on a particularly bad day it is nearly impossible not to smile back.

REFERENCES

Bigham, Will. 2007. "Pitzer College Class Studies YouTube Craze." *Inland Valley Daily Bulletin* (Ontario, CA) (September 13). *Newspaper Source.* EBSCOhost. Available through subscription: http://search.ebscohost.com (accessed November 28, 2008).

Big Think. "Big Think: F.A.Q." bigthink.com. Available: www.bigthink.com/ About (accessed October 10, 2008).

Byrne, Richard. "Great Alternatives to YouTube." Free Technology for Teachers (2008). Available: http://freetech4teachers.pbwiki.com/Great+Alternative s+to+YouTube (accessed November 28, 2008).

Center for Social Media. "The Code of Best Practices in Fair Use for Media Literacy Education." Washington, DC: Center for Social Media (November 2008). Available: www.centerforsocialmedia.org/resources/publications/ code_for_media_literacy_education (accessed November 30, 2008).

Christensen, Christian. 2007. "YouTube: The Evolution of Media?" *Screen Education* 45 (January): 36–40. Available through subscription: http://search. ebscohost.com (accessed July 30, 2008).

comScore. 2006. "comScore Data Confirms Reports of 100 Million Worldwide Daily Video Streams from "YouTube.com in July 2006." Reston, VA: comScore.com (October 11, 2006). Available: www.comscore.com/press/release. asp?press=1023 (accessed November 3, 2008).

comScore. 2008. "YouTube Draws 5 Billion U.S. Online Video Views in July 2008." Reston, VA: comScore (September 10, 2008). Available: www.comscore. com/press/release.asp?press=2444 (accessed November 10, 2008).

Creative Commons. "About." CreativeCommons.org. Available: http://creative-commons.org/About/ (accessed March 25, 2009).

EDUCAUSE. "Seven Things You Should Know about Ustream" EDUCAUSE. com (October 21, 2008). Available: http://net.educause.edu/ir/library/pdf/ ELI7042.pdf (accessed November 28, 2008).

FindLaw. 2007. "Viacom Files Copyright Infringement Lawsuit Against YouTube and Google Over Unauthorized Use of the Company's Shows." Findlaw. com (March 13, 2007). Available: http://news.findlaw.com/nytimes/docs/ google/viacomyoutube31307cmp.html (accessed November 3, 2008).

"Google to Acquire YouTube for $1.65 Billion in Stock." Mountain View, CA: Google (October 9, 2006). Available: www.google.com/intl/en/press/press-rel/google_youtube.html (accessed November 13 2008).

Grossman, Lev. 2006a. "Best Invention: YouTube." Time (November 13). Available: www.time.com/time/2006/techguide/Bestinventions/inventions/ youtube.html (accessed October 28, 2008).

Grossman, Lev. 2006b. Time's Person of the Year: You. *Time* (December 17). Available: www.time.com/time/magazine/Article/0,9171,1569514,00.html (accessed April 25, 2008).

Helft, Miguel. "Google Told to Turn Over User Date of YouTube." *New York Times* (July 4, 2008). Available: www.nytimes.com/2008/07/04/technology/ 04youtube.html (accessed November 3, 2008).

Hinderliter, Robert. 2007. "The History of YouTube [Video]." Digital Ethnography @ Kansas State University (May 18). Available: www.youtube.com/ watch?v=x2NQiVcdZRY (accessed October 25, 2008).

Hopkins, Jim. "Surprise! There's a Third YouTube Co-founder." *USAToday* (October 11, 2006). Available: www.usatoday.com/tech/news/2006-10-11-youtube-karim_x.htm (accessed November 3, 2008).

Media Education Lab. "Teaching Tools to Reduce Copyright Confusion." Temple University. Available: http://mediaeducationlab.com/index.php (accessed November 30, 2008).

"Moving Image Archive." Internet Archive. Available: www.archive.org/details/movies (accessed November 30, 2008).

Nielsen News. "Top Web Brands Among U.S. Internet Users: October 2008." Nielsen News (November 13, 2008). Available: http://Blog.nielsen.com/nielsenwire/tag/youtube/ (accessed November 20, 2008).

Peters, Jeremy. "Viacom Sues Google over YouTube Clips." *New York Times* (March 14, 2007). Available: www.nytimes.com/2007/03/14/Business/14viacom.web.html (accessed November 3, 2008).

"Prelinger Archives." Internet Archive. Available: www.archive.org/details/prelinger (accessed November 28, 2008).

Skiba, Diane. 2007. "Nursing Education 2.0: YouTube." Nursing Education Perspectives 28, no. 2 (March/April): 101–102.

Stelter, Brian. "Some Media Companies Choose to Profit from Pirated YouTube Clips." *New York Times* (August 15, 2008). Available: www.nytimes.com/2008/08/16/technology/16tube.html?_r=1&oref=slogin_(accessed November 20, 2008).

Tarrant, Jon. 2008. "Geek Speak–Flash and Grab for Free Videos" *Times Educational Supplement* (September): 52.

Teacher Tube. "About Us." teachertube.com (2009). Available: www.teachertube.com/About.php (accessed March 25, 2009).

TimeWarner. "CNN, YouTube Team Up to Host First-Ever Voter-Generated Presidential Debates. TimeWarner.com (June 14, 2007). Available: www.timewarner.com/corp/newsroom/pr/0,20812,1633139,00.html (accessed November 26, 2008).

"Top Web Brands Among U.S. Internet Users: October 2008." Nielsen News (November 13, 2008). Available: http://Blog.nielsen.com/nielsenwire/tag/youtube/ (accessed November 20, 2008).

Trier, James. 2007. "Cool Engagements with YouTube: Part 2." *Journal of Adolescent and Adult Literacy* 50, no. 5 (February): 408–412. Available: http://search.ebscohost.com/login.aspx?direct=true&db=aph&AN=24572529&site=ehost-liveCut (accessed July 30, 2008).

Wesch, Michael. 2007. "A Vision of Students Today [Video]." Kansas State University (October 12). Available: www.youtube.com/watch?v=dGCJ46vyR9o&feature=channel (accessed October 10, 2008).

Yadav, Sid. "YouTube—The Complete Profile." Rev2.org (October 2, 2006). Available: www.rev2.org/2006/10/02/youtube-the-complete-profile (accessed October 10, 2008).

Zappone, Christian. "Help! YouTube Is Killing My Business!" CNNMoney.com (October 12, 2006). Available: http://money.cnn.com/2006/10/12/news/companies/utube/index.htm (accessed November 10, 2008).

Chapter 9

Google and Wikipedia: Friends or Foes?

Jeffrey Knapp

INTRODUCTION

For many librarians, the words "Google" and "Wikipedia" call to mind a whole world of anxieties about their profession that have festered since widespread use of the Internet bloomed in the mid-1990s: "Will librarians be out of work?" "Will the public still need libraries?" "Do people understand what they're getting on the Internet?" Of course, Google and Wikipedia are not the sum total of what is available online; but the overwhelming dominance of Google in the Internet search market has made it, by default, the term often used by people who are simply trying to communicate the fact that they searched for something online: "I Googled it." Wikipedia's dominance is not a result of it being a finder of knowledge, but as a knowledge source. Its massive coverage of topics from academic to popular, along with its overall accessibility and ease of use have made it a favorite destination for both the student and casual learner alike.

There are plenty of reasons behind librarians' anxieties about Google and Wikipedia, some of which will be discussed here. However, the primary question we are asking is whether these resources are tools to be embraced, or enemies to be countered. The only way to approach this question properly is to take a step back from our knee-jerk reactions and take a look "under the hood" of Google and Wikipedia to see how they work. Whether they are deemed "Friend" or "Foe," there is no question that both of these resources are amazingly popular, especially among Gen M. If "Friends," we must know them in order to use them more effectively; if "Foe," we must understand them to counter them more effectively.

Google has become so ubiquitous as a search engine that it is difficult to differentiate it from the Web itself. Both seem inextricably linked, almost as if they were born together. Indeed, future generations after Gen M will only be more likely to feel this way. Since Google has moved to a place in our collective consciousness where we tend to no longer question its results or how it arrived at them, it is that much more important that we do so. Let us place Google in historical context so that we can remind ourselves why it works as well as it does.

Before Google, the Internet search field was scattered. There were many different search engines (Lycos, AltaVista, Excite, and Yahoo!, among many others) competing for eyeballs, and they all had their own supposedly unique ways of finding what people were looking for. The technology that was used by most of these search engines at that time usually placed a heavy emphasis on the number of times a searched term appeared on a page in order to list it in your results. In other words, a person searching for "dog collars," would get pages that listed the words "dog" and "collars" most often as the most highly ranked results. While this worked acceptably in the earlier days of the Web, a number of problems became evident as the total size of the Web grew and users became more savvy as to how to "game" the system to get their pages to display prominently.

The first problem had to do with early search engines' reliance on text matching to rank results. Early Web searchers were educated in the seeming relationship of every word in the English language to some sort of sexual practice: in the prior "dog collar" example, a searcher looking for a pet accessory would undoubtedly be served a link concerning sadomasochism. Since a page's text was one of the few things that early search engines tested for, results like this were bound to happen. Web page owners then started to include extraordinarily long lists of words in their page titles, sometimes even including text in the same color as the page's background, so that readers would not be able to see it, but search engines could pick it up as text occurrences on their page, which hopefully would boost their results.

In 1998, Larry Page and Sergey Brin started Google, Inc. using search algorithms they developed at Stanford (Miller, 2008). While Google's technology and search algorithms are proprietary and therefore secret, the three basic ideas behind how Google works are as follows:

- Text analysis: Google looks for not only matching words, but also examines how and where those words are used. So if words are matched that are in larger type (possibly indicating a page heading) or are in close proximity to each other, that page may be considered more relevant to the search query. Neighboring pages on the same Web site are also examined for relevance (Miller, 2008: 21).
- Links and link text: Google examines the links that are present on the page and the text of those links (Miller, 2008: 21). Do the links go to sites that are also relevant to the search? If so, then the site in question may be considered more relevant to the search. How does the text that is hyperlinked relate to the page it links to? If enough sites have the text "Passport Information" hyperlinked on a page, and those links take you to the State Department Web site, then the State Department Web site will be highly ranked in searches for passport information.
- PageRank: Perhaps the most secret portion of Google's methodology, PageRank will boost a page's ranking in the search results based on the number of other pages that link to it (Miller, 2008: 21). When users first started to discover Google, some experts and librarians sniffed at such a ranking system as being little better than a popularity contest, making Google an unreliable resource. This is, however, how Google has managed to leverage the "wisdom of crowds" concept (discussed in more detail later) that has proven to yield astonishingly accurate information and results without the input of experts, albeit under certain conditions.

And, ultimately, it is not only how Google goes about ranking its results, it is the fact that they are ranked at all that has made Google such a success. In so many cases, a searcher can find the information one is looking for, and often from a reputable source, on the first page of results. Indeed, there are many Internet users who rarely bother to record a URL for a useful site anymore—they simply type their search terms into Google, and they know it will show up in the results.

GOOGLE: STRENGTHS AND WEAKNESSES

There is no question that Google is the dominant player in the Internet search market. And for good reason: all scholarly concerns aside, people find what they are looking for with Google. The name of the author who was on Oprah last week, a site that sells that gadget we need to buy, the address of our local congressman—it is all very easy to pull up. Even proper spelling is optional. As long as you get a few of the letters in the proper order, Google will offer other possibilities with "Did you mean _____?"

Even in the scholarly realm, Google is gaining credibility. With Google Scholar, many scholars have found a tool for searching scholarly literature in a streamlined way. They can search a large body of scholarly literature with a single interface, which is an important benefit when you consider the increasingly large role that interdisciplinary research is playing in academia. Researchers can now find articles in disciplinary literature that they would not even have considered before by using discipline-specific indexes and databases. And if convenience is an issue, they can click directly into the subscription database that offers the full text of the articles if their institution utilizes any kind of link resolver (such as *SFX* or *LinkSource*).

Yet Google is not omnipotent or infallible. As with all search engines, Google can only find what exists in a static state on its own servers. We often forget that Google is not searching the entire Web in real time when a search is conducted. It is really just searching an index of Web pages residing on its own servers, which have been indexed by Google's "web crawlers" that systematically browse the Web. Therefore, any site that generates information dynamically from a large data set and requires the user to enter a query to access it, may not be represented well (Miller, 2008).

Of course, this also means that Google can only find pages that allow their Web crawlers in to index them. This means that subscription-based resources or any that require login credentials will not be represented in search results, unless, of course, they work out an arrangement with Google. Increasingly, Google is making arrangements with information vendors to allow its Web crawlers to access their servers to index them, even though users may need to pay the vendor to access the actual content.

Google has proven to be relatively resistant to manipulation of its results from outside, as in the methods mentioned earlier. However, there have been instances of chicanery. "Google bombing" entered the American lexicon in 2003, when typing the words "miserable failure" into Google brought you to the official White House biography of President George W. Bush. How was this done? A computer programmer, who was clearly not fond of the president, added the words "miserable failure" to his site and hyperlinked the text to the president's biography page. He then contacted other like-minded people who had blogs and other highly trafficked sites and urged them to do the same. Over time, the PageRank algorithm boosted the president's biography as the top hit for a "miserable failure" search (Hansell, 2003). Google initially did not consider it a problem to be fixed, since its system was technically working as it was designed. It was not until 2007 that Google finally modified its secret algorithm to prevent this from happening; no doubt due to other "bombs" that had proliferated on the Web (Cohen, 2007).

Which finally leads us to the ultimate reason librarians and other educators feel ambivalent toward Google as a tool for finding information: despite its great results, they are not quite sure what is going on "under the hood." Going back to the earliest forms of electronic searching, even though the search process could sometimes be frustrating, a librarian could always figure out fairly easily what the problem with the search was. Perhaps a word was misspelled, or a field was wrong. While problems like these were annoying, it at least gave the seasoned searcher a sense of control. Literature searches in scholarly databases could be (and were) described in clinical, scientific terms: "Search conducted in index q on date v for articles with terms x, y, and z in the descriptor field, published between date a and date b. There were m articles retrieved, of which p were relevant." It was systematic and comforting to the scholarly community. Anyone could duplicate the search parameters and be able to see exactly the set of articles that were reviewed.

By using Google or even Google Scholar, however, the search function is a commercial secret. You can make general assumptions, but on any given day, as a result of many different variables including citation analyses of published articles, results may differ. The systematic and transparent nature is simply not there. The scholar is easily left with the feeling that he/she could be missing something relevant—even when Google retrieves 187,000 pages in 0.24 seconds.

Educators must acknowledge these (or any other) feelings they have about Google in order to successfully address its use to students in classroom. Only then will they be able to formulate a response to the questions from their students, such as "Why can't I use Google? What's wrong with it?"

Unlike Google, which is technically an indexer of information, Wikipedia is actually made up of *content*. What kind of content? It depends on whom you ask, but in terms of quantity, Wikipedia.org reports close to 2.5 million articles in English alone, as of this writing. Wikipedia had its start in 2001 when an options trader named Jimmy Wales and Larry Sanger wanted to design an online encyclopedia using Wiki software. That is, an encyclopedia that would be writable and editable by anyone.

When it began, many thought the idea to be preposterous. However, to the surprise of most, it has become one of the top 10 most visited sites on the Web (Rainie and Tancer, 2007).

Here's how it works. Anyone can register with Wikipedia and proceed to write or edit any article he/she wants. Others can then edit those articles or that person can make the edits.. People can set up a "watchlist" that notifies them whenever a change is made to an article, or when discussion takes place on it (each article features a "history" tab that lists the editing history of the article, and a "discussion" tab, where users can discuss the topic and negotiate terminology, layout, or anything else related to the article). What's fascinating about the whole process is that it does not result in informational anarchy, as many thought it would. Because everyone has the same powers to write and edit content, and everyone has the ability to be immediately notified when edits are made, an order emerges from this chaos.

In a *Wired* magazine article, Daniel Pink (2005) describes a "fairly typical instance" of "vandalism" on a Wikipedia article: At 11:20 one morning, the entry for "Islam" was replaced with a "single scatological word." The article was then corrected, or "reverted" back to its original state, at 11:22. At 11:25 it was vandalized again, and then reverted again at 11:26. A study of Wikipedia has shown that cases of "mass deletions" of content were corrected in a median time of 2.8 minutes. If a deletion or edit was accompanied by an obscenity, the median time dropped to 1.7 minutes (Pink, 2005). Hence, as long as there are users who care and are vigilant in the face of such vandalism, offensive editing with faulty information can be kept to a minimum.

In order for users to succeed and have their viewpoints continue to be expressed in an article, users have to be able to "play well with others" and be able to negotiate the wording of contributions under contentious circumstances (Weinberger, 2007: 136). A good example of this negotiation is in the entry for "Swift Vets and POWs for Truth," about the political group that formed to oppose John Kerry's candidacy for president in 2004. This article, which at this writing is over four years old, is still being edited up to twenty times a month. Some of the negotiated terms include whether Kerry received "combat" medals or "service" medals

(Weinberger, 2007). Interestingly, for all the edit history this article has, the article, in fact, reads from a fairly Neutral Point of View (NPOV), which is what Wikipedia wants the goal of all articles to be.

Wikipedia is not completely lawless. There are various safeguards in place, such as the "locking down" of articles for a period of time if too much "vandalism" is taking place on them, and the ability of users to report others for vandalism and having them blocked from editing articles. To warn readers of potential problems with the quality of information in some articles, a number of warning notes can precede an article, such as "The neutrality and factual accuracy of this article are disputed" or "This article is a frequent source of heated debate" (Weinberger, 2007: 140).

So when is an article "done?" Basically, never. Wikipedia articles are no more "done" than the status of human knowledge is ever "done." It changes and shifts, new points of view develop and rise to the surface, outlooks change as the result of new discoveries, and so on. Where a printed encyclopedia remains static in the face of changing knowledge, Wikipedia articles change with the ebb and flow. Wikipedia's founder, Jimmy Wales, is interested primarily in articles having a Neutral Point of View and has said, "An article is neutral when people have stopped changing it" (Weinberger, 2007: 136). In other words, an article has reached some level of consensus and stability when the dust settles and the edits stop—which leads us to the fascinating concept of the "wisdom of crowds."

WISDOM OF CROWDS

An important feature that Google and Wikipedia share is the use of the "wisdom of crowds" concept to organize and evaluate knowledge and information, which contrasts with the "single smart person" method used in the past. Rather than hire armies of catalogers and bibliographers to describe Web pages and add subject headings to them so they can be searched using controlled vocabularies, Google allows the massive interconnectedness of the Internet and the way people direct each other to helpful information to create its own order by using computer algorithms. A Web page will show up at the top of a results list if enough sites with enough Web traffic link to it using the right terminology. Rather than hire armies of scholars to write 2.5 million articles about subjects as diverse as quantum physics and "New York State Route 32," Wikipedia allows the world of Internet users to settle issues of knowledge by writing, editing, and arguing it among themselves.

As crazy as this seems to most people, the wisdom of crowds has the potential to create astonishingly accurate results when applied to knowledge and information. In his book, *The Wisdom of Crowds*, James Surowiecki (2004) provides many examples of instances where the knowledge of a group of "average" people was more accurate than that of experts. He includes the example of the submarine USS *Scorpion*, which sank in the North Atlantic in 1968. The U.S. Navy believed it could be anywhere within a 20-mile-wide circle. Rather than consult three or four experts to estimate its location, they assembled a diverse team including mathematicians, submarine experts, and salvage experts. Each person wagered on what each thought was the submarine's final location. All of the guesses were then incorporated into a formula, which averaged them out into a single location. When the *Scorpion* was found, it was 220 yards from that estimated location (Surowiecki, 2004).

Surowiecki (2004) also cites the classic "guess how many jelly beans are in the bowl" contest. If all of the guesses are averaged together, the result is often closer to the actual number than any single guess. By decentralizing and accounting for diverse points of view, the wisdom of crowds can produce very accurate results.

As interesting a concept as this is, it is not as simple as it sounds. In order for the wisdom of crowds to work successfully, there must be a very broad diversity of input ("cognitive diversity") and feedback must be given, to nudge the results in the proper direction (Surowiecki, 2004). These conditions are frequently present in online communities, which may be one of the reasons that the wisdom of crowds has gotten so much attention since the advent of the Internet. However, cognitive diversity and feedback are not present in all cases—and even when they do exist, they take time to manifest themselves. Using Wikipedia as an example, if an article is written on August 1 and sees a great deal of diversity of input and feedback over the following three months, resulting in a quality article on November 1, that does not help the student looking at it on September 5.

Something else that must be present in order for crowd wisdom to operate effectively is individuality (Catone, 2008). A corollary to cognitive diversity, individuality dictates that all actors in an effective crowd situation must act based entirely on their own knowledge and perspectives, without influence from others. Without individuality, "groupthink" becomes a possibility and results can be skewed. The aforementioned

Google-bombing episode would be an example of this: Google's results for "miserable failure" were skewed by a person convincing others to code the necessary links into their highly rated Web sites. Without that person's influence, it is unlikely that the crowd would have initiated the activity needed to make this happen.

Nonetheless, crowd wisdom has intrigued enough people that the bastion of traditional knowledge resources, *Encyclopaedia Britannica*, has actually announced that it will be incorporating wiki-like features in its online product, albeit with certain safeguards to ensure that a stable body of articles is always available (Van Buskirk, 2008). It is likely that this move has been prompted more as a way to increase traffic at its site—the wiki model certainly has a social aspect to it, and social networking sites are clearly popular Web destinations.

An analogy to economics can be made here: the traditional academic model that emphasizes academic achievement and credentials can be compared to a socialist-style command economy with experts doing all the planning and making all the decisions about production, while Google and Wikipedia can be compared to a completely unrestrained market economy, where production is determined by the innumerable decisions made by individuals in the marketplace. Neither scenario in its purest form is a very good one, but adopting certain aspects of each—a market economy with some experts providing guidance and safeguards—is a decent compromise. Scholars will generally blanch at the thought of "market forces" determining the state of Knowledge and Truth, and this would be a difficult argument to make. But there are clearly aspects of crowd wisdom that deserve further consideration in academia.

Ultimately, what dismays educators is that Google and Wikipedia are flourishing in the field of knowledge and information retrieval without the benefit of traditional scholarship—the very thing that gives educators and scholars their authority in academia. This is an important fact for educators to acknowledge when they consider how they feel about these resources.

WIKIPEDIA: THE GOOD AND THE BAD

Certainly one of the strong points of Wikipedia is the speed with which it can be updated and corrected (or vandalized, depending on your point of view). As mentioned earlier, examples abound that show how quickly articles have been corrected after someone deletes or otherwise vandalizes articles; but what about the actual accuracy of the content in Wikipedia?

In 2005, the journal *Nature* did a study comparing the accuracy of science articles on Wikipedia and *Encyclopaedia Britannica* (*EB*). Entries were chosen from both sources and sent to a relevant expert for peer review. Reviewers were not told which source the articles came from. Of the 42 reviews that were returned, there were eight "serious errors, such as misinterpretations of important concepts," four from each source. There were also less serious "factual errors, omissions or misleading statements" present in both of the sources, 162 in Wikipedia and 123 in *EB*. Overall, Wikipedia averaged about four inaccuracies per article, *EB* about three (Giles, 2005: 900–901). In other words, although *EB* fared better in the study than Wikipedia, the difference in the results seemed negligible when you considered that one resource was written and edited by scholars and experts, while the other was written by no one particular author.

EB shot back with a report of its own (*Encyclopaedia Britannica*, 2006), voicing its objections to, among other things, the facts that:

- all the data were not shared or made public (the *Nature* article about the study was a mere two pages long);
- *Nature* did not check the assertions of its reviewers;
- *Nature* "failed to distinguish minor inaccuracies from major errors"; and
- *Nature* counted "errors" and "critical omissions" that "did not exist" (i.e., there was disagreement between the study's reviewers and *EB*'s editors as to what is appropriate for an encyclopedia article).

Nature's editors published a brief response to *EB*'s report, standing by its study, and emphasizing that the reviewers were blinded and did not know from which source each of the articles came (*Nature*, 2006). While *Nature*'s study certainly highlighted the quality of information that is possible through a crowd-sourced encyclopedia—and garnered plenty of attention in the media—its weakness from a librarian's point of view was that it was more of a quantitative study than qualitative. Knowledge has many shades of meaning, and it is difficult to fit some of the examples from this study into black-and-white comparison figures. Were the articles of one resource easier for a layperson to read and understand? Were the articles well written and organized? Several of the reviewers in the study commented that the Wikipedia articles were poorly structured and confusing, pointing out that in some articles there was undue prominence given to controversial scientific theories (Giles, 2005). Thus, while the issue of quality was acknowledged in the article about the study, it was not a part of the study itself.

Lucy Holman Rector (2008), a librarian, did a study in which nine articles were evaluated between Wikipedia, *EB*, and two other subject-specific resources. Rather than a straight comparison of number of inaccuracies, however, Rector assigned an "accuracy rate" to each of the sources in the comparison. This rate was figured as the number of facts listed in each article, divided by the number of inaccuracies and unverifiable facts. Using this methodology, Wikipedia had the lowest accuracy rate of 80 percent, while *EB* had the highest with 96 percent.

Perhaps no example highlights Wikipedia's weakness more than the "Seigenthaler Affair." In 2005, John Seigenthaler Sr. discovered that his biography on Wikipedia noted that he was believed "to have been directly involved in the Kennedy assassinations of both John and his brother Bobby" but that "nothing was ever proven" (Seelye, 2005). Seigenthaler is a former newspaper editor and had been a very good friend of Robert F. Kennedy, actually serving as a one his pallbearers. What was distressing about the situation was not only the fact that such erroneous information existed, but that it had been there for a number of months, unedited. Although some will herald Wikipedia's speed of updating and self-regulation by the crowd, this instance casts a light on the fact that not all articles and subjects have a vigilant crowd looking out for them. What worked in the earlier example of vandalism of "Islam," a religion with millions of adherents worldwide, did not work very well for a retired newspaper editor and associate of an assassinated presidential candidate.

Compounding the problems of erroneous information is the amazing speed with which the Internet magnifies and duplicates the errors. John Seigenthaler was notified of his Wikipedia entry by his son, who found the same text duplicated on Reference.com and Answers.com (Seigenthaler, 2007: 32). An article from the *Washington Post* states it this way: " . . . without peer review, it's so easy to be wrong, and for your wrongness to become the top Google hit on a subject, and for your wrongness to be repeated by other people who think it's right, until everyone decides that it's raining in Phoenix" (Anonymous, 2008). And Wikipedia is very good at creating top Google hits on subjects. Wikipedia is a highly interconnected resource, very large in size, with lots of Internet traffic. It has plenty of "see also" links to other articles within it, and those links have straightforward, subject-based text links that work very well with Google's page ranking system. A Pew study revealed that during one week, 70 percent of visits to Wikipedia came from search engines (Rainie and Tancer, 2007).

And so, as fascinating as Wikipedia is from a social/knowledge perspective, even at its best it is analogous to watching an electrocardiogram. There's a wealth of information to be had, if you understand what you are looking at, and you can observe changes and new developments every second. But if you have little interest in the details of how everything works, you might want to talk to the doctor if you want to know how healthy your heart is.

PERSPECTIVES

In the media and in scholarly literature, there are two camps set up on the "Friend or Foe" question. One side sees Google and Wikipedia in the "new paradigm" image that was so popular in the late 1990s at the height of the Internet bubble. It posited that everything about the Internet was brand new—it was an entirely new universe, and therefore none of the old rules mattered anymore. This side sees Wikipedia and Google as breaking new ground, and creating a whole new reality for the world—who needs so-called scholars and experts if the crowd can achieve similar results without them? As could be expected, such perspectives are more common in the non-scholarly literature (Weinberger, 2007; Surowiecki, 2004; Pink, 2005).

In general, and also as could be expected, scholarly opinions about Wikipedia tend more to the other side of the spectrum, the side that believes that it is a serious resource. A significant portion of non-scholarly literature (blogs, newspaper and magazine articles, etc.) falls into this category as well (Anonymous, 2008; Carr, 2008; Catone, 2008), so in other words, more published opinion seems to be against Wikipedia as a reliable source of knowledge. But while there may not be as many voices explicitly supporting Wikipedia, we cannot ignore the fact that it is consistently one of the top 10 visited sites on the Internet (Rainie and Tancer, 2007).

Most of the arguments against the use of Google and Wikipedia for educational or scholarly use are actually leveled against the Internet as a whole, with Google and Wikipedia taking the brunt by virtue of their prominent positions within it. Mark Herring (2007) covers this ground quite well in his book *Fool's Gold: Why the Internet Is No Substitute for a Library*. Overall, a key theme in Herring's book is the decline in reading skills and whether it is possible to learn and read critically from the Web. This is an important question that deserves plenty of attention. Even the popular press is talking about this, proof that people outside of academia are taking note of the fact that the use of the Internet, with immediate hyperlinks, is shortening our attention spans, and might even be changing the way we think and process information (Carr, 2008). The immediacy of information on the Internet makes us impatient to always move on to the next page. As quickly as the page arrives in front of us, the belief that something else, something better, is just another click away—and the page we were looking at is gone just as quickly as it came.

Herring makes an excellent distinction between "knowledge" and "information" (2007: 27). He argues that the Web works well in dealing with information, if you define that term as "any bit of datum, right or wrong, factual or not, fraudulent or accurate." Knowledge, he says, is more than this. It includes aspects of appropriateness, balance, and value—which the Web is not very good at discerning.

Along these same lines, many undergraduate students are utilizing a sort of "data mining" technique when it comes to doing research. They use Google-like search strategies to find their sources, and then skim to find a supportive or useful paragraph for citing, and then move on. The prospect of reading a 22-page scholarly article from beginning to end to enhance their knowledge of a subject is not an attractive prospect. It is clear that members of Gen M are comfortable using the Web and mastering the social networking aspect of it. Even if they are finding high-quality scholarly sources, they are not necessarily able to use them well (George, 2007; Thomas and McDonald, 2005). Alvarez and Dimmock also weigh in on this, reporting that faculty members are more concerned about the writing and critical thinking skills of their students than their ability to locate the best sources (2007: 5). Current undergraduate students "lack sophisticated analytical and interpretive skills they would need to see implicit and explicit relations between the sources or to distinguish between strong and weak arguments" (Alvarez and Dimmock, 2007: 5).

Herring sharply criticizes Wikipedia specifically as an extremely unreliable resource (Herring, 2007: 27–30). He ridicules the disclaimer that Wikipedia has on its site, warning users that "Most educators and professionals do not consider it appropriate to use tertiary sources such as encyclopedias as the sole source for any information . . ." as utter nonsense and nothing less than an admission by Wikipedia itself that it is a flawed resource. Herring goes on to describe numerous high-quality scholarly encyclopedias. However, although Wikipedia may be conveniently overemphasizing this fact to enhance credibility, it is not unheard of for many college and university faculty to not allow their students to cite from encyclopedias, regardless of whether they are Wikipedia, *Britannica*, or *International Encyclopedia of the Social Sciences*. Many a librarian has tried to suggest an encyclopedia to an undergraduate for background information on a topic only to be told, "My professor won't let us use encyclopedias." This proscription by faculty is most likely aimed at keeping students from regurgitating facts along the lines of a grade-school-book report. However, it has the unintended consequence of disqualifying some very high quality, scholarly encyclopedias that can help introduce students to more complicated concepts found in the scholarly literature.

On the positive end of the spectrum for Wikipedia, there are those who praise its forthrightness in disclosing its weaknesses as a scholarly source (see "Wikipedia: About" at http://en.wikipedia.org/wiki/Wikipedia:About). David Weinberger argues that in some ways Wikipedia has even more credibility than traditional sources because it is so open about its limitations (Weinberger, 2007: 141). It would be hard to imagine *Britannica* placing similar disclaimer notes at the beginning of its articles, he argues, if there was some general disagreement about it. It is commendable for Wikipedia to disclose its limitations as a scholarly source, but it is not a great selling point. Wikipedia's Sandra Ordonez told InsideHigherEd.com that although "Wikipedia is the ideal place to start your research and get a global picture of a topic, we recommend that students check the facts they find in Wikipedia against other sources" (Harris, 2007: para. 4). Here Ordonez hits upon what is really the ideal method of covering Wikipedia in the classroom: admitting that is a very helpful introductory resource for getting perspective and identifying possible directions to go for more detailed study—but emphasizing the fact that it should be treated with caution.

WHY GEN M LIKES GOOGLE AND WIKIPEDIA

Forty-four percent of adult Internet users ages 18–29 avail the Internet to look for information on Wikipedia. (Rainie and Tancer, 2007: 1). It is important to consider some of the reasons that Gen M might find Google and Wikipedia so appealing. By understanding some of these reasons, librarians and other educators can more effectively help Gen M to use Google and Wikipedia more responsibly.

The most obvious reason that Gen M prefers to use Google and Wikipedia would be the "path of least resistance" factor. Neither Google nor Wikipedia require any login procedure to use, they have simple URLs, and anything found using them can be e-mailed, IM'd, or texted to themselves or friends freely and without learning any new kind of user interface. Students of this generation value mobility in accessing their information and dislike anything that ties them down to a physical location (Thomas and McDonald, 2005). They can be in daily contact with friends who are at other colleges and universities. Can they share something they found in their library's database with them? Only if their friend's college library subscribes to that database, with the same collections packages and options—and even then it probably will not be a matter of simply sending a URL. The friend will have to run the same search and know which of the results to choose, which is a waste of time and patience that many of these students do not have.

Other reasons that Wikipedia and Google are appealing to Gen M are features that exist in electronic information in general. For example, according to Richard T. Sweeney, Gen M "want[s] to learn, but they want to learn only what they have to learn . . ." (Carlson, 2005: para. 28). Electronic information is very easy to slice up and search, making it easier to assimilate only what one has to learn. Similarly, electronic information found on Google and Wikipedia is inherently easy to cut, paste, copy, and remix, features that are desired by Gen M (Thomas and McDonald, 2005).

Speed and currency are strong factors as well. Students want their information fast, and have few qualms about sacrificing reliability and credibility in exchange for faster, more convenient, and easier to use information (Herring, 2007: 124). There is a common belief among Gen M that printed books are immediately out of date when they are on the shelf (Anonymous, 2008), whereas online information is constantly updated. Some clarification to these students about the "shelf life" of knowledge—that, for example, a survey about the Internet habits of teenagers has a longer useful life than, say, the score of last night's ball-game—might be in order.

The social nature of Gen M must be clearly understood by those who wish to reach them. Gen M students have frequently been given group assignments coming up through school and college courses more frequently including group projects and team presentations (George, 2007). There is a strong "peer group dynamic" instilled in this generation. Similarly, with their high mobility and connectivity, they not only study together in physical groups, but also are frequently instant messaging and text messaging each other throughout the process (Weinberger, 2007). They care a lot about what their friends think, and they look for recommendations from them (Perez, 2008)—not that caring about what one's friends think is unique to this generation of young adults, of course, but their connectivity to each other amplifies the impact of friends' opinions within this group. It is this peer group dynamic and constant feedback from friends that reinforces the logic of socially networked resources like Google and Wikipedia. After all, they might argue, if the vast cloud of Internet users have all collaborated on Wikipedia, offering recommended changes and constant feedback, and the universe of interconnected Web sites have pointed to the best sites to visit on Google, they would be the best places for searching for knowledge, right? Using socially networked information sources feels perfectly natural to them.

It should be noted however, that this social dimension to determining the credibility of information is not unique to Gen M, and actually has some history in psychology. In Farhad Manjoo's *True Enough: Learning to Live in a Post-Fact Society* (2008), he tells of an experiment that was done in the early years of World War II by Kurt Lewin, an eminent psychologist. At that time, the War Department was unsure if America's food supply would hold out in the event that the war dragged on for many years, so it considered a campaign to convince women, the primary meal preparers at the time, to cook organ meats (kidneys, hearts, brains), which are an excellent source of protein. Lewin devised a series of experiments to determine the best way to convince women to prepare organ meats for meals. Organ meats were uncommon in the average American diet, and considered to be lower-class fare. Lewin tested two different strategies on two groups of female Red Cross volunteers. In the first group, a nutrition expert lectured the women on how and why they should prepare these foods, and gave them recipes to try. In the second group, a researcher would start the women off by talking about why the diet change would be necessary, and then ask the women to discuss it among themselves (the researcher answered questions when necessary). Of all the women who participated in the study, those who were in the group discussion were five times more likely to change their diet than those who were lectured to by an expert (Manjoo, 2008). Thus, with certain kinds of knowledge at least, the ability to discuss, negotiate, and share was more persuasive than being lectured by an expert—even in the 1940s. This is similar to what happens online in social networking sites: people get to discuss, share concerns, and be convinced by their peers—except that it happens much more quickly, without the hassles of a psychologist setting up an experiment and finding volunteers. It has become an automated part of the culture. Educators traditionally sell the idea that the "best" information comes from experts, so this may become an increasing challenge going forward.

GOOGLE AND WIKIPEDIA ARE NOT OUR FOES

Google and Wikipedia are fascinating and useful resources for finding and gathering knowledge. They are not the foes of educators. The "foe" that must be fought is information illiteracy. Google and Wikipedia can be compared to the gun control debate. "Guns don't kill people, people kill people" is a common refrain. Google and Wikipedia themselves don't create bad or misleading information, people do. In the hands of experienced professionals with good intentions (say, police officers), a gun can protect people and even save lives. In the hands of a person with malicious intent, it can be dangerous, to say the least. The same can be said of Google and Wikipedia in the place of guns.

Granted, a common response in the gun control debate is "Guns don't kill people, *people with guns* kill people." In other words, that guns (or Google and Wikipedia) share some responsibility for dangerous or adverse results purely because of their ability to expedite the process exponentially. Perhaps this is true. However, the fact is that Google and Wikipedia are not going away anytime soon, nor does their popularity show any signs of waning. Ever since information began to migrate from the printed page to pixels on a screen, users have lost contextual clues to help them evaluate the quality of a source. Librarians and other educators have understood the importance of information literacy—the ability to evaluate information resources regardless of their format—for a long time. Google and Wikipedia have now made the issue more pressing, and a bit more difficult.

PLACE THEM IN THE PROPER CONTEXT

No amount of finger-wagging or outright prohibition is going to make students stop using Google or Wikipedia. Gen M has a reputation for needing to know why—that is, telling them they cannot use Google or Wikipedia is not enough. They will need to know a reason. Many of them are not overly concerned with excelling at scholarship in the traditional way—they want to get through college and move on. They will not blindly follow authority figures just because of their status (Perez, 2008). Furthermore, if your reason is not convincing, they will abide your rules only so far as it gets them a good grade in your class: for example, they may still use Google and Wikipedia, but cite the information to other sources.

The good news is that Google and Wikipedia can play a role in scholarly research if educators make clear to students what that role is. As seemingly wide open and uncontrolled as Wikipedia seems, most articles do include citations that lead elsewhere to other more authoritative sources (Shaw, 2008). Ironically, for as much as Google and Wikipedia are treated as scourges in academia, some statistics show that resources like them may be contributing to greater use of libraries. According to a Pew study from 2007, Internet users ages 18–30 are actually the most likely to have visited a public library in the past year (62 percent), compared to 59 percent for Gen X (31–42), and 57 percent for 43–52 (Estabrook, Witt, and Rainie, 2007: 10). It is possible that Google and Wikipedia are driving some traffic to libraries, from people in search of authoritative sources listed online that are not actually available online (at least not for free).

Introductory information that can help students acquire background knowledge of a new topic is another strong suit of sources like Google (Thelwall, 2005). Remember Google's page ranking system: introductory material will tend to appeal to a wide audience and therefore a large number of sites are likely to link to it, which will result in a higher page rank (Thelwall, 2005). Students should be encouraged to do some "introductory" or "casual" research before actually delving into the specifics of research assignments—let them go to Wikipedia or Google, or any of the many excellent encyclopedias, general or specialized, about a topic. This may give them some easy-to-digest introductory material that can help to guide their initial steps, such as titles of seminal works in a field or key people. Information like this will not need to be cited necessarily, but can be a very effective "bridge" between the knowledge a college sophomore understands and the knowledge that is being published in scholarly journals.

From the perspective of overall knowledge, one of Wikipedia's strengths is the sheer volume of information available, from academic information to popular culture references (which is always helpful when working with college students). Wikipedia covers thousands of topics that one would never find in an encyclopedia like *Britannica*. Shaw offers the example of "turducken" (a roasted de-boned turkey stuffed with a duck that has been stuffed with a chicken). If someone had never heard the term before, Wikipedia could give them a valuable starting point—the history of the dish and even some recommended recipes (Shaw, 2008). While not a scholarly example, perhaps, it still shows an important role that Wikipedia can play in helping to make sense of new information.

STRATEGIES

The most important thing to bear in mind when dealing with Wikipedia and Google in the classroom is to acknowledge them. No matter what your beliefs are regarding their usefulness in academic research—even if you plan to prohibit your students from using them entirely—you must be prepared to defend your decision and explain convincingly why they should not use them. If you cannot explain your decision convincingly, then tell them your prohibition is an exercise in personal discipline. Failure to acknowledge these popular sources will only undercut your credibility with this generation of students, who tend to consider their Internet searching skills to be much better than they really are. Many of them have the too-common perception that libraries are only about books—not realizing that librarians were working with electronic information long before many of them were born.

Do not bad-mouth Google and Wikipedia before these students. The better course of action is to fit them into the context of scholarly research: tell them what these sources are good at—and what to be cautious of. Give them specific strategies for using them effectively in this context (Harris, 2007).

Some examples of strategies to teach for Google include the "Advanced Search" option and Google Scholar. The "Advanced Search" option is unfamiliar to many because it occupies so little space on the standard Google search page. Clicking on the link to the Advanced Search screen takes users to a broader interface. The interface is more complicated than the eminently simple and uncluttered search box everyone is familiar with, but it helps visually to give the user some structure by which to construct his/her search. Here, users are given the option of limiting their searches to different domains, for example, ".edu" or ".gov" sites, which often provide more academic information than broader searches, or searching only in the titles of pages, which can also help to limit a lot of clutter in their results. Google Scholar is another way to lure students into using scholarly sources. With an interface that is similar enough to the one they are familiar with, students will feel more comfortable using it, and it can at least serve as a way to get them into the right ballpark (Cathcart and Roberts, 2005).

With Wikipedia, tell them the potential pitfalls of using it. If students find an intriguing bit of knowledge in a Wikipedia page that will help their research, tell them to look up whatever citation is given for it. If there is no citation, then it is likely that the information could be problematic and not widely accepted. If the citations all tend to go to private Internet sites that lack academic credentials, this is also problematic. Have them review the "History" and "Discussion" tabs for the article: Has it been actively edited and worked on recently? Is it a controversial topic? Is there a lot of emotion in the discussion page? Explain that the process of what goes on with Wikipedia articles is similar to the scholarly communications process. New knowledge is created and published, other scholars respond to the knowledge, supporting it or refuting it, other scholars contribute, and over time, consensus is reached. The main differences between Wikipedia and the scholarly communications process is that Wikipedia moves exponentially quicker, and there is no formal academic authority or credentials involved on Wikipedia—issues that students must be made to realize are problems when they are trying to do college-level work.

Google and Wikipedia are fascinating resources that have a potential for misuse. They are not the foes of educators. They can be made into friends by learning about them, using them, discussing them in the classroom, and placing them in the proper context as introductory gateways to more advanced knowledge.

REFERENCES

Alvarez, Barbara, and Nora Dimmock. 2007. "Faculty Expectations of Student Research." In *Studying Students: The Undergraduate Research Project at the University of Rochester* (pp. 1– 6), edited by Nancy Fried Foster and Susan Gibbons. Chicago: Association of College and Research Libraries. Available: www.ala.org/Ala/Acrl/Acrlpubs/downloadables/Foster-Gibbons_cmpd.pdf (accessed October 12, 2008.

Carlson, Scott. 2005. "The Net Generation in the Classroom." *Chronicle of Higher Education* 52, no. 7 (October 7): A34–A37.

Carr, Nicholas. 2008. "Is Google Making Us Stupid?: What the Internet Is Doing to Our Brains." *The Atlantic* 301, no. 6 (July/August). Available: www.the-atlantic.com/doc/200807/google (accessed October 12, 2008).

Cathcart, Rachael, and Amanda Roberts. 2005. "Evaluating Google Scholar as a Tool for Information Literacy." In *Libraries and Google* (pp. 167–176), edited by William Miller and Rita M. Pellen. Binghamton, NY: The Haworth Press.

Catone, Josh. 2008. "Sometimes Crowds Aren't That Wise." ReadWriteWeb (May 26). Available: www.readwriteweb.com/Archives/sometimes_crowds_arent_that_wise.php (accessed October 11, 2008).

Cohen, Noam. 2007. "Google Halts 'Miserable Failure' Link to President Bush." *New York Times* (January 29): C6.

Encyclopaedia Britannica, Inc. 2006. "Fatally Flawed: Refuting the Recent Study on Encyclopedic Accuracy by the Journal *Nature*." [Chicago] (March). Available: corporate.britannica.com/britannica_nature_response.pdf (accessed October 12, 2008).

Estabrook, Leigh, Evans Witt, and Lee Rainie. 2007. "Online Activities & Pursuits: Information Searches that Solve Problems." Washington, DC: Pew Internet and American Life Project and the University of Illinois Urbana-Champaign Graduate School of Library and Information Science (December 30). Available: www.pewinternet.org/PPF/r/231/report_display.asp (accessed October 12, 2008).

George, Sarada. 2007. "How Today's Students Differ." In *Studying Students: The Undergraduate Research Project at the University of Rochester* (pp. 63–71), edited by Nancy Fried Foster and Susan Gibbons. Chicago: Association of College and Research Libraries. Available: www.ala.org/Ala/Acrl/Acrlpubs/downloadables/Foster-Gibbons_cmpd.pdf (accessed October 12, 2008.

Giles, Jim. 2005. "Internet Encyclopaedias Go Head to Head." *Nature* 438, no. 7070 (December 15): 900–901.

Hansell, Saul. 2003. "Foes of Bush Enlist Google to Make Point." *New York Times* (December 8): C8.

Harris, Chris. 2007. "Can We Make Peace with Wikipedia?" *School Library Journal* 53, no. 6 (June): 26.

Herring, Mark Youngblood. 2007. *Fool's Gold: Why the Internet Is No Substitute for a Library*. Jefferson, NC: McFarland.

Hesse, Monica. 2008. "Can You Handle It?: Better Yet: Do You Know It When You See It?" *Washington Post* (April 27): M01.

Manjoo, Farhad. 2008. *True Enough: Learning to Live in a Post-fact Society*. Hoboken, NJ: Wiley.

Miller, Michael. 2008. *Googlepedia: The Ultimate Google Resource*. 2nd ed. Indianapolis, IN: Que Pub.

Nature. 2006. "Britannica Attacks." *Nature* 440, no. 7084 (March 30): 582.

Perez, Sarah. 2008. "Why Gen Y Is Going to Change the Web." *ReadWriteWeb*. (May 15). Available: www.readwriteweb.com/Archives/why_gen_y_is_going_to_change_the_web.php (accessed October 12, 2008).

Pink, Daniel H. 2005. "The Book Stops Here." *Wired* (March). Available: www.wired.com/wired/Archive/13.03/wiki.html (accessed October 12, 2008).

Rainie, Lee, and Bill Tancer. 2007. "Online Activities & Pursuits: *Wikipedia Users*." Washington, DC: Pew Internet and American Life Project (April 24).

Available: www.pewinternet.org/PPF/r/212/report_display.asp (accessed October 12, 2008)

Rector, Lucy Holman. 2008. "Comparison of Wikipedia and Other Encyclopedias for Accuracy, Breadth, and Depth in Historical Articles." *Reference Services Review* 36, no. 1: 7–22.

Seelye, Katharine Q. 2005. "Snared in the Web of a Wikipedia Liar." *New York Times* (December 4): 4.1.

Seigenthaler, John. 2007. "Wikipedia Is a Flawed Research Tool." In *User-generated Content* (pp. 31–34), edited by Roman Espejo. Farmington Hills, MI: Greenhaven.

Shaw, Donna. 2008. "Wikipedia in the Newsroom." *American Journalism Review* 30, no. 1 (March): 40.

Surowiecki, James. 2004. *The Wisdom of Crowds: Why the Many Are Smarter than the Few and How Collective Wisdom Shapes Business, Economies, Societies and Nations.* New York: Doubleday.

Thelwall, Mike. 2005. "Directing Students to New Information Types: A New Role for Google in Literature Searches?" In *Libraries and Google* (pp. 159–166), edited by William Miller and Rita M. Pellen. Binghamton, NY: Haworth.

Thomas, Chuck, and Robert H. McDonald. 2005. *Millennial Net Value(s): Disconnects between Libraries and the Information Age Mindset.* Florida State University D-Scholarship Repository. ScientificCommons. Available: en.scientificcommons.org/8897565 (accessed October 12, 2008).

Van Buskirk, Eliot. 2008. "Encyclopaedia Britannica to Follow Modified Wikipedia Model." Epicenter: Wired Blog Network (June 9). Available: blog.wired.com/business/2008/06/ency.html (accessed October 12, 2008).

Weinberger, David. 2007. *Everything Is Miscellaneous: The Power of the New Digital Disorder.* 1st ed. New York: Times Books.

Chapter 10

It's Not About the Game

Nicholas Schiller
Carole Svensson

INTRODUCTION

This chapter addresses librarians connecting to the Generation Media (Gen M)—which could easily be called the gaming generation—with information literacy. At its heart, it is not really about games; it is about maximizing student learning. We will cover quite a bit about video games, the culture of gaming, and the people who play games. We will also discuss how games teach and how students have come to prefer certain methods of learning because of the hours they have spent in games. We are not, however, going to cover using games in the classroom or designing games that teach. There may be some excellent learning opportunities from those kinds of inquiry, but our experiences, both as gamers and as librarians, have led us to believe that librarians and educators becoming literate in the media of games and using what they learn from games to inform their teaching will have a greater effect on student learning than instructors replacing effective pedagogical techniques with the latest fad.

Our focus is on a generation of students who have played thousands of hours of video games. We want to discover what they have learned from games and how these games have taught them how to navigate complicated systems. We hope that these insights will be useful to educators and librarians engaged in the process of teaching Gen M students information literacy. To start, it is important to understand the relationship members of Gen M have with games, including aspects of the gaming culture and its conventions. We also need to understand how information literacy instructors can integrate these understandings into their various classrooms. After all, it's not about the game; it's about pedagogical encounters with a generation of students who happen to play games.

THE IMPACT OF VIDEO GAMES ON GEN M

Members of Gen M have been playing computer and video games for most of their young lives. In fact, the beginnings of Gen M coincide with the introduction of the Nintendo Entertainment System (NES) to the United States market in 1987 (McGill, 1988). What does this mean? It can be difficult for those of us who came of age in an era where many types of media were not interactive to grasp the full impact video games have had on the generations of students who have grown up with games. The comparative impact has been as significant for this generation as television was for Generation X or LP records were for the Baby Boomers. Take a moment and think back to yourself in your teenage years. How important was music in forming your burgeoning identity? What role did television play in how you saw yourself and the world? John Beck and Mitchell Wade, two researchers who investigated the impact of video games on the work habits of today's employees, came to the conclusion that the impact of video games on Generation M is greater than the impacts that other forms of media had on previous generations.

It is difficult to measure the impact of media types across generations, but consider the following. The LP record was introduced in 1949, and eighteen years later *Sergeant Pepper's Lonely Hearts Club Band* was released. The album and the medium it was released on defined the generation as they passed through adolescence. *Sesame Street* first aired in 1969 and helped Generation X to learn how to read and count. A dozen years later, as Generation X reached their teens and young adulthood, television had 24-hour access to cable news on CNN and MTV was sending music and youth culture into family rooms across America. These media and the ways they presented information to the young people of the day helped to define entire generations. Video games are significant forces in the development of the core identity of members of Gen M. Librarians who can understand this can use what we know of games as a powerful tool in teaching this cohort.

Gen M is roughly defined as children born between the mid-1980s and the mid-to-late 1990s. As previously noted, this coincides with the introduction of Nintendo to America. The NES marked the beginning of video games as a media outlet capable of competing with television, film, radio, and print media. In May 2008, the video game Grand Theft Auto IV (GTA IV) grossed more than $500 million on its opening week. This was the highest recorded opening of any entertainment product (van Lent, 2008), breaking a record set in 2007 by another video game, Halo 3. (This record may not account for the book *Harry Potter and the Deathly Hallows*, which reported 11 million first-day sales to 3.6 million for GTA IV) (2008).

Video games are big business, but these numbers do not fully convey the influence they have on markets and minds. Both the Halo and Grand Theft Auto games that set entertainment sales records are rated 17+ by the ESRB (Entertainment Software Rating Board), an industry group that provides age-appropriate ratings for video games, similar to the rating provided for the film industry by the MPAA (Motion Picture Association of America). If the guidelines are being enforced, this excludes half of the Gen Ms who were too young to purchase the game. However, there are many other indicators that help us trace the full cultural impact of video games on this generation.

In 2006, Americans spent more money on retail video games than they did at the movie box office (2008). This does not mean that games have overtaken the movie industry for size and popularity, but a shift in momentum is clear. Video games were nonexistent as a media thirty years ago; now they are challenging the largest and most established media for popularity, profitability, and centrality in our culture. Video games have arrived in a way that may be invisible to those of us who are not targets of their marketing efforts and who have not lived our entire lives in a world where games rival music, film, and television as media outlets. Educators and librarians who came of age before the mid-1980s have not previously been target markets for video games and, as such, are likely less attuned to their pervasive cultural influence.

The influence of games increases as we measure the younger players. When we look at older demographics, video games are important, but gaming is significantly more important to males than to females. According the Nielsen report on the state of the console, 63 percent of all Americans between the ages of 18 and 34 have access to a video game console in their homes. (This study does not account for computer games or other platforms). In this group, 68 percent of males have access to game consoles in the home compared to 58 percent of females. When we look at the data for Generation M, access to video games increases to 80 percent for ages 12–17, and the difference in access between males and females is insignificant (Nielsen Company, 2007). The numbers tell us that games are popular and important. They also indicate that games have a progressively greater impact as we look at younger demographics. Video games are a central cultural artifact in the lives of Generation M. They are significant in ways it is difficult for members of older generations to comprehend. The *New York Times* ran this quotation from an eager Halo fan waiting for the game to go on sale:

> "Halo is the 'Star Wars' of this generation," Mr. Gunther added. "Thirty years ago my father waited in line to see 'Star Wars,' and I know I'll tell my kids I stood in line to buy Halo 3. It's like saying you were at Woodstock or something." (Schiesel et al., 2007: C1)

The question that arises is: how can educators and librarians make use of this information?

USE OF VIDEO GAMES BY LIBRARIANS AND EDUCATORS

Now that we can see that video and computer games are a central part of the Gen M experience, how do we make use of this information? Should video games be important to librarians and other educators? Why should those who seek to educate this generation of students pay any more attention to video games than we have paid to popular music, film, or television in the past? What is it about games that make an understanding of gaming literacy worth the effort? We certainly do not want to suggest that everything that is popular with students should find its way into the classroom or library. After all, there are many things that are popular with Gen M that we do not choose to integrate into our pedagogies and curricula—reality television, for example. Popularity alone is not enough. In the next section we investigate how video games teach and affect learning style preferences in ways that educators can exploit in teaching information literacy skills.

Games have been around as long as civilization. Cultural theorist Johan Huizinga, in his book, *Homo Ludens*, describes play as a central defining characteristic of humanity (Huizinga, 1955). What then makes video games so special? The answer is nothing and everything. Engaged, imaginative, immersive play has always been an important aspect of learning, and video games are not unique in having these qualities. For this media-focused generation, video games have developed into a mature media that is a central part of how they have been trained to gather, evaluate, and process information. In short, educators and librarians should pay attention to video games because paying attention to video games can help us engage Gen M in higher quality learning.

James Paul Gee notes:

> The designers of many good video games have hit on profoundly good methods of getting people to learn and enjoy learning. They have had to since games that were hard to learn didn't get played and the companies that made them lost money. Furthermore, it turns out that these learning methods are similar in many respects to cutting-edge principles being discovered in research on human learning. (Gee, 2007: 29)

Video games are a path to increased student learning. Good video games do a good job of teaching and good video game players do a good job of learning when they play games. In addition, video game designers are a valuable source of pedagogical insight for librarians and other educators.

Another aspect of video games that makes them worth careful inspection is that they are social learning environments. Those of us outside the gaming generation may remember video games as a largely solitary activity, but the Nielsen report on the State of the Console reveals that 4.4 million households have their video game consoles connected to the Internet (Nielsen Company, 2007). This figure does not include the newest generation of consoles or people who play games on their computers. Worldwide, 16 million people are currently subscribed (MMOGCHART. com, April 2008) to massively multiplayer online role-playing games (MMORPGs). Not only are our students playing games, but they are also playing games together. This kind of collaboration has an effect on how students work and learn together. Think of the difference between a class reading *Romeo and Juliet* together and a group that learns lines and blocking, builds sets, and puts on a production. Collaboration and relying on other students in the class can lead to a richer learning experience. Students who are comfortable learning and working in groups are capable of very different kinds of learning than students who are primarily comfortable reading texts by themselves. Those who play games online have developed and practiced those kinds of collaborative learning skills.

Yet another reason that video games are worth the notice of educators is that these games are teaching our students the kind of intellectual skills that we want them to learn. Well-designed games played in a thoughtful and reflective manner can provide training in active and critical thinking skills (Gee, 2003). Video games may often be childish, but they are not easy. Playing games develops abilities to rapidly acquire new information, evaluate it, and then make rational decisions based on that evaluation. Those of us who are interested in creating a generation of information-literate students, students who acquire information from a variety of sources, evaluate it based on a set of criteria, and then draw rational conclusions and develop complex arguments based on the evidence they have gathered and evaluated would do well to examine how games teach players to do these same things. If we divorce the content of the information from the processes used and skills required to successfully complete well-designed video games, if we set aside the fact that the games are about zombies, space aliens, and elves, we become able to see that students who play games have been engaged in complex learning exercises. We can use these collective experiences to direct our students to performing similar tasks in their academic research.

Looking beyond surface content is a necessary skill for educational professionals who are curious about video games and pedagogy. Just as information literacy skills exist independent of particular academic disciplines, many of the skills taught by games are independent of the games' content as well. At first glance it may seem that defending the realm of Azeroth from Orcish invasion (or plotting the Orcish takeover of Azeroth for that matter) has little to do with information literacy. However, if we ignore the content and focus our attention on the cognitive skills involved in successfully playing games, educators will see that many Gen M students have developed complex information acquisition and evaluation skills. What they may lack is the ability to transfer those skills to the academic context. This is where librarians and educators who understand both information literacy and video gaming can help students the most. Transferring information and skills from one context to another is an activity high up on Bloom's Taxonomy, (Anderson and Krathwohrl, 2001) but if we can build on skills students have happily worked to acquire, we can help students get to that point much more quickly than if we simply dismiss games as childish and irrelevant.

WHAT IS A VIDEO GAME ANYWAY?

Up to this point, we have used the term, "video game," fairly loosely. It is important to provide some kind of definition and description for a continued discussion. When we write about video games, we are referring to a very large set of entertainments that can be enjoyed on an extremely wide range of devices. Video games at their most basic require three things: a video display, a computing unit, and a control interface. A broad range of devices and platforms can be used to play games. Mobile phones have these three requirements and many people happily play games on their phones. Indeed, even portable music players and digital cameras have all the requirements be considered platforms for video games and modifications are available that allow people to play games on these devices (Pash, 2008).

Mainstream video game play tends to take place on personal computers or on dedicated video game machines. Game devices that connect to users' televisions and stereos are known as video game consoles or just consoles. The current generation of video game consoles includes Nintendo's Wii, Sony's Playstation 3, and Microsoft's Xbox 360. Games are also widely available for personal computers (PCs) as well. Most commercial games for PC are released for the Microsoft Windows operating system but games are available for Mac OSX, Linux, and other operating systems. Portable devices dedicated to video games, such as the Nintendo DS and Gameboy systems and the Sony Playstation Portable (PSP) also have significant followings.

Our definition of video game includes games played on a computer or computing device and games played on home and portable video game consoles. However, as we investigate the impact that thousands of hours spent playing video games have made on the development of Gen M, we will focus on the unique aspects of video games including the characteristics that they do not share with traditional, non-computerized games. The key distinguishing feature of video games is that they are interactive simulations. While textual critics and theorists may tell us that all texts require interaction between the reader and the text, video games take a radical next step. Video games respond in real-time to input and choices made by the player. The action and narrative in a video game is determined by choices made by the players as much as by choices made by the team that designed the game. This participatory aspect of the video game media sets them apart from more passive media such as film or print. Beck and Wade note that "even as adults, we learn only about 10 percent of what we watch, but over 70 percent of what we do. And in the formative years, learning from games may be even more powerful" (Beck and Wade, 2006: xi). The active and participatory nature of video games makes them uniquely suited for teaching and learning.

Behind this general definition of video games there lies a tremendous amount of diversity and complexity. Games can be divided into Byzantine classifications based on platform, genre, or nature of origin. For example, when talking to a hard core gamer, a Japanese role-playing game (JRPG) connotes a very different gaming experience and design conventions than a role-playing game (RPG) designed in the United States. There are first-person shooters (FPS), real time strategy games (RTS), 4X games, platform games, adventure games, puzzle games, casual games and others. There are subgenres and divisions inside these. By and large, we want to limit our observations to general concepts shared by most, if not all, video games. However, we will pay special attention to one significant genre of games that is relatively new to the scene and pushes the interactivity and social learning aspects of gaming to new areas. Massively multiplayer online role-playing games (MMORPGs) are a special kind of games that create special kinds of learning environments. Outside of that one particular set of games, we will limit our observations to principles that can be derived from analyzing video games as a whole. In other words, we will draw our conclusions from the medium of video games as a whole rather than from individual games or genres of games.

Interactivity is one of the hallmarks of playing a video game. Playing a game places the player in a very different place than the reader of a text or the viewer of a film. As mentioned above, the outcome of a narrative or plot in a game is in part determined by the choices the players make. This degree of control and engagement with a text, likely has significant effects on how these students interact with the texts they are assigned to read and engage in conversation with and about in college. A significant part of information literacy instruction at the college level involves instructing students on how to read content from the scholarly press. Specifically, it involves introducing new students to the ongoing scholarly conversations recorded by the journals and helping them transition from the reading skills they bring to college into the reading skills necessary to participate in the scholarly conversations taking place around them. Gen M have grown up influencing the outcome of the stories they have "read" and are very likely to have developed both reading skills and areas of need that attentive educators can use to increase the effectiveness of their instruction.

When playing a game, by and large, the player is a hero of the story. Unlike other kinds of games such as soccer, charades, tag, or poker, video games tend to have a narrative and the player is usually found at the center of that narrative. Whether the game is a fantasy role-playing game, a science-fiction shooter, a city-building simulator, a historical strategy war game, or a cartoon platform frolic there is almost always some kind of story and the player is almost always the protagonist. This can be an important realization when the new "game" the students are trying to learn is the Academy and new undergraduates are about as far from being the heroes of the Academy's story as one can possibly get. Librarians can help students identify their roles in the conversation and this can build the motivation needed for students to "level up" and contribute at much higher levels than they otherwise would.

Another thing that video games have in common is that every problem has a solution (Beck and Wade, 2006). Every problem a player faces in a game becomes a puzzle. Solving the puzzle is the point of playing. In a game, if a player comes across a puzzle that cannot be solved, then the player may rightly feel that the game is somehow broken or poorly designed. Logic, clues, and the skills taught by previous puzzles in a game are all that are needed to solve any problem. In the world of video games everything is fair and everything is logical. Often there is only one correct answer to a particular scenario. The player typically is trying to solve a puzzle designed by another human being; it may be a labyrinth or a mystery, but there is always a solution. Players who have learned to solve these kinds of puzzles may be easily frustrated when the "puzzles" set before them by their instructors do not have ready answers. The trial and error skills used by video games may fail them when solutions become more ambiguous. All problems in video games have a solution, and all solutions are either right or wrong. When students who are also gamers encounter puzzles that have multiple correct answers that depend on the justification offered by the student, they may feel confused or cheated. Educators who are aware of this can intervene and help these students make the leap from simple puzzles to the more complex world of arguments and evidence.

A third key aspect to video games is that they keep score. Video game players are used to earning points or rewards for their efforts. The game-world offers nearly constant feedback. When players do something "wrong" in a game they are almost always given immediate negative feedback. Often, this feedback is immediate and harsh; their character or avatar is killed when they make a mistake. When the punishment for missing the mark is death, it is hard to ignore the fact that one has made a mistake. Basically, screw up and you die. When presented with clear and immediate feedback of this nature, gamers learn quickly when it is time to adopt a new strategy or tactical approach to a problem. Often when defending a line of reasoning with evidence or even when searching a database or OPAC, our students are not provided with feedback on the success of their efforts, let alone given immediate warning that they have missed the mark. It can be daunting and unnerving for novice searchers to invest hours of time in research without any of the signals they have been trained to rely on. Games teach by trial and error, but academic work often doesn't communicate error with the immediacy of video games. It is not completely clear whether video games use trial and error because they have found that Gen M players prefer to learn that way or if members of Gen M have come to prefer trial and error because they have played thousands of hours of video games. It is clear that both games and members of Gen M rely heavily on trial and error for teaching and learning (Prensky, 1998). Savvy educators can take advantage of this to help students learn to read the signs and feedback from their searching and self-correct when their search strategies are not working as intended.

ANALYZING GAMES

Note to our readers: if you find yourself feeling skeptical about some of the claims advanced about video games so far, you are in good company. The authors join you in a spirit of general skepticism regarding out-sized and hyperbolic claims made about the latest fads for libraries or educational theory. Video games are no exception. This is not to say that we don't feel strongly that video games have much to offer library and education professionals, we just don't expect you to take our claims at face value. Ideally, we'd like this chapter to inform you and stimulate your curiosity about connections between the best-designed video games and solid classroom practice. In order for that to take place, we are going to need a methodology for "reading" video games. Games are new for many of us and, as with all media, a solid methodology for analyzing them can help us identify what aspects of their design are significant.

Individual video games are texts and, as education professionals, we all have developed highly advanced methods for reading, studying, and learning from texts. The first rule for analyzing a video game is to use the tools we already have in place for analyzing literature, film, and other texts or art forms. On a personal note, as a new undergraduate, I (NS) was introduced to close reading of texts through the classic title, *How to Read a Book*, authored by the University of Chicago's Mortimer Adler and Charles Van Doren. Among the advice and reading skills described in *How to Read a Book* is the concept of multiple readings of a text for multiple purposes (Adler and Van Doren, 1972). For example, one should read a text through in order to get a feel for the unified message of the title, but on a second reading break the whole down into its component arguments. Tactics like this can work very well for analyzing video games as well as books. When examining a game, on the first play-through a critical player should suspend analysis as much as possible and simply play the game. By suspending disbelief and analysis and immersing one's self in the game, the critic allows the game to reveal itself. Then, on a second playing of the game, having established a familiarity with the game's rules and features, the critic is free to devote attention to the underlying pedagogical structures of the game. The use of multiple play-ings for multiple purposes has served this librarian-gamer well. Unlike my coauthor I have played computer games since my teen years, but I am not a terribly skilled player. Suspending analysis until I've gained an understanding of the game's mechanic and narrative helps make the initial playing much more immersive and fun and the second analytical playing more informative and revealing.

How to Read a Book teaches that not only are there many ways of reading a text, but there are many reasons for reading a text, as well. As a general rule, the method chosen to analyze a particular text should suit the kind of insight the reader hopes to gain. "Hence, as books differ in the kinds of knowledge they have to communicate, they proceed to instruct us differently; and, if we are to follow them, we must learn to read each kind in an appropriate manner" (Adler and Van Doren, 1972: 74). Seeing as how our purpose in this case is to "read" games for what they have to teach us about pedagogy and learning, it follows that we should apply what we already know about instructional design to our analysis of video games. There are many valid approaches to instructional design for information literacy instruction. The following example is taken from my own training; readers should use it as an example of how to adapt a methodology for designing instruction into a methodology for analyzing video games rather than a fixed rule. The use of Adler and Van Doren's method and the following five questions are expanded on in "A Portal to Student Learning: What Instruction Librarians Can Learn from Video Game Design" (Schiller, 2008).

The ACRL Institute for Information Literacy's Immersion Program provides a solid and popular guide for librarians designing teaching sessions. From this curriculum, the Five Questions for Outcomes/ Assessment Instructional Design (ACRL Immersion Curriculum) are particularly suited for adaptation to video game analysis. The five questions are:

1. What do you want the student to be able to do? (This is the outcome.)
2. What does the student need to know in order to do this well? (This is the curriculum.)
3. What activity will facilitate the learning? (This is the pedagogy.)
4. How will the student demonstrate the learning? (This is the assessment.)
5. How will I know the student has done this well? (This is the criterion.) (Gilchrist, 1999)

These five rules have been highly practical when used during lesson preparation. By providing answers to each of these five questions instruction is focused on specific outcomes and related material; that which distracts from a clear understanding of the central point is stripped away. In addition, they are an aid to building assessment into every session. However, they can also be used to reverse-engineer learning situations and direct our analysis so that we reveal the structures of unfamiliar teaching methods. For example, on a second playing of a particular video game, an educator can isolate a particular level or sequence in a game and apply these five questions to the game. What do the game designers want the player to be able to do in this situation? What does the player need to know in order to master the skill? How does the game get the player to practice the skill or teach the concept in question? How does the player demonstrate mastery of the required skill? How does the game reward or punish success or failures?

Video games usually do not advertise themselves as learning laboratories or tightly structured lesson-plans. However, very often the best examples of video game design reveal a sound understanding of teaching and learning principles coupled with creative and innovative solutions to pedagogical problems. By using what we already know about instructional design, learning theory, and pedagogical methods, educators and librarians can decode video games and see the design structures underneath the cute cartoon characters, fantastic settings, and violent action that present themselves to surface analysis. The sections that follow provide descriptions of teaching methods, pedagogies, and principles we discovered as we analyzed video games.

LEARNING PRINCIPLES AND INSTRUCTIONAL APPLICATIONS

Trial and Error

Principle

Perhaps the single most heavily used pedagogical technique in video games is trial and error. Gamers can show tremendous persistence after failure because games teach them to keep trying until they get it right. While searching, students may easily grow frustrated and quit, but well-designed games have discovered the knack for keeping players' interest despite or even because of failure. The way this works is that players are given a goal, a set of tools or skills at their disposal and a challenge that prevents them from achieving the goal without solving some sort of puzzle or problem. The necessary conditions for this kind of persistence seem to include a clear goal that the player understands and accepts, a challenge that follows a consistent set of rules, and clear communication of failure and/or success. As long as players understand and accept the goal and the challenge follows the rules of the game, players seem willing to persist through any number of failures until they achieve success.

For example, if a player in a game is attempting to rescue a princess from a tower surrounded by an army of trolls, a player might try fighting with the trolls, negotiating with them, sneaking past them, etc., until he or she finally arrives at the correct solution of bribing the trolls with food. As long as the puzzle seems fair and reasonable, failure can be a learning experience rather than a barrier.

Classroom Application

Do you suppose that he would have attempted to look for, or learn, what he thought he knew, though he did not, before he was thrown into perplexity, became aware of his ignorance, and felt a desire to know? (Plato, Meno84d)

In this section of dialogue, Socrates explains what is at the heart of the Socratic method and also at the heart of any kind of trial and error learning. Without awareness of our ignorance or failures, we have little motivation to seek better answers or solutions to problems. Video games provide the motivation for striving for improvement by clearly communicating how the player is doing at all times. Each failure communicates something significant. When educators teach information literacy instruction sessions, helping students understand what a failed search looks like can be as important as or more so than communicating what a successful search looks like. Until our students learn to recognize the signs of a failed search, they may simply be satisfied with whatever results Google, Academic Search, or our catalogs return for their first keywords. Hence, if library instructors can find more ways to clearly tell students, "No, that is not quite right, please try again," we may be able to tap into the remarkable ability of video games to motivate students to persistence after failure.

Environmental Pedagogy/Design Pedagogy

Principle
When analyzing games, it is useful to treat them similarly than we do other texts. However, because of their visual nature, games are less textual than written media. When game designers need to communicate concepts or principles to players, they often use visual communication techniques. That is to say, when they want to tell the players "turn right at the intersection" they often will use visual or environmental cues rather than writing or speaking the words "turn left." By using cues or clues rather than words, game designers add an element of discovery into their training. Players must interpret the environment to discover the needed action. This places the player in the role of a discoverer or an active learner rather than a passive participant who is merely following orders.

Classroom Application
Indirect communication can be difficult to implement. A major key to using the *design* of learning environments as a teaching tool instead of the *content* of our learning environments is to focus on the learning outcomes we are aiming for. For example, if our end goal is for students to know what a subject heading can do for them, speaking or writing this content will suffice. However, if our end goal is for students to be

able to use subject headings to expand their searches, we may find that adding visual cues to our Web pages, interfaces, or class handouts may lead to better retention and implementation of the desired skill.

If we keep in mind Dale's Cone of Experience, the concept that humans tend to recall more of what they actively participate in compared to their recall of experience of abstract activities, such as written or spoken language, we can see the value of guiding our students into discovery as compared to relating content verbally (Dale, 1970). If educators take care to design our Web pages, search interfaces, and handouts using visual cues to guide our students into discovery, we can take advantage of a learning behavior students will have encountered in their gaming experiences.

Button-Mashing and Gating

Principle

A common behavior in video game players when confronted with a difficult puzzle is button-mashing. Button-mashing involves randomly pressing buttons or controls in hopes of accidentally stumbling upon the solution to a puzzle. This can present problems, especially when players advance through a game by means of button-mashing without actually developing the necessary skills to solve the game's puzzles. The designers of the game, Portal, observed button-mashing players and discovered that button-mashers can advance in a game beyond their skill level. Then, when they face a particularly difficult challenge, they are ill equipped to solve it and can quit in frustration. The Portal designers combat this issue by building in "gates" or challenges that require the demonstration of certain skills and cannot be circumvented by button-mashing to ensure that players develop the skills they need (Valve, 2007).

Classroom Application

Game designers build in gates, or points that force a player to dem-onstrate skill acquisition before advancing. Librarians who are providing instruction sessions in other faculty members' courses rarely have the necessary control over the content or search environment to build in such stops. However, we can learn from game designers and focus on self-assessment when presenting research strategies. If we encourage our students to ask themselves "what worked" and, more important, "what didn't work" with their searches, we can help them learn to recognize the signs of a weak or failed search strategy. Contemporary search interfaces including Google's Web search and confederated search products for our databases often have the side-effect of making every search, no matter how poorly conceived, appear successful. Since Gen M students may have a strong preference for trial and error learning, any steps we can take to help them recognize a failed search will pay off.

These principles and their application to the library classroom are an introduction to the pedagogy of games. Librarians will likely recognize some of the principles and perhaps have employed them in their own classrooms. So they will be familiar even if we have never been taught by a game that employed them. Gen M students have likely spent significant time learning and being entertained by games that use these principles to train players. Educators who develop game-literacy will be able to understand the learning preferences of these students from a different perspective. If we take on the roles of diligent students of well-designed games, we will gain insight into what it feels like to learn skills this way. This perspective can be extremely valuable when we are trying to help students bridge the gap between what they know when they come to our institutions and what they need to know to be successful student researchers.

The next section will introduce a specialized genre of games that has exciting implications for teaching and learning. Massively Multiplayer Online Roleplaying Games or MMORPGs are online environments where thousands of gamers meet in online communities. Just as video games broke new ground by making the "reading" of a "text" more interactive, MMORPGs take this a step farther and introduce the experience of communities to the picture. The text of a single-player video game is constructed by the interplay between a player and the world designed by the game makers. In a MMORPG, the designer and the player create the text, but there is a social body, as well, which influences choices, values, and outcomes in the game. This third layer of influence on the text of a game is rich with implication for educators. Learning in a peer group is a very different experience from learning on one's own.

MMORPGs

> I respecced [*sic*] a few times during the leveling process, finding the burst damage offered by Assassination only slightly better than a good Combat build. However, I must admit that the Combat spec granted a bit more survivability (but it wasn't nearly as fun to play!) Eventually (around level 50) I settled on a Subtlety/Assassination

build and I haven't looked back. So as far as I'm concerned, rogues seem to level quickly regardless of their builds (although the Subtlety tree is less viable at the lower levels in my opinion). (Warcraftpets. com, 2008)

What?! Like the trombone "voice" of Charlie Brown's teacher's in the "Peanuts" specials, the above paragraph glides over our brains as if it were another language. And, indeed, it is another language, the language of a World of Warcraft (WoW) player, one of the most popular Massively Multiplayer Online Roleplaying Games in the world (MMOGCHART. com, 2008). Many of our students are MMORPG players, and just as the above description of a Rogue class's ability to level quickly befuddles us, the description of a database and its features can glide over our video game-playing students' brains without any connection. Using the language and pedagogy of the MMORPG world can help us to connect to our students and help them understand the world of information literacy.

A Librarian's Journey into the World of MMORPGs
(Note: This section is written by Carole Svensson and based on her own experiences with World of Warcraft.)

I am not a gamer. I am a librarian. I have never before played video games, or role-playing games. When I'm looking for entertainment I prefer foreign films to playing games. However, I was recently ill for several months, during which time a colleague introduced me to the MMORPG World of Warcraft. It was an excellent way to pass the time when daytime TV couldn't provide the intellectual stimulation usually presented by work as an academic librarian. I entered the new and intimidating semiotic domain of gamers.

According to John Paul Gee's definition of *semiotic domain*, "an area or set of activities where people think, act, and value in certain ways" (2003: 19), I fully occupy the semiotic domain of librarianship. Therefore, as I cautiously made my way into the semiotic domain of WoW, I saw it all through my librarian eyes, and my librarian eyes saw a highly complex online environment that had to introduce novice players to it in such a way as not to scare them off. Immediately, I thought of my large research library's resources, accessed via a very complex online environment that often intimidates novice researchers—back to the safety of Google.

It is not a big stretch to make the analogy that the modern library is a MMORPG, a complex online environment that requires interacting with other "players" (fellow researchers) with more expertise, learning a new way of thinking, "leveling up" your skills to improve your experience, and gain more "loot" (good resources) (Dickey, 2007). In a MMORPG, you are online with thousands of your player peers. In the library, you are online with thousands of your scholar peers. The techniques used for success in a MMORPG are directly transferable to those that are required for success in the classroom, or in doing research. And the pedagogical principles that are used to explicate those techniques make sense to our students. They enable us to speak the language of our Gen M students and connect their experience to the library world.

Obviously, the classroom setting is not going to parallel directly the online experience. However, it is not necessary to emulate every aspect in order to engage students the way they are engaged when they play video games. "Successful e-learners possess qualities similar to those who frequently play videos games: they are independent, possess a thoughtful learning style and are self-motivated by the ability to utilize interactive technology in new and innovative ways" (Kenny and Gunter, 2007: 8).

Next, let us compare how professional teachers in the classroom and peer mentors in games approach instruction. We'll look at the Madeline Hunters' Instructional Design Model as presented by Dr. Rodney P. Reigle (Reigle and Matejka, 2005) and *The Art of War: Can't Tell a Night Elf from a Nether Dragon? Here's a Player's Primer* (Levine, 2007). The former is a brief for teachers on instructional design, the latter is a help document written by a non-academic to help folks new to WoW make their way in that world. Hunters' model uses technical language to describe a formal approach to instruction. Teachers begin with an anticipatory set (AS) to introduce the topic; they set out a purpose, define models, and allow input. Students participate in guided and independent practice sessions while teachers occasionally check for understanding (CFU) to ensure information transfer is successful. Finally, closure is reached (Reigle and Matejka, 2005). It turns out that the informal introduction to the World of Warcraft contains the same basic elements structured in a similar fashion. Both begin by giving indicators of the learning to come; focus and commitment are needed. Both set out formal structures or "mastery of your domain" as necessary steps to understanding the content to come.

In both settings, the importance of having a mentor model demonstrate how tasks are performed successfully is paramount. Independent practice, feedback, and assessment are found in both of these sources and both build in some kind of closure while keeping the learning experience alive. Closure is a definitive word for what is actually an open concept:

the class may end, but the learning continues. The progressions parallel each other and underscore two things: the pedagogy underlying the development of a good game environment and the need for mentorship and collaboration to succeed in a MMORPG. Obviously, information literacy instruction already has a solid pedagogical foundation. However, an emphasis on collaboration and mentorship is not always present. These concepts are often secondary content for an instructor—but they are everyday practice for students who text, blog, instant message (IM), and communicate constantly with their friends during life, during work, during school (even while the instructor is talking, much to our chagrin) and while playing. Whether consulting a friend for dating advice, figuring out how to complete a quest in WoW, or doing homework, students today turn to their peers first.

This observation is particularly meaningful when considering how game designers construct the learning and how we can use the same principles in teaching information literacy. Principles such as *Mentorship, Deemphasizing Authority Distinctions, Emphasizing Peer Knowledge, Socializing and Community* can be interpreted and applied to the classroom setting.

Collaboration and Apprenticeship

Principle

Members of Gen M rarely work alone; they work with friends or those who are working on the same tasks, either in physical proximity or an IM away; Gen Ms are constantly connected to peers with whom they can commiserate and consult. Traditional library research is a solitary experience. Librarians frequently hear the students lament: "I just spent three hours searching and couldn't find anything." A brief conversation with a peer who's successfully working on the same project could get them started and a conversation with a librarian would likely quickly yield a plethora of resources. As I (CS) made my way through the WoW world, I IM'ed friends, called them, played while I sat next to them, or consulted my new "friends," via their Web sites, wikis, or forums. WoW became less intimidating to me with their encouragement and guidance. However, when I tried out another MMORPG, EVE online, I was alone. None of my old or newfound friends played it, and I had no one to provide mentorship, or with whom to apprentice. I set up a character, started the game. I stared at it, trying to figure out what my first step should be. Then I logged out and went back to WoW, where I had someone to ask for help.

Classroom Application
One principal that is not difficult to apply is to make most exercises a process of working with a teammate (or teammates) that has been selected to address the identified skills needed to provide a similar experience. Two approaches that may vary from common library instruction practice: it's useful to have the students self-select their groups, as they would in an MMORPG. Also, working with the students as a class to identify and list the skills they will need, such as critical thinking and problem solving, enables the students to have a sense of control over their group destinies.

Deemphasizing Authority Distinctions/Emphasizing Peer Knowledge

Principle
When working through a MMORPG, there is no single authority source, such as an instructor or professor. Players look to other players, online resources such as forums, wikis, or in-game chat. In addition, there are many books that teach "hacks," which are workarounds, or programming add-ons that assist the player in completing tasks. Players prefer to turn to each other—official help is the last resort, just as often a teacher or librarian is. And this isn't surprising when all of the peer-provided resources are so readily accessible, and all of the authoritative resources require some sort of extra effort, however small. The players must create a help ticket in order to receive an official response, just as they have to go physically to the reference desk, visit during office hours, or send an e-mail message. Conversely, according to one study (Nardi, Ly, and Harris, 2007), the average response rate from other players in-game is 32 seconds. When thousands of avid players are anxious to display their knowledge, a 32-second response time is no surprise. In academia, students often need to wait until an authority (professor or librarian) can get back to them. Typically the response time is well in excess of 32 seconds and, therefore, is a wait that seems like an eternity especially with so many other stimuli vying for attention.

Classroom Application
It is difficult to find a correlate in the classroom; students are likely to seek the "authority" if one is available in person or online, or consult

one's peers on an individual basis. There are no peer-initiated resources such as wikis or knowledge bases to consult. This can lead to the student feeling like the needed knowledge is occult, in the truest sense—hidden from view, and just as mysterious to access. Some partial solutions do exist. Classroom management systems such as Blackboard provide discussion boards and an instructor can require that students participate in these discussions. But the differences are obvious: they are class specific, and access goes away when the class is over. Students can't point friends to it or add to it themselves. They are required to add content—not driven by some inner urge to share (and show-off) their expertise as they are in such resources as the WoW wiki. A better strategy for educators would be to incorporate into their instruction a social networking tool that students could use to share their researching expertise, such as a searchable bulletin board.

Parsing Out Learning/Using the "Level" Concept

Principle

When a player enters the World of Warcraft, he/she is assigned tasks that are equivalent to his/her identified level. A player can't achieve a level 25 task when that player is only a level 5. WoW only shows the parts of the World to which the player has been. These are identified by the skill levels needed for success (i.e., survival) so that the player doesn't venture accidentally into danger. Sometimes players will venture into a more difficult zone purposely to challenge themselves, or go with a higher-level friend who is there to protect and guide them. The guidance is crucial. An example of this kind of guided learning conversation in WoW (Steinkuehler, 2008: 17) can look like this:

Myrondonia: I know a secret
JellyBean: what?
Myrondonia: hold your mouse key down . . . wait
JellyBean: wow
Myrondonia: there you go
JellyBean: that's so cool!
Myrondonia: another rule
JellyBean: ok
Myrondonia: quickly use your mouse cursors over the dead bodies
   . . . make sure they didn't drop
JellyBean: oh wow

While the content of this conversation clearly diverges from what can be heard in the reference section of a library, nonetheless, it is easy to see the commonalities. It is a wonderful experience for both parties when students help each other "level" their research knowledge. Everyone comes away with a sense of accomplishment and pride.

Classroom Application

This principle relies heavily on the idea of collaboration and apprenticeship. Well-designed exercises build a foundation of information literacy and strengthen individual skills through working with others and observing and emulating their skills. The focus falls on process rather than content. While this makes grading more qualitative than quantitative and thereby increase grading times, the results are valuable. The assessment for success is not *the* answer, but instead a clearly recorded step-by-step process with a viable answer.

Socializing/Community

Principle

One magazine editor comments, "the real takeway from a good swordfight session in World of Warcraft is its masterful community building" (Bernstein, 2006: 16). As seen in the previous principle, many WoW players spend copious amounts of time and energy to build resources for other players; everything from wikis, discussion boards, dedicated Web sites, or even software that improves play. Why? They *belong* to the community, just as students often feel a sense of belonging to a university community. How, then can educators translate this sense of belonging to the classroom?

Classroom Application

This principle is built upon many of the others. By providing a strong collaborative environment where students get to know each other and work together to think critically and solve problems using all of the resources provided them, educators can create a sense of community with their students. It requires time and commitment on the part of the instructor and, most importantly, a desire on the part of the students. Through creative teaching techniques, educators can help to create that desire and thereby engender self-motivated students.

CHALLENGES

Clearly, most of these principles work together and are difficult to separate. Whether gamers or non-gamers, librarians and educators need to examine student's behaviors in complex gaming environments and consider how they can use them to inform traditional classroom activities and teaching for the Gen M student. Transitioning the pedagogical principles from game play to classroom implementation presents several challenges.

Intrinsic Motivation and Rewards

Players choose to play a game. Students rarely choose to do research above and beyond Google. Above and beyond the external motivation of grades, instructors need to somehow 'gift' their passion for the topic to their students. An important way to achieve intrinsic motivation is to guide the students to an understanding of the value of the pursuit. In WoW, as a player gains experience, he earns money and "stuff" (swords, armor, elixirs, etc.). Activities are rewarded in tangible and measurable ways. This, like the intrinsic motivation to start the game in the first place, is virtually impossible to duplicate in a classroom setting. Grades are clearly measurable and tangible; they just aren't all that fun and not intrinsically motivated.

In Michele Dickey's article "Game Design and Learning," she proposes that choice is one method for building intrinsic motivation:

> [P]layers are presented with a choice of many quests and they choose the quests they would like to complete. Successful completion of smaller quests allows players' characters to gain points and attain advanced levels, which, in turn, provide players with a choice of increasingly more difficult tasks. Malone and Lepper argue that choice is a significant variable in fostering motivation when learners are given a range of choice and provided with a sufficient structure with which to make choices." (Dickey, 2007: 264)

Earlier, we discussed the need to let students build the list of critical skills, and identify those with whom they wish to build those skills. In addition, providing flexibility and adaptability in the methods that are used to teach the content can help students feel that they are making decisions that are vital to the learning process, selecting their "quests" and working hard to fulfill them.

Persistence Through Failure

Despite being killed over and over and over again (a player must run back to her body from a cemetery before she can be "resurrected"), a player will persevere. Similarly, despite no results search after search, librarians will persevere with reference questions. There are many intangibles in this drive, which can be difficult to translate pedagogically. However, one of the key intangibles is the belief of eventual success. No matter how often a player or a librarian fails to get a useful result, each knows that eventually her expertise will not fail despite setbacks. WoW players know that the game designers want them to succeed; if for some reason a poorly designed quest has slipped through, multitudes of players who have struggled with it will report the flaw. In WoW, a player in trouble knows what to do: get some help or consider tackling a lower-level challenge until enough experience is gained to address the higher-level challenge. Students in the classroom, who have built a record of success through apprenticeship and collaboration, should be able to discern the need for help and seek it from an appropriate source: instructor, librarian, a peer, or (gasp!) a reference source.

CONCLUSION

There is a growing body of scholarship examining the use of educational games based on MMORPGs to teach subjects such as science (NASA, 2008). There's even been some examination of how MMORPG pedagogical principles can be applied in the classroom for a variety of subjects. However, there have been few, if any, connections made to information literacy instruction. While Second Life is rife with libraries and librarians, they are essentially providing the same old instruction in a new medium. It feels forced—an artificial "virtual reality" overlay on traditional approaches.

It is time to think differently, not only about how we present our message, but what our message is. MMORPG teaching principles are not a replacement for good teaching, or traditional teaching tools. These new approaches are a supplement and a way to reach students who think differently from previous generations. Consider: skills learned in WoW are directly transferable to other MMORPGs and basic skills for searching one database are directly transferable to another. It's time to help our students make the leap from their world of play to the world of learning. Once they know how to learn, the world of scholarship is open to them.

REFERENCES

Adler, Mortimer Jerome, and Charles Van Doren. 1972. *How to Read a Book*. New York: Simon and Schuster.

Anderson, Lauren, and David R. Krathwohl. 2001. *A Taxonomy for Learning, Teaching, and Assessing: A Revision of Bloom's Taxonomy of Educational Objectives*. New York: Longman.

Beck, John, and Mitchell Wade. 2006. *The Kids are Alright: How the Gamer Generation Is Changing the Workplace*. Boston: McGraw-Hill.

Bernstein, Jared. 2006. "In Sites." *EContent* (December): 12–16.

Dale, Edgar. 1970. "A Truncated Section of the Cone of Experience." *Theory into Practice* 9, no. 2 (April): 96–100.

Dickey, Michelle. 2007. "Game Design and Learning: A Conjectural Analysis of How Massively Mutiple Online Role-Playing Games (MMORPGs) Foster Intrinsic Motivation." *Educational Technology, Research and Development* 55, no. 3 (June): 253–273.

Gee, James Paul. 2003. *What Video Games Have to Teach Us about Learning and Literacy*. New York: Palgrave Macmillan.

Gee, James Paul. 2007. *Good Video Games and Good Learning: Collected Essays on Video Games, Learning and Literacy*. New York: Peter Lang.

Gilchrist, Deb. 1999. "Outcomes Assessment from the Inside Out." Paper presented at the Library and Media Directors Council of Washington State. Yakima, WA. May 4, 1999.

Huizinga, Johan. 1955. *Homo Ludens: A Study of the Play-Element in Culture*. Boston: Beacon Press.

Kenny, Robert, and Glenda Gunter. 2007. "Endogenous Fantasy-Based Serious Games: Intrinsic Motivation and Learning." *International Journal of Social Sciences* 2, no. 1 (January): 8–13.

Levine, Robert. 2007. "Spoils of Warcraft." *Fortune* (March 19): 151–156.

McGill, Douglas C. 1988. "Nintendo Scores Big." *New York Times* (December 4): F1.

MMOGCHART.com. "MMOG Active Subscriptions World of Warcraft." Available: www.mmogchart.com/Chart11.html (accessed November 28, 2008).

MMOGCHART.com. "MMOG Subscriptions Market Share–April 2008." Available: www.mmogchart.com/Chart7.html (accessed November 28, 2008).

Nardi, Bonnie A., Stella Ly, and Justin Harris. 2007. "Learning Conversations in World of Warcraft." Proceedings of the 40th Hawaii International Conference on System Sciences. January 3–6, 2007, Waikoloa, Hawaii.

NASA. 2008. "Request for Proposals to Partner with NASA on the Development of a Massive Multiplayer Online Game to Support STEM Learning." NASA Learning Technologies. Available: http://ipp.gsfc.nasa.gov/mmo/MMO_RFP.pdf (accessed November 29, 2008).

The Nielsen Company. 2007. "The State of the Console." The Nielsen Company. Available: www.nielsenmedia.com/nc/nmr_static/docs/Nielsen_Report_State_Console_03507.pdf (accessed November 28, 2008).

Pash, Adam. "Camera Hacks: Turn Your Point-and-Shoot into a Super-Camera." Lifehacker.com (May 6, 2007). Available: http://lifehacker.com/387380/turn-your-point+and+shoot-into-a-super+camera (accessed November 28, 2008).

Plato. 1989. *The Collected Dialogues of Plato, Including the Letters*. Bollingen Series 71. Princeton, NJ: Princeton University Press.

Prensky, Marc. 1998. "Twitch Speed." *Across the Board* (January): 14–20.

Riegle, Dr. Rodney P., and Wesley A. Matejka. 2005. "Dying to Learn: Instructional Design and MMORPGs." Paper presented at the 21st Annual Conference on Distance Teaching and Learning. Madison, WI.

Schiesel, Seth, Geannina Munizaga, J. Michael Kennedy, and Rachel Pomerance. 2007. "Reward for Fans, and Microsoft." *New York Times* (September 26): C1.

Schiller, Nicholas. 2008. "A Portal to Student Learning: What Instruction Librarians Can Learn from Video Game Design." *Reference Services Review* 36, no. 4 (December): 351–365.

Steinkuehler, Constance. 2008. "Massively Multiplayer Online Games as an Educational Technology: An Outline for Research." *Educational Technology* 48, no.1 (January): 10–21.

Valve Software [Firm]. 2007. "Portal, The Orange Box" [Video Game]. Valve Software: Bellevue, WA.

van Lent, Michael. 2008. "The Business of Fun." *Computer* 41, no. 2 (February): 101-103.

Warcraftpets.com. "Nine Warcraft Classes Ranked: Leveling Speed." Available: www.warcraftpets.com/guides/other/leveling.asp (accessed November 28, 2008).

Chapter 11

Comics Go Digital: The Rise of Webcomics

Tyler Rousseau

AN INTRODUCTION TO THE RISE OF WEBCOMICS

Getting published has never been easy. It is even tougher for artists wanting to break into the comic industry, due to the few publishing companies that invest in the format. Local newspapers tend to print only syndicated comics from well-known strips and only occasionally give local and independent artists a chance to show their work. Because of this, independent comics have always had a certain prominence in comic culture. In previous generations, aspiring artists had to invest personal funds into their publication and distribute wherever they hoped they could find a readership. Often, these publications did not make enough money to cover the initial cost of printing. Therefore, many died out within the first couple of publications (Guigar et al., 2008).

In hopes of providing a better chance of success, Generation M, and now even its bordering generations, are taking their comics in a new direction. By shedding themselves of the traditional paper medium and bypassing standard publication processes, Gen M artists (M-Artists) are attempting to improve their readership, lower production costs while increasing sales, and vastly improve the geographic distribution of their work by taking their creations to the Internet. For the Gen M comic artist, Webcomics are quickly becoming a more accepted route of publication in lieu of traditional means (Campbell, 2006; Worton, 2008).

Since the creation of the Webcomic in the 1990s (Campbell, 2006), this format has been growing in popularity both among artists and readers. As Web 2.0 technologies continue to improve in quality and decline in cost, there is a greater incentive for M-Artists to move from the paper-based publications into the digital realm, especially among independent and beginning artists.

Gen M is leading the charge in the rising popularity of Webcomics as both creators and readers. The ability to freely access these comics on various Web sites and devices, without necessarily having to download the information or subscribe to services, is a textbook example of how the Gen M culture prefers to handle their content. For the M-Artists, it presents the opportunity to publish their comics on many Web sites and social networks for little to no cost, little effort, and with far less editing than traditional means (Barnes, 2008; Weinryb, 2008).

It is difficult to say how many Webcomics are in existence. Estimates start at the low end of 7,000 for regularly updated serials (Manley, 2007) and soar to well over 70,000, if all registered names are counted (Shableski, 2008). It is even more difficult to determine how many people are reading them. In a poll conducted by Blank Label Comics, it was estimated that 30 percent of comic readers view more than 20 comics per day. In an e-mail correspondence, John Shableski, a representative of Diamond Book Distributors, was asked about Webcomic statistics. He responded, "Webcomic publishing is exploding to where we have lost track." (2008). Furthermore, there is a small group of people who may read the comics section or editorial cartoons of a newspaper, but not consider themselves actual comic readers.

Despite the difficulty with numbers, it is evident among artists and publishers that the Webcomic creations of M-Artists are rivaling their paper-format predecessors for several reasons:

- Webcomics enjoy an audience that is not necessarily related to comic book readership (2008).
- The cost for both the artist and reader is far less.
- Acquiring, reading, and finding Webcomics is far easier for the reader.
- Distributing Webcomics requires less time and money (although promoting Webcomics still requires time and focus).
- Production of Webcomics tends to go through far less editing and artistic compromise.

Figure 11.1. Bill Barnes' Webcomic, *Unshelved*

Note: Bill Barnes, author of *Unshelved*, is one of the few Webcomic artists who has created a sustaining Webcomic.

For both professional and independent artists, there are definite benefits to working in the digital realm. These include the advantages in software and hardware for creation, distribution factors with reaching a larger fan base, and definitely lesser risk in financial investments. Readers of Webcomics also find benefits in the digital realm including a larger selection, various methods of reading and subscribing and, again, less financial investment.

In this do-it-yourself, control-it-yourself age of technology, Gen M is quickly becoming the leader in this new model of publication. In the publication, *A History of Webcomics*, Campbell clearly sees that there is little stronghold by the pioneers of this format and that readers are showing greater interest in viewing newer and fresher comics (Campbell, 2006). This chapter will examine the reasons why this generation is bypassing traditional means of publication and moving into the digital realm, such as Bill Barnes did with his "Unshelved" Webcomic (see Figure 11.1).

ARTISTIC BENEFITS OF WEBCOMICS

"NO EDITORS."

This answer was unanimous from all Webcomic artists who were interviewed for this chapter. It was also the biggest incentive and/or satisfaction for artists who tried their hands with the traditional publication route. The ability to maintain control of one's creation from beginning to finish is an extremely enticing motivator for artists to take their work online.

Editors usually tend to be supporters of their clients' work, but their primary goal is sales. If this means they need to tweak pictures, storylines, and content in order to generate more appeal to a larger audience, the changes will be made in spite of the artist's original idea. Sometimes, this can lead the artists to feel that the integrity of their work has been compromised or that the work is no longer their own. The difficulty of this also comes with the fact that many extremely popular books have gone through an exceptionally long process of rejections before getting published; J. K. Rowling estimates she received more than 100 rejection letters for her cultural phenomenon known as "Harry Potter." This tends to leave many people wondering what exactly the wisdom of an editor is when he/she can be so wrong about such exceptionally popular works.

M-Artists, like their generational cohorts, tend to be extremely self-assured of their quality of work and ability to succeed. They do not need the acceptance of a company to know that they may have a potentially good idea or product; they are willing to put it out for the public to decide. Typically casted as being naturally wary, they do not inherently believe that the traditional model of doing things is in their best interest (i.e., publishing companies are in it for the money, not for the writer or artist).

Webcomics are the exclusive creation of the artists involved. Posting a comic does not require the approval of an editor or the Web publisher (but may require the work to be tagged as 'mature' if the content deems it necessary). The end result for artists is a greater control of their work, its destiny, and the feeling that, if the work is truly great, it will be known regardless of its format.

Webcomic artist Boxy Brown, an M-Artist himself and creator of *Bellen!* (see Figure 11.2), talked about potential frustrations that writers have going the traditional publication route. "Going the traditional route is way more rigorous. Knowing myself, I would have gotten discouraged after getting a lot of rejection letters from editors" (Brown, 2008). The alternative was receiving the instant gratification of online publishing and seeing his readership build. At the time of this publication, "Bellen!" has produced more than 400 comic strips and been included in four books as well.

Not only is artistic control in the hands of the artist, so, too, are the characters and stories created, which is not necessarily the case for comic writers. In the early 1990s, some of Marvel Comics' and DC Comics' most popular writers grew continually frustrated with the publishing corpora-

Figure 11.2: Box Brown's Webcomic, *Bellen!*

Note: Webcomic *Bellen!* has existed for over three years.

tions due to residual rights. During this time, when a new character was created, that character became the property of the company, not the artist. In addition, this meant that the creating artists were not earning much residual from the sales of the comics, action figures, and so forth.

The result was a break from traditional means. Todd MacFarlane and other artists left their major publishing companies and formed Image Comics. The key selling point was that all creative works were the property of the artist. While Marvel and DC still maintain a stronghold on comic publishing, Image has produced some of the most notable new superheroes in the past 18 years, including Spawn, Savage Dragon, Witchblade, and The Walking Dead.

In many ways, Image became a model for the do-it-yourself method of business for the M-Artist. It demonstrates that a company can be quite lucrative, even with artists maintaining property rights. This ideal of creative rights has carried into Webcomics and proves to be beneficial to both the artist and the publisher. M-Artists have taken this model even further by essentially relieving publishing companies of almost any say in the creation of paper comics, with the exception of overall publication costs (and even this can be negotiable). The result is greater control for Generation M, as well as financial incentives.

FINANCIAL BENEFITS OF WEBCOMICS

While independent publications have definite benefits for creative control, very few independent comics earn enough money to sustain themselves. Most comic artists have to invest personal funds into their publications and hope in the long run that the comic will gain enough popularity to become financially self-sustaining. Due to the overall costs of publishing, many comics do not make it past the first couple of issues as the amount of money required to independently publish one's work is significantly more than the money earned from sales.

According to the online digital publication company Ka Blam (www.kablam.com), 300 copies of a 32-page (standard comic book length) black-and-white comic will cost just over $500 to print. This amount would be required for each continuing serial publication. In order to make enough profit to cover the costs of the following publication, artists would have to sell every single copy of their book for $3.50, which is a little more expensive than most popular comic publications. If artists decided to risk publishing a meatier version of their comic, the printing costs for a 160-page comic would cost about $3,500 for an initial run. In order to make enough funds to cover the initial costs and the costs of the next publication, artists would have to sell every book for $23.00. Using either publication model, it is easy to see how quickly and easily finances can cripple a person's publication attempts. Neither of these sales numbers takes into account profit margins that a comic book store would want to include on the sale.

"There are almost no financial risks involved with doing Webcomics," says Dave Roman, who, in addition to working with Nickelodeon Magazine, has made a significant name for himself with his Webcomic, *Astronaut Elementary* (see Figure 11.3). Roman continues, "People can post their comics on free services or blogs or sites designed for hosting comics like www.webcomicsnation.com and www.comicspace.com" (Roman, 2008). As Roman indicates, there are various sites aimed at comic writers that require no monthly or annual fee in order to maintain the site. Some may require the artist to have either a concept or a few pre-made panels submitted as part of his/her application but, once accepted, the services rendered by the hosting site are free with only standard contractual obligations. The work also belongs to the artist, not the site. The hosting site itself tends to make its money by placing Web ads on the site and various contributions. This becomes a win-win situation for both host and user as they both attain benefits.

Figure 11.3. Dave Roman's Webcomic, *Astronaut Elementary*

Source: *Astronaut Elementary* is a registered trademark and copyright of Dave Roman 2009.

Web 2.0 technologies changed the way in which M-Artists need to do business. As the new business model for social networks, blogs, and aggregator sites demonstrates, little investment needs to be made by the users of a particular Web site. Webcomics, therefore, are an ideal solution to the aforementioned publishing problems, as they require very little financial investment in order to publish and/or maintain themselves.

This freedom from financial investment tends to entice more of the up-and-coming artists into creating Webcomics. Since there is little to no money involved in the hosting services, artists are not limited by their personal finances or ability raise money. This type of digital publication is also not limited to the amount of physical copies that can be produced for distribution. The artist needs only to place his/her comic on the Web and it can be viewed by anyone. After the comic is posted and progress has been monitored, the artist can then decide if producing a paper version of the comic would be profitable.

For the reader, the financial benefits come from not having to spend money on the comic itself. A 1995 study by DC comics estimated that 37 percent of readers purchase more than $100 worth of comics a month (Carlson, 2007). Considering the amount of money these dedicated readers already spend on readership, there is a reluctance to invest even more money in a new and untested comic.

Again, M-Artists recognize that Webcomics are a great alternative choice for readers as there is no financial risk. Readers can go online and browse various comics and their archives to determine if something is worth reading. If they do like a comic, they can subscribe to it, read it with frequency, and make a more informed decision of whether or not they want to purchase a bound copy of the comic.

DISTRIBUTIVE BENEFITS OF GOING ONLINE

Large conglomerate companies like Barnes & Noble or Borders generally do not purchase independent publications nor allow independent artists to sell their comics in the store. This means that comic writers have to try to sell their comics through other independent bookshops, comic stores, or by other creative means. Considering the general strain that the large chain stores have been putting on independent companies over the past couple years, this is by no means an ideal situation for an artist looking to get their work to an audience.

Most comic artists have full-time jobs in order to make ends meet (this is one thing that has not changed for the Gen M-Artist) and distributing comics can require much more time than they may have. Most towns do not have a comic shop, and that requires the artist to travel in order to push distribution. If the artist has a subscription service set up with stores and customers, this may require a lot of time simply keeping track of these services. The ability to post comics in a single place and have them be distributed by other means is a very enticing one to the busy artist.

M-Artists have an advantage in that they understand the abilities of using 2.0 technologies in order to advance their work. Most Webcomics are housed on Web sites whose background is designed like a blog. By design, the site will keep a running archive of previous works by the artist. This backlog of comics is something that is difficult to do in the real world as, spatially, there simply is not enough room for a comic shop or bookstore to keep an entire series of most publications.

The limitations of distribution geographically are also corrected by Webcomics. Once the comic is posted, it can be viewed by anyone and through various sites and social networks (if they are set up by the artist). Through the use of an RSS (Rich Site Summary) feed, typically supplied by most blogs and social networks nowadays, the artist can allow the comic to be housed at a central location and then read at various locations. This cross posting allows the artist to distribute his/her work with far less effort than traditional publication requires. The ability to copy and paste a comic from a site onto another person's site also means that the distribution of an artist's comic may expand further than they realize as well.

Ultimately, using these various posts creates a far larger readership and fan base than most artists would experience otherwise. Boxy Brown states that his work is able to reach comic enthusiasts worldwide. When asked about his fan base, he jokes, "It turns out that Australians like my comic as well" (Brown, 2008). For a readership that is estimated to be a few thousand, it is clear to see just how important maximizing the readership of an independent is. M-Artists, like Boxy, have not only learned to use the technologies they have grown up with, but have learned how best to use them in order to maximize their own potential. M-Artists understand that a Web-based comic can potentially increase the distribution and readership of the work at a much faster rate than the traditional means, and can allow the artist to have more time in order to work on the story and characters and less on the worry of distributions. To turn this scenario around for the Web-reader, Webcomics allow enthusiasts to find comics that would normally never make it to their region in paper form.

PUBLISHING BENEFITS OF GOING ONLINE

This method of publishing falls well into the preferred models of Gen M-Artists: creations that are do-it-yourself, organic in feel, and allowed to change over time in order to best use resources and please users. Gen M-Artists are content to dedicate themselves to personal endeavors, particularly ones that allow attention and feedback from other users. The instant gratification from seeing their work online combined with the instant feedback from users means that more productions from these artists will likely follow (Campbell, 2006).

Webcomic sites that are being used by the M-Artists, like blogs and Web sites, usually contain software that allows the administrators to see how many people are visiting the site, how many pages are being accessed, how many people subscribe to the site, as well as from where users are accessing the site. By using these statistics, Web artists can make better informed decisions about when to post new comics, how to modify stories, and if they should take a chance at producing a trade paperback.

Webcomics offer an advantage to M-Artists through feedback that can be given by the fan base. Webcomics, like blogs, often offer a spot at the end of the comic for the reader to provide comments and suggestions. This can help the artist determine what storylines and character developments to follow or, for that matter, what artistic stylings to use for the comic (initial runs of comics are often scratchy in feel but become cleaner and more refined as the story progresses).

Webcomics also offer an advantage of piecemeal publications. M-Artists do not have to have a completed library of comics in order to put their work online. As a comic is created, it can be posted at the artist's convenience. Once enough comics are created, artists can then collect the already completed works and put them into a trade paperback publication.

This method eases the time constraints for M-Artists that are often associated with traditional publication practices. Since, as mentioned before, Webcomics are often produced on the artist's free time, which means artists do not have to feel pressured into pushing out comics at the need of a publisher, but instead at the pace that their routine allows.

TECHNOLOGICAL IMPROVEMENTS THAT CHANGED COMICS

Perhaps the greatest advantage that Gen M has over earlier generations is the usability and affordability of technology. Previously, users had to be familiar with the inner workings of technology in order to use it to its fullest ability. Web developers—and even the most recreational user who wanted to create a Web page—had to be well versed in a coding language in order to create a Web site.

Today's 2.0 technologies are able to implement these changes without the administrator having to do more than create a post. The algorithms working in the background of these sites means that the user does not need to know about the inner workings or have special knowledge in Web development. With a simple click or uploading of pictures, users can take generic sites and make them completely customized to their liking.

While Gen M is known for its ability to multitask to some degree and use multiple technologies, 2.0 technologies are known for being multidimensional in use and application and highly customizable to the preference of the individual user (i.e., cell phones can have specialized ringtones, access the Web, take pictures, and play music). This flexibility in technological application has led to many ways in which the artist can create and advertise his/her Webcomics, which has led to completely new forms of artistry.

The basic hardware needed to create a Webcomic is well within the price range of most people. At the most basic set up, a scanner and Internet connection are all that is needed to post a comic online. A basic search of major retail stores (Walmart, Target, Best Buy, and Kmart) shows that each one has at least two scanners for less than $100. High-speed Internet connections are available for as little as $35 per month. At well under the price of an initial run of paper-bound comics, artists can publish the same work online and potentially have far more people reading their comic.

If an artist wants to try his/her hand with digital drawing tools, these, too, can be found for a reasonable price. Wacom, generally known for professional-grade pen tablets, has recently created a more recreational version for aspiring enthusiasts. The product, called Bamboo (www. wacom.com/bambootablet), runs as little as $79, comes with drawing software, and requires no programs to download in order to run it (i.e., plug and play device). If the artist would like to buy drawing software, he or she can choose from myriad options. There is a dramatic difference in prices between lower-end and higher-end programs. However, an independent artist does not need to buy the most expensive software in order to create a quality Webcomic. For most artists, the quality of the artwork comes directly from ability first; the software and tools are just extensions for their work.

Web 2.0 technologies have made it easier for readers to find and access Webcomics as well. Tagging by genre and subject is the most common way that Webcomics are classified online. Depending on the site, these tags can be created by the reader or the artist. The ability to classify comics by their subject matter rather than by lumping them together under a general heading of "graphic novels" or "comics" is a considerable convenience to the user. Subscription services and RSS feeds make keeping track of new comics much easier. These services mean that readers do not have to check sites constantly to see if a new comic has been posted. Having the comic, when published, sent to the user provides not only a convenience to the reader but also benefits the artist as it helps prevent the reader from forgetting about the comic.

Since aggregators and subscription services are all handled online, this means that the reader can access the information on a variety of technologies. Computers, cell phones, gaming consoles, and mp3 players, as long as they can download or access the Internet, all have the capability of viewing a Webcomic. This allows fans to access their favorite strips whenever and wherever the user may be.

CONCLUSION

Both Webcomics and comics are growing in popularity and are gaining acceptance into mainstream culture. Some of the largest blockbusters of the past ten years have been adapted storylines from comic books (e.g., X-Men, History of Violence, Ghost World); and some of the most popu-

Figure 11.4.   A Self-portrait of the Author, Tyler Rousseau: The Triangle Man

lar blockbusters and TV shows have been turned into graphic novels (e.g., *Indiana Jones, Buffy the Vampire Slayer*). Certain books, like Stephen King's *Dark Tower* series, have been made into comic format as well. By all means, comics are seen by the entertainment industry as a lucrative format to lure fans.

The line between comics and Webcomics is thinning, too. Published authors, like Scott Adams (*Dilbert*), offer their entire collection of comics online and viewable to anyone. The critically acclaimed graphic novel, *Shooting War,* written by Anthony Lappé and illustrated by Dan Goldman, started as a Webcomic.

As our culture keeps turning towards digital resources for its information and entertainment needs, it seems only logical that artists will continue to follow the trend of the Gen M pioneers: M-Artists. The major comic book publishing companies, DC and Marvel, taking notice of the technological trends of their readers and artists, have started moving some comics to the digital realm, while publishing others exclusively through this format (e.g., Zuda Comics). Among artists, it is assumed that this new generation will not only continue to work through the digital realm but will also push the new movements of digital artwork.

REFERENCES

Barnes, Bill. Interview by author. E-mail correspondence. Trenton, NJ., June 14, 2008.

Brown, Boxy. Interview by author. E-mail correspondence. Trenton, NJ., June 10, 2008.

Campbell, T. 2006. *A History of Webcomics*. San Antonio: Antarctic.

Carlson, Johanna. "Superhero Comic Reader Stats." Comics Worth Reading (May 10, 2007). Available: http://comicsworthreading.com/2007/05/10/superhero-comic-reader-stats/ (accessed August 21, 2008).

Guigar, Brad, Dave Kellet, Scott Kurtz, and Kris Straub. 2008. *How to Make Webcomics*. Berkeley, CA: Image Comics.

Manley, Joey. "The Number of Webcomics in the World." TalkAboutComics Blog (January 3, 2007). Available: www.talkaboutcomics.com/blog/?p=766 (accessed August 20, 2008).

Roman, David. "Interview with Dave Roman." Interview by author. The Rock & Roll Librarian and skalogy.podomatic.com (April 10, 2006). Available: http://libraryrock.wordpress.com/2006/04/10/interview-with-dave-roman-podcast/ (accessed October 10, 2008).

Shableski, John. Interview by author. E-mail correspondence. Trenton, NJ., June 15, 2008.

Weinryb, Avi. "Web Comics: An Unlimited Audience" (June 15, 2008). Available: www.comicbookbin.com/Unlimited_Audience001.html (accessed August 17, 2008).

Worton, Steve. 2008. *Webcomics 2.0: An Insider's Guide to Writing, Drawing and Promoting Your Own Webcomics*. Boston: Course Technology PTR.

Chapter 12

The Emerging Gen M Ecology: What Will Their World Look Like?

Stephen Abram

INTRODUCTION

The Gen M community and our libraries must be prepared for the world that people will encounter, not for one that existed in the past. This chapter will focus on the potential ecology for Gen M in the years 2020–2025, which is about when current Gen M members will hit the main stride of their lives as workers, scholars, consumers, professionals, and parents—when they are approximately in their late 20s to early-to-mid-40s. Can strategies be built now to lay a strong foundation for these folks to be very successful in a world of too many media formats, too much information, stimulation, technology, and ever-present advertising?

THE FUTURE: AN ENVIRONMENTAL SCAN FOR THE GEN M COMMUNITY

The Global Economy

In 2009, the world is entering a period of enormous and exciting change—far greater than anything ever experienced to date. Major forecasters, such as the Gartner Group and Morgan Stanley, have noted that these changes will be transformational on a global scale. The world, in general, has grown accustomed to a period of continuous economic expansion for decades—arguably one of the most peaceful and longest expansionist economies in modern history. Up until this time, with the recent upheaval in the world economy, Gen M has really never known a period of severe economic contraction. In addition to the global economic issues, war, terrorism, climate change, and social disruption (e.g., food and resource shortages) will likely characterize the second decade of this millennium. Struggles that will have an impact on Gen M will also include the ecology or Green movement, as well as global resource sharing. Major global corporations, including those in the information, entertainment, and technology sectors, in addition to serious legal trends to change the laws governing intellectual property and copyright, are causing a sea of change in the legal context of national and international protections for content and research. By 2020, it is expected that many of these issues will have been addressed or be well on the way to stabilization. Therefore, Gen M is likely just hitting their mid-careers in a world that has been through a decade or more of serious disruption in terms of the ability to secure economic success. This should be a positive development for this generation of learners as long as they have kept up their skills and competencies, and they are prepared to build a new information and knowledge-based global economy.

The Social Context

By 2020–2025, there will have been a huge consolidation within the social networking space, just as search consolidated in the first decade of this millennium. Gen M will have priority access to the consumer market and e-commerce and drive some developments of expectations for work and learning collaborative social environments—just as the Internet/Web drove expectations for intranets. The world will be infinitely globally connected, and individual and professional brands will be as important as corporate brands. Many Gen M members will be sought after for their individual skills and competencies, as well as their access to their personal networks.

The Technology Context

By 2008, some of the new modalities could already be seen emerging in the gaming environment. This was clearly visible in the convergence of interactive and creative features and functions as they emerged in high growth Web sites like MySpace, YouTube, Second Life, Google Lively, Active Worlds, Facebook, Ning, Twitter, Meebo, and others. Context is the word of the day here. Such technologies, as listed below, serve as the emerging foundation for Web 2.0, where Web 2.0 "describes the changing trends in the use of World Wide Web technology and Web design that aim to enhance creativity, secure information sharing, collaboration and functionality of the Web" (Wikipedia, 2008a).

Technologies that will drive the decade preceding 2020 include RSS, wikis, blogs, social networks, social bookmarking, and photo applications—technologies that many within the Gen M community have enthusiastically embraced. But it will extend further than those to increased personalization in profiles, alert capabilities and reviews, ratings, and commentary on all Web sites. Creation and collaboration will also be on the rise with open access, open source, and open content leading to new, simple, and revised programming methods like AJAX, J2EE, widgets, gadgets, Mashups, and APIs. Advances in personal devices will exceed current expectations of iPhones and Kindles. Peter Kaufman predicts that an iPod-size device will be able to hold one year's worth of video (8,760 hours) by 2012; all the commercial music ever created by 2015; and all the content ever created (in all media) by 2020 (Kaufman, 2007).

A technology framework and ecology in 2020 that is very different than most dreams today can be expected, one characterized by unlimited content and connectedness, and ease-of-use that are truly personalized. Ubiquity will also drive major changes in key behaviors around collaboration, discovery, entertainment, research, work life, and learning.

Information 3.0

Information 3.0 is the step that evolves out of Web 2.0 in the second decade. The term Web 2.0 has been around since about October 2004. The Masters of Media blog at the University of Amsterdam states that "the characteristics of Web 2.0 are: rich user experience, user participation, dynamic content, metadata, Web standards and scalability. Further characteristics, such as openness, freedom and collective intelligence by way of user participation, can also be viewed as essential attributes of Web 2.0" (Batermadjian, 2008; Best, 2006). Web 2.0 lays a foundation to go much further than this, actually beyond an application focus. It is really about the "hot" Web—"hot" in the McLuhanesque sense of the hot and cold or the warm and cool aspects of technology (McLuhan, 1964;

Wolfe, 2004). Interactivity, as epitomized by the social Web, makes the Web warmer or hotter. This fairly recent aspect of the Web (e.g., MySpace, Facebook, and YouTube) supports not just individual personal interactions but also the social construct of society: businesses, schools, clubs, and associations. Of course, the Web is already interactive in a cooler transactional sense, with instantaneous response and the ability to surf Web sites. Web 1.0 was based on the paradigm of Web sites, e-mail, search engine ads, and surfing transactions, whereas Web 2.0 is about the more social aspects of interactivity. It is about conversations, interpersonal networking, personalization, and individualism. In the library world, this has relevance not just for public Web portals, but also for workplace intranets. The underlying imperative is for greater social cohesiveness in virtual teams and global content engagement. The contemporary Gen M student needs the interactive experience of the Web, not just its content, to learn and succeed.

For this coming decade, the technology infrastructure of Web 2.0 will remain to be complex and constantly in flux; it will be in a Renaissance mode. In some ways, the mosaic tiles that form this technological infrastructure exist now and are just starting to create the bigger picture. This bigger picture is Information 3.0. It is the Web that is focused on *transformations* and not just interactions. The emerging "cloud computing" environment—which creates a Web-based operating system for applications such as word processing, spreadsheets, e-mail, readers, and presentations—is an early indicator of this trend. Perhaps it will look something like the MIT Croquet Project (a " deeply collaborative multi-user online virtual world"), describing an exciting potential scenario of what Information 3.0 might look like (The Croquet Consortium, accessed 2008) for the future Gen M community.

Imagine the merger of Google Earth and Second Life to truly create a parallel world experience—Second Earth? Information 3.0 and the social Web will probably be even more distributed in form than Web 2.0. Perhaps some of the Web 2.0 applications will disappear or merge into a new integrated whole. Web services or the emerging semantic Web may replace such things as social networking sites and repositories. Either way, it rises to a new plateau in terms of the user experience and user control.

This change is fundamentally about a transition of the Web site- and e-mail-centric world from one that is mostly about information content (and largely textual information) to one where the content is combined with functionality and targeted applications that meet the needs of society and individuals in context. It is primarily about a much higher level of interactivity and deeper user experiences. Web 2.0 is ultimately about a social phenomenon—not just about networked social experiences, but also about the distribution and creation of Web content itself. It moves the Web experience into a place that more closely resembles an academic learning and collaboration environment than information delivery or e-commerce, thus becoming a learning, decision-making, and social collaboration ecology. To enable this new world, a more organized Web with a plethora of new modalities of categorized content and more developed deep-linking Web architecture and a greater variety of Web display modes (e.g., visualization) will be seen.

What is truly exciting is that Web 2.0 and Information 3.0 are just the titles of conversations. Everyone can participate and influence the development of this next generation of the Web and thus may influence the building of the world where Gen M members will reside for most of their lives.

TECHNOLOGY AS A DRIVER OF CHANGE

Several key and already apparent technologies will be principal change agents. These social technologies that connect people and allow greater collaboration are found in many types of social institutions. Libraries are social institutions, as are schools, colleges, universities, hospitals, businesses, and associations. The friend-driven applications seen in 2008 are being used right now in all of these institutions, and they are merely the beginning of a long-term development of a collaborative platform for social good that has arisen out of the Web. This is a key driver of changes in society of the coming decade. Socially driven content and advanced recommendation engines and environments will be critical in dealing with a world of too much information and too much choice. By 2020, this environment will be considered essential to work and learning.

Over the past few decades, a huge amount of full text content has emerged. By 2020, the world will be one of essentially unlimited content. Enough books, journal articles, video, music, podcasts, and recordings will have been converted and made searchable to make the seeking of the edge of the information universe a largely academic effort. Indeed, the critical skills will be filtering, choosing, and evaluating content. A historical shift from hard-to-find to hard-to-winnow will thus occur.

Also emerging is a next-generation search environment that is all about building on the traditional list display with more visual interfaces, an expanded and informed faceted display, and taxonomies and tag folksonomies driving selection and word or tag clouds (see definition of "word cloud" in Wikipedia, 2008b). All of this will allow for a discovery leap that is greater than the leap from index metadata to full-text searching in the last century.

Related to the emergence of a next generation search display is the role XML and Unicode are going to play in this information and technology architecture. Each will result in the ability to create easily and efficiently electronic experiences that will seamlessly display on any device and in any character set for any language. Each standard is essential to the globalization of the Internet environment.

The early results from tagging systems like Flickr, del.icio.us, Digg, or Connotea and research trails software like Zotero and RefWorks illustrate the beginning of a shift to users building trusted cohort networks and content selection systems. The research and development and consumer and academic opportunities here will be more fully evident by 2020. The threat to traditional juried publishing is clear, and new processes for judging preprints and research will emerge out of these technologies.

The cloud is another major trend in computing that will reach major mindshare by the end of the next decade. The desktop computer is not going away, but as bandwidth speeds increase, more and more computing can be done in the network of computers sitting in data centers—aka, the cloud. Much of the cloud will be supported by ads, and this 'free' service will draw a majority of users to it. Early entrants are services like Zoho or Google Docs. Once participation in the cloud begins, it is all about network operations and the attendant collection of user behavioral data. For libraries, schools, and universities, this will astronomically reduce the cost of software eco-systems and result in a level playing field for more users and learners.

Personalization has been touted as the big killer application. Originally, this was imagined as a personal homepage that users constructed themselves. By 2020, personal and professional social networking pages that allow for the building of a personal range of applications will dominate. The social collection of user behavior data will be providing news, and these sites will be providing locally significant information, like ads, weather, and security alerts, driven by GIS (Geographic Information Systems) locally aware devices. Some of this will involve the use of advanced presence management systems that look a lot like Twitter, Plurk, or the Facebook presence application—as such people will be able to deal with team- and classroom-oriented behavior and collaboration. Mash-ups or downloadable applications for social networks will number in the millions.

Hardware also plays a role in the 2020 environment. What the mobile device will ultimately look like has not yet been seen. iPhones hint at this, but it is more likely that the cloud will play a much bigger role, and download activities will decrease. The multifunction device might also go the way of the vintage HiFi/TV/Radio hybrid furniture of the 1960s, which were replaced by component systems. In this mobile world, the issue of next generation monitors arises. Plasma screens for large display will be better, but the display environment will expand to include e-paper in black and white and color, with displays that can be projected anywhere from mobile devices using projectors that are no bigger than a sugar cube. Combined with voice response interfaces and keyboards, as well as keyboards that can be projected using laser technology, the functionality of mobile devices will exceed that of today's desktops and laptops. Bandwidth issues will be much farther advanced by 2020. Fast, ubiquitous networks will be available in many flavors—over air, telephone, cable, TV signal, satellite, and standard electrical wires. In addition to improvements in battery life and size, enhancing mobility of devices, there will also be new ways of addressing the provision of electricity, including charging pads and green-oriented solar panel chargers. Overall, this will result in much more portable devices, and the nomadic service and information anticipation will grow as an expectation—especially for mobile workers and students.

FUTURE LEARNING ENVIRONMENT FOR GEN M

In 2020, lifelong learning is not only a good personal value; it is also an essential thread to anyone's career, essential to the competitive advantage of nations and trading blocs. All governments must focus on all aspects of lifelong education and preparation for society and work including K–12, college, university, vocational, workplace, and continuing education strategies. Libraries are integral to these strategies.

To that effect, the Ontario School Libraries Association has worked to code the expectations of our learners to learning standard outcomes and to help them build their information literacy skills in a planned, staged, and effective manner. Each stage of life and school comes with its own set of new skill requirements to achieve success across the curriculum, and this curriculum recognizes the need for and importance of programs that facilitate learning literacy skills and translating those to real-life situations. It also includes learning problem-solving skills and processes, using both critical and creative thinking skills. Emphasis is given to including parents, teachers, and other professionals, such as librarians, in the learning program (Information Studies Writing Team, 1998).

FUTURE WORKPLACE AND ORGANIZATIONAL ENVIRONMENT FOR GEN M

Many of the other trends outlined in this chapter will characterize the workplace. If Gen M is prepared for this world, then this group will be more successful. The major trends include a significantly more mobile workforce that works from home more often, and often in a hybrid situation with an office. It will be a workforce that is promoted more quickly into managerial work due to the large retirement bulge in the senior staff cohort. This workforce will be truly global and work with people around the world. It will be more diverse, multilingual, and collaborative, and it will be about the network instead of the individual. This will be a world where job mobility is quite extreme, and where some workers—especially those whose skills are in high demand and for which there are shortages—are employed by multiple employers. A world where advanced information literacy competencies, teaching skills, coaching skills, and social skills are valued, measured, and rewarded. In short, the world will require talented people with a suite of competencies and the flexibility and nimbleness to move with the times and succeed in a knowledge-based enterprise.

FUTURE OF SCHOLARSHIP AND RESEARCH & DEVELOPMENT FOR GEN M

Gen M will have the world of information and data at its fingertips as no other generation has ever had or experienced. This will change many aspects of the scholarly world. Juried scholarly publishing is changing radically as they explore open access models and the role of preprints. This will change the entire citation indicator model, which influences tenure and publishing decisions. Microfilm of the old days is being converted, and there are now hundreds of full runs of major and local newspapers available for free text searching. Also, other content that was previously difficult to access, such as historical ads, pictures, and more, has become accessible. The ability to search the full text of hundreds of millions of digitized books and an even greater number of articles will materially change scholarship resources and decisions. Young scholars will choose different thesis and dissertation topics due to the availability and accessibility of material previously difficult to access. Radical national licensing programs will encourage access from smaller higher education institutions and put them onto a competitive field with larger universities, including the Ivy League schools. National conversion programs will encourage access to the world of scholarly content in countries that may not share Western traditions. Multicultural research institutions will find this very useful. In collaboration with each other, universities and colleges will build advanced, mission-specific, and user-friendly scholarly portals and workstations. The key emerging tools of targeted federated search, fuzzy logic search, taxonomy-driven faceted display, and automated translation and OpenURL resolvers will come into service and support of the scholar.

FUTURE OF LIBRARIES AND LIBRARIANS AND OTHER INFORMATION PROFESSIONALS

What must libraries do today to prepare for this emerging ecology of new technologies, generation, and economies? Can libraries reinvent their traditional strengths as the organization of information, metadata, technology and research, reference, and education?

Library 2.0 and the Information World

Arguably, the library and information professional world generally deals with a savvier audience of users relative to the general consumer demographic and tends to the digital divide issues of the more challenged user. Librarians can often inform users and train them in the newest technologies that can have an impact on their success as well as society as a whole. For those users who can quickly become comfortable using technologies such as wikis, RSS, instant messaging, news aggregators, and blogs, librarians can help them to leverage these in making a difference in reaching their goals and libraries' institutional or enterprise goals. For those libraries that block access to the newest applications, they are positioning their technological presence as one that is poor. This is not a good position to take as a bridge in the digital divide for their communities.

Library 2.0 is another conversation. This narrative is mainly around the concept of how to use the Web 2.0 opportunities in a library environment. It is an exciting concept and one which can start a conversation that creates the next generation of library Web sites, databases, online public access catalogs (OPACs), intranets, and portals in a way that allows the end user to thrive and survive (and libraries along with them). It is also a conversation about some of the human aspects of this emerging environment. The hope is that an era is beginning where the user experience for learning and research will finally top the technology.

Clearly, every one of the Web 2.0 technologies listed in this chapter could be useful in an enterprise, institutional research, or community environment, and these technologies could be driven or introduced by the library. The beauty of Web 2.0 and Library 2.0 is the level of integration and interoperability that is designed into the interface through portals or intranets. That is where the real power to enhance the user experience is. In order to take advantage of the concepts inherent in Library 2.0, it is imperative to not shy away from adding advanced functionality and features directly into the content. This would provide the context and workflow-oriented features that users will demand or are demanding already. The beachfront on this trend is seen in services like Second Life Library 2.0, Google Open Social, Google Open Handset Alliance (Android), the Open Content Alliance, and the MySpace SDK and Facebook F8 development platforms.

As predicted in a recent 2008 *Searcher* magazine article, "Reference is the place to watch for change and innovation in libraries. Indeed, all this 2.0 talk is all about the real nature of the customer relationship—in person *and* virtual. The IT and metadata types were dealing well with a fairly predictable future—one driven by the consumer space and [fairly] reaction-driven, one with standards and rules and not influenced by messy human behaviors .... It cannot be denied that traditional reference stats are down, though, this is not the case with our research requests, training activities, and one-on-one contact" with students at academic libraries and public library patrons (Abram, 2008: 43). In addition, Web site hits (and return Web visits/hits) to public library Web resources, not to mention their circulation statistics, are also on the rise, as are most academic and public libraries' gate counts (Abram, 2008).

"After more than 20 years of primarily working on the infrastructure of libraries—servers, Web sites, wireless, electronic content licensing, broadband, access, security, viruses, etc.—a real tipping point has been reached. In 2008, the real action in our world of libraries is moving from the back office to the front desk, from a technology-centric strategy to one where the real needs of clients must predominate. Aligning technology with user behaviors is no longer sufficient for success. Librarians need to understand and understand deeply the role of the library in end-users' lives, work, research, and play. This is critical to long-term success and failure is not an option" (Abram, 2008: 44).

Possible Future Scenarios for Reference Services to Gen M

What are the possible future scenarios for reference services that the Gen M population might see? "Will [libraries] offer a one-stop solution of computer, social, circulation, education, and research in the reference space? Can this goal for critical segments of library users, such as R&D staff or higher-education students, be attained? Can [libraries] elegantly blend the physical commons with the virtual commons?" (Abram, 2008: 45).

   This author believes that the future environment will be more like a mosaic or hybrid of services. "Don Beagle's (2006) book, *The Information Commons Guidebook*, offers a fine survey of the emerging opportunities with this strategy [or idea in mind. His book] seems to align very well with the [concept of] simplifying reference and research relationships and the alignment [of libraries with their] host institution's funding strategies and visions" (Abram, 2008: 45). E-learning, embedded librarians, and remote librarianship are a few of these emerging opportunities, briefly mentioned below.

   For instance, e-learning is truly the "major trend in the corporate and academic spaces. In this environment, learners have their major relationship with the learning space at the lesson level" (Abram, 2008: 45). Can libraries collaborate "with the e-learning developers and offer context-sensitive help in such courses? For this scenario to succeed, strategic relationships must be developed and, indeed, deep partnerships with the e-learning developers, department heads, and deans" (Abram, 2008: 45) must be formed.

   Regarding embedded public services librarians, this author believes it is imperative for these front-line instruction and reference librarians to have a seat at-the-table in their academic, public, school, or work environment. They can do this by strategically focusing on both long-term assignments aligned with the organization's major goals—especially those concerning information literacy—as well as being key professional team members on academic policy committees and learning and student experience task forces, contributing to the quality of system-wide decision making impacting learning initiatives (Abram, 2008).

Last but not least is the scenario concerning the remote librarian, connecting to users through digital devices and e-services. "This scenario depends on understanding the potential [for] personal devices—laptops, smart phones, PDAs—to dominate as *the* device[s]. Such emerging service technologies, such as microblogging, Twitter, and text messaging . . . offer great opportunities for [librarians and other educators] to be at the point of every user's need" (Abram, 2008: 46). The ideas and scenarios listed above provide suggestions for how libraries of all types may address the needs of Gen M members in the digital world that they will inhabit and help create.

CONCLUSION: TO BECOME A LIBRARIAN 2.0

All of the changes presented above cannot occur without some improvements in the capacity, competences, aptitudes, and attitudes of all library employees. Librarians have a once-in-a-generation opportunity to invent a new future. This Librarian 2.0 is the guru of the information age and, as such, Librarian 2.0 strives to understand the power and opportunities of Web 2.0 and Library 2.0 tools. They will strive to connect people and technology and information in context and not shy away from the nontraditional. They will teach users the skills they need and connect those users to relevant experts and communities. Libraries will house collections of e-resources and print that are seamlessly integrated, and are container and format agnostic. Librarians will be device independent to use and deliver the desired content to every type of device, even the latest tools of communication. Librarians will also work to develop targeted federated search, adopt the OpenURL standard, and encourage user-driven metadata, content, and commentary.

First and foremost, the Librarian 2.0 should understand the users at a deep level—not just as pointers and clickers—but also as end-users in terms of their goals and aspirations, workflows, and social and content needs. Librarian 2.0 needs to be where the user is, when the user is there. This is an immersion environment to which librarians are eminently qualified to contribute. Aspects of librarian-influenced e-learning and distance education as implemented by institutions and communities should allow contributions to the preparation of our users to acquire and improve their skills and competencies.

It is essential that librarians start preparing to become Librarian 2.0 now. The Web 2.0 movement is laying the groundwork for exponential business growth and another major shift in the way users live, learn, work, and play. Librarians have the ability, insight, and knowledge to influence the creation of this new dynamic—and guarantee the future of the profession. To prepare the next generation, the members of Gen M, for this new world so that they can be successful in it, librarians must start now.

REFERENCES

Abram, Stephen. 2008. "Evolution to Revolution to Chaos? Reference in Transition." *Searcher: The Magazine for Database Professionals* 16, no.8 (September): 42–48.

Batermadjian, Maggie. "Web 2.0 + Second Life." Masters of Media blog (September 22, 2008). Available: http://mastersofmedia.hum.uva.nl/2008/09/22/web-20second-life/ (accessed October 23, 2008).

Beagle, Donald Robert. 2006. *Information Commons Guidebook*. New York: Neal-Schuman.

Best, David. 2006. "Web 2.0 Next Big Thing or Next Big Internet Bubble?" Lecture Web Information Systems. Technische Universiteit Eindhoven (January 11). Available: http://page.mi.fu-berlin.de/~best/uni/WIS/Web2.pdf (accessed October 28, 2008).

"The Croquet Consortium." Durham: Duke University Office of Information Technology (December 16, 2007). Available: opencroquet.org/index.php/Main_Page (accessed August 15, 2008).

Information Studies Writing Team. "Information Studies, Kindergarten to Grade 12: Curriculum for Schools and School Library Information Centres." Ontario School Library Association (May 1998). Available: www.accessola.com/action/positions/info_studies/html/intro.html (accessed August 13, 2008).

Kaufman, Peter. 2007. "Online Digital Video—Educational Developments and Opportunities." Presentation at the international JISC Digitisation Conference, Cardiff, Wales (July 20). Available: www.jisc.ac.uk/media/documents/programmes/digitisation/jiscdigicon07p12kaufman.ppt#259,1,Slide%201 (accessed August 14, 2008).

McLuhan, Marshall. 1964. *Understanding Media: The Extensions of Man*. Cambridge, MA: MIT Press.

Wikipedia. "Web 2.0." (November 14, 2008a). Available: http://en.wikipedia.
org/wiki/Web_2.0 (accessed November 15, 2008).
Wikipedia. "Word Cloud" (November 7, 2008b). Available: http://en.wikipedia.
org/wiki/Word_cloud (accessed August 12, 2008).
Wolfe, Tom. 2004. "McLuhan's New World." *Wilson Quarterly* 28, no. 2: 18–25.

SELECTED RECOMMENDED READINGS

Abram, Stephen. 2006. "Millennials: Deal with Them." *Texas Library Journal* 82,
no. 3: 100–103.
Abram, Stephen, and Judy Luther. 2004. "Born with the Chip." *Library Journal* 129,
no. 8 (May 1): 34–37. Available: www.libraryjournal.com/article/CA411572.
html (accessed August 8, 2008).
"Creating and Connecting//Research and Guidelines on Online Social—and
Educational—Networking." Alexandria, VA: National School Boards Asso-
ciation. Available: www.nsba.org/site/docs/41400/41340.pdf (accessed
August 20, 2008).
De Rosa, Cathy, Joanne Cantrell, Diane Cellentani, Janet Hawk, Lillie Jenkins, and
Alane Wilson. 2005. *Perceptions of Libraries and Information Resources (2005):
A Report to the OCLC Membership.* Dublin, OH: Online Computer Library
Center (December). Available: www.oclc.org/reports/2005perceptions.htm
(accessed November 11, 2008).
De Rosa, Cathy, Joanne Cantrell, Janet Hawk, and Alane Wilson. 2006. *College
Students' Perceptions of Libraries and Information Resources.* Dublin, OH: Online
Computer Library Center (May). Available: www.oclc.org/reports/percep-
tionscollege.htm (accessed November 11, 2008).
Federman, Mark. 2007. "Why Johnny and Janey Can't Read, and Why Mr. and
Ms. Smith Can't Teach: The Challenge of Multiple Media Literacies in a
Tumultuous Time." Paper presented at the annual meeting of the Calgary
City Teachers' Convention Association, Calgary, Alberta, Canada (February
14–15). Available: http://individual.utoronto.ca/markfederman/Why-
JohnnyandJaneyCantRead.pdf#search=%22Mark%20Federman%2C%20W
hy%20Johnny%20and%20Janey%20Can%E2%80%99t%20Read%20and%20
%22 (accessed October 10, 2008).
Johnson, Steven. 2005. *Everything Bad Is Good for You: How Today's Popular Culture
Is Actually Making Us Smarter.* New York: Riverhead Books.
Lenhart, Amanda, and Mary Madden. 2007. "Teens, Privacy and Online Social
Networks: How Teens Manage Their Online Identities and Personal Informa-
tion in the Age of MySpace." Washington, DC: Pew Internet and American
Life Project (April 18). Available: www.pewinternet.org/pdfs/PIP_Teens_
Privacy_SNS_Report_Final.pdf (accessed August 23, 2008).
Levitt, Steven D., and Stephen J. Dubner. 2005. *Freakonomics: A Rogue Economist
Explores the Hidden Side of Everything.* New York: William Morrow.
Oblinger, Diana. 2003. "Boomers, Gen-Xers, and Millennials: Understanding the
'New Students.'" *EDUCAUSE Review* 38, no. 4 (July/August): 36–40, 42, 44–

45. Available: www.educause.edu/ir/library/pdf/ERM0342.pdf#search=
percent22oblinger percent22 (accessed August 10, 2008).

Oblinger, Diana, and James Oblinger, eds. 2005. *Educating the Net Generation.*
Boulder, CO: EDUCAUSE. Available: www.educause.edu/educatingthenet-
gen/ (accessed August 11, 2008).

Prensky, Marc. 2001. "Digital Natives, Digital Immigrants." *On the Horizon* 9,
no. 5 (October): 1–6. Available: www.marcprensky.com/writing/Pren-
sky%20-%20Digital%20Natives,%20Digital%20Immigrants%20-%20Part1.
pdf (accessed August 12, 2008).

Prensky, Marc. 2006. "Listen to the Natives." *Educational Leadership* 63, no.4
(December/January): 8–13.

Sweeney, Richard. 2006. "Millennial Behaviors & Demographics." Newark, NJ:
New Jersey Institute of Technology (December 22). Available: http://library1.
njit.edu/staff-folders/sweeney/Millennials/Article-Millennial-Behaviors.
doc (accessed August 18, 2008).

Thierer, Adam. "Social Networking and Age Verification: Many Hard Questions; No Easy Solutions." Washington, DC: The Progress and Freedom
Foundation (March 2007). Available: www.pff.org/issues-pubs/pops/
pop14.5ageverification.pdf (accessed August 25, 2008).

SELECTED RECOMMENDED RESOURCES

"Classroom 2.0." Available: www.classroom20.com (accessed August 28, 2008).

"Library 2.0." Available: http://library20.ning.com/ (accessed August 23,
2008).

"Library 2.0 Services to Teens—A Listing." (February 15, 2006). Available: www.
yalibrarian.com/wordpress/2006/02/library-20-services-to-teens-a-listing/
(accessed August 23, 2008).

"Library 2.0 Services to Teens—Best Practices." Available: www.libsuccess.
org/index.php?title=Library_2.0_Best_Practices_to_Teens (accessed August
25, 2008).

"Online Social Networks." Chicago: American Library Association (April 17,
2008). Available: http://www.ala.org/ala/aboutala/offices/oif/ifissues/
onlinesocialnetworks.cfm (accessed August 25, 2008).

SirsiDynix. "SchoolRooms: A New Learning Portal for the K–12 Community."
(November 2006). Available: www.schoolrooms.net/index.php (accessed
October 16, 2008).

"Social Networking: A Guide for Teens." Chicago: Young Adult Library Services
Association. Available: www.ala.org/ala/mgrps/divs/yalsa/profdev/
teen_sn_brochure.pdf (accessed August 25, 2008).

"Teens and Social Networking in School and Public Libraries Toolkit." Chicago:
Young Adult Library Services Association (January 2008). Available: www.
ala.org/ala/mgrps/divs/yalsa/profdev/SocialNetworkingToolkit_Jan08.
pdf (accessed August 25, 2008).

"Ypulse." Available: www.ypulse.com/ (accessed August 15, 2008).

PART III:

Pedagogy—Current and Imagined

Chapter 13

Gen M(obile): Learning Applications for Mobile Technology in Higher Education

Boris Vilic

Robert J. Lackie

INTRODUCTION

As Gen M's insatiable demand for technology resources continues to increase, many institutions of higher education have introduced mobile learning into their "brick and click" classrooms as ways of providing students with ubiquitous access to education. Mobile learning (or m-learning) is a new learning modality where access to educational content is facilitated by means of mobile devices, such as cell phones, MP3 players, and PDAs, thus effectively enabling students to access learning materials anytime, anywhere, and any while (Walker, 2006).

Even though early m-learning applications emerged in the 1970s, it was not until the technological advances of the twenty-first century occurred that we witnessed a proliferation of relatively inexpensive mobile technologies move into the classroom (Sharples, 2007; Sharples, Taylor, and Vavoula, 2007). The advent of powerful pocket-sized devices, such as personal digital assistants (PDAs) and smart phones, enabled innovative educators to utilize these emerging technological tools to deliver interactive educational content that was no longer constrained by a learner's ability to access a physical classroom or Internet connection.

Thus, a range of learning applications utilizing mobile devices began to emerge in the late 1990s. For example, the much-touted Duke University project, which employed iPods to deliver educational content to students, sought to provide incoming students with a means of recording (and retrieving) course content (Belanger, 2005). Likewise, Rider University's Westminster Choir College made available podcasts that feature the College's prominent faculty and guest speakers (Westminster, 2007). And, Northern Alberta Institute of Technology developed m-learning content for PDAs that included full chapter reviews, streaming video, quizzes, glossary of terms, and interactive exercises and games to help increase learning outcomes in an introductory accounting course (mLearning, 2002). These examples and others, which will be further explored in this chapter, illustrate how m-learning can be used to augment and/or supplement classroom learning, games, and competition in learning, distance learning, and laboratory and field trip learning.

IT IS THE DAWNING OF THE AGE OF . . . MOBILE LEARNING

In the early 1970s, Xerox's research labs introduced the harbinger of mobile technology—the Dynabook—whose purpose was to provide users with a book-like, interactive personal computer. At the time, the concept of what is now considered a "laptop" was truly revolutionary. Inspired by the work of his colleagues on teaching children how to use computers, Xerox scientist Alan Kay, who invented the Dynabook, resolved to provide a learning tool for children, stating that "the potential of computers as an aid to learning was, in itself, a validation of them" (Kay, accessed 2008, under "The Music of Ideas"). Thus, by providing students with text, visual animation, and audio capabilities in an easy-to-carry (or book-like) device, Kay and Xerox set the stage for the subsequent introduction of mobile technologies.

The validation of Kay's vision of computers as a viable learning tool became apparent with the introduction of Milton Bradley's Simon. This electronic (and mobile!) device, designed to foster rhythm and memorization skills, was first unveiled in New York's Studio 54 in 1978 and quickly became the symbol of the 1980s pop culture. Adored by children and adults alike, the game's red, blue, green, and yellow buttons introduced the concept of rudimentary m-learning to millions of households. Following the success of Simon and its smaller version, Pocket Simon, released in the 1980s, many other mobile gaming devices began to consume the market, consequently becoming an integral part of Gen M's childhood experiences.

In the 1990s and early 2000s, a widespread proliferation of mobile devices that could carry on tasks once only associated with personal computers was witnessed (Weinstein, 2006). As the popularity of these devices—called personal digital assistants or PDAs—increased (and their prices and sizes decreased), innovative educators began to utilize these devices to provide students with access to myriad educational software applications. These included the following: (a) *entertainment software* used to deliver games and simulations; (b) *reference software* such as encyclopedias and reference books; (c) *productivity software* used for word processing, spreadsheets, databases, Web browsing, and e-mail; and (d) *specialty software* for video and audio editing, presentation graphics, drawing and painting, and project management, among others (Williams and Sawyer, 2005).

Recently, however, smart phones—devices that merge the functionality of cell phones, music players, and PDAs—quickly became the mobile devices of choice as they enabled users to carry only one, rather than many, devices. The introduction of Apple's iPhone in 2007 demonstrated the voracious demand for such mobile technology; with more than half a million units sold during opening weekend alone, buyers were attracted to the iPhone's ability to access e-mail, text, photos, music, videos, calendar, Internet and phone service, and more (Cable News Network, 2007). Using smart phones for applications other than telephony has become relatively commonplace as 69 million Americans utilize smart phones for Web browsing, 66 million for playing games, 20 million for watching TV or video clips, and 7 million for listening to the radio (Limbo, 2008). The unprecedented adoption of such mobile devices, the International Data Corporation predicts, is likely to continue to increase in the foreseeable future; shipments of devices "will grow from 80.9 million in 2006 to 304.4 million in 2011" (IDC, 2007, under "Abstract"). It is also important to note that the use of mobile applications, such as mobile browsing, does not seem to be limited to high-income populations: The Nielsen Company found that "24 percent of all mobile Internet users have household incomes of $100,000 or more, [and that] approximately the same portion of mobile Internet users have a household income of under $50,000 (26 percent)" (Covey, 2008: 5).

MOBILE LEARNING AND THE HIGHER EDUCATION LANDSCAPE

The technological advances that resulted in powerful mobile devices (e.g., palmtops, PDAs, and smart phones) paved a path for educators to provide students with ubiquitous educational content (Motiwalla, 2007), thus introducing the concept of m-learning to the higher education landscape. At the same time, students entering the higher education landscape exhibited an increasing demand for technical resources, with m-learning and its related tools and technologies being recognized as useful by colleges and universities and becoming quickly and widely embraced by the Gen M community (Fox, 2007; Jacob and Issac, 2007; Kurubacak, 2007; Kvavik, Caruso, and Morgan, 2004; Roberts, 2005). These Gen M students were found to "like to receive information quickly and have little tolerance for delays; parallel process and multitask . . . function best when connected to a network; like to receive instant gratification and frequent rewards; and prefer games to serious work" (Kvavik, Caruso, and Morgan, 2004: 29).

Furthermore, the digital divide (a concept describing the unequal access to and skills in using technology) among our higher education student population has begun to disappear. In a recent 2007 study involving 27,846 students from 103 higher education institutions, EDUCAUSE found that virtually all student respondents (98.4 percent) possessed a personal computer and that a majority of these students (61 percent) thought technology could improve their learning outcomes (Caruso and Salaway, 2007: 1). Students from 40 higher education institutions who took part in all three (2005–2007) surveys also became more mobile with "laptop ownership increasing from 52.8 percent in 2005 to 75.8 percent in 2007" and smart phone usage expanding "from 7.8 percent in 2006 to 10.1 percent in 2007" (Salaway et al., 2007: 10). In addition, the Pew Internet and American Life Project found that American young adults would have an easier time giving up Internet, television, and e-mail than their cell phones (Horrigan, 2008).

However, these increases in students' mastery of technology and of their expectation to use technology in the classroom are not the only reasons why institutions began to introduce m-learning to their curricula.

They also found that m-learning can have a positive impact on their efforts to recruit students. Thus, several institutions have utilized m-learning to differentiate themselves among their peer institutions, whether by providing free iPods or PDAs to entering freshmen, or by podcasting lectures and special events for the general public (Van Eck, 2007).

Mobile Learning in the Classroom

Since mobile learning is becoming increasingly common in higher education, it is important to note that m-learning unlike distance learning is not a disparate teaching modality. It can be used to supplement and enhance the teaching and learning processes in the traditional and online classrooms.

Elements of the learning environment that can be effectively presented (and accessed) by means of m-learning technologies include textual content, communication tools, and multimedia content. **Textual content** such as course syllabi, written lectures, book reviews, and chapter overviews can be downloaded on a mobile device to give students access to such material regardless of their ability to access a computer. This textual content can also be dynamic (when the mobile device is used to access blogs, RSS feeds, and wikis) and searchable (when the mobile device is used to provide access to encyclopedias and reference books). **Communication tools,** such as e-mail and online discussion boards, can also be accessed through mobile devices, thus giving students an unprecedented ability to engage in the learning process with their peers and with the instructor regardless of their ability to access a computer. **Multimedia content** can be used to make learning fun and/or engaging through electronic learning games, flash cards, video clips, podcasts, etc. It can also provide students with access to complex learning simulations, for example, enabling a nursing student to review, on a mobile learning device, how to assess a patient.

All of these elements of the learning environment, arguably, merely extend the course management system's capabilities (e.g., Blackboard) when Internet connectivity and access to a computer are not readily available (e.g., while waiting at the airport, while walking a dog, etc.). However, m-learning can also surpass the features of a traditional course management system. For example, mobile devices can be used to provide students with a database interface for use in a laboratory or fieldwork setting; the data collected can then be integrated with data collected by other students in a central database. Furthermore, m-learning can capitalize on the personal information management features of mobile devices (e.g., to-do lists, calendar, or contact lists) to guide students in developing good learning habits.

In addition, because of the technical capabilities of mobile devices, the educational content developed for use on them can also be "'personalized' [in addition to being] 'bite-sized,' and 'portable'" (Traxler, 2007: 4). For example, m-learning can be used to enable instructors to record student interaction with educational content and subsequently to assess student performance, utilizing that data to provide individualized content designed for the individual student (Virvou and Alepsis, 2005).

Thus, mobile learning applications could be differentiated by their intent (Goh and Kinshuk, 2006):

- **Games and Competition in Learning:** electronic flash cards or more complex learning games can help students memorize course concepts in an environment to which they are accustomed (given that most Gen M students grew up with electronic games).
- **Classroom Learning:** mobile devices can be utilized to provide a quizzing mechanism in class, enabling the instructor to instantly poll students. Furthermore, mobile devices can be used as reference tools (rather than carrying several books to the classroom).
- **Laboratory and Field Trip Learning:** students can utilize mobile devices to gather and analyze data in a field or laboratory setting.
- **Distance Learning:** mobile devices can provide anytime, anywhere, any while access to the course management system (CMS) and can also be utilized to supplement the CMS courses (for example, through audio study guides and learning games).

Mobile Learning Examples in Higher Education

Myriad institutions within the higher education landscape have successfully and creatively introduced m-learning initiatives to supplement and enhance the teaching and learning process, in brick and click classrooms alike. The following colleges and universities represent institutions that have addressed and achieved, to some degree, mobile learning for their students. These higher education examples demonstrate the ability of m-learning to deliver 'un-tethered' (i.e., not reliant on one's ability to access the Internet) and ubiquitous educational resources, thus providing their students and faculty with the access they need and demand to the learning environment—anytime, anywhere, and any while:

Baruch College of the City University of New York, through its Air Baruch program, enables students to "check the availability of loaner laptops and study rooms [at the library], view course announcements, connect with faculty and fellow students, and receive timely alerts from the university . . ." (AllBusiness, 2006: 2). The University, an early adopter of campus-integrated cell phone use for its constituents, thus capitalized on the widespread use of cell phones among its students (and others) to help foster a sense of connection to the University, as well as provide its many commuters and adjunct faculty with ubiquitous access to campus resources (Fox, 2007).

Baylor University's Crouch Fine Arts Library introduced Audio Reserves To Go to give students access to podcasts of music assignments outside of the physical library space. By renting iPods to students, the library has found that students utilized non-learning spaces (such as walking to and from class) for learning. The library also utilizes iPod's *Notes* feature to equip its iPods with the listing of all assignments in all music courses offered in a semester; thus giving students unprecedented access to learning materials (Stephens, 2005).

Duke University was among higher education pioneers to utilize m-learning to attract incoming students. Its much-touted iPod project sought to enable students to record, store, and retrieve course content (Belanger, 2005). However, students themselves expanded the original intent of the program and "collected and created primary source materials of cultural settings, conducted interviews of experts, and produced podcasts and audioblogs that were linked and downloadable from course Web sites" (Boettcher, 2005, under "Pilot to Watch: Duke").

Duquesne University's Learning-on-the-Go project connects the University's course management system (CMS), Blackboard, to a student's PDA. The program was originally created to help members of our military serving on active duty in Iraq and Afghanistan enroll and actively participate in a degree program (Zlatos, 2005). By synchronizing their mobile devices with computers, students are able to download the CMS content (e.g., course content, discussion areas, e-mail) to their PDAs and upload all of their work (e.g., replies to discussion messages, e-mail messages, etc.) to the CMS (Boettcher, 2005; Hodes, 2007).

Georgia College and State University's iVillage is an iPod-based mobile learning application, created in the fall 2005 semester, which combines the iPods with the University's course management system to create a virtual-equivalent to a learning community (GCSU, 2006a). For example, the University used iPods in math classes to show students how a graph is created incrementally in an animated environment, rather than having students only refer to a static version of a completely created graph (GCSU, 2006b). In addition, students at GCSU can easily download "films to their video-capable iPods for a history class, and a psychology [professor's] podcasts [of] the week's most frequently asked questions" (Fox, 2007: 13).

Johns Hopkins University is developing a mobility framework to extend personalized campus portal information (such as news, information, and tools) to students for use on cell phones, smart phones, and PDAs. Recognizing that mobile devices have become "a way of life for many of [its] students, faculty and administrators," the University considers this project as a means to adapting to "sociological and technological changes occurring in the real world" (Schaffhauser, 2008, under "Johns Hopkins").

Marist College's study abroad students have used iPods since late 2005 to interview local residents in the countries of study about topics assigned by their faculty. Students then post the podcasts of their interviews to a course management system—thus enabling their peers, who are concurrently pursing study abroad in disparate countries, to compare how different cultures respond to a topic (Franklin, 2005).

Rider University's Westminster Choir College created Westminster-to-Go in 2006, a collection of podcasts (available to the general public) that feature Rider University's prominent faculty and guest speakers (e.g., famous composers). Each podcast provides current students with a unique opportunity to hear a leading expert's commentary, while also advertising the College's acclaimed programs to prospective students and the interested general public (Westminster, 2007).

Seneca College and the **Northern Alberta Institute of Technology** (NAIT), in collaboration with publishing and technology companies, deployed (in 2002!) a mobile learning game for accounting students: Tetraccounting. The PDA-based game mimics the game of Tetris and allows students to learn to differentiate between "debits" and "credits" in a fun environment (mLearning, 2002).

Robert Morris University utilizes PDAs to enable its nursing students to access drug information, disease diagnoses, medical definitions, etc. in clinical and classroom settings. By utilizing their mobile devices, students no longer have to carry several large books to their clinical assignments (RMU, accessed 2008).

Southeastern Louisiana University's Sims Memorial Library has allowed students since 2005 to text a librarian by using their cell phones, in addition to providing telephone, e-mail, and chat access to the library. The Library encourages students to utilize the texting service "for asking quick, simple questions that can be answered in short responses (160 characters or less)" (Sims, 2008, under "When Should You Use the Service?").

University of Pittsburgh utilizes iQuiz, a quizzing engine developed by Apple for its popular iPods. For example, Rimanakuna, a vocabulary quiz generator developed by a graduate student in the University's Linguistics Department, provides technologically–driven "flash cards" to help students memorize complex linguistic concepts by explaining word paradigms and conjugation rules (Littell, accessed 2008).

University of West Florida has created Pocket Campus, or a PDA-version of a correspondence course. Through Pocket Campus, students can access video lectures, quizzes, simulations, and so on, and they can complete the entire course without ever accessing the Internet (UWF, accessed 2008).

Wake Forest University's PocketClassroom utilizes PocketPCs and the University's wireless network to enable "students to send private messages to their professor . . . and [to let] the professor conduct impromptu quizzes" during class (Mansell, 2002, under "WFU Uses Hand-held"). Beginning in 2001, the WFU faculty members were thus able to gauge instantaneously whether the students were actively participating in the class and whether they comprehended the material. In addition, their MobileU pilot program, rolled out in 2005, provided more smart phone services "focusing on mobile messaging, mobile access to information such as calendars, campus announcements, and real-time location of the campus shuttle bus . . . [and their library] created a MobileU-friendly version of its Web site using a mobile style sheet . . ." (Fox, 2007: 12).

MOBILE LEARNING FUTURE

Because of computer-games, our grandchildren are now growing up with an indelible addiction to computers. For better or for worse, in sickness or in health, till death do us part, humans and computers are now joined together more durably than husbands and wives. (Dyson, 2008, under "The Domestication of Biotechnology")

As technological advances continue to permeate every fabric of our lives, as Dyson suggests above, and as mobile devices become increasingly

ubiquitous, it is important for institutions of higher education to capitalize on students' expectations of technologically supported learning to
introduce mobile learning applications that add value to the teaching-
learning process. This "monumental frontier" presents educators with an
opportunity "to take advantage of the trails being blazed by consumer
markets" (Fox, 2007: 16).

It is not far fetched to imagine a world where computer monitors are replaced with head mounted displays that resemble ordinary
glasses and produce a "visual effect [equivalent] to watching a 62-inch
screen" and with the sound system so advanced that it results in "the
overall illusion of . . . a complete high-end home theater except that
it weighs less than four ounces and can be held in the palm of your
hand" ("Eyeball-to-Screen," 1999: 1). Or, a world where smart watches
provide access to "global positioning system (GPS) receivers, Internet
connections, Bluetooth attachments, and low-resolution cameras," and
more (Widhalm, 2007: B1), replacing smart phones and other mobile
devices. After all, to imagine such a world, one only has to review the
latest headlines in the news or browse the hi-tech gadget section of one's
favorite online store.

It may be harder, though, to imagine a world where body implants
replace mobile devices, or a world where keyboards become a thing of the
past because of body implants that are able to detect finger movements
on a virtual keyboard that is only visible to the person wearing a digital
contact lens. Or, a world where the interaction between a professor and
a student is so individualized that it meets the needs of every student
regardless of the class size; and a world where faculty are able to "technologically" detect the content areas that their students are struggling
with—whether by detecting a change in a student's typing pattern, time
spent on reviewing the material, or even the amount of perspiration
while listening to a lecture—and are consequently able to automatically
personalize and individualize the learning experience for each student.
It may be as hard to imagine such as world as it was to imagine flying
to the moon and back at the beginning of the last century!

However, rather than waiting for further technological advances to
occur, many institutions of higher education, as evident by the mobile
learning applications described in this chapter, have already begun to
embrace the potential that mobile technology brings. These institutions
recognized that m-learning can indeed improve our processes, whether
outside the classroom by providing students with access to room sched-
ules, laptop rentals, etc., or inside by providing students with ubiquitous
access to course materials, or tools for improved data gathering. Unlike

distance learning, m-learning is not a new learning modality, but rather a means of supplementing instruction with the potential of increasing the learning outcomes of students—something all educators strive toward in the higher education arena.

If the examples mentioned in this chapter are uninspiring, consider talking to third-graders. Their ideas on how to utilize mobile learning technology can be surprising, much like Shea O'Gorman (a third-grader who sent a letter to Apple's CEO Steve Jobs with suggestions on how to improve the iPod) managed to surprise Apple—enough so to receive a cease-and-desist letter from Apple's general counsel for fear that her ideas, if implemented, could enable her to claim intellectual property rights against the company (Marsal, 2006). One has to remember, after all, that Shea and her friends will enter the halls of higher education in less than a decade and all involved should be prepared for them. Educators need to emulate the multitude of colleges and universities discussed earlier that have successfully and creatively introduced m-learning initiatives to supplement and enhance the teaching and learning process. However, fortunately for all in higher education, no one is alone in the quest to implement and improve m-learning initiatives.

In a recent *USA Today* article, the author acknowledges that many companies, organizations, and institutions are scrambling to vastly advance their m-learning technology and applications. Enterprising Web search providers such as Google, MSN, and Yahoo! certainly see the "mobile Web [as] an advertising gold mine just waiting to happen. [In fact,] the fledgling mobile search industry generated about $700 million in ad revenue in 2007, JupiterResearch estimates. By 2012, revenue is expected to hit $2.2 billion and keep rising" (Cauley, 2008: B2). *USA Today* also mentions that Yahoo!'s mobile search solution might be its OneSearch with Voice system, which will combine Web search with its much-improved voice recognition technology. Likewise, Google, not to be outdone by other search and ad revenue leaders, has implemented its own open wireless operating system, called Android. Both search engines' mobile solutions are expected to be available to the general mobile community in 2009.

CONCLUSION

Educators and administrators can certainly continue to learn from Google's, Yahoo!'s, and many other companies' and universities' successful mobile technology and m-learning efforts. Perhaps, though, those interested in m-learning initiatives should also listen to ideas from third-graders like Shea O'Gorman, from military personnel worldwide taking m-learning courses, and from the ever-increasing number of mobile technology users, many of whom are Gen M students. Neil Howe and William Strauss, infamous for several well-known studies on gauging and interpreting trends concerning American generations, including Gen M , outline a dynamic, hopeful vision for the future of and impact of this particular community:

> Indeed, [Gen M(illennials)] have a solid chance to become America's next great generation, as celebrated for their collective deeds a hundred years from now as the generation of John Kennedy, Ronald Reagan, Joe DiMaggio, and Jimmy Stewart is celebrated today, . . . [introducing] itself to the nation and [pushing] the nation into a new era. (Howe and Strauss, 2000: 5)

Howe and Strauss do paint a very positive picture for Gen M's future, arguing that this generation is poised for a bright future, being fairly ambitious, optimistic, team-oriented, and confident in their approach to life, not to mention, mobile. Even if one is a bit skeptical about some of the predictions outlined in this chapter, consider the fact that mobile technology has already become an integral part of Gen M students' lives (Salaway et al., 2007). These learning-on-the-go students are already here, with many more planning on gracing these "brick and click" halls. Is higher education ready to connect with Gen M(obile) students and give them what they want—easy access to education anytime, anywhere, and any while?

REFERENCES

AllBusiness. "Baruch College and Rave Wireless, Inc. Put the Campus on Mobile Phones." Business Wire (August 28, 2006): 1–4. Available: www.allbusiness.com/media-telecommunications/5352344-1.html (accessed July 18, 2008).

Belanger, Yvonne. "Duke University iPod First Year Experience Final Evaluation Report: Summary." Duke University Center for Instructional Technology (June 2005). Available: http://cit.duke.edu/pdf/reports/ipod_initiative_04_05.pdf (accessed July 29, 2008).

Boettcher, Judith V. 2005. "Watch These Pilots." Campus Technology (September/October). Available: http://campustechnology.com/articles/40510/ (accessed July 20, 2008).

Cable News Network. "iPhone Sales Said to Hit Half-million." CNNMoney.com (July 2, 2007). Available: http://money.cnn.com/2007/07/02/technology/iphone_sales/index.htm (accessed July 10, 2008).

Caruso, Judith Borreson, and Gail Salaway. "ECAR Roadmap: The ECAR Study of Undergraduate Students and Information Technology, 2007." Boulder, CO: EDUCAUSE Center for Applied Research (September 2007). Available: www2.nau.edu/~provo-p/pacac/subcommittees/learning_spaces/07students_IT_road_map.pdf (accessed August 2, 2008).

Cauley, Leslie. 2008. "Are Google, Yahoo the Next Dinosaurs?: Many on the Hunt for a Way to Cash in on Wireless Search." *USA Today* (June 9): B1-2.

Covey, Nic. "Critical Mass: The Worldwide State of the Mobile Web." The Nielsen Company (July 2008). Available: www.nielsenmobile.com/documents/CriticalMass.pdf (accessed July 17, 2008).

Dyson, Freeman. 2008. "Freeman Dyson's Four Heresies." *U.S. 1: Princeton's Business and Entertainment Newspaper* (June 18). Available: www.princetoninfo.com/index.php?option=com_us1more&Itemid=6&key=06-16-2008%20Dyson (accessed August 7, 2008).

"Eyeball-to-Screen." 1999. *The (Oklahoma City) Journal Record* (December 3): 1.

Fox, Megan K. 2007. "The Mobile Age." In *Information Tomorrow: Reflections on Technology and the Future of Public and Academic Libraries* (pp. 3–18), edited by Rachel Singer Gordon. Medford, NJ: Information Today.

Franklin, Meg. "Marist Abroad Program: Unit 1 Language and History." Marist College (December 30, 2005). Available: www.marist.edu/international/unit1.html (accessed August 3, 2008).

GCSU. " iPilots." Georgia College and State University (2006b). Available: http://ipod.gcsu.edu/iPilots/index.html (accessed August 4, 2008).

GCSU. "Our iPod Story." Georgia College and State University (2006a). Available: http://ipod.gcsu.edu/GCSU%20iPod%20Story/index.html (accessed August 4, 2008).

Goh, Tiong, and Kinshuk. 2006. "Getting Ready For Mobile Learning—Adaptation Perspective." *Journal of Educational Multimedia and Hypermedia* 15, no. 2: 175–198. (Note that Kinshuk is the only name provided on all of Kinshuk's articles and book chapters; he does not ever provide a first name or initial for any publications, but sometimes provides Dr. Kinshuk).

Hodes, Benjamin. "Learning-on-the-Go: Anytime, Anywhere Access to Course and Study Materials." Sloan-C (September 23, 2007). Available: http://sloan-consortium.org/node/339 (accessed August 4, 2008).

Horrigan, John. "Pew Internet Project Data Memo: Mobile Access to Data and Information." Washington, DC: Pew Internet and American Life Project (March 2008). Available: http://pewinternet.org/pdfs/PIP_Mobile.Data.Access.pdf (accessed July 17, 2008).

Howe, Neil, and William Strauss. 2000. *Millennials Rising: The Next Great Generation*. New York: Vintage Books.

IDC. "Handheld Device Vendors Benefit from Dell's Departure, But Overall Market Still in Decline, Says IDC." International Data Corporation (August 8, 2007). Available: www.idc.com/getdoc.jsp?containerId=prUS20815207 (accessed July 11, 2008).

Jacob, Seibu Mary, and Biju Issac. 2007. "Mobile Learning Culture and Effects in Higher Education." *IEEE Multidisciplinary Engineering Education Magazine* 2, no. 2 (June): 19–21. Available: www.ewh.ieee.org/soc/e/sac/meem/public/old_issue/vol02iss02/MEEM020204.pdf (accessed July 23, 2008).

Kay, Alan C. "The Dynabook Revisited: A Conversation with Alan Kay." The Book and the Computer. Available: www.squeakland.org/resources/articles/article.jsp?id=1007 (accessed August 1, 2008).

Kurubacak, Gulsun. 2007. "Identify Research Priorities and Needs for Mobile Learning Technologies in Open and Distance Education: A Delphi Study." *International Journal of Teaching and Learning in Higher Education* 19, no 3. Available: www.eric.ed.gov/ERICDocs/data/ericdocs2sql/content_storage_01/0000019b/80/28/06/c0.pdf (accessed August 30, 2008).

Kvavik, Robert B., Judith B. Caruso, and Glenda Morgan. 2004. "ECAR Study of Students and Information Technology, 2004: Convenience, Connection, and Control." Research Study Volume 5. Boulder, CO: EDUCAUSE Center for Applied Research. Available: http://net.educause.edu/ir/library/pdf/ers0405/rs/ers0405w.pdf (accessed August 2, 2008).

Limbo, Inc. "Mobil Advertising Report: First Quarter 2008." Mobile Marketing Association: Global (March 2008). Available: http://mmaglobal.com/Limbo_Mobile_Advertising_Report_Q1_2008.pdf (accessed August 1, 2008).

Littell, Patrick. "Rimanakuna: A Vocabulary Quiz Generator for iQuiz." University of Pittsburgh, Linguistics Department. Available: http://littell.nfshost.com/cgi-bin/index.cgi?d=rimanakuna (accessed August 6, 2008).

Mansell, Sarah S. "WFU Uses Hand-held Technology to Enhance Class Participation." *Wake Forest University News Service* (July 17, 2002). Available: www.wfu.edu/wfunews/2002/071702.html (accessed July 7, 2008).

Marsal, Katie. "Apple Calls Meeting After Making Little Girl Cry." AppleInsider News and Analysis (April 14, 2006). Available: www.appleinsider.com/print.php?id=1672 (accessed August 7, 2008).

mLearning Consortium. "mContent Objects: Why mLearning?" McGraw-Hill Ryerson (2002). Available: www.mcgrawhill.ca/college/mlearning/ (accessed August 5, 2008).

Motiwalla, Luvai F. 2007. "Mobile Learning: A Framework and Evaluation." *Computers & Education* 49, no. 3 (November): 581–596.

RMU. "Nursing PDAs: Help and Support." Robert Morris University. Available: www.rmu.edu/OnTheMove/findoutmore.open_page?iPage=66346 (accessed August 2, 2008).

Roberts, Gregory R. 2005. "Technology and Learning Expectations of the Net Generation." In *Educating the Net Generation* (pp. 3.1–3.7), edited by Diana G. Oblinger and James L. Oblinger. Boulder, CO: EDUCAUSE. Available: http://net.educause.edu/ir/library/pdf/pub7101c.pdf (accessed July 16, 2008).

Salaway, Gail, Judith Borreson Caruso, Mark R. Nelson, and Chris Dede. "ECAR Study of Undergraduate Students and Information Technology, 2007." Research Study Volume 6. Boulder, CO: EDUCAUSE Center for Applied Research (2007). Available: http://net.educause.edu/ir/library/pdf/ers0706/rs/ers0706w.pdf (accessed August 4, 2008).

Schaffhauser, Dian. 2008. "John Hopkins Goes Mobile on uPortal." *Campus Tech-*

nology (April 23). Available: http://campustechnology.com/articles/61188/ (accessed August 4, 2008).

Sharples, Mike. 2007. "A Short History of Mobile Learning and Some Issues to Consider." Paper presented at the annual meeting of the mLearn International Conference on Mobile Learning: Doctoral Consortium, Melbourne, Australia (October 16). Available: www.slideshare.net//of-mobile-learning-mlearn-2007-doctoral-consortium-oct-2007 (accessed July 1, 2008).

Sharples, Mike, Josie Taylor, and Giasemi Vavoula. 2007. "A Theory of Learning for the Mobile Age." In *The Sage Handbook of Elearning Research* (pp. 221–247), edited by Richard Andrews and Caroline A. Haythornthwaite. London: Sage.

Sims Memorial Library. "Text A Librarian." Southeastern Louisiana University (2008). Available: www.selu.edu/library/askref/text/index.html (accessed August 5, 2008).

Stephens, Michael. "Libraries Doing Cool Things with iPods." Tame the Web: Libraries and Technology (February 23, 2005). Available: http://tametheweb.com/2005/02/libraries_doing_cool_things_wi.html (accessed July 20, 2008).

Traxler, John. 2007. "Defining, Discussing and Evaluating Mobile Learning: The Moving Finger Writes and Having Writ . . ." *International Review of Research in Open and Distance Learning* 8, no. 2 (June): 1–12. Available: www.irrodl. org/index.php/irrodl/article/view/346/882 (accessed July 7, 2008).

UWF. "PDA Course Demo." University of West Florida Pocket Campus. Available: http://onlinecampus.uwf.edu/pocketcampus/About/EME6428/index.cfm (accessed July 7, 2008).

Van Eck, Richard. 2007. "Recommended Reading: Gamers Go to College." Review of *Gamers Go to College*, by Craig Westman and Penny Bouman. *EDUCAUSE Quarterly* 30, no. 1: 71–72.

Virvou, Maria, and Eythimios Alepis. 2005. "Mobile Educational Features in Authoring Tools for Personalised Tutoring." *Computers and Education* 44, no. 1: 53–68.

Walker, Kevin. 2006. "Introduction: Mapping the Landscape of Mobile Learning." In *Big Issues in Mobile Learning: Report of a Workshop by the Kaleidoscope Network of Excellence Mobile Learning Initiative* (pp. 3–4), edited by Mike Sharples. Nottingham, UK: University of Nottingham.

Weinstein, Margery. 2006. "Going Mobile." *Training* 43, no. 9 (September): 24–29.

Westminster College of the Arts. "Westminster-To-Go Podcasts." Rider University (2007). Available: www.rider.edu/888_13267.htm (accessed August 2, 2008).

Widhalm, Shelley. 2007. "The Watch Comes Back for Seconds: Accessory Adapts in Battle with Cell Phone Over Time-telling." *Washington Times* (January 18): B1.

Williams, Brian K., and Stacey S. Sawyer. 2005. *Using Information Technology: A Practical Introduction to Computers & Communications*. New York: McGraw-Hill Technology Education.

Zlatos, Bill. 2005. "Combat Doesn't Slow Down These Students." *Pittsburgh Post-Gazette* (June 16). Available: www.pittsburghlive.com/x/pittsburghtrib/s_344561. html (accessed July 2, 2008).

Chapter 14

Technology and Pedagogy: The Best of Both for Gen M Students

Lauren Pressley

INTRODUCTION

Education is an especially exciting field these days: there is an ever-increasing list of inexpensive and easy-to-use tools, and new educational technologies abound. Teachers and librarians are examining their work, and looking for ways to adapt to these cultural and technological changes.

Some look at ways to incorporate technology into their work with great enthusiasm while others take a more wait-to-see-evidence attitude. This chapter is written for both of those groups. Technology enthusiasts will hopefully find relevant supporting evidence that can be helpful to modify their teaching to the technological expectations of today's students. However, this chapter will also argue that it is important to look at learning outcomes and to use the technologies that help reach these goals and objectives. Surely, blending both useful technology and strong pedagogy is the way to create an educational environment that will be most effective for today's students.

Educators need to adapt constantly to stay relevant and useful in students' lives, especially Gen M students who have grown up with the emerging technologies and now operate in a very different information environment than the one familiar to most of their educators. This chapter will discuss these different environments. It will cover how the learning environment is changing, what educational theory has to say about the changes, and provide some suggestions for adapting current pedagogy to Gen M students' technological expectations.

THE LEARNING ENVIRONMENT

Many of today's classrooms still look just like the ones from decades past: rows of desks with the teacher lecturing from a station at the front. This model was developed in an era of mass education, when the focus was on one-size-fits-all lectures and the teacher was the "sage on the stage." It made perfect sense for the agrarian/industrial society that it prepared students to enter (Wallis, Steptoe, and Miranda, 2006).

However, Gen M will be entering a global, knowledge-based economy. Education theory has suggested that teachers become 'guides on the side,' facilitating rather than lecturing. This movement represents an interest in individualized, student-centered education. Though many classrooms look traditional, what is happening inside them has changed. There is an increased emphasis on active learning and collaborative projects. Teachers are adapting their pedagogy to reach their students more effectively.

RAPID TECHNOLOGICAL CHANGE

It is frequently noted that this is an era of accelerated and unprecedented change. Technology that is ubiquitous did not exist twenty, ten, or, in some cases, even two years ago. Most Gen M students do not remember when Google did not exist. Researchers are looking into how these changes impact learning, and as of yet there are no definitive answers. Certainly growing up with Google is different from growing up without it. Its very existence has a strong cultural impact—the Internet, with sites like Google, has dramatically changed communication, relationships, and notions of privacy.

Recent research verifies that communication practices among Gen M members are changing. According to the 2007 Pew Internet and American Life Project report, *Teens and Social Media*, teens prefer communicating by phone. The preferred phone might be a landline or it might be a cell phone, depending on what is available, but they like communicating synchronously by voice. Their least favorite form of communication is e-mail (Lenhart et al., 2007). What does this mean for educators? Baby Boomers and Gen Y came of age with e-mail, or adopted e-mail later in their careers. Many prefer e-mails to other types of instant communication. It is important for educators to be mindful of this difference in attitude. If students more strongly prefer a communication medium, its use should be considered.

There are also some notable trends in how members of Gen M use social networking Web sites like MySpace and Facebook. According to the Pew Internet and American Life study, *Digital Footprints: Online Identity Management and Search in the Age of Transparency*, over half of all college students have created online profiles while only 15 percent of adults ages 30–49 have joined the networks, and even fewer of those 50 and above have participated (Madden et al., 2007). We can see from this that over half of all college students are comfortable with using Web sites in this way, and are likely more comfortable than their instructors are in these environments.

Another generational trend that is useful for educators and librarians to note is that the number one reason teenagers join social networks is to extend the friendships they have in real life. The number one reason people 50 years old and older join social networks is to be part of a community or group, to make friends (De Rosa et al., 2007). These very different motivations are something that educators should be mindful of when using a Web site to extend the classroom experience to an online environment. The 2007 OCLC (Online Computer Library Center) report, *Sharing, Privacy and Trust in Our Networked World*, showed that teens and college-age students are most familiar with social networking sites, followed by commercial sites like Amazon or eBay, whereas people age 22 and older are most familiar with commercial sites followed by social networking ones (De Rosa et al., 2007). Gen M students are typically very comfortable with social networking sites, which enhances the utility of those sites for educators as an element for online course development.

According to the 2007 OCLC report on sharing, 64 percent of college students say that search engines "fit perfectly with [their] lifestyle," whereas only 30 percent say the same for online libraries. (De Rosa et al., 2006: 3–21). This information is useful to both educators and librarians and may have implications for online learning management systems, such as Blackboard or Moodle. Since these sites are largely based on the traditional classroom model perhaps educators should be looking for ways to create something that more closely emulates a Web 2.0 world.

THE READ/WRITE WEB

The Web is transitioning to what programmers call a read/write environment. Initially, the Web, like television, radio, and newspapers, was a one-way communication channel. It was necessary to know programming in order to add content to the Web. Anyone with an Internet connection could read the content, but only a select few were able to contribute. Over time, there has been a revolutionary shift—now anyone can add content as well as read it. The Internet as a two-way communication channel is the only Internet that Gen M knows.

Communication media in general has moved toward being interactive. Early on, people passively received news from sources like newspapers, radio, and television without being able to say much in response (the exceptions were call-ins and editorial letters, but even those were screened). The Web has changed all that. Where once only reporters could write the news now any blogger can question, comment, and post alternative versions of news on the Internet. In some cases, a media station or publication might even respond to these online comments. The two-way communication of the Internet has profoundly changed traditional media.

So what does it mean to us that students have grown up in this technologically advanced environment? How do they contribute to the Internet? According to the 2007 Pew Internet and American Life Project study on *Teens and Social Media*, from 2004 to 2006 there was a 5 percent increase among teens who contribute to five or more sites (Lenhart et al., 2007). Most students contribute to a number of different types of sites. Of students who use social networking sites, 73 percent post pictures for others, 53 percent share their artistic work, and 42 percent create or maintain a Web site (Lenhart et al., 2007). These statistics indicate that many students are contributing to online communities, and many know how to code a Web site from scratch. To participate in multiple places on the Web, members of Gen M need to create and edit profiles in a number of spaces. It is worth remembering, however, that although many members of Gen M are quite comfortable with new technologies, each individual has his or her own comfort level with technology. Some students will adapt more easily than others, and some will be more technologically literate than others. Good teaching practices require an awareness of both individual differences in proficiencies and online access. Some classroom assignments may need to be modified assignments in order that all students may participate.

COMMUNITY

Social networking software has allowed people to form specialized communities according to their interests. In social spaces like MySpace and Facebook users can post profile information, send messages, and play games. Interest-based networks like Last.fm and Ravelry allow users to share information related to a theme. For example, Last.fm users post lists of music they have listened to in order to find bands liked by people with similar tastes. Ravelry members are knitters who share their projects, yarn collections, and photos of their finished products. These networks allow people to connect with people who have common interests across great distances.

This community-building nature of the Internet has implications for online teaching and learning. Students can potentially form interest groups around the topic of a particular course. They might chose to be in the class or they might be required to enroll in it, but for the duration of the course, all students have the same goal: to do what is necessary to learn the material or make a good grade. A savvy educator can use some of the same principles that drive social networking sites for a class's online presence by utilizing online tools to create interest groups around a subject area.

For example, a language class in literature can meet half time in-person for lecture, and half time in an online environment. The traditional lecture might have the appearance of a traditional language lecture, but the online sessions could utilize the technology to communicate across distances and involve native speakers of the language who wish to improve their English. A literature class might include online discussions that give rise to discussion topics for the next class. A science lab group might use a wiki to develop a lab manual and in-depth reporting on more experiments than any individual class member could carry out in a semester. In each of these scenarios, the course is being adapted to make use of some of the communicative, asynchronous, collaborative aspects of new communication technologies. Creating course experiences using the best of social networking allows students to use networking capabilities in order to learn academic content.

EDUCATIONAL THEORY

Understanding the contemporary learning environment is one aspect of positioning oneself to best meet the needs of Gen M students. Another area worth exploring is educational theory. Many terms are tossed around when discussing how to incorporate technology to enhance teaching for this techno-savvy generation. This section will discuss the terminology associated with technology-enhanced education as well as some of the educational theories that build the foundation of contemporary education.

Education Technology Terms

Though the traditional classroom still exists, educators have been experimenting with adapted models for some time. In the early days of distance learning, where education takes place away from the classroom, there were mail-order courses in which correspondence took place on paper via the physical mail. This evolved when audio and video became an option and teachers mailed lectures in addition to paper-based text. Once cable and networking were available, people sent video through cable or the Internet. At times, this might even be conducted synchronously, with a local classroom and a classroom at a distance, watching the lecture on the television in real time. Distance education has evolved to an almost entirely online environment, which is frequently referred to as "e-learning."

"Blended learning" takes the best of both traditional education and e-learning and puts them together in one course environment. In these cases, classes meet regularly and an instructor might even give traditional lectures in class, but there is also an online component. A lecturing professor might encourage discussion in the Learning Management System, or he/she might create smaller groups to work collaboratively on a number of projects. A professor might choose to post PowerPoint slides on a Web site for students to read between classes, and use class time for discussion and active learning assignments. In these examples of blended learning, classes meet both traditionally in classrooms, as well as online.

"Hybrid learning" is like blended learning, but goes a step further. In these courses, a class might meet online in place of some in-person classes. This has practical benefits such as allowing for more flexible scheduling for busy students, the ability to schedule more than one class per classroom per timeslot, as well as giving the professor the opportunity to think creatively about the restructuring of the course.

Education Theory Terms

This section provides a very basic overview of the major theoretical models used in the field of education. Entire graduate level courses are taught on each of these topics; however, the scope of this section is to provide only enough information for a discussion of these terms in conjunction with e-learning.

Behaviorism is a nineteenth-century theory of psychology based in the work of thinkers such as Ivan Pavlov and B. F. Skinner. Behaviorists focus on the behaviors of an individual. Operant conditioning is used to produce a desired response. Pavlov, for example, trained dogs to salivate when he rang a bell. Educational behaviorists, however, are interested in what they can do to get a student to respond with a correct answer at the correct time. Though many educational theorists today are interested in newer approaches, behaviorism still surfaces at education conferences. There are many behaviors that instructors would like their students to adopt, such as raising their hands to talk in the classroom, participating in discussions, and visiting the course Web sites regularly. Understanding some of the basic principles of behaviorism can help encourage these types of actions.

Over time, psychologists and teachers became more interested in what was going on inside the student's head, and theories began to shift toward the internal workings of the mind. This line of thought manifested in psychology as Cognitivism in the work of Jean Piaget, among others, and found its way into the field of education with the work of Constructivist thinkers. Constructivist education is based on the idea that people construct meaning from what they know; and so in order to learn, they have to be able to incorporate new information into their current understanding of the world. In this model, teachers are facilitators that guide the class rather than lecturers, who speak in front of the class. This movement is strong in contemporary education, and one that can be seen clearly in courses with prerequisites and library instruction sessions that are custom tailored to a specific course and assignment.

A radical theory, but one that is particularly relevant to those interested in incorporating relevant technology for Gen M, is Connectivism. This model is largely the work of George Siemens, who advocates for a model that incorporates theories of chaos, networking, complexity, and self-organization (Siemens, 2004). One might think of Connectivism as an extended model of Constructivism. Connectivist thinkers would recommend that educators take Constructivism a step further to incorporate informal learning, a focus on knowing how to learn, and create a system that is based on a personal network of learners (2004). This informal system of learning can be particularly useful in library settings as online tutorials, and informal sessions via chat or e-mail would fit into this system.

TECHNOLOGY TO SUPPORT PEDAGOGY

There are many reasons to consider using technology to make education more relevant to Gen M students. Many institutions have embraced educational technology for practical reasons; online courses save classroom space and allow busy students to have a more flexible schedule. Gen M students also have expectations that encourage educational institutions to move toward a blended learning environment; students are used to interacting in online spaces, they go online to socialize and share ideas. Educators need to consider that if they do not adapt to this environment, their course methodology and content may seem irrelevant and less than useful to their Gen M students. Giving students the opportunity to interact online can be argued to have pedagogical value. Constructivists would want to learn more about what students know before teaching a new unit and could use an online environment to build on their existing understanding of the discipline. The Connectivist model creates networks within the class and encourages seeking out good information online that can be brought back into the course environment.

Online discussions also give students an asynchronous way of sharing ideas that allows them the opportunity to reflect on new ideas before contributing in class. Many instructors offer anecdotal evidence of how this is good for shy students, but we also know that some of our more vocal students could stand to spend some time thinking before sharing an answer, too. Online classroom space also allows students to build more meaningful relationships with one another and with the professor. Though a typical class might allow for a little in-class interaction, an online extension can allow for an exchange of ideas and much more discussion among students and the professor. In this manner, professors can have more personal one-on-one conversations with students and get to know them better.

Getting Started with Technology in (and out of) the Classroom

A number of solutions exist for educators who want to incorporate more technology into their teaching. The best recommendation is to start slow. This involves finding a tool that looks useful and determining the best ways to incorporate it.

Luckily, in this time of technological advances, a number of technology solutions are available to users for little or no cost. These include hosted blogs; wikis; and videos such as the blogs at wordpress.com; wikis at pbwiki; and videos at YouTube, as well as other new Web 2.0 tools where the only cost is the time it takes to set up an account on the Web site. Of course, when obtaining a tool inexpensively online, a number of issues should be considered: Does it offer the ability to change things quickly? Does it do things personally without relying on campus IT? Will it help students gain skills they can use outside of class? Where to host the site is another issue to consider. Off-site (off-campus) hosting limits archiving capabilities and increases privacy concerns. Some institutions have very specific policies about hosting local information. It is worth looking into specific organizational rules and culture prior to making such decisions.

As with any technology or tool, there are always pros and cons. Well-thought-out educational goals and objectives help to guide pedagogical decision making.

Examples of Technology in (and out of) the Classroom

One aspect of traditional education that many professors want to replicate in the online world is synchronous discussion, or conversation that happens in real time across a distance. In these settings, conversations can be one-on-one or held in large groups. One way to hold these is through text-based chat, though voice is increasingly an option. Use of real-time video exchanges will be more popular in the coming years. Some professors are beginning to hold office hours in a chat program, so that students with instant messaging programs can contact their professor in a way that is comfortable and less threatening. Many libraries are offering chat reference for this reason as well.

Sometimes asynchronous discussion makes more sense. In these settings, people leave messages for one another at different times. Whenever students check in they read all the messages that have been left since their last login. Asynchronous conversation can take place in a discussion board for a Learning Management System, in the comments section of a blog, and in the collaborative space of a wiki. New tools, from Google Docs to new microblogging sites like Twitter, make this an increasing option.

A world of multimedia hosting options is available today that did not exist just a few years ago. Google Calendar provides an interactive means of sharing class meetings and assignments. Web 2.0 features allow educators to embed the content directly into a course Web site—including images, videos, and PowerPoint presentations—so that students do not have to leave the course Web site to complete the assignment. This method can appeal to students of multiple learning styles as well as make the course Web site more engaging. Web 2.0 features also permit additional feedback mechanisms for student response. In a face-to-face class, a teacher has the benefit of real-time student reaction. Are students confused, engaged, or bored? In an online environment, feedback mechanisms help instructors adjust their teaching methods.

Finally, good online pedagogy dictates that the instructor provide a well-organized, collaborative space to house the course content. Through the thoughtful organization of educational content into one convenient location, an instructor can ascertain that students will be able to access the information they need in order to be successful. Instructors use Learning Management Systems, wikis, blogs, and even simple Web sites as a home base for the course, embedding a wide variety of content in the main page. Ultimately, by bringing together disparate tools into one place, an instructor creates something greater than each of its parts, which can be conducive in motivating students to learn.

Gen M students are different from their predecessors. Their different experiences and expectations have shaped their worldview and perceptions of education. Through an understanding of these students, the application of educational theory, and informed use of available technologies educators can adapt to meet the needs of this new generation in creative and interesting ways.

REFERENCES

De Rosa, Cathy, Joanne Cantrell, Andy Havens, Janet Hawk, and Lillie Jenkins. 2007. *Sharing Privacy and Trust in Our Networked World*. Dublin, OH: OCLC. Available: www.oclc.org/reports/pdfs/sharing.pdf (accessed October 22, 2008).

De Rosa, Cathy, Joanne Cantrell, Janet Hawk, and Alane Wilson. 2006. *College Students' Perceptions of Libraries and Information Resources*. Dublin, OH: OCLC. Available: www.oclc.org/reports/pdfs/studentperceptions.pdf (accessed October 22, 2008).

Lenhart, Amanda, Mary Madden, Alexandra Rankin Macgill, and Aaron Smith. 2007. *Teens and Social Media: The Use of Social Media Gains a Greater Foothold in Teen Life as They Embrace the Conversational Nature of Interactive Online Media*. Washington, DC: Pew Internet and American Life Project. Available: www.pewinternet. org/pdfs/PIP_Teens_Social_Media_Final.pdf (accessed October 22, 2008).

Madden, Mary, Susannah Fox, Aaron Smith, and Jessica Vitak. 2007. *Digital Footprints: Online Identity Management and Search in the Age of Transparency*. Washington, DC: Pew Internet and American Life Project. Available: www.pewinternet.org/pdfs/ PIP_Digital_Footprints.pdf (accessed October 22, 2008).

Siemens, George. 2004. "Connectivism: A Learning Theory for the Digital Age." *elearnspace: everything elearning* (December 12). Available: www.elearnspace. org/Articles/connectivism.htm (accessed October 22, 2008).

Wallis, Claudia, Sonja Steptoe, and Carolina A. Miranda. 2006. "How to Bring Our Schools Out of the 20th Century." *Time* 168, no. 25 (December 18): 50–56.

Chapter 15

Teaching Gen M Through Cooperative Learning

Sharon L. Morrison
Susan L. Webb

INTRODUCTION

Learning is an important field of study in psychology that focuses on the process by which changes in behavior result from experience or practice. Learning, as defined, is a change or modification in a behavioral tendency resulting from instruction, study, or the learner's experience or interaction with the social, emotional, cognitive, and physical environment. If learning is to be a sustainable, lifelong, renewable process, learners need to acquire and apply productively new knowledge and skills as they grow, mature, and adapt successfully to changes and challenges. The readiness to learn is a large component of efficient learning. Also important is motivation. The means of acquiring motivation are either the promise of a reward or threat of punishment. Numerous research studies have shown that reward is better than punishment. Many people recognize the direct effects of reward more easily than punishment and perceive the by-products of reward as more favorable. Thus, success consists of reaching a goal that learners set for themselves and failure consists of not reaching that goal. An ideal learning situation is one in which learners set progressively more difficult goals for themselves, and keep at the task until they succeed.

Skill learning or active learning, the first method of education used by mankind, employs a wide variety of techniques that includes group discussion (large or small), demonstration, role playing, hands-on projects, teacher-driven questioning, and teaching others (cooperative learning). Michael Lorenzen (2001) wrote that the goal is to bring students into the process of their own education. This style of learning is much preferred to the traditional lecture and demonstration method that is the most prevalent teaching method in education today. Johnson, Johnson, and Smith (1991) found in their research that lecture promotes the acquisition of facts rather than the development of higher cognitive processes such as analyzing, synthesizing, and evaluation. The following are useful guidelines in the learning of discrete skills:

- Work in short practice sessions to ensure quick learning of the task.
- Imitate experts.
- Perform a new activity rather than only watching or listening to someone.
- Break a task into distinctive parts making it easier to learn.
- Practice difficult parts of a task separately and then try to incorporate them into the task as a whole.
- The more meaningful the task, the easier it is learned, especially when the task is related to previously learned skills.

Immediate feedback on performance is beneficial to the success of the task. Transfer of training occurs when new learning can profit from an existing knowledge base because mastering one skill lays the foundation for additional learning. The three factors involved are: (a) positive, not negative, transfer of training; (b) general principles learned in one task and applied to another task; and (c) good study habits learned in one task that help to learn another task.

The learning pyramid described in *How the Brain Learns* and devised in the 1960s by the National Training Laboratories of Bethel, Maine, provides information on the retention of learning after exposing students to different teaching methods (Sousa, 2006). The results showed that the learner's ability to retain information is dependent on the type of teaching method. Lecture involving verbal processing with little student active participation or mental rehearsal produced the lowest degree of retention for most learners. As students became more involved in the learning process through verbal and visual processing, learning retention increased. It was determined that the best way to learn was to prepare to teach someone else the learned skills. This is one of the major components of cooperative learning groups and helps to explain the effectiveness of this instructional technique.

COOPERATIVE LEARNING DEFINED

Cooperative learning is the collaboration within an instructional setting among members of small groups to achieve stated learner outcomes to enhance their own and their teammates' learning. Students are encouraged to function interdependently by sharing resources, working toward a common goal, and depending on other students for acknowledgement and recognition. Two key characteristics of cooperative learning are positive interdependence and individual accountability. These outcomes include the ability to recognize and define a problem and formulate a strategy resulting in a solution. Thus, it was determined to use integrated information literacy initiatives to provide library instruction.

Students today have grown up in a world of cell phones, the Internet, and interactive television and games, and, consequently, they want immediate feedback at their own fingertips. Because the Gen M learner has specific behavioral characteristics, librarians need to tap into their unique learning styles. Instruction needs to be novel, fast paced, relevant, social, and technical. Academic librarians generally have insufficient information about how students typically think; therefore, it is important for instruction librarians to shift from the traditional approach of lecturing to a more student-centered integrated learning environment. Among the benefits of cooperative learning are:

- Students have the opportunity to develop social skills; thereby becoming more considerate, better listeners, and better communicators;
- Students develop leadership, decision-making, and conflict-management skills;
- Students become better able to explain information literacy techniques in language that their peers can readily understand, thus creating an atmosphere of achievement;
- Students build an atmosphere of positive interdependence and individual accountability;
- Students have the opportunity to reflect on their own effectiveness within a group setting;

- Student learner outcomes include improved academic performance with increased self-confidence and motivation.

Information literacy is generally accepted as an essential ingredient in higher education curriculum; however, the traditional model of finding books, microfiche, government documents, and database access to articles needs to be re-evaluated in light of today's information society. Information literacy skills are essential for navigating this new environment. Since purposeful library research is one way to become information literate, Southeastern Oklahoma State University decided to move toward inquiry-based learning, highlighting the building of competency skills by having students use information resources in a problem-solving strategy. They found, evaluated, and used information along with technology skills to produce an online library tutorial to help other students navigate the information highway. The learning outcomes included in the Information Literacy Competency Standards developed by ACRL along with the stated Orientation/College Success course goals established a baseline for assessment.

The ACRL document *Information Literacy Competency Standards for Higher Education* outlines five standards. The information-literate student:

- Determines the nature and extent of the information needed;
- Accesses needed information effectively and efficiently;
- Evaluates information and its sources critically and incorporates selected information into his or her knowledge base and value system;
- Individually or as a member of a group, uses information effectively to accomplish a specific purpose;
- Understands many of the economic, legal, and social issues surrounding the use of information and accesses and uses information ethically and legally (ACRL, 2000: 2–3).

CASE STUDY: SOUTHEASTERN OKLAHOMA STATE UNIVERSITY

Background

Southeastern Oklahoma State University is a small regional university that serves southeastern Oklahoma and northeastern Texas. The environment is primarily rural. A substantial number of students are the first in their family to attend any college or university and an equally substantial number are nontraditional students. A nontraditional student is one who enters college at an age older than 18. The University's fall 2007 semester enrollment statistics were as follows: total enrollment for fall 2007 was 4,002; 35.1 percent of all students were age 21 or below; 27.9 percent of all students were age 21–23; 37 percent of all students were age 23 or above; total enrollment for the freshman class was 1,294 with 600 males and 694 females; the average age of incoming freshmen was 20.7. By almost any agreed starting year (typically 1982), 63 percent of all enrolled students fall squarely into Generation M.

College Success classes are recommended for all incoming freshmen and are required for those students enrolled in remedial classes; for students whose score on the ACT test is 19 or below; and for all undecided majors. In addition, classes will disperse into specific sections to give incoming freshmen a sense of community. For example, there are sections for athletics, music, aviation, President's Leadership Council, honors, education, residence life, nontraditional, and undecided majors. Our study concentrated on the honors group and the undecided majors group.

At Southeastern Oklahoma State University, students enrolled in an Orientation/College Success course receive an introduction to using the library for research to help them become engaged in intellectual inquiry. The library instruction sessions are an essential portion of this course. The library component of each course consists of five consecutive sessions taught by librarians with various specialties conducting individual classes. On days one and five, pre- and post-information literacy quizzes are administered to individual students. Also on day five, a homework assignment that covers resources presented by the peer groups measures each student's progress. These three instruments become the assessment portion of the final grade for the Orientation/College Success course.

Information Literacy/Cooperative Learning Study

Two groups of students were selected to participate in the study. The control group consisted of one class of students enrolled in the honors program and one class of students with the designation of undecided majors. The control group consisted of 47 students. The same make-up of students was in the experimental/cooperative-learning group, although that group consisted of 57 students. The same two librarians worked with these groups of students, meeting with the classes five consecutive times during the semester. The entrance requirements for inclusion in the study were as follows. Criteria for the honors students included a 25 ACT score, an interview, a written essay, and a recommendation by the Academic Advising Center. Undecided majors were required to have an ACT score below 25 and a recommendation from the Academic Advising Center.

Class goals and student learner outcomes for both groups were the same, to enable the student:

1. To become acquainted with selected library resources.
2. To locate, evaluate, and effectively use information.
3. To collect the resources necessary to write a research paper.
4. To become an independent library user.

Assessment for both groups was the same. The control group and the experimental/cooperative-learning group were to complete a worksheet that would measure their application of the information learned in the most expeditious manner. The teaching method for the control group of honors and undecided majors was the traditional lecture, demonstration, and hands-on method. The instruction emphasized what the librarians wanted the students to know. At the conclusion of five days of instruction that included one workday, each class member completed a worksheet. The method for the study group was the cooperative learning teaching method and team problem solving. The process followed will describe the class structure, the student-generated PowerPoint tutorials, and the assessment instruments used for team and overall project evaluation. At the conclusion of the five days, each student had to complete the same worksheet as the traditionally taught class.

The Assignment

The instruction librarians formulated a real-life problem and assignment to be solved. The focus for the problem's solution would be within resources that could typically be used for any library assignment. The rationale was that students should be able to transfer the knowledge or skill set learned in the College Success class to other library-related assignments. The scenario and the problem to be solved were read aloud to the class on the first day.

The Scenario

Sharon selected gender discrimination in higher education as her ORIE (orientation) research topic. Since the first day of Dr. Smith's class, she felt that he rarely asked girls questions, just the guys. Whenever girls joined the class discussion, their comments were either dismissed as not relevant or not treated with the same respect as the guys. Sharon had made these claims to him before, but they were dismissed out of hand. Therefore, she decided to research the topic and present her findings to Dr. Smith and let him know that the problem was not just a class problem, but systematic. The trouble was that Sharon did not have a clue as to where to start. A friend told her to Google "gender discrimination" and that she would be able to get everything that she needed there. She found 4,840,000 hits—that was about 4,839,900 more than she wanted, and most of the hits were about discrimination in the workplace. About to give up, she remembered to read the class instructions on how to gather information for the research paper. "The library!!! Why did I not think of that? Wouldn't you know, Dr. Smith wants a minimum of ten sources and he was very specific about which sources. He wants books, magazine articles, journal articles (is there a difference?), newspaper articles, and an Internet Web site. Who knew there were so many places to get information? Soooooo, it is off to the library!!!!"

The Problem to Be Solved

Working in small groups, the class will compile a typed bibliography for Sharon's research paper on gender discrimination in higher education. The bibliography will consist of the following:

- One book and one reference book;
- Three magazine/journal articles (one peer-reviewed) from Academic Search Premier;
- Two scholarly articles from Wilson Select Plus;
- One Newsbank article;
- Two Internet sites (.edu, .gov, or .org).

The Method

The class divided into five equal and interdependent groups with each group assigned a specific library resource to investigate. The only stipulation was that each group had to have at least one person who was proficient in PowerPoint. To help with the research, each group had a tip sheet to complete that covered the scope and specific features of the resource. After completing the tip sheet, the groups were to use the information gathered to prepare a PowerPoint presentation to present to the class. It is important to note that no instruction was given to the individual groups on what to emphasize to the class. The students were to select and teach the class what they considered important or what they considered was necessary for success; however, the librarians were available for clarification and discussion.

The following specific roles were assigned to members of each group:

- Facilitator: responsible for making sure the assignment is completed;
- Recorder: responsible for taking notes and completing the tip sheets;
- Presentation organizer: responsible for preparing the PowerPoint presentation;
- Presenter: responsible for making the class presentation;
- Observer/bibliography compiler: responsible for balancing group dynamics and reporting, at the end of the group work, on what went well and what could be improved; responsible for compiling a typed bibliography using APA style.

The schedule for the honors class and the undecided majors class was the same. Day one was the organizational day with the librarians explaining the process and answering any questions. Days two and three were for the groups to do their investigation and prepare their Power-Point presentations. The individual groups gave their presentations on days four and five. At the conclusion of day five, a worksheet given for homework provides assessment of skills learned.

Outcomes

The inter-rater reliability rubrics devised were for peer, student, and instructor evaluations. Student's evaluations were for their work within the group, their peers rated each group, and each group had an instructor evaluation. Peer and instructor evaluations rated the preparation, organization, technical specifications, mechanics, and overall presenta-

Table 15.1. Peer and Instructor Evaluation

Peer Evaluations		Instructor Evaluations	
Group 5	Average 15	Group 3 & 5	Average 14.6
Group 3	Average 14.2	Group 2	Average 14.3
Group 4	Average 13.7	Group 4	Average 13.3
Group 2	Average 12.9	Group 1	Average 11
Group 1	Average 12.6		

tion. Individual evaluations considered contributions, attitude, focus, and working with others. This procedure became part of the overall assessment of the project. Table 15.1 shows the results of the honors class inter-rater reliability rubric. Each group could receive a maximum of 15 points.

The worksheet, assigned as homework, became the application portion of the project. Students in the control group of honors taught by using the traditional model scored an average of 65 percent on their worksheet, whereas the honors class taught using cooperative learning and peer teaching scored an average of 91 percent. The undecided majors classes drew the same correlation. The traditionally taught class scored an average of 55 percent, whereas the cooperative learning peer teaching class scored an average of 65 percent.

Benefits/Conclusions

Online tutorials are effective instructional tools because they allow student convenience (available 24/7) for distance education classes as well as traditional classes especially when they target specific resources. The student-generated tutorials are on the library's Web site (Internet Resources, 2008). In addition, as the instruction librarians prepare online interactive tutorials for specific classes, they embed within their syllabi the student-generated tutorials, as well as the worksheet assignments (Business Bibliography, 2008).

This model of instruction created tremendous enthusiasm from students for their projects. Students learned how to navigate the Henry G. Bennett Web site, locate and utilize resources, evaluate Web sites for authority, accuracy, currency, usability, and cite sources. They learned to trust the information they found from the library databases more than

Figure 15.1. Cooperative Learning/Traditional Teaching

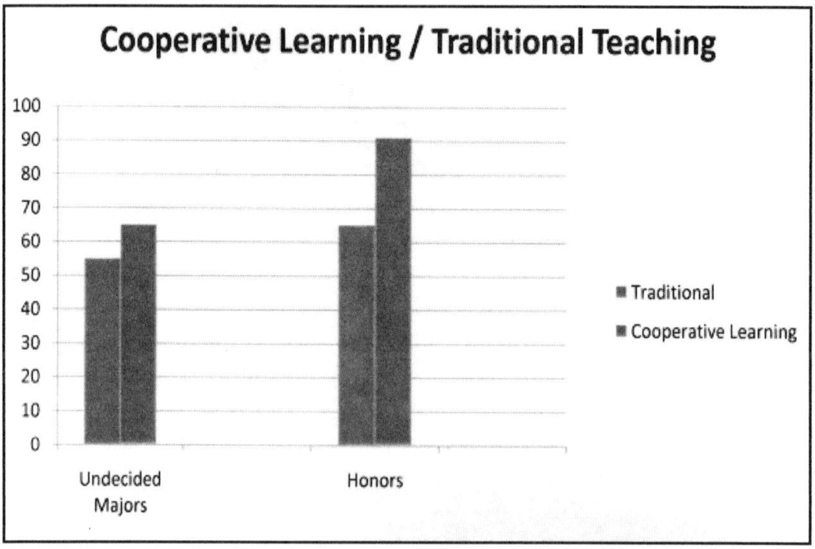

what they found on the Internet and to seek help from the librarians for assistance in the research process. Benefits to the students included increased achievement, improved attitudes toward assignments, positive motivation, enhanced interpersonal skills, and the realization that the participation of all group members was necessary for the group to accomplish its learning task successfully. Students acquired and demonstrated proficiency in oral and written communication, critical analysis and reasoning, and technological competency while learning information literacy skills. The students saw concretely how the skills they learned in this class had broader application to their information needs in other classes and they saw the library as a place with practical resources for locating materials to help them. Through the library unit, these students have established a connection to the library and its librarians.

LOOKING FORWARD

Due to more and more emphasis placed on online education classes, the authors believe that a change is coming to most institutions with the delivery method of their information literacy program. The trend is toward embedding information literacy in the curriculum through collaboration with individual faculty and, at least in some institutions, throughout the whole institution. Ideally, information literacy will fully integrate into the curriculum at all stages of each individual's program. The emphasis on lifelong learning is conducive to a teaching and learning environment that is growing more receptive to the idea of sustainable information literacy programs. The best means of ensuring curriculum-embedded information literacy instruction on an institution-wide scale is to have it recognized as a core educational value in the institution's academic mission and an essential element of all academic curricula, regardless of discipline.

REFERENCES

ACRL. "Information Literacy Competency Standards for Higher Education." Chicago: Association of College and Research Libraries (January 18, 2000). Available: www.ala.org/ala/mgrps/divs/acrl/standards/informationliteracycompetency.cfm (accessed October 24, 2008).

"Business Bibliography for Business 1133." Durant, OK: Southeastern Oklahoma State University (June 23, 2008). Available: www.se.edu/lib/introtobusiness.htm (accessed October 24, 2008).

"Internet Resources." Durant, OK: Southeastern Oklahoma State University (March 27, 2008). Available: www.se.edu/lib/studentppt.htm (accessed October 24, 2008).

Johnson, David, Roger Johnson, and Karl Smith. 1991. *Active Learning: Cooperation in the College Classroom*. Edina, MN: Interaction Books.

Lorenzen, Michael. 2001. "Active Learning and Library Instruction." *Illinois Libraries* 83, no. 2 (Spring): 19–24.

Sousa, David A. 2006. *How the Brain Learns*. Thousand Oaks, CA: Corwin Press.

ADDITIONAL READING

Ellis, Susan S., and Susan F. Whalen. 1990. *Cooperative Learning: Getting Started*. New York: Scholastic.

Halpern, Diane F. 1994. *Changing College Classrooms: New Teaching and Learning Strategies for an Increasingly Complex World*. San Francisco: Jossey-Bass.

Lyman, Lawrence, and Harvey C. Foyle. 1990. *Cooperative Grouping for Interactive Learning: Students, Teachers, and Administrators*. Washington, DC: National Education Association.

McGlynn, Angela Provitera. 2005. "Teaching Millennials, Our Newest Cultural Cohort." *Education Digest: Essential Readings Condensed for Quick Review* 71, no. 4: 12–16.

McGuinness, Claire. 2007. "Exploring Strategies for Integrated Information Literacy." *Communications in Information Literacy* 1, no. 1 (Spring): 26–38.

Meyers, Chet. 1986. *Teaching Students to Think Critically: A Guide for Faculty in All Disciplines.* San Francisco: Jossey-Bass.

Philip, Abrami C., Catherine Poulsen, and Bette Chambers. 2004. "Teacher Motivation to Implement an Educational Innovation: Factors Differentiating Users and Non-Users of Cooperative Learning." *Educational Psychology* 24, no. 2: 201–216.

Slavin, Robert E. 1990. *Cooperative Learning: Theory, Research, and Practice.* Englewood Cliffs, NJ: Prentice Hall.

Upcraft, M. Lee, John M. Gardner, and Betsy O. Barefoot. 2005. *Challenging & Supporting the First-Year Student: A Handbook for Improving the First Year of College.* San Francisco: Jossey-Bass.

Chapter 16

Screencasting: Extending Your Educational Environment

Steve Garwood

INTRODUCTION

"A screencast is a digital recording of computer screen output, also known as a video screen capture, often containing audio narration" (Wikipedia, 2008a, under "Screencast"). In more general terms, a screencasting program will record everything done on screen, as well as spoken into a microphone, in real time. The program will then produce the recording as some type of audio/video file.

Jon Udell, a columnist who solicited his blog-reading audience to come up with a name for the emerging technology, originally coined the term screencasting. (Udell, 2004). This 2004 blog post shows many of the early names that were considered. Udell's "Heavy Metal Umlaut" screencast, which shows the evolution of a Wikipedia article, is an early example of a screencast (Udell, 2005).

Screencasting has been used for software demonstrations and tutorials, and distance education librarians find it a valuable tool. In the past few years, tools have evolved to truly take advantage of the online medium. The quality of the video and audio capture, along with easy recording and production, combine to make this an easy software approach to use and share.

Currently, one of the interesting uses of screencasting software is to record screen actions in online gaming environments. It is not just software companies and educational institutions who are researching and using screencasts. Gamers are using this software to prove success with a game, to explain areas where they are having problems, or to share techniques and approaches with fellow gamers.

Libraries and educational institutions may not have taken advantage of screencasting and video content because the majority of users find it difficult to view video content over the Web. Services, such as YouTube, TeacherTube, Joost, blip.tv, vimeo.com, and so on, are eliminating the objections to viewing video content on the Internet, while broadband penetration into the home market is enabling quick and easy viewing. According to the Increased Use of Video Sharing Sites report released by the Pew Internet and American Life Project, "48 percent of Internet users have been to video-sharing sites such as YouTube. The daily traffic to such sites on a typical day has doubled in the past year" (Rainie, 2008: 1). Furthermore, a study by the Leichtman Research Group has found "high-speed (broadband) Internet accounts for over 70 percent of all online subscribers at home" (Leichtman, 2008, under "Research Study 2008 Brochure").

The Pew Internet and American Life Project also reports: young adults (ages 18–29) are among the most voracious video viewers; three in four young adult Internet users (76 percent) report online consumption of video; and, videos with educational content are equally as popular among the general population of Internet users (Rainie, 2008). With the combination of increased broadband and interest in video-based resources (even educational), the time is right for libraries, schools, and other educational settings to use the medium of video to promote, teach, inform, and communicate. With these statistics, librarians and educators should see that the users are waiting for them to make these screencast resources available.

ADVANTAGES, DISADVANTAGES, AND AWARENESS ISSUES IN SCREENCAST CREATION AND USE

When evaluating any tool for potential use in libraries and educational settings, it is wise to weigh the advantages and disadvantages. In addition, when using tools where the primary output will be to the Web, awareness of issues such as accessibility and baselines of user technology are also important considerations.

Advantages

Numerous advantages can be gained with the effective use of screencasts. From meeting users where they are, to increasing the appearance of librarians and educators as technology savvy, to the ability to save time and money, screencasting can be an incredibly valuable tool to add to your technology toolbox.

Meet users where they are, when they're there: Screencasts can generally be placed at a user's point of need; for example, on a "results not found" page or on a page that links to a database or other information source. They can also be grouped together as a larger page dedicated to learning a topic or tool. As an additional advantage, all of the approaches above can be accommodated as links to the same screencast and could be placed in multiple locations. The 24 hours a day, 7 days a week, and 365 days a year availability of screencasts determine that users can always get help in their time of need.

Create it once, use it over and over: If the resource that is being displayed or demonstrated does not change from assignment to assignment, quarter to quarter, or semester to semester, why not reuse the created video? In addition, if examples in recordings are general videos, they can be used for multiple audiences/classes.

Record brief segments and mix and match recordings: Higher-end screencasting programs can edit recordings into another production, mixing and matching to create new content. This creates more general, broader scope recordings, while allowing the addition of specific examples tailored to certain audiences.

Serve those who WILL NOT come and ask: For many reasons such as time, embarrassment, language or cultural barriers, some users will not speak up when they have a question. Whether users view an available screencast when they are confused or screencasts are used to answer a question via e-mail or IM, the information can reach those who will not come into the library or approach the Reference/Information Desk.

Add "personality" and human voice: Screencasts can add personality and flair to information literacy lessons and general library skills training. The use of an encouraging voice, color, and/or movement can add a comforting quality to material that is rarely easy to create in print.

Screencasts give librarians and educators a voice, something that can say, "We're here and we're here to help."

Show that libraries and educational institutions are tech savvy: Screencasting is an easy-to-use technology tool. Since screencasts incorporate audio and video for Web use, libraries and educational institutions can take a step up from "flat" Web pages or help guides that are simply text and pictures. A true sign of the possible increase in the technological reputations of librarians and educators will be when educational screencasts go "viral" when a big paper or project is due.

Users can repeat an entire screencast or just parts: Especially for content that is new or complex, one great advantage of screencasts is the ability to replay them, possibly as a class lecture, until the message, skill, or concept becomes clear.

Reach beyond your "intended" audience: Screencasts are primarily recorded to teach information retrieval skills or information literacy lessons for students directly involved with projects. However, these lessons can also find their way to other family members, especially parents of children learning these skills and/or partners/group-mates of those doing projects. Also, they can help those who just happen to find them on the Web.

Librarians/educators can do "old" things in new ways: Although direct information literacy lessons can be a great use for screencasting technology, other direct and indirect uses can be applied. For example, screencasts can be used to grade or review assignments to give students more feedback. A screencast can also be used with a general/anonymous assignment to better enable teachers to explain what they are looking for and why.

Staff time saver: Screencasts can pick up some of the burden of teaching the same class repeatedly. Although screencasts cannot completely alleviate demands on staff time, they can help re-prioritize time. Not everyone needs to be an expert on all things. Using screencasts, subject and resource experts can record lessons/explanations that others can refer to when needed.

Fairly inexpensive approach to extend teaching/training: At a cost of about $250 for an educational license, screencasting programs can provide a quick and impressive return on the investment. As a screencast is viewed more over time or for every time a screencast enables a staff member to pre-teach a topic and reinforce with hands-on practice, value grows. Although nothing can replace a direct human touch, screencasts can enable one human to be in more than one place at a time.

Flexibility of delivery method: Depending on the software used to create the screencast, files can be downloaded from the Web and watched on a user's computer or mobile device, watched online with a browser or media player, presented on CD, or any combination thereof. Different tools will approach this in different ways with some being more flexible with publishing formats. However, with the availability of third-party products to convert file formats for different uses, this is becoming less of an evaluation area for various software packages.

Files can be given to students to remix or mash up content: With the higher end screencasting programs, students could be given video, audio, image and other files to mix and reuse to create and teach lessons of their own.

Disadvantages

For all of the advantages that come with screencasting, there are also some disadvantages. Some of these disadvantages are technological in nature, wheres others are based in the time commitment to learn a new tool and/or how to properly integrate that tool. No matter the type of disadvantage, serious decisions must be made which will affect the type and quality of recordings.

Something new to learn (learning curve issues): To achieve effective results when using screencasting technology, a new program's interface, or interfaces if more than one program is used, can take time to learn. In addition, learning how the software works, the terminology that the software/technology uses, and how to achieve the best results are all time intensive. Last, there are general usability issues with online video and audio presentation that need to be taken into account.

Time to create recordings (thought and planning to get the lesson across): Some "point of need" screencasts can be easy to create and share, but, in general, screencasting should be part of an overall strategy to educate and train users/students. This requires time and planning. Plans should include what is being recorded, and in what order, as well as any issues or ideas that should be highlighted.

Things change: Companies love to change their interfaces. Though this does not happen daily, if there is a 10-video series explaining an online database, and that database changes its search and results screens, the videos will need to be changed or updated. This is when it is a good idea to have saved original outlines or scripts, so that only the visual aspects will need to be updated, and not the whole process begun from scratch.

Only one-way communication: No matter how great screencasting programs are at "showing and telling" or how many interactivity tools they add to help assist learning, all screencasting programs are still a one-way communication tool. This can be especially limiting when working in a setting where communication needs to be two-way or synchronous.

User bandwidth/computing ability/plug-in concerns: Although this can be mitigated in school or on campus, the very large files that are produced by the combination of audio and video make it important for users to have a high speed DSL or cable connection in the home. As more videos are created, and as more people simultaneously watch them, a school or library server/connection could be taxed beyond its capabilities. A user's computer must also be able to handle video and have the proper player, program, or browser plug-in to view files. This is becoming less of an issue, but potential limitations exist.

Awareness Issues

The following items are not necessarily advantages or disadvantages, but merely things that should be considered when utilizing screencasts. Accessibility and overall access are two large considerations that need to be weighed when working with a technology that can and will be used primarily online.

Section 508/Accessibility Compliance: Compliance with section 508 of the Rehabilitation Act is important for libraries and educational institutions, as barriers should not be added to acquiring information skills simply because of a technological approach to teaching them. Higher-end screencasting software packages like Camtasia and Captivate have documentation and built-in features (i.e., captioning) to help users comply with Section 508/accessibility regulations and concerns, but many screencasting products do not.

Digital divide: For those with no computer or Internet access at home, or even slow or unreliable access, screencasts may not be the best approach as students will not be able to properly view recordings. This makes it all the more important to have a low-tech solution available as well (e.g., handouts with screen captures that can be linked or handed out in class or in the library).

EDUCATIONAL ASPECTS OF SCREENCASTING

Strong pedagogical reasons exist for a library to create online multimedia tutorials and pathfinders. They are responsive to a number of educational theories and can successfully reach a broad range of learner types concurrently (Hook, 2002). Thoughtful planning of screencasts combined with strategic placement and promotion of materials can go a long way to increasing information literacy and the particular skills necessary to becoming a skilled searcher and evaluator of information.

One area that is often difficult to internalize is the differences and similarities between using screencasts for "help" based situations, where a single short screencast would suffice, and broader information literacy lessons that may combine skills and theories/concepts. Also potentially confusing is how screencasts are used in the broader context. Screencasts can be primary material (especially for those who teach online), supplemental material (lessons that students can review prior to or after bibliographic instruction or an information literacy session), or both. Screencasts are great for both, but each may have a different focus depending on the overall plan of the educational setting.

As with many tools within the field of educational technology, librarians and educators must remember that screencasts do not replace planning and that a screencast may not be enough to get the lesson or message across. Creating a screencast is not teaching or training; screencasts should be utilized in the same manner as other pedagogical tools or approaches. Being aware of the shared content, the context in which it needs to be learned, and the varied abilities and experiences of students and users all come in to play. Screencasting can be part of a constructive learning experience, but it is only a part.

One of the most important facts to remember when considering learners is that, generally, more than one type of learner exists and each will learn a bit differently. Utilizing screencasts as a part of teaching, and taking learning styles into account within screencasts, can go a long way to helping people create the knowledge they need.

Visual learners: Screencasts are inherently visual and thus are fantastic to use with those who learn best in this manner. Two important areas to focus on are using a pointer to point at what is being described and ensuring a screencast's capture area is large enough for viewers to see what is being described. Some screencasting tools will allow the use of callouts and captions that can be added to help those who are text-based learners or who like visual pointers. Last, providing an outline, flow chart, and/or script as a separate link can let those who prefer to read digest the material this way.

Auditory learners: Although screencasts can be done without audio, users will generally expect audio and will usually think something is wrong if they do not hear it. As this function-ability exists in just about all screencasting programs and because many people learn by what they hear, audio is an effective and important addition to a screencast. Moreover, using detailed explanations of steps and illustrative terminology to describe what is being watched make a message or lesson clearer.

Experiential learners: Keeping two or more windows open: one window that contains the screencast and the other that contains the application or service that the learner is trying to learn is a fairly common practice of those learning particular skills from screencasts. With this approach, learners can watch and try as many times as they require. Because of this, the screencast can become much more than a video to watch, taking on the role of "teacher." The ability to utilize a screencasting program, such as Adobe Captivate, to create a lesson where users need to interact with the screencast in order to complete a lesson can add a level of experience where users do not need to own a particular software product or have access to a service in order to learn about it.

Pacing/chunking: Cognitive Load Theory generally states that people learn better when they can build on what they already understand. However, the more a person has to learn in a shorter amount of time, the more difficult it is to process that information in working memory (Wikipedia, 2008b). The incorporation of screencasts can help tremendously to assist learners in building on knowledge they already have and allowing them to gain knowledge at their own pace. Care must be taken when creating screencasts for information literacy to ensure that skills and concepts are not taken for granted and that steps work well together.

Relating the learning to the learner's goals: Utilizing screencasts to explain/show the learners what they need to know/do in the context of what they are doing will help the learner to internalize the information. While some screencast lessons can be more general (e.g., logging in to a library's Online Public Access Catalog [OPAC]), as the lessons get more detailed or as more pertinent examples are given, relating examples to the learners' goals should be considered. While this may mean the creation of more screencasts, it could also mean increased learning and retention.

State dependent learning: Screencasts can easily assist learners to learn anywhere at any time. While learners may be pressed into learning in a certain way or in a specific location because of time constraints, there also exists the possibility that the learners will be able to seek the environment, time, mood, and so on, at which they know they learn the best.

Teaching students to screencast: Especially in online classes, student use of screencasting software can be a powerful approach to collaborative learning and sharing. By using screencasts, students can show where they are stuck with an application or with the use of a skill. Screencasting can also be helpful for presentations, especially when a student is nervous about speaking to an audience or possibly faces an issue with social anxiety disorder. Last, collaborating students could each be held responsible for a portion of a screencast, making it difficult for any one student to "slack off" and take credit for others' work.

INFORMATION LITERACY/LIBRARY FUNCTIONS THAT CAN BE ADDRESSED

The applications for screencasting technology in library and educational settings are just starting to be developed. It would be presumptive to suggest a "best" approach of what should be done. With that said, it would be a good idea to think of multiple marketing approaches for advertising screencasts. Do not assume that everyone will find the screencasts by following a particular path on a library Web site, and remember that some will use one lesson and want to learn much more, while others will want to learn only the basics in order to accomplish a simple task (e.g., locating the full text of a journal article). The possibilities are only limited by the developer's time, resourcefulness, and the medium. The key is to try new things and share the successes with the world.

One of the best places to start with screencasts would be by helping users with those Frequently Asked Questions (FAQs) within the library or in the classroom, such as these examples: "What's a thesis statement?" "What's a journal article?" "How do I search for a journal/journal article?" "How do I find a book in the catalog?" "What do I do if I cannot find a particular book?" "How do I cite an interview using APA style?" From FAQs, the particulars of conducting searches in certain sources, evaluating sources, and other more in-depth topics can be covered and educators/librarians can begin to put together complete information literacy lessons.

In addition to the above, librarians and educators can use screencasting software for several other purposes:

- *A virtual library tour:* Higher-end screencasting programs allow mixing of audio, video, screen-based video, images, and more. A dynamic and informative tour is easily created.

- *A "sources for a project" tour:* Let people know what sources could or should be used for a project. Teachers or librarians could easily create these to highlight books in the catalog, subjects to be searched, Web sites, and useful online databases that would be valuable for a project.
- *Source/service awareness:* Especially in a library setting, a short screencast could be created and easily added to a Web site or blog when a new source or online service becomes available.

SERVING SCREENCASTS TO THE PUBLIC

How screencasts can be served to the public depends on several factors. Some of these factors are based on utility for users, some are based on access rights and practical concerns of changing the design, layout, and/or content of an OPAC, bibliographic database, or other proprietary system, and some are based on the technological solutions available at the library or educational setting. In addition, the purpose of the screencasts can have a large impact on the method of delivery. One thing to keep in mind is that how and where screencasts are served can strongly influence if and how materials are used. Making the use of screencasts as easy as possible and/or ensuring that screencasts can be used in a way that the intended audience prefers should be a strong consideration for those creating them.

Students or other users may be learning from scratch, reviewing, or may be simply "stuck" when utilizing online resources. Putting links to screencasts or a page of screencast content based on where students are and what they need to accomplish can greatly help to ensure success. Besides "where" to put a link, thought should also be put into "how" students will utilize the content. Content can be viewed via a link that opens a pop-up window, a downloadable file they can save and watch on their computer, or even preloaded on a computer in the classroom or library that students can view and review via a simple click.

Placing a link in a particular location on a Web page or computer can be limited by the user's ability or by rights of ownership. While links can almost always be placed on a Web page the library or school maintains, it may not be possible to add a link on an OPAC or an online database page.

The purpose of the screencast can determine where it should naturally go as well. Individual screencasts can be part of larger lessons or full classes where content could be listed on a Web page and learners could proceed in an orderly fashion from one lesson to the next. Screencasts can also be seen as single item products used to serve a particular finite need (e.g., renew an item in a library catalog—a useful link to have on a library catalog page, FAQ, or even a main library home page).

For an online instructor, screencasts can be a primary way of presenting content and explaining concepts, theories, and practices. In this type of setting, an online teacher/professor/librarian would treat screencasts just as they would treat a lecture or presentation. Within classes, there can also be short "how-to" type screencasts that act as primers to labs or homework projects and can help students learn new software or online services.

Creating a set of screencasts on a common topic and listing them on a Web page or wiki is a very common approach. An example would be the Video Guide to the OhioLink Catalog (OhioLink, accessed 2008). This is an excellent way to keep everything together, but linking directly to certain screencasts from places where students/users might be when they run into difficulty would be very helpful as well. Most of the above suggestions are based on the idea of linking to content hosted on the library server or a media host like YouTube, blip.tv, or ourmedia.org, but there are other possibilities as well.

Collections of screencasts could also be packaged together on a CD/DVD to act as a takeaway for students when they leave bibliographic instruction/information literacy classes and/or packaged for parents, teachers, or other interested parties to pickup. A CD/DVD of screencasts created by a library or information literacy person could also be distributed or loaned to teachers to show in class or before a class comes to the library so that time in the library could be directed to hands-on application of what was demonstrated/explained in the screencasts.

Content can also be created and vodcast using a library server to host the files and an RSS feed to which users could subscribe. This could also be done by using one of the many video hosting services that exist on the Web, such as blip.tv, YouTube, or ourmedia.org. This might be a particularly helpful approach for classes that meet over a period of time or to address those tech-savvy Gen M users who may want to use video aggregators like Miro.com, iTunes, or their iPod.

SCREENCASTING SOFTWARE AND SERVICES

Each screencasting product has specific features, strengths, and weaknesses that require an understanding of the results that the person creating the screencast would want to achieve BEFORE purchasing any particular software. Possibly the best general advice would be to ascertain the final desired results, the method of serving the content, such as links on a page or a vodcast, as well as the budget, and then begin to review the software programs to find the best fit. A quality, but somewhat dated, review of products is available in the online review: Best Screencasting Tool (DonationCoder.com, 2005). Table 16.1 indicates some of the most popular software/services now available.

Camtasia by TechSmith is a robust tool for creating screencasts that one would want to refer to repeatedly and/or produce in multiple file formats (e.g., Flash for Web-use or QuickTime for vodcasts/streaming). Among the various screencasting programs, Camtasia allows the most flexibility in the creation of various file formats (e.g., .swf, .flv, .wmv, .mov, .avi, and .m4v files). The recording and production process is easy to learn and even various editing features, such as creating callouts or pan-and-zoom effects as well as caption features, are easy to use.

Adobe's Captivate is another rich screencasting tool. Captivate generally allows more interactivity for software tutorials and demos. Using Captivate, a screen recording similar to that which can be done with Camtasia can be created or interactive elements can be added to create a simulation exercise where users must interact with the screencast to complete a task. With this ability comes a steeper learning curve, but nothing that cannot be overcome. Captivate will produce files as .swf and .exe, but not as many formats as Camtasia.

As of this writing, Camtasia and Captivate are, unfortunately, not available for Macintosh computers. When a screencast is needed from a Mac, a good tool of choice would be Snapz Pro X by Ambrosia Software. Snapz Pro X is a strong and easy-to-use tool; however, it produces video only to the QuickTime (.mov) format. Screenflow by Vara Software is a newer product that has been getting good reviews on the Web; it is available only for Mac OS X Leopard, but still represents the strides that manufacturers are making to address the Macintosh market.

A source of screencast best practice examples, lynda.com, makes excellent use of Camtasia, Captivate, and Snapz Pro X. The lynda.com site has detailed tutorials and lessons on all types of software at all levels of expertise. Subscriptions to this site can get you access to a detailed

Table 16.1. Popular Screencasting Programs

Product	Company	Platform	URL	Price/Edu*
Camtasia	TechSmith	Windows	http://techsmith.com/camtasia.asp	$299/$179
Jing	TechSmith	Windows/Mac	http://jingproject.com/	Free (for now)
Captivate	Adobe	Windows	http://adobe.com/products/captivate/	$699/$249
Snapz Pro X	Ambrosia Software	Mac	http://ambrosiasw.com/utilities/snapzprox/	$69
Screenflow	Vara Software	Mac	http://varasoftware.com/products/screenflow/	$99
ViewletCam	Qarbon	Windows	http://qarbon.com/presentation-software/vc/	$179/$139
BB Flashback	Blueberry Software	Windows	http://bbsoftware.co.uk/BBFlashBack.aspx	$225/up to 40% off
Wink	DebugMode	Windows/Linux	http://debugmode.com/wink/	Free
CamStudio	SourceForge	Windows/Linux	http://sourceforge.net/projects/camstudio/	Free

*As of 6/30/08, prices taken from manufacturers' sites.

tutorial on the use of Captivate and can also act as a guide to creating professional screencasts (lynda.com, accessed 2008).

Jing by TechSmith (Windows and Macintosh compliant) is a perfect tool for "point of need" screencasts and can be used when an IM or e-mail call for help arrives that could be more easily answered by a screencast than a text-based message. Jing has a couple of useful and unique features. A screencast can be recorded quickly with Jing and automatically uploaded to screencast.com. When the upload process is complete, Jing automatically puts the URL of where the screencast is located in the clipboard, which can then be pasted into an e-mail or IM window to share easily with a student/colleague. While Jing will only produce a .swf file or .png file for image capture, the .swf format is the most universally supported, and recordings that are uploaded to screencast.com can be easily managed and shared. Two limitations of Jing are that recordings can be a maximum of 5 minutes and the Jing brand/logo will appear on all screencasts.

EXAMPLES OF HOW LIBRARIES ARE ALREADY USING SCREENCASTS

As this is a fairly new approach for libraries, it is not surprising that many libraries are not taking advantage of this technology yet. Also, many libraries/librarians that are working with this technology put their screencasts inside course management systems (CMS), which make them visible only to those who can access the CMS.

The sites below are just a sample of some of the innovative things that libraries are doing with screencasting technology. Much of what can be seen are approaches to dealing with many common library/information literacy questions such as item holds, renewals, and database and catalog searching. Some also have short tutorials on software programs or Web-based services.

Academic Libraries

- Blake Library at the University of Maine at Fort Kent
  www.umfk.maine.edu/infoserv/library/resources/tutorials/
- University of Calgary Library
  http://library.ucalgary.ca/tutorials/

- Montana State University
  www.lib.montana.edu/tutorials/
- Seattle Community Colleges
  http://seattlecentral.edu/library/passport/
- University of Nevada, Las Vegas
  www.library.unlv.edu/help/tutorial/

Public Libraries

- Calgary Public Library
  www2.calgarypubliclibrary.com/library/tutorials.htm
- Enoch Pratt Free Public Library: Show-Me-Guides
  www.prattlibrary.org/findanswers/how_to.aspx?id=15078
- Flint Public Library: Make a Simple Chart/Graph with Microsoft
  Word
  www.flint.lib.mi.us/kidsweb/extras/makeachart/index.html
- Orange County (FL) Public Libraries: Online Tutorials
  www.ocls.info/Virtual/tutorials/default.asp?bhcp=1
- Rockaway Township (NJ) Free Public Library: Online Tutorials
  www.rtlibrary.org/Howtos.html

GETTING THE MOST FROM YOUR SCREENCASTS

Following are suggestions, ideas, and practical tips for getting the most
from screencasts. Most of the advice focuses on the end user and what
he/she will see and hear.

Window Sizes

When preparing a screencast, thinking about the audience and how
they are going to be seeing and using the information shared will have
a large impact. Some important questions to ask are: Do they need to
clearly read what is being typed? Is what is being shown large enough
that it can work in a smaller window? What is the most common screen
resolution of those who are going to be seeing the screencasts?

At present, these are most common resolutions (width x height) that
come to this author's principal Web site (in order): 1024x768, 1280x1024,
and 1280x800. Based on this, creating screencasts that are 800x600 is
perhaps the most usable. If someone does come to the site with 800x600

resolution, he or she can still view the screencast. Those with higher resolutions will be able to easily see the material presented without any scrolling. It is simple to set up a pop-up window that contains the screencast without worrying about whether or not it will fit onto the screen. Also, the size is comfortable for demonstrations as it is generally easy to see.

There are other size considerations as well. General size for embedding a video in a browser window tends to be 640x480 or 320x240, blog post size tends to be 400x300, iPod Video (not iPhone) settings are 320x240, and YouTube will basically make the embed size of any video about 425x355. One of the main benefits with using higher-end screencasting programs like Camtasia is the ability to record a video at one size and then produce it at other sizes. Features like Zoom-n-Pan allow zooming in on areas of a video when the overall size of the video needs to be smaller than when it was originally recorded. However, it is still a good idea to consider what size the video will be when the end user is viewing it and plan accordingly.

If unsure of how to resize windows so that it fits the desired dimensions, there are a few solutions. One of the easiest solutions is to use a program called Sizer (www.brianapps.net/sizer.html), which is a freeware application that allows quick and easy resizing of windows to exact dimensions. Another freeware tool is PixelRuler (www.mioplanet.com/products/pixelruler/), which you can use to measure any window or the content of a window to determine its dimensions. Some screencasting programs will also allow users to resize their window via their interface.

Scripts/Outlines/Sequencing

Scripts: Some people love using scripts and some do not. There are strong reasons for using a script. A script can make a screencast sound more polished, keep a voice from stammering, and ensure the use of proper terminology. Using a script can make certain that none of the points are missed. Lastly, one of the best reasons to use a script is that scripts can be used to create other educational materials (e.g., traditional screen capture tutorials), or simply provide another resource for text-based learners.

Outlines: Many of those who screencast, especially those who do not use a script, will use an outline. With an outline, the user can delineate the major points to make in the screencast to be recorded. While this might be unnecessary in "single step" videos (e.g., bolding text in

Word), it can be necessary if recording something where multiple things are covered in a short video, such as a video on "Microsoft Word 2007: What's the Ribbon?".

Sequencing: Just as lesson plans need to be sequenced to ensure that important information is not skipped and to guarantee a base of understanding/competence before moving forward, screencasts/videos should be thought of as a sequence. Breaking things down into smaller steps and recording shorter videos, which will load faster, is often a better idea than recording long videos where someone might miss an essential piece in a barrage of information. An example would be a lesson on searching a library catalog: instead of a long video that details every possibility, shorter videos on specific searching options will let users pick what they want to see and not have to hope to find what they are looking for in a longer video.

Other Considerations

Check the microphone: Nothing is worse than recording a 5-, 10-, or 15-minute screencast and then discovering that audio was not recorded. Dubbing/narrating after the fact is something to be avoided. Making sure the microphone is plugged in and doing a sample recording to check the audio level is an important step in saving time and frustration.

Remember how to pause and stop: It is easy to quickly pause and resume recording, which is especially useful in the midst of a fit of coughing or when the phone rings.

Quick Tips

- Respect your users/viewers. Remember, screencasts are created for those who need to/want to learn something.
- Go slow. It will help the quality of the recording and the ability of those watching to absorb the content.
- Files are big, attention spans short. Keep recordings short or break them up.
- Do not forget about loading to services like YouTube, blip.tv, and screencast.com as alternatives/additions to a library server for storing screencasts.
- Prepare the storyboard, outline, and script, and then do a dry run.
- Have a quality microphone. Nothing helps voice quality more than a quality microphone (a USB microphone is highly recommended).

- Do not spend a lot of time editing little things. The information/teaching is what is important, not whether there is an "um" once or twice.
- Have some water handy. Better to pause and take a sip than sound like a sip is needed.
- People will use a library card number if you show it, so demonstrate with a fake one or destroy the one used.
- Where possible, brand the screencast using a watermark or other technique to better establish accurate, official information.

REFERENCES

DonationCoder.com. "Best Screencasting Tool." (June 6, 2005). Available: www.donationcoder.com/Reviews/Archive/ScreenCasting/index.html (accessed October 19, 2008).

Hook, Peter. 2002. "Creating an Online Tutorial and Pathfinder." *Law Library Journal* 94, no. 2: 243–257.

Leichtman Research Group. "Broadband Internet Access & Services in the Home: Research Study 2008." (March 2008). Available: www.leichtmanresearch.com/research/bband_home_brochure.pdf (accessed October 9, 2008).

lynda.com. "Learning @ Your Own Pace." Available: http://lynda.com/ (accessed November 9, 2008).

OhioLink. "Video Guide to the OhioLINK Catalog." Available: http://dmc.ohiolink.edu/help/VidHelpHTML/ (accessed October 20, 2008).

Rainie, Lee. "Increased Use of Video Sharing Sites." Washington, DC: Pew Internet and the American Life Project (January 9, 2008). Available: www.pewinternet.org/pdfs/Pew_Videosharing_memo_Jan08.pdf (accessed November 11, 2008).

Udell, John. "Heavy Metal Umlaut: The Movie." *InfoWorld* (January 22, 2005). Available: http://weblog.infoworld.com/udell/2005/01/22.html (accessed October 9, 2008).

Udell, John. "Name That Genre: Screencast." *InfoWorld* (November 17, 2004). Available: http://weblog.infoworld.com/udell/2004/11/17.html (accessed October 9, 2008).

Wikipedia. "Cognitive Load." (November 2, 2008b). Available: http://en.wikipedia.org/wiki/Cognitive_load (accessed November 10, 2008).

Wikipedia. "Screencast." (October 11, 2008a). Available: http://en.wikipedia.org/wiki/Screencast (accessed November 9, 2008).

SELECTED RECOMMENDED READINGS

Baillin, Alan, and Aisha Pena. 2007. "Online Library Tutorials, Narratives, and Scripts." *Journal of Academic Librarianship* 33, no. 1: 106–117.

Brown, Judy, and Lu Jiayun. 2001. "Designing Better Online Teaching Material." *ACM SIGCSE Bulletin* 33, no. 1: 352–356.

Dewald, Nancy. 1999. "Transporting Good Library Instruction Practices into the Web Environment: An Analysis of Online Tutorials." *Journal of Academic Librarianship* 25, no. 1: 26–32.

EDUCAUSE Learning Initiative. "7 Things You Should Know about Screencasting." Washington, DC: EDUCAUSE CONNECT (March 2006). Available: http://connect.educause.edu/Library/ELI/7ThingsYouShouldKnowAbout/39389 (accessed October 4, 2008).

Farkas, Meredith. 2007. "Chapter 12: Screencasting and Vodcasting." *Social Software in Libraries: Building Collaboration, Communication, and Community Online*. Medford, NJ: Information Today, 197–210.

Lindsay, Elizabeth, Lara Cummings, and Corey Johnson. 2006. "If You Build It, Will They Learn? Assessing Online Information Literacy Tutorials." *College & Research Libraries* 67, no. 5: 429–445.

Nichols, James, Barbara Shaffer, and Karen Shockey. 2003. "Changing the Face of Instruction: Is Online or In-Class More Effective?" *College & Research Libraries* 64, no. 5: 378–388.

Notess, Greg. 2005. "Casting the Net: Podcasting and Screencasting." *Online* 29, no. 6: 43–45.

Roberts, Gary. 2005. "Instructional Technology That's Hip High-Tech." *Computers in Libraries* 25, no. 10: 26–28.

Zhang, Li. "Effectively Incorporating Instructional Media into Web-based Information Literacy." *The Electronic Library* 24, no. 3: 294306.

SELECTED RECOMMENDED RESOURCES

"A.N.T.S.: Animated Tutorial Sharing Project." Available: http://ants.wetpaint.com/ (accessed October 4, 2008).

Garwood, Steve. "Screencasting Wiki." Available: http://screencasting.pbwiki.com (accessed October 4, 2008).

Kanter, Beth. "Screencasting: The Latest in Technology Training." Screencasting for Nonprofits. Available: http://screencastingprimer.wikispaces.com/ (accessed October 4, 2008).

Notess, Greg. "LibCasting." Available: www.notess.com/screencasting/ (accessed October 4, 2008).

Pival, Paul R. "Show and Tell the Easy Way—Introduction to Screencasting." SirsiDynix Institute (November 8, 2006). Available: www.sirsidynixinstitute.com/seminar_page.php?sid=71 (accessed November 2, 2008).

Prange, Laurie, and Barbara Sobol. 2008. "Develop Your Instructional Palate with Online Tutorials: A Balanced Blend of Theory and Practice." Presentation at the annual meeting of the WILU 2008: 37th Workshop on Instruction in Library Use, Kelowna, British Columbia, Canada (May 22). Available: http://eprints.rclis.org/archive/00013500/ (accessed October 29, 2008).

Weber, Betsy. "Screencasting Tips for Beginners." TechSmith. Available: www.presentersuniversity.com/visuals_screencasting.php (accessed November 7, 2008).

Chapter 17

How I Learned to Stop Worrying and Love Google and Wikipedia: Two Classroom Exercises and Some Musings and Trends

Mitch Fontenot

INTRODUCTION

We all do it. Some of us may not think about it, others may feel guilty as a result of it, but we all do it. We (and certainly our undergraduate students as well as some graduate students and faculty) all use Google and Wikipedia for scholarly research at times instead of using a proper database or alternative online encyclopedia, respectively. In light of this fact, I constructed an exercise to show students the superiority of Google Scholar to traditional mainstay Google. I trump that card when I show them how Academic Search Complete or Web of Science tops Google Scholar. I also designed an exercise demonstrating the difference between using Wikipedia and an online encyclopedia such as World Book Online. These mini-exercises were researched, designed, and conducted in my Library and Information Science 1001 classes to undergraduates to attempt to prove my point.

PEDAGOGY OF THESE EXERCISES AND THE ASSOCIATION OF COLLEGE AND RESEARCH LIBRARIES' INFORMATION LITERACY STANDARDS

How and why did I develop these exercises? After years of hearing librarians complaining and condemning simultaneously with students extolling the virtues of Google and Wikipedia for research papers, I thought it was time to formulate exercises to spark, encourage, and emphasize both sides of the debate. Standard Two of the Association of College and Research Libraries' (2000) *Information Literacy Competency Standards for Higher Education* (www.ala.org/ala/mgrps/divs/acrl/standards/informationliteracycompetency.cfm) states that, "the information literate student accesses needed information effectively and efficiently." In everyday working and researching the literature as well as in my humble opinion, using Google and Wikipedia for college- and university-level research papers is not accessing information effectively or efficiently. Judging by conversations with students and especially my seven teenage nieces and nephews, they will not stop using Google and Wikipedia anytime in the near future. I surmised that by comparison and fostering a classroom debate, I could show them the advantage of a database after teaching them evaluation criteria such as relevance, currency, completeness, authority, and scope, among others. I enhance that hypothesis with the fact that whereas a database such as Academic Search Complete or Web of Science may even have prepublication data (i.e., articles that will be published in the near future) for "free," that Google and Google Scholar do not. I convey to them that Google may have a high error rate for scholarly research (see the excellent University of California Berkeley Library Web sites on Search Engines at http://www.lib.berkeley.edu/TeachingLib/Guides/Internet/SearchEngines.html and show them to your students) and does not link to current articles, mainly only the older (i.e., free) stuff. I first wrote about this exercise in a small article for the American Library Association's Library Instruction Round Table (LIRT) newsletter, LIRT News (www.3.baylor.edu/LIRT/lirtnews/) in September 2007, and it is the basis for this chapter (LIRT, 2007).

HISTORY OF LIS 1001 PROGRAM

Louisiana State University Libraries has a decades-long history of teaching library research and information literacy. The course is titled Library and Instruction Science (LIS) 1001, which is a one-hour credit course available to undergraduates (Louisiana State, 2009d). The course is taught in the fall and spring semesters in both live and online environments, and online during the summer. Live classes are limited to 21 students in an electronic classroom setting with individual computer workstations. Online classes are limited to 50 students. A variety of instructors teach the course in both environments and each lends his or her own unique talents and "slant" to the course, but there are a core of topics for both the live and online versions that all are is encouraged to cover in their own unique way. These include, but are not limited to, such topics as the nature of libraries in general, LSU Libraries' home page (www.lib.lsu.edu) and online catalog, evaluation of information resources, periodicals (scholarly and popular), specific databases such as Web of Science, Lexis-Nexis Academic Universe, CQ Researcher, Vanderbilt's Television News Archive (especially for Mass Communications majors, who as a department are required to take LIS 1001), Academic Search Complete, JSTOR, Project Muse, print reference tools (with an accompanying reference scavenger hunt and a requirement of no online research accepted for this exercise), government publications, the Internet, and the evaluation of Web sites and search engines. Classes are held twice a week for a half semester, in order that we can allow twice as many students to take the course.

My version or "slant" on the course emphasizes the concept of information literacy in accordance with the Association of College and Research Libraries' *Information Literacy Competency Standards for Higher Education*. Topics taught include, but are not limited to, evaluation criteria for scholarly research, periodicals research, online catalog and database searching, search engines and Web sites, government information, the Internet, etc. Students leave the course, hopefully, with a thorough understanding of the principles of information literacy, and a fundamental knowledge of various research methods. In the midst of all of this, I usually place these exercises after we have had our lesson on evaluation criteria, and many times in tandem with the individual lessons on Academic Search Complete or Web of Science and print reference tools.

THE GOOGLE EXERCISE

While demonstrating our library's home page (www.lib.lsu.edu), I show students the section titled "Ready Reference" (Louisiana State, 2009b) and then "Search Engines" (Louisiana State, 2009c), which lists the librarians' favorite and, hopefully, best search engines under various categories such as "Academic Search Engines" (Louisiana State, 2009a). Just before doing this, however, I ask them, "How many of you have used Google?" All of their hands, including mine, go up. I ask them to take a look at the list of the academic search engines and see if any of them look promising or familiar. They always notice Google Scholar (scholar.google.com), and a few of them may have actually used it, but for the most part after using this exercise for two years, this is rare.

Just prior to introducing Academic Search Complete or Web of Science, and after having them use Google Scholar, I ask students to tell me how it looks in comparison to regular Google. They usually answer that the search interface looks identical (i.e., the same "look and feel") to regular Google. We run a search and I ask them to comment on their search results. By this time in the class, they are, or at least should be, well versed in evaluation criteria for books, periodical articles, Web sites, and search engines. They notice that the list of search hits is not the usual disorganized result of two million hits that you find on regular Google; but rather fewer, cleaner, and somewhat better organized and/or aesthetically pleasing, and generally more scholarly looking in nature (e.g., educational and governmental Web sites) to traditional, mainstream Google search results. I ask about the currency of their results and they notice that they are not chronologically arranged (as results are usually displayed from our online catalog or most database search hit lists) and—lo and behold—they are three to five years out of date on the average (i.e., in their vernacular, old stuff)! An enterprising student or two may notice the "Recent Article" feature at the top of the Google Scholar screen (as I fervently hope they do), but they are then dismayed to find out that they may have to pay for the full text of many of these "recent" articles, unlike the articles from the library's databases that are "free" to them.

COMPARISON OF GOOGLE SCHOLAR TO DATABASES

We then move on to Academic Search Complete or Web of Science. I ask students to run the identical search as they did in Google Scholar. They may be amazed as to how easy some of these databases are to search, even if they do have to think about and formulate their search using Boolean operators or search connectors. Using a well-designed database may not be as easy as using Google, but it may help the students make critical, analytical leaps from thinking of research in terms of its general subject to its more specific aspects or subtopics as opposed to just a deluge of keywords. More often than not, they are amazed as to the currency of the articles, some of which are slated for publication months in advance (if not a year), the fact that they are arranged chronologically from the most current backwards to the oldest with complete and concise citation information and, especially, that the articles are scholarly and overall more relevant to their research—not to mention "free" and possibly full text.

This is a simple exercise overall, yes, but an effective one. If, by means of this exercise, I can get students to take the "baby steps" of information literacy towards Google Scholar and, subsequently, "adult steps" to Academic Search Complete or Web of Science, I consider this exercise and this aspect of my job somewhat of a success.

WIKIPEDIA VS. WORLD BOOK ONLINE INTRODUCTION

The teaching of Wikipedia as a resource that is not best or one that should be taken as a first step for scholarly research is a tougher challenge than Google in certain respects. I begin first by directing the students to the information pages of Wikipedia, which, in all likelihood most, if not all of them, have never read. Unlike Google, Wikipedia is refreshingly, albeit disarmingly, frank in its disclaimers as to the limitations of its service regarding scholarly research. For example, under its General Disclaimer section (Wikipedia, 2009a) it prominently displays the message "WIKI-PEDIA MAKES NO GUARANTEE OF VALIDITY," with sections titled "No formal peer review" and "No contract; limited license" and "Not professional advice." In its section titled "Researching with Wikipedia" (Wikipedia, 2009b) it states, "You should not use only Wikipedia for primary research (unless you are writing a paper about Wikipedia). In all academic institutions, Wikipedia, along with most encyclopedias, is unacceptable as a major source for a research paper." Wikipedia also includes two highly detailed sections on "Why Wikipedia is so great" (Wikipedia, 2009d) and "Why Wikipedia is not so great" (Wikipedia, 2009e). Four pages of information detail Wikipedia's greatness as to "editability" by practically anyone, organization, comprehensiveness, and depth (over two and a half million English articles alone as of the writing of this article), and steps to stop "destructive edits" or vandalism. On the other hand, 12 pages of information detail why Wikipedia is not so great, mentioning challenges and concerns about accuracy, completeness, negative cultural and social, non-bias, overall quality, among others.

WIKIPEDIA VS. WORLD BOOK ONLINE EXERCISE

After the class on print reference tools and research, including encyclopedias, I then ask students to run identical searches in Wikipedia and an online encyclopedia such as World Book Online, to which our libraries subscribe. In searching for a topic that they could use and also one that would be of interest to them, and after much discussion, we came up with the topic of *video gaming*. I ask the students to run a search or searches, find an appropriate encyclopedia entry in both Wikipedia and World Book and analyze the results in accordance with ACRL Standard Two (as with the Google exercise) and draw upon the lessons about evaluation criteria as to relevancy, authoritativeness, completeness, currency, and scope. I even go so far (or so little) as to ask them how the article looks, the aesthetic use, and the ease of navigation throughout a possibly lengthy article.

The students noted some interesting details. They found that (as of the writing of this article), that Wikipedia gave them three possible search hits whereas World Book offered twelve. They also noted that the three Wikipedia hits seemed to be more on point while World Book had located some not so relevant hits in its list of 12, namely such search "hits" as Mississippi, Manon Lescaut (an opera), and Missouri, to name a few. The students chose "Video game" (Wikipedia, 2009c) as the article to analyze from Wikipedia, and "Electronic game" (Squire, Kurt) from World Book Online for comparison and evaluation purposes.

When they access and read both articles, the questions of authoritativeness and completeness strongly come into play. Students have noted that whereas the article from Wikipedia looks like it has been contributed to by many people, by examining the References section they find it does not readily give any information as to the level of expertise of these contributors such as occupation or title. Students simultaneously note that the article from World Book Online on "Electronic game" is written by one author, Dr. Kurt Squire, assistant professor of Educational Communications Technology, Curriculum and Instruction, at the University of Wisconsin at Madison. Students usually give the World Book Online article a high reliability and authoritativeness vote on this basis since its author is a professor at a major university. They have maintained that they would have to do further investigation into the numerous sources from the References section of the Wikipedia article since it does not readily describe their professional affiliations as title, occupation, etc. This gives me the opportunity to emphasize Wikipedia's simultaneous great strength as well as its weakness. Anyone, no matter how well qualified or not, can contribute to the community encyclopedia that is Wikipedia. Steps have been taken to curb Wikipedia "vandalism," such as registering its contributors, but there is still the possibility for bias and/or error as in all research sources, which students need to be made aware of through competent and constant information literacy education.

Both articles are of relatively equal length, with the Wikipedia article at 11 pages and the World Book Online article at 13. Students have noted that based on the lesson of scholarly versus popular publications as well as the nature of reference tools, that these two articles are probably more scholarly than popular in nature. My lesson on periodicals includes the characteristics of scholarly articles; peer review, written in technical jargon for a limited amount of persons interested in the subject, lengthy in nature, etc., in comparison to that of popular articles; no peer review, written in everyday, simple language for as many people to read as possible, and relatively few pages in nature. They have also noted that there is a sidebar to the various sections of the article with clickable links for easier navigation through the article. When it comes to the true in-depth analytical evaluation of the article however, the students have come up with some very interesting points. They have noted that the World Book Online article, contributed to by a solo author, seemed to flow more smoothly than that of the Wikipedia article, which they felt was filled with a lot of great (as well as not so great) facts but seemed to meander. They have also thought that both history sections about the creation and development of video gaming were good, but that the article from Wikipedia seemed to be presented in much greater detail. Some of the students also thought that the article in World Book Online, written by an educational communications and technology professor, seemed to reflect it and that the writing was a little staid, like a boring lecture in class (with no offense to the author). The section on Theory on page 4 in the Wikipedia article and the difference between the attitudes of narrativists who see "video games as a storytelling medium," and ludologists, who "argue that a video game is first and foremost a game" (en.wikipedia.org/wiki/Video_gaming) created some debate among the few sociology and psychology students I usually have enrolled in a given semester. The sections on controversy also tended to spark some serious debate, as to whether gaming is harmful; whether it promotes addictive behavior, insensitivity to violence, poor health habits, social isolationism, and denigrates certain members of society. On the other side of the debate, students also argued that video games could be helpful if they improve analytical skills, manual dexterity, and cognitive reasoning through having to learn the game and participate with members of society, sometimes literally throughout the world. This is commonly referred to as massively multiplayer online role-player games or MMORPGS, and most of the students tended to take the latter, more positive view of video gaming.

What excites them the most and swayed their arguments, however, is the number of convenient *"see also"* hypertexting links throughout the main article. Students love the fact that with a simple click they can easily "branch off " to other related topics such as: the history of video games, genres, game development and modifications, cheating (gasp!), multiplayers, benefits, controversy, and a list of bestselling videogames, just to name a few. Students love this ability of Wikipedia especially when the section they have read has either not quite given them enough information or has sparked their interest in a more specific aspect of their topic (i.e., Wikipedia can help build some rudimentary research skills such as general-to-specific topic building). At this point in the exercise/ debate, I attempt to emphasize that while electronic research is a good thing (and probably the only kind of research that, in all likelihood, they have ever done), the big white research boxes that we euphemistically know as Google (I often encourage my students to think outside the Google box, literally and figuratively) and, to a lesser degree, Wikipedia, do not necessarily hone research and analytical skills. They do not force or, perhaps better stated, train students to think from a general subject, such as gaming, to a more specific or precise aspect of it, such as theory or controversy. Some roll their eyes in dismay, or even drop my class, from day one when I tell them that one-third of my class—three out of nine assignments, four out of 12 lectures, materials, notes, etc., are based on print research. I always try to emphasize, sometimes my words falling on deaf ears, that true, effective, scholarly research greatly depends upon a thorough balance of knowledge between online or electronic and print research, and that there may be research situations, believe it or not, in which print research is superior, that is, to be what is truly considered information literate.

THE SCHOLARLY LITERATURE ON GOOGLE AND WIKIPEDIA

Golderman and Connolly (2007: 22) in *Library Journal* suggest using Google Scholar "ironically enough" as a way of weaning students from reliance on Google for scholarly research. "Hook" them with a demonstration on the extreme currency and quality of databases such as Academic Search Complete and Web of Knowledge. Atwater-Singer (2006: 11) writes about "googlewhacking" in *Indiana Libraries* to exploit Google in the instruction classroom. On the flip side of these approaches, Cathcart and Roberts (2005, 10: 171) in *Internet Reference Service Quarterly* warn that Google Scholar promotes the incorrect notion that "most information on the World Wide Web is online, full text, and free."

Searching Ebsco's *Library and Information Science Technology and Abstracts (LISTA)* and Wilson's *Library Literature and Information Science Full Text* databases on students' use of Wikipedia turned up some interesting articles and differences of opinion on the subject. Opinions tend to run the gamut of a hard line stance of not allowing them to use Wikipedia to cajoling them, if you will and as I do, into using Wikipedia as a starting point in their research in order to expose them to using databases that the library owns. Bennington's (2008) article in *American Libraries* takes the approach of having them use Wikipedia as a starting point toward acquiring information literacy skills. Murley (2008) in *Law Library Journal* goes even a step further in "defending" Wikipedia at the law school educational level. On the other end of the educational time spectrum, Achterman (2005; 2006) writes two articles on "surviving" Wikipedia in 2005 and the going "beyond" Wikipedia in 2006 at the high school level that illustrate that need for librarians and teachers to work together on the Wikipedia challenge, realizing that if they are going to use it for research regardless, perhaps education and collaboration is the key to guiding novice researchers in the right direction towards information literacy. On the alternative, Waters (2007) makes a strong argument as to why Wikipedia should not be used for scholarly research in discussing the details of the Middlebury College History Department's decision not to accept Wikipedia citations in student papers. On a more informal note, in personal conversations with high school students, more of them mention that there seems to be an increase in the banning of Wikipedia for student research papers in high schools.

ASSESSMENT

At the present time, I have not yet performed formal assessments on whether my exercise works. However, via the online class roster and e-mail, I have kept in contact with some students over the past two years, and for the most part the conversations have been positive with such statements as, "I write much better papers" and "I wish I had taken this class in my freshmen year instead of waiting or putting it off until my last semester" and "My research papers have gone up about one letter grade since I took this course." We do have pre- and post-tests of ten questions to judge the effectiveness of LIS 1001 overall, and these have been mostly positive over the years, but it is my plan to develop some sort of assessment test to judge the effectiveness of one or both tests in the near future.

HOW BEST TO PROCEED

Having reviewed the literature and conversed informally with students, my opinion is that speaking out directly against Google and Wikipedia will never suffice. Cajole them, if you will, into using Google and Wikipedia as a first step toward finding more current and reliable information. Refer to Google and Wikipedia as ready reference tools like an almanac at the ready reference desk that should be used as a first step to lead to more scholarly, reputable information. Convey to students the advantages as well as the inaccuracies and blatant mistakes in both, and nudge them toward using more reliable databases in a step-by-step process (i.e., what I euphemistically call information literacy parenting). Show them the "disclaimers" on Wikipedia. Convey to them that anyone, a novice or expert, can contribute to Wikipedia and that its accuracy rate is lower in comparison to such encyclopedias such as World Book Online or Encyclopedia Britannica (Giles, 2005).

Google and/or Wikipedia will never go away, or at least their successors will not.

Encourage students to use other online encyclopedias. Wikipedia "deftly" claims that errors can be and are quickly removed from their encyclopedia in comparison to paper encyclopedias, but does not seem to compare itself to online encyclopedias such as Encyclopedia Britannica or World Book Online. Build a healthy cynicism with your students about the limitations and currency of computerized databases. Do not allow them to deify the computer and/or databases or better still, encourage them to deify research skills and/or information literacy.

REFERENCES

Achterman, Doug. 2005. "Surviving Wikipedia: Improving Student Search Habits through Information Literacy and Teacher Collaboration." *Knowledge Quest* 33, no. 5 (May/June): 38–40.

Achterman, Doug. 2006. "Beyond Wikipedia." *Teacher Librarian* 34, no. 2 (December): 19–22.

Association of College and Research Libraries. 2000. *Information Literacy Competency Standards for Higher Education.* Chicago, IL: American Library Association. Available: www.ala.org/ala/mgrps/divs/acrl/standards/informationliteracycompetency.cfm (accessed November 18, 2009).

Atwater-Singer, Meg. 2006. "Googlewhacking: Exploiting Google in an Instruction Classroom." *Indiana Libraries* 25, no. 4: 11–14.

Bennington, Adam. 2008. "Dissecting the Web through Wikipedia." *American Libraries* 39, no. 7 (August): 46–49.

Cathcart, Rachael, and Amanda Roberts. 2005. "Evaluating Google Scholar as a Tool for Information Literacy." *Internet Reference Services Quarterly* 10, no.3/4: 167–176.

Giles, Jim. 2005. "Internet Encyclopedias Go Head to Head." *Nature* 438 (December 15): 900–901.

Golderman, Gail, and Bruce Connolly. 2007. "Who Cited This?" *Library Journal Net Connect* 132 (Winter): 18–26.

Google Scholar. Available: http://scholar.google.com (accessed November 18, 2009).

LIRT. 2007. Library Instruction Round Table (LIRT) News. Chicago, IL: American Library Association. Available: www3.baylor.edu/LIRT/lirtnews/ (accessed November 18, 2009).

Louisiana State University Libraries. Home page. Section on Academic Search Engines. Available: www.lib.lsu.edu/general/internet_searchacademic.html (accessed November 18, 2009a).

Louisiana State University Libraries. Home Page. Section on Ready Reference Sources. Available: www.lib.lsu.edu/ref/readyref.html (accessed November 18, 2009b).

Louisiana State University Libraries. Home Page. Section on Search Engines. Available: www.lib.lsu.edu/general/internet_search.html (accessed November 18, 2009c).

Louisiana State University Libraries. Library and Instruction Science (LIS) 1001 Course. Available: www.lib.lsu.edu/instruction/lis1001/lis1001.html (accessed November 18, 2009d).

Murley, Diane. 2008. "In Defense of Wikipedia." *Law Library Journal* 100: 593–599.

Squire, Kurt. "Electronic Game." *World Book Online Reference Center.* (October 30, 2008). (www.worldbookonline.com/wb/Article?id=ar752699).

University of California Berkeley Library. Home page. Section on Search Engines. Available: www.lib.berkeley.edu/TeachingLib/Guides/Internet/SearchEngines.html (accessed November 18, 2009).

Waters, Neil L. 2007. "Why You Can't Cite Wikipedia in My Class." *Communications of the ACM (Association for Computing Machinery)* 50, no. 9 (September): 15–17.

Wikipedia. General Disclaimer Section. Available: en.wikipedia.org/wiki/Wikipedia:Disclaimers (accessed November 18, 2009a).

Wikipedia. Researching with Wikipedia Section. Available: en.wikipedia.org/wiki/Wikipedia:Researching_with_Wikipedia (accessed November 18, 2009b).

Wikipedia. Video Game Article. Available: en.wikipedia.org/wiki/Video_game (accessed November 18, 2009c).

Wikipedia. Why Wikipedia Is So Great Section. Available: en.wikipedia.org/wiki/Wikipedia:Why_Wikipedia_is_so_great (accessed November 18, 2009d).

Wikipedia. Why Wikipedia Is Not So Great Section. Available: en.wikipedia.org/wiki/Wikipedia:Why_Wikipedia_is_not_so_great (accessed November 18, 2009e)

Chapter 18

Teaching Information Ethics: The Guided Research Paper

Joseph F. Joiner

INTRODUCTION: INTERGENERALITY

Originally, this chapter was slated as a guide to assist instructors and students in the areas of ethics and honesty, with respect to Gen M. While reviewing the literature, however, it quickly became apparent that many others are more qualified on the subject of ethical behavior. Any guide I devised would only be a rehash of their research. Humbled by this revelation, I turn to my own trials, tribulations, and triumphs as a university instructor. This understanding of my experiences is intergenerational in nature and is a representation of two generations interacting and interfacing, Baby Boomers and Gen M, jockeying for control of the mouse, as it were. Gen M utilizes the information highway to provide the most efficient, and sometimes quickest, reward. The Baby Boomer attempts to pass on those ethical behaviors that will hopefully promote and enhance academic integrity.

Baby Boomers

According to Faber (2001), even though individual members of a generation share the same age, no one generation itself should be identified as a single-minded homogeneous set defined by a "single defining generational experience" (212), because no single event significantly impacts all members in the same manner. Mannheim (as cited in Faber, 2001) postulates that a generational cohort contains only those [age-related] individuals who have taken "part in similar . . . defining social and intellectual activities, events, or movements of a common time and space" (295). From such group interactions, Robins and Wilner (as cited in Johnson and Romanello, 2005) contend that "each generation eventually develops and cultivates a [distinct] 'peer personality' because individuals [of a generational cohort] share 'an age location in history' that lends itself to a 'collective mind set'" (212), which develops as a result of each generation's place in human history between other cohorts. Nonetheless, since all defining generational endeavors derive as a collective process in a multigenerational environment, rather than in an isolated decision-making outpost, defining events and corresponding attitudes from preceding and following generations continually influence and reshape each other through time.

The Baby Boomer generation has been defined as those individuals born between 1943 and 1960 to gainfully employed future-optimistic parents who, contrary to earlier child-rearing practices, have indulged their children and allowed for more freedom of expression. Consequently, as the Baby Boomers came of age during the turbulent times of the civil rights movement, the Vietnam War, and Watergate in the United States, this tolerant parenting style laid the groundwork for the development of a collective Baby Boomer mind-set that found their parents' world wanting and in need of social revision. Distrusting established institutions and believing they could improve their world, and, in an attempt to surpass traditionally restrictive familial and occupational imposts, Baby Boomers, as young adults, have detached themselves from their extended families and set forth to reduce future extended family sizes, challenge the status quo, and attack age-long oppressions. In an attempt to appease their cynical and idealistic nature, as they continue to age and mature, fostered by a deterministic and devoted work ethic, Baby Boomers have successfully integrated their identity and self-worth with their careers and professions (DeBard, 2004; Johnson and Romanello, 2005).

Whether categorized as a hippie or yuppie, self-indulgence—a buy now, pay later attitude—has also persisted as a major peer-personality trait for most Baby Boomers. Despite this narcissistic self-view, with respect to their children, Baby Boomers emphasize control, safety, rules, and discipline—a do-as-I say, not-as-I-did type of philosophy (Ortner, 1998). As parents, they expect their children to learn, grow, and gain independence as young adults, thereby liberating the middle-aged Baby

Boomers to explore new self-indulgent interest prior to old age and death (DeBard, 2004).

Gen M

Johnson and Romanello (2005) define the Millennial generation, Gen M, as those individuals born between 1982 and 2002. Exhaustively planning, intentionally conceiving, and continuously nurturing them throughout their childhood and adolescence, Baby Boomer parents have repeatedly told the Millennial generation "all of their lives that they are special" (DeBard, 2004: 35). Such devoted concern for Gen M offspring's continued welfare and safety has dubbed them as the 'baby on board' and 'have you hugged your kid today' generation" (Johnson and Romanello, 2005: 213). Their parents have chosen to rear Gen M in a sheltered and affirming, yet structured—zero tolerance—environment, wishing for them to be "smart, powerful, and dutiful" (213). Duly influenced by this structured parental affirmation, members of Gen M have become "optimistic, assertive, positive, and friendly" (213), have come to expect good news, have been encouraged to believe in themselves, and have come to expect their life's work to grant them substantial rewards and monetary riches. Lancaster and Stillman; and Sax contend:

> [Members of Gen M] are confident of their ability to match the effort required to meet the expectations others place upon them and are motivated to do so as long as their own expectations of beneficial outcomes are met [; however, they] have come to expect high grades as a way of validating their achievement; on the other hand, they will only do what is expected of them to achieve these outcomes. (as cited in DeBard, 2004: 36, 41)

Howe and Strauss (as cited in DeBard, 2004) postulate that, regulated by a decree of expected social conformity, while striving toward their life's goals, Gen M prefer the rules and regulations associated with an integrated team-oriented approach, as they "expect such actions and projects to be highly structured because they do not like to work without a net" (38). In practice, Gen M's greatest challenge does not appear to be the lesson content, but rather the need to "navigate the . . . divergent values practiced and espoused by those who do not share the characteristics ascribed to the Millennials" (Lancaster and Stillman, as cited in DeBard, 2004, 39). Howe and Strauss, Martin and Tulgan, and Sax (as cited in DeBard, 2004: 35–38) further add that the sheltered members of Gen M

> have come to accept social rules that have been imposed upon them because the Baby Boomer authority figures who have defined the rules also have power and resources to support such good behavior by supporting those who follow convention. . . . [having] been encouraged to follow the rules . . . they expect the rules to be clearly communicated and enforced with due process. . . . [Gen M will show] a lack of tolerance for aberrant behavior . . . as long as the rewards for behavior are known to all.

GENERATIONAL ETHICS

Plagiarism

Ruggiero defines ethics as "the study of right and wrong conduct" (2008: 5), and "unethical decisions can be defined as going against the normal behaviors of society (Detert, Trevino, and Sweitzer, as cited in Graham, 2008: 3). Ruggiero further asserts that ethics should focus on situations "in which there is a choice of behavior involving human values" (2008: 5). Accordingly, the discipline of ethics collects, evaluates, and interprets data related to cultural beliefs and behaviors. From such data, ethics determines which beliefs and behaviors are morally correct, regardless of sanctioned cultural paradigms. Throughout history, preceding generations have painstakingly attempted to impart the virtues and rubrics of ethical mores to their succeeding generations. Due to its profound and far-reaching effects on the continued legitimacy of academic integrity, the ethical conduct of intellectual honesty, and the perplexities, dilemmas and implications associated with contrary behavior, that is, plagiarism, continue to demand ethical consideration from postmodern scholars and student alike. Ruggiero writes:

> Once ideas are put into words and published, they become intellectual property, and the author has the same rights over them as he or she has over material property. . . . Anyone who has ever wracked his or her brain trying to solve a problem or trying to put an idea into clear and meaningful words can appreciate how difficult mental effort can be. (2008: 15)

Any individual who, knowing or unknowingly, quotes or paraphrases another author's written words and ideas without properly citing him or her as the true owner of the intellectual property in any academic exercise has committed academic dishonesty, or plagiarism (Rutgers, 2004).

Despite repeated efforts to identify and curtail plagiarism, any human endeavor dependent upon oral and written forms of language to communicate philosophical ideas, research data, and theoretical concepts remains at risk. As evidence, daily newspapers continuously report suspected and confirmed incidents of single and multiple episodes of plagiarism by members of all academic and non-academic undertakings (Dionne, 1987; McGrath, 2007; Roberts, 2008; Stolberg, 2008). Based on academic integrity literature and university professor accounts, Hayes and Introna (2005) report an increase in plagiarism among postmodern college students. In an attempt to identify the prevalence of cut-and-paste Internet plagiarism, the researchers of one study have concluded that 38 percent of those undergraduate students surveyed admitted to this type of unethical behavior (Rimer, 2003). Another survey has determined that "only 27% of college students thought cutting and pasting someone else's work was 'serious cheating'" (Thompson, 2006: 2429). McCabe (as cited in Rimer, 2003) contends that many students believe that Internet material does not need to be cited because it is public knowledge.

Intergenerational comparison of the difference in levels of academic integrity conducted by McCabe, Treviño, and Butterfield (2001) further demonstrates the prevalence of increased academic cheating over a 30-year period by college students. In an attempt to identify the possibility of any significant difference in the levels of ethical behavior between contemporary students and college students from the 1960s, Webster and Harmon (2002) have compared data from questionnaires given to samples of college students from the two respective generations. Based on student answers, the authors claim that contemporary college students admitted to an increase in a Machiavellian mentality over college students attending college in the 1960s. According to Granitz and Loewy (2006), people influenced by and adhering to a Machiavellian mind-set are motivated by perceived self-interests. Such individuals "employ aggressive, manipulative, exploitive, and devious methods to achieve goals without regard for the feelings, rights, and needs of others" (Webster and Hammon, 2002: 435). These data suggest the potential for a decrease in ethical behavior among younger adults in the university, workplace, and societal environs.

Nonetheless, the mere fact of the generation's makeup and historical position does not automatically render a foolproof maxim that conclusively determines a cause-and-effect relationship between the individuals and their ethical behavior. Regardless of a generation's prevalent mindset on ethical behavior, not all students act unethically. Bennett (as cited in Nadelson, 2007) found that some students act ethically because they do not want to face the consequences of such behavior. Feeling a sense of loyalty toward their instructors, fellow classmates, and themselves, others defer from dishonest scholastic behavior. In fact, Princeton University students have organized and held a campus-wide assembly in order to educate the student body on the merits of academic integrity (Rimer, 2003). Nadelson (2007) adds that institutional honor codes play an important factor, which regulates both student and faculty ethical behavior. Liddell and Fong further contend, "[honor and ethics] policies . . . can be effective in helping students understand what constitutes plagiarism and how to avoid it" (2008: 5). McCabe, Butterfield, and Treviño add that in institutions with honor codes, instructors have "more positive attitudes toward their schools academic policies and are more willing to allow the system to take care of monitoring and disciplinary activities" (as cited in Nadelson, 2007: 6). Nadelson (2007) further reports that instructors can serve as role models and foster ethical behavior from their students when they maintain an emotional and physical availability with their students. Despite these findings, however, some students do act unethically; therefore, educators, reviewers, and editors need to remain vigilant to ensure writers reference all intellectual property, because "Manuscripts cannot be clones either in skeleton or in soul" (Boquiren, Creed, and Shapiro, 2006: 431).

Cyber-Plagiarism

Rettie (2002) asserts, "the effect of the Internet is not ubiquitous" (255), because not all individuals, families, or cultures are able to or choose to be connected to the Internet. Regardless of these varying demographics, Horn writes, "Information technology will change everything in the world in which we live. There will be no institution, no person and no government that will be unaffected" (as cited in Rettie, 2002: 254) Gen M is a title used by scholars, researchers, and demographers to describe the cohort of individuals who have grown up with ready access to the Internet. Members of Gen M have (typically) grown up in a technologically rich home and school environment. Unlike their parents, they operate the computer and access the Internet deftly with authoritative mastery. This skill-reversal phenomenon elevates the young people to mentors and demotes the parents to the pupil.

In the postmodern academic world, the Internet renders a dual service as both research and teaching tool. Consequently, the Internet not only provides an efficient resource for information retrieval, it also presents an opportunistic haven for plagiarism. Granitz and Loewy report, "through online term paper mills . . . Google searches . . . and library databases, students literally have a world of information at their fingertips. The Internet has made cyber-cheating as simple as a mouse click" (2006: 293, 296). Although in actuality, the true amount of cyber-plagiarism occurring among students remains unclear, limited research data finds that 41 percent of undergraduate students and 25 percent of graduate students polled report that they have plagiarized by cutting and pasting from both written and Internet sources as least once in their academic careers (Center for Academic Integrity, as cited in Granitz and Loewy, 2006; Muha, as cited in Thompson, 2006).

Electronic paper mills, which are highly profitable Internet sources that provide online prefabricated and custom written assignments, compound the problem of Internet-facilitated plagiarism ("Plagiarism and the Internet," as cited in Granitz and Loewy, 2006). In an attempt to detect and circumvent this vexing postmodern cyber-resource, many colleges and universities subscribe to electronic text matching services provided by such Internet sites as Turnitin.com. As a prerequisite to handing in research assignments, students must first transfer an electronic version of their term paper into the text matching service's data bank. This provides professors with a technological resource to reduce incidents of plagiarism. Raw (as cited in Regan, 2008) reports that 100,000 papers from 7,000 institutions are uploaded daily into Turnitin.com's database. Such vigilant behavior should significantly counter and thwart the paper mills' advantage. Unfortunately, by ceasing the printing of mass-produced, identifiable cut-and-pasted papers, an increasing number of electronic paper mills have met the challenge and evolved into "professionally designed sites touting custom writing services" by hiring graduate students and professional writers to pen completely untraceable papers, which severely hinders the instructor's attempt to halt such technically proficient unethical behavior (Thompson, 2006: 2442; Regan, 2008). Warn also reports, "plagiarism detection software can provide some real teeth to warnings about plagiarism since verbatim copying is easily detected. However, the software does not detect all plagiarism and, in particular, will miss paraphrased material and material not previously submitted" (Thompson, 2006: 201).

SYSTEMIC VARIABLES

Students

Because human behavior is based on a complex system of cultural influences, no one influential factor determines students' ethical decision-making processes (Hayes and Introna, 2005; Taylor, Paterson, Usick, and Smith as cited in Nadelson, 2007). Students plagiarize for various reasons from planned deception to course-work overload, to mandatory-course dissatisfaction to time mismanagement to simple misunderstanding of citation rules. They may understand the differences between paraphrasing and plagiarism, but their writing mirrors the cited author's words too closely. Some students may surmise—correctly or not—that they can outwit their inferior technologically adept professor. In one study, McCabe (as cited in Rimer, 2003) reports, "one student wrote, 'If professors cannot detect a paper from an Internet source, that is a flaw in the grader, or professor'." Academic cheating may also be accepted practices among fellow students (Carroll, as cited in Hayes and Introna, 2005; Granitz, and Loewy, 2006; Roig, 2001; Thompson, 2006).

In an attempt to identify ethical-reasoning theories employed by students, Granitz and Loewy (2006) performed a content analysis of plagiarism cases at a large West Coast American University. The authors have identified three major reasons as to why students cheat—Deontology, Situational Ethics, and Machiavellianism. From the sample of students questioned, 41 percent reported ignorance, or deontology, as the reasoning behind their plagiarism. Proponents of a deontological perspective believe that a student only cheats when he or she knows and understands the guidelines for plagiarism. If a student plagiarizes, but "didn't know what plagiarism was [or] . . . didn't know that plagiarism was wrong" (297), then the student cannot be guilty of plagiarism. Approximately 20 percent of the students sampled have stated that they knew the rules for plagiarism at the outset of the writing assignment; however, they justify the ethical dishonesty as a result of a contextual dilemma arising during the time period in which the paper was written. From this situational ethics perspective, behavior results from the contingencies of the social situation. The contextual stress the writer faces during the writing process causes the unethical behavior, that is, "My kid was sick" (299). If the situation presents no stressful factors, the student does not resort to unethical behavior. Third, 18 percent of students who plagiarized acted unethically from a Machiavellian, or self-interest, perspective. These students justify their behavior if they do not get caught, and if they happen to get caught, they blame others as the reason for the unethical behavior; i.e., "Look how clever I am . . . I can plagiarize, do well, and not get caught. [or] It's the teacher's fault" (299).

Families and Cultures

Regardless of the numerous justifications for both ethical and unethical behavior, students first begin to learn the rules associated with ethical behavior from their families and the cultures in which they operate. These rules begin to take root in the minds of the students at a young age and further develop through time and experience from family role models and cultural norms. Thompson (2006) believes, "Students are confused about or uninterested in the expectations for ethical behavior and that such confusion begins well before students are in college" (2006: 2441). Mathieson and Tyler have reported that some university faculty believe that it is a waste of time teaching ethics to young collegiate adults, because "Values are formed in childhood. Neither companies nor . . . schools can do anything about it. Therefore, changing behavior is impossible" (2008: 2). When surveyed, a college student has written, "You can't stop it [Academic Cheating] . . . . Some people were just raised that way" (Rimer, 2003, 2). Furthermore, Thompson (2006) reports incidents in which parents also either hired an editor to write their child's paper or wrote the paper for the child. May Akabogu-Collins researched and reported incidents of parental unethical behavior with respect to their children's collegiate papers. Akabogu-Collins, "herself a professor, insisted that she would still provide her son's essay with some 'motherly editing'" (Akabogu-Collins, as cited in Thompson, 2006: 2441).

Interestingly enough, some acts of conscious plagiarism are to be understood from long-standing cultural bias. Hayes and Introna (2005) have found that foreign students studying at American colleges and universities find the West's approach to learning at odds with their cultural experiences. In China, consciously plagiarizing another's words is a form of respect. In Asia and Greece, students understand the teacher as the unquestioned authority and the text's author as the presumed expert, so, as a rule, the students need only to memorize the teacher's and author's words. With students for whom English is a second language, they may find themselves under pressure from linguistic constraints. The rules for writing in the foreign language can prove to be a daunting process, so the student willfully plagiarizes. Foreign students may be under pressure to perform well because families, industry, or governments fund their educations, and so they plagiarize in order to maintain a high GPA.

Academia

Either prior to or at the collegiate level, most students understand that to paraphrase means to reword another's central idea into the student's own words and give the cited author credit for the passage. First, unfortunately, Roig finds that "there appears to be no general operational definition for paraphrasing" (2001: 10), and there are "few . . . existing definitions of paraphrasing in traditional writing guides [that] operationalize" (2001: 3) terms such as plagiarism. As a result, there is no rule that defines "the exact degree to which text must be modified to be classified as correctly paraphrased" (2001: 3). Warn also contends that the "existing categories of plagiarism appear too broad to provide useful tools for analyzing actual incidents of plagiarism" (2006: 197). Second, at times, there appears to be confusion regarding whether or not the cited passage is paraphrasing or summarizing. While paraphrasing is the restatement of another's words, summarization "condenses larger amounts of text into a few sentences for the purposes of conveying the main points of the original" (Roig, 2001: 9). The question to be answered is whether or not the students understand the difference between paraphrasing and summarizing. Third, college professors, themselves, do not all agree on the exact operational definition of plagiarism. In a study of rewritten versions of a paragraph from a journal article, college professors, when asked to consider if the re-worded paragraph was plagiarized, did not always agree the student's rewording was plagiarism, even with professors within the same academic discipline. Compounding this problem, all professors do not adhere to the same writing practices in their classrooms. Equally important, professors from different disciplines appear to define plagiarism differently (Roig, 2001).

Unfortunately, the struggle to maintain high ethical standards moves beyond the context of the student–professor relationship and into the realm of university policies. Thompson (2006) reports that shifts in university administration policies may actually encourage unethical behavior. Some contemporary colleges and universities have shifted from a student-as-student to a student-as-customer attitude. As such, students are no longer granted academic admission at the pleasure of the faculty but are catered to from a retail perspective in which the student, as the customer, is always right and is to be appeased as such, regardless of ethical conduct. In an attempt to remain financially solvent, following other postmodern business practices, many colleges and universities outsource course teaching to adjunct faculty. These part-time lecturers may lack the educational training, as well as the technological and time resources that full-time faculty members have at their disposal to investigate possible instances of plagiarism.

Many university faculty and administration do continue to address ethical issues through various educational approaches and punitive sanctions. As a minimum, some universities, such as Rutgers University, develop academic integrity policies that provide a consistent guidepost for both faculty and students (Rutgers, 2004). Liddell and Fong (2008) contend that some educational institutions utilize the academic integrity policy after the fact and address plagiarism from a reactive position once the student has committed an unethical act. Only after the student has been suspected of plagiarism, scholastic standing committees invoke the academic integrity policy to review the case, and, from which, the student can receive one of various pre-ordained academic penalties ranging from a failing grade for the paper or class to expulsion from the institution. Other institutions, from a proactive stance, cultivate and reinforce ethical behavior as part of the instructional process. They develop programs, workshops, and tutorials in which students are instructed on what defines plagiarism and which strategies are used preventing it. (Bowman, 2004; Liddell and Fong, 2008). Instructors are encouraged to be available to their students, both online and during office hours, and to work closely with their students throughout the entire writing process, not just the final grading procedure (Pfeuffer-Scherer, 2004). From this, the students and faculty enhance and maintain the academic integrity of their institution.

THE BABY BOOMER VS. THE GEN M EXPERIENCE

I think a generational cohort exists more so as systemic qualitative mind set rather than a linear quantitative age group. Since I was born in the mid-1950s, I am classified as a Baby Boomer, but while growing up, I never fully believed, nor felt, I was a member of that generation—

I sometimes still think of myself from another cohort. Baby Boomers have reached their 60s, and I have just arrived at the mid-century mark. Ten year's difference can be a big gap, especially during childhood and adolescence. Growing up, I perceived Baby Boomers as those children born to the World War II generation, who came of age during the Vietnam War. My parents were young teenagers during World War II, and I graduated from high school a year after the Vietnam War ended. My graduating class was the first of the post-Vietnam War 18-year-old-males not required to register for selective service, which further widened the gap between my age group from those who I thought of as Baby Boomers. As a young teenager, I believed the real Baby Boomers were the hippies and yuppies that fought and protested the Vietnam War. These people were the older brothers and sisters of my friends. I saw them as adults. In fact, it was not until I entered middle age that I realized they were only teenagers, like me, at the time.

Growing up in a Northeast American blue-collar river community, I cannot say that in my limited experience I had observed a true representative sample of the Baby Boomers, either. The World War II generation of men in my community mostly worked blue-collar and factory jobs, and the women were stay-at-home moms. The Baby Boomers born from the World War II generation in my community grew up hearing of heroic acts and learning community pride from their fathers as they regaled their offspring with intrepid wartime yarns in the American Legion and VFW halls. From this experience, most of the young impressionable males believed it was their patriotic duty to enlist and fight in the Vietnam War. The hippies I knew seemed more occupied with unbridled sex and illicit drug use than challenging the tyrannies of the establishment. I thought only the Baby Boomer veterans dedicated themselves to changing the world for the better, not the self-absorbed hippies.

Today, I strongly identify with and practice many of the ethical beliefs and values of the Baby Boomer generation. Regardless of my parent's age and my place on the Baby-Boomer time line, being part of a multigenerational community, I received many of life's instructions and lessons from the World War II generation. In hindsight, I realized they took pride in teaching ideals meant to produce an ethical lifestyle: a do-what-you're-suppose-to-do tenet. What was I supposed to do? The men and women of World War II lovingly planted and relentlessly nurtured a "Work hard and be honest" rule into my young psyche during my formative years. In late 1970s, which seemed a highly unethical time of aftershocks from the deception and violence of the Vietnam era, I often observed those who did subscribe to those high ideals that were taught to me by the World War II generation pay the price for their honesty and forthrightness. At the time, society did not seem to want anyone to hold up a mirror to its unchecked Machiavellian behavior. Luckily, with time, societal attitudes have changed for the better; however, the experience has left me, as with other middle-aged Baby Boomers, sometimes cynical and impatient with young Gen Ms as they grow and attempt to reshape the world according to their own prevailing generational ideas and self-interests. Rather than as a parent, my direct experience with Gen M has been as a part-time university lecturer. For the first course I instructed, I created a one-page syllabus, which simply identified the course text, daily lecture material, and mid- and final exam and research paper dates. I believed there was no need to micro-manage the course, because, no doubt, these were highly motivated college students who could and would self-regulate their behavior. After all, they must have had a higher calling to learn for the ascetic value of knowing. Since the course was a four-week summer session, I integrated the mid-term and final exam into a two-part cumulative paper, each of which was a take-home assignment. The day after the mid-term, I explained the main premise of the final exam to the class. Having the information they needed for their take-home final, two-thirds of the students stopped attending the lectures. This became my first understanding that some Gen Ms would only do what was expected of them and no more.

I also required both exams be written in an accepted version of the American Psychological Association's (APA) format, which requires submitted manuscripts to follow a coherent detailed structure. For most of the students, APA formatting only meant a double-spaced paper. From this abject experience, I realized that if I expected members of Gen M to perform at a standard necessary to compete in the post-undergraduate environment, I would need to abandon my minimalist approach and invest additional time developing a detailed, comprehensive lesson plan.

I think the decision to commit more time to the Gen M student was the stepping-stone that converted my thinking to the parenting Baby-Boomer mind-set. Our rolls began to mimic that of a parent and child relationship. As with any structured relationship, if I expected the students (children) to comply, as the instructor (parent), I had to develop, set, and enforce a coherent set of rules. I expanded my syllabus sevenfold, specifically detailing attendance and grading policies, lecture readings, paper, and exam guidelines. As the students found loopholes in my syllabus, I revised and revised. As an unexpected outcome of this process, students began informing their fellow classmates about my stringent regulations, and those who preferred not to invest a significant amount of time toward this regimen refrained from enrolling in my courses. This invaluable consequence provided both the students and I with an academic environment, in which I quickly learned that the students were eager to comply; however, they expected me to provide them with a thought-provoking, multifaceted course outline that substantially rewarded them for their investment.

The greatest challenge had been, and still remains, the paper assignments. Initially, I viewed research and writing deficits as a lack of attention to detail, and I reacted to the errors by punitively grading mistakes and omissions, which quickly became counterproductive. After further evaluation, in order to develop a proactive stance, I concluded that some students needed more research, review, and manuscript instructional training, which I alone could not provide. With respect to writing skills, I realized that despite their identical class ranking, they were a heterogeneous group. Many did not enter the university as freshman following the prescribed writing courses. A significant portion entered the university after attending two-year colleges. I sought help from the university's student writing resource center, which enthusiastically provided the students with valuable paper-editing skills. To encourage the students to utilize the writing center, I refrained from being their primary paper editor. For those who utilized the resource, their writing skills began to improve significantly.

In graduate school, my professors demanded a high standard of APA-formatting skills. No student can master the American Psychological Association's publication manual in one sitting. APA-formatting proficiency is a perpetual process. Most of my fellow graduate students and I agreed that, despite the degree of training we received in undergraduate school, we still had more to learn. As an undergraduate instructor, I believe students should become proficient with APA formatting prior to graduate school. As such, I have created an outline of the manual and present a procedural-guideline lecture in each course. Since any group of students possesses varying degrees of paper-writing skills, sacrificing course content lecture time can be problematic. Given the choice during the course, most students prefer to have their individual paper issues addressed during lecture time and not during the instructor's office hours. Unfortunately, this process requires a serious time commitment that is needed to cover course material. Initially, I utilized student e-mails to help alleviate the problem. Since students often write their final draft during the week or weekend prior to the assignment's due date, I found myself frequently monitoring student e-mail traffic. As often as possible, I collected papers during the first class session after a weekend, which gave me more time to answer questions. Recently, Rutgers University added an online course management program, which provides a valuable instructional resource to instructors and students. The program furnishes the students and instructor with an online discussion and chat room modality, in which the students can present any issue for review and clarification. All class members can simultaneously view and respond to their fellow students' questions or comments. Since I began utilizing the program, I found, in most cases, I only needed to monitor student questions, because they often would help each other before I had time to respond. During a previous semester, of the two courses I instructed, only one class utilized the course management program. Their grades significantly outranked the group who did not.

The most daunting and intricate part of the paper assignment has been issues regarding the Internet and literature review. Seeking updated academic literature-reviewing procedures, I reached out to the university library staff for guidance. I began sacrificing a lecture period from each course in order to have the research librarians retrain the students and myself in the skills of Internet-based literature database research. I also provide a copy of each course's paper guidelines to the research librarian assigned to my department so he/she may help students one-on-one. At present, the university library staff continues to provide invaluable training to students.

From this valued instructional process, I additionally began to comprehend not only the research and instructional potential of the Internet, but also the copious possibilities for unethical behavior, most important, plagiarism. I also realized how technologically inept and unprepared I was to detect and thwart such behavior. Once I started tending to suspect passages from student papers, I quickly learned that plagiarism was more prevalent than I could have suspected. I have witnessed plagiarism ranging from one passage not being cited to an entire paper being a cut-and-pasted version of another author's paper. When questioned, one student reported receiving "editing help" from a parent who possessed a graduate degree. How many papers have been turned in that were bought or retrieved from another source in my tenure? I will not venture a guess. Without full evidence, I could err in either direction. I continually attempt to address the issue with the assistance of a Turnitin.

com account. Regardless of the degree of citation error, when challenged, every student thus far has issued forth with the deontology defense—"I didn't know I was plagiarizing." Whether being realistic or cynical, I still find this a difficult proposition to believe in all cases.

After my initial doubtful reactions to the high prevalence of deontological reasoning, I initiated a fourfold attempt to alleviate the confusion surrounding citation protocol. First, I lectured on the rules for directly quoting and paraphrasing, showing examples from previous papers. Second, if, while grading a paper, I had some concerns regarding citation errors, I handed back the paper without posting a grade and requested the student present the cited material. This requires students to meet with me during office hours and rectify the confusion. Initially, I found that some students often resented this post-assignment procedure. For some students, once they handed in the paper, they believed they owed no other responsibility toward its grade, and they have expressed so emphatically in the student course evaluations. Although the reviewing process takes time and has required patience on my part, I have received enough positive feedback from those students who are truly confused with the citation process and truly want to develop their paper skills.

Third, my students and I do not operate in a vacuum. We are part of a larger system governed by rules of academic integrity. As an alumnus of the program in which I instruct, my connection to the university goes beyond the classroom. The distinguished reputation of the undergraduate program played no small part in my acceptance into graduate programs, and I feel a debt of obligation toward the university. Providing the students with the same potential for success by maintaining ethical standards affords me the opportunity to repay my alma mater for my academic career. As such, I have a responsibility to the intergenerational university community to enforce the policy on academic integrity.

Although, in most cases, the majority of students make only minor citation errors, which can be addressed and corrected with a one-on-one tutorial session. Sometimes the violation requires the paper be submitted for a university review, which is not a positive experience for either the student or me. Prior to submitting a paper, I consult with the departmental chairperson and office of the dean for the faculty of arts and sciences to determine the need for university review. From the support, I have often been able to reduce the stress of the proceedings and have gained valuable insight, which I have utilized as preventative measure during paper guideline instructional time.

Finally, I make the paper content and structure as specific as possible in an attempt to prevent students from recycling old assignments and downloading papers from the online paper mills. Initially, I resisted this decision, because I wanted to promote creativity by having students review, research, and write on a course–related topic that interests them. With each course paper, I have to continually find the new equation that balances out student interest and ethical concerns. This process continues.

AFTERTHOUGHTS

As you no doubt have noticed, regarding plagiarism, I have not developed a profoundly conclusive guide. I am only rehashing timeless academic issues and postulates that we attempt to utilize and circumvent student unethical behavior. Bowman writes, "Good teaching practices are hard to define" (2004: 51), and I am not immune from this statement. With respect to teaching ethical behavior, I have found that there are no quick and easy answers, and somewhere within us, we all know this statement to be true. I have no control over the students' familial or cultural lessons. I cannot stop a student from using a "parental" editor. I cannot stop a student from buying a custom paper. In fact, I would need student assistance if I wanted to locate a resource on the Internet that provides such a service. How many of my former students have turned in a purchased or plagiarized paper and received a grade without my detection? I do not know. I hope not too many. Has the time that I have spent instructing the students paid off ethically? I know it has. How so? The citation errors from students who take multiple courses with me have decreased. So, what can I add here to the existing literature? It takes a community to raise a child.

REFERENCES

Boquiren, F., F. Creed, and C. Shapiro. 2006. "Plagiarism: Digging to the Root of the Problem." *Journal of Psychosomatic Research* 61: 431.

Bowman, Vibiana. 2004 "Intellectual Honesty: Selling It!" In *The Plagiarism Plague: A Resource Guide and CD-ROM Tutorial for Educators and Librarians* (pp. 51–60), edited by Vibiana Bowman. New York: Neal-Schuman.

DeBard, R. 2004. "Millennials Coming to College." *New Directions for Student Services* 106 (Summer): 33–44.

Dionne, E. J. 1987. "Biden Was Accused of Plagiarism in Law School." *New York*

Times (February 17). Available: www.nytimes.com (accessed October 28. 2008).

Faber, B. D. 2001. "Gen/Ethics? Organizational Ethics and Student and Instructor Conflict in Workplace Training." *Technical Communication Quarterly* 10, no. 3: 291–318.

Graham, R. 2008. "Plagiarism and Ethics." Unpublished manuscript. Rutgers: The State University of New Jersey, Camden Campus.

Granitz, N., and D. Loewy. 2006. "Applying Ethical Theories: Interpreting and Responding to Student Plagiarism." *Journal of Business Ethics* 72: 293–306.

Hayes, N., and L. D. Introna. 2005. "Cultural Values, Plagiarism, and Fairness: When Plagiarism Gets in the Way of Learning." *Ethics & Behavior* 15, no. 3: 213–231.

Johnson, S. A., and M. L. Romanello. 2005. "Generational Diversity: Teaching and Learning Approaches." *Nurse Educator* 30, no. 50: 212–216.

Liddell, J., and V. Fong. 2008. "Honesty, Integrity, and Plagiarism: The Role of Student Values in Prevention." *Plagiary: Cross-Disciplinary Studies in Plagiarism, Fabrication, and Falsification* 3, no. 1: 1–5.

Mathieson, K., and C. Tyler. 2008. "'We Don't Need No Stinking Ethics': The Struggle Continues." *Journal of College & Character* 9, no. 4: 1–12.

McCabe, D. L., L K. Treviño, and K. D. Butterfield. 2001. "Cheating in Academic Institutions: A Decade of Research." *Ethics & Behavior* 11, no. 13: 219–232.

McGrath, C. 2007. "Plagiarism: Everybody into the Pool." *New York Times* (January 7). Available: www.nytimes.com (accessed October 27, 2008).

Nadelson, S. 2007. "Academic Misconduct by University Students: Faculty Perceptions and Responses." *Plagiary: Cross-Disciplinary Studies in Plagiarism, Fabrication, and Falsification* 2: 67–76.

Ortner, S. B. 1998. "Generation X: Anthropology in a Media-saturated World." *Cultural Anthropology* 13, no. 3: 414–440.

Pfeuffer-Scherer, D. 2004. "Academic Remedies: A Survey of University Policies on Intellectual Honesty." In *The Plagiarism Plague: A Resource Guide and CD-ROM Tutorial for Educators and Librarians* (pp.105–124), edited by Vibiana Bowman. New York: Neal-Schuman.

Regan, J. 2008. "Curing the Cold but Killing the Patient: Turnitin.com, Online Paper Mills, and the Outsourcing of Academic Work." *Plagiary: Cross–Disciplinary Studies in Plagiarism, Fabrication, and Falsification* 3, no. 2: 1–11.

Rettie, R. 2002. "Net Generation Culture." *Journal of Electronic Commerce Research* 3, no. 4: 254–264.

Rimer, S. 2003. "A Campus Fad That's Being Copied: Internet Plagiarism Seems on the Rise." *New York Times* (September 3). Available: www.nytimes.com (accessed October 27, 2008).

Roberts, S. 2008. "In Politics, Inspiration or Plagiarism Is a Fine Line." *New York Times* (February 20). Available: www.nytimes.com (accessed June 1, 2008).

Roig, M. 2001. "Plagiarism and Paraphrasing Criteria of College and University Professors." *Ethics & Behavior* 11, no. 3: 307–323.

Ruggiero, V. R. 2008. *Thinking Critically about Ethical Issues*. 7th ed. New York: McGraw-Hill.

Rutgers: The State University of New Jersey, Faculty of Arts and Sciences. 2004.

Policy on Academic Integrity for Undergraduate and Graduate Students. Available: www.camden.rutgers.edu/RUCAM/Academic-Integrity-Policy.php (accessed October 27, 2008).

Stolberg, S. G. 2008. "Bush Aide Resigns after Admitting Plagiarism." *New York Times* (March 1). Available: www.nytimes.com (accessed October 27, 2008).

Thompson, C. 2006. "Unintended Lessons: Plagiarism and the University." *Teachers College Record* 108, no. 12: 2439–2449.

Warn, J. 2006. "Plagiarism Software: No Magic Bullet!" *Higher Education Research & Development* 25, no. 2: 195–208.

Webster, R. L., and H. A. Harmon. 2002. "Comparing Levels of Machiavellianism of Today's College Students with College Students of the 1960s." *Teaching Business Ethics* 6: 435–445.

Chapter 19

Information Literacy vs. Computer Literacy: The First-Year Experience as a Teaching Tool

Beth Larkee

INTRODUCTION

Gen M students often underestimate their need for information. Many assume all knowledge is online and freely available through an easily searchable interface. But in the scholarly writing process, finding the information is only half the equation; it is how it is used that counts. As first defined by the American Library Association in 1989 and reaffirmed in the *Information Literacy Competency Standards for Higher Education* in 2000, the information literate person is someone who can "recognize when information is needed and have the ability to locate, evaluate, and use effectively the needed information." (American Library Association, 2000: 1). Conventional wisdom holds that most incoming first-year students are computer savvy; however, that assumption does not always hold true. Computer skill assessment and training is the recommended practice for ensuring that students can avail themselves of the technologies used at their university (Junco, 2005). One of the major challenges for educators who work with Gen M students, especially incoming freshmen, is to help these students to understand and master the differences between computer literacy and information literacy.

As an academic librarian, it is my personal experience that many of the first-year students I teach are surprised at the amount of information contained in the library's password-protected subscription databases. Databases such as these are part of the Internet often referred to as the "Invisible Web" or the "Deep Web." Because they are password protected these resources are typically not freely available through search engines such as Google and Yahoo!. Estimates regarding the size of the Invisible Web vary greatly. A 2006 study estimates the academic Invisible Web may contain between 20 and 100 billion documents (Lewandowski and Mayr, 2006). The lack of accessibility to this material through the major search engines makes counts nearly impossible. Egger-Sider and Devine compare the Invisible Web to Goliath, "a giant, albeit a cumbersome giant, lacking a single search tool, dwarfing the Web that is accessible to Google" (2005: 90). Search engines, like Google, are easy to access and easy to use. While most college librarians can relate from personal experience that students repeatedly use Google over any library database, the Pew Internet and American Life Project has the proof. This 2002 study reports that 73 percent of students used Internet resources as their first stop in information searching versus only 9 percent who tried library resources first (Jones et al., 2002: 3). It is the role of educators to show what is available and to guide them to the best and most appropriate resources—in short to teach information literacy.

One challenge is to "catch" incoming freshman in order to install good scholarly habits from the outset—first semester, first year. Collaboration between librarians and faculty is one way to meet this challenge of achieving information literacy by providing them with high quality assignments, introducing them to the appropriate sources, and meeting measurable objectives.

In this chapter, I will demonstrate how First-Year Seminars can provide a solid foundation through in-depth subject-specific research. Specifically, how it is important to reach every first-year student in his/her first semester, through collaboration between the faculty and librarians. This foundation will carry students through four years of college and continue into their professional lives. Technology, essential to the Gen M student, can be used both inside and outside of the classroom to support a fluid, mobile learning environment. I will discuss the lessons learned during our first attempt to measure the progress of the students, and what we came away with from the experience drawn from our own assessments, formal and informal. We continue to use these results to modify our instruction and best serve students in their information literacy journey.

THE FIRST-YEAR EXPERIENCE: OVERVIEW

A popular trend among universities is to implement a First-Year Seminar or Experience program, and with good reason. Studies such as Porter and Swing's show that students enrolled in these programs are less likely to drop out than students in universities without such programs (2006). However, the First-Year Seminar serves a broader purpose than merely a retention device; it is a pedagogical tool for instilling excellence in undergraduate scholarship.

According to a survey by the National Resource Center for The First-Year Experience and Students in Transition, First-Year Seminars have been implemented at nearly 85 percent of college campuses. Less than half (47.8 percent) of these have been around for more than a decade (National Resource Center, 2006). While these seminars exist in a variety of formats the National Resource Center listed three main course objectives that the schools reported (2006): to develop academic skills (64.2 percent); to provide an orientation to campus resources and services (52.9 percent); and for self-exploration/personal development (36.9 percent). Of course, the faculty cannot do it alone and collaboration between faculty and librarians will benefit students and the university as a whole. As one educator put it, "What is needed is an even further expansion of the role of librarian as educator. Therefore, the place of the library needs to figure into the overall educational goals of any college or university. A library instruction program for first-year students must be understood in the context of the total activities of the student, the library and the curriculum" (Watts, 2005: 339).

Some universities have taken innovative approaches to the traditional library orientation, for example, Eckerd College (St. Petersburg, Florida). Here students attend an orientation held in August, three weeks before the returning students, called "Autumn Term." These students work closely with the librarians to complete the four areas of the technology requirement: word processing, e-mail and listservs, use of library systems, and use of the Internet for academic research (Schwartz and Siegel, 2005). Thus, all Eckerd freshmen receive a solid foundation regarding the skills they need for academic research before the start of the regular semester.

Another trend, especially at larger institutions, is to designate a First-Year Seminar librarian. This librarian focuses on freshman instruction and orientation as well as traditional library functions such as reference. Some schools, such as the University of Cincinnati, have the First-Year Experience librarian report directly to the administrators of the First-Year program. This person teaches nearly 100 instruction sessions to the first-year students. Other programs, as at the University of Montana, have the First-Year Seminar librarian serve more as a coordinator, and run a "train-the-trainer" program for colleagues (Boff et al., 2007). Either way, the library is fully integrated into the First-Year Seminar curriculum by means of a dedicated professional. Smaller universities more typically rely on dividing up instruction responsibilities between all librarians.

Across all campuses, large or small, one point remains consistent for the incoming first-year student: that student needs academic support from faculty, administrators, and librarians outside the confines of the traditional classroom. One approach is to meet the students in the places where the students are, particularly online. Faculty and librarians have incorporated virtual office hours either through e-mail, IM, or online sites such as Facebook or through classroom management tools (Erickson, 2006; Balkun, 2007). Whatever the support system, traditional or technological, the intent is to help the student in the transition process between high school and college. Many Gen M students show a proclivity toward new gadgets and a desire to embrace new technologies, but they still need a basic foundation in the scholarly writing process to begin their college careers successfully (Oblinger and Oblinger, 2005). The earlier they receive that foundation, the better.

THE FIRST-YEAR EXPERIENCE: A CASE STUDY

I am a librarian at Hollins University, a private liberal arts women's college in Southern Virginia. Hollins is a small university with approximately 800 residential undergraduate women with an average GPA of 3.5 and an additional 250 students in its co-ed graduate program. It has a proportionally small library instruction staff of seven, each responsible for a division of the subject areas. I teach the natural sciences, math, psychology, and computer science, the smallest division of the school.

Hollins began its First-Year Seminar program in 2007, designing many of the seminars to be interdisciplinary and team-taught by two faculty members from different departments. All 16 of these required First-Year Seminars are taught simultaneously, in 90-minute sessions, two times per week. This schedule is easy for the students' planning, as there will not be conflicts with other courses. However, the schedule is a major challenge for the library since the majority of instruction sessions are scheduled in the first six weeks of the semester. Librarians are restrained by having only one computer-equipped classroom space within the library and that is in high demand. The First Year Seminar requires more coordination than the average class to ensure a similar experience on the part of the faculty and librarians as we try to provide an even level of understanding across the disciplines. This instruction serves as a foundation on which we build future advanced instruction sessions. For example, all seminars are required to fulfill the "Applied Research Techniques" component and each division librarian works with a faculty member on the specifics for their subject. To help ease the transition into university life and research, each First-Year Seminar is assigned an upper-class student, called the Student Success Leader, to serve as a mentor and provide additional peer support for the new student in his/her first semester.

Of the 16 First-Year Seminars offered at Hollins, 15 are for the traditional 18-year-old freshman, but one is unique. This final seminar is for the nontraditional student. Typically this student is a woman with a job and a family, usually of the Gen X or Boomer generation, who has taken time off since high school and is entering college at a later stage in life. These students, referred to as Horizon students, range in age from their late 20s to retirees, and other than their First-Year Seminar will attend classes with the Gen M students. The Horizon student seminar is specifically designed for the student who has been away from the academic environment for a time and who may be unfamiliar with new educational technologies. In addition to teaching Horizon students information literacy skills, such as how to critically evaluate a source, our goal is to also boost their computer skills, increase their comfort level with technology they need to produce a well-written, well-researched scholarly document.

Course management systems are one technology that has become increasingly more common in the last ten years. Hollins uses Blackboard, one of the more popular systems available. These systems were originally designed for online course work; however, course management systems are frequently being used to augment on-campus instruction. This mixing of face-to-face classroom instruction with online tools such as asynchronous bulletin board discussions is often called blended learning.

Many Gen M students come to college with the technological, multitasking skills needed for participating in such blended learning already in place. They are often comfortable with intersecting the online environment of social networking sites and mobile technologies, such as texting, with everyday face-to-face interactions. The objective for the Gen M student is to transfer the technological knowledge to the educational realm, which can become a real challenge for individuals of older, Gen X and Boomer generations. Unlike the "Net native" Gen M students, who have constructed what they know about technology from an early age, older students may be playing "catch-up" in the acquisition of such skills. The Horizon program is meant to address this perceived need.

Libraries are at the forefront in adapting and promulgating the educational uses of Web 2.0 technologies. Hollins, along with a large number of other academic libraries, has implemented reference instant messaging services. Through the service, Hollins students can reach a Hollins librarian quickly and not an anonymous online service. A big advantage for our students is that if they are IMing us from the third-floor stacks because they can't find a book, we can go up and help them face to face. This is important since many first-year students come to campus with the mind set that information should be easily accessible and that different resources should be interconnected. This is an idea that can be reflected in the close instructional collaboration between librarians and faculty. The main instrument of this collaboration is planning.

I try to meet with First-Year Seminar instructors in my division of math, science, psychology, and computer science before the semester begins, and incorporate the library instruction into the syllabus. A key component is to structure the library experience around the classroom assignment. This direct correlation between bibliographic instruction and practical application in producing a paper for class generates higher interest and participation on the part of the student. For example, one class assignment was for students to write a biography on a historical woman scientist. Students were allowed to choose from a list. As the professor had included me in the Blackboard course management online discussion, so I was familiar with the assignment, and the choices on the list. I modeled my lesson as a walk-through of the actual steps needed to research one of the choices on the list. My post-assessment indicated that the majority of students rated my instruction session as "Extremely Useful" on a scale of "Not Useful," "Moderately Useful," "Useful," and

"Extremely Useful." I credit this to the fact that the teaching was directly related exactly to what they needed for the assignment.

The benefits of the librarian-faculty relationship are tremendous for students. One faculty member remarked that her First-Year Seminar students were producing better papers and citing more scholarly sources by the end of the course than her upper-class students. She was proud to report that a student in her First-Year Seminar won first place in the College Undergraduate category in a national mathematics essay contest. The knowledge base and skills that a student gains in the First-Year Seminar carries forward throughout the next four years.

I noticed the difference in information literacy levels the semester after we began the First Year Seminar program at Hollins. I was teaching an instruction session for a mid-level biology course. Students were both lower and upper level undergraduates, but I could immediately identify who had received library instruction sessions in the past. I was able to verify their library background experience during post-session assessment. I asked, "What did you learn about research techniques and the library that you didn't know before attending this session, if anything?" and "What would you change about the session you attended today?" About half of the students commented that the session had been useful, as they didn't even know about the online resources, or that they could order items through interlibrary loan if we did not own them. The other half said they already were familiar with the library services and were interested in learning advanced techniques for locating biology research materials. Such feedback supports that all students could greatly benefit from an immersion experience in information literacy such as the First-Year Seminar.

At Hollins University, the First-Year Seminar is a team effort on the part of the library, but one seminar was particularly memorable. We taught three 90-minute instruction sessions based in a course about notable women in science and math. The first instruction session emphasized information literacy and focused on evaluating sources for the class project on the basis of authority, objectivity, currency, and coverage. We applied these core questions to online and print resources; the students located and critically analyzed materials. One highly successful assignment a colleague and I developed for this First-Year Seminar focused on the *process* of how students found information. Students were required to create a bibliography of at least ten sources and asked to identify how they found each source. Sample statements included: "I found this Web page using Google with the search: *Rachel Carson*" or "I found this book in the library catalog using a subject search: *Women Scientists—Biography*." Other students noted that they used the library's electronic resources Web page and found an entry in *Biographies Plus*, a subscription database. Students were required to find a mix of print and electronic resources, and write a few sentences about why each resource was appropriate for the assignment. Students were given a passing grade or an opportunity to redo the assignment. Librarians graded the assignments, wrote comments, gave suggestions for sources other than Wikipedia, and offered individual research help. Several students came in for follow-up visits, but from subsequent interaction with these students, it was evident that they were on the right track. The teaching faculty graded the second part of the assignment, a traditional research paper using the ten sources from their bibliography. The professors indicated that papers were scholarly and well done as a result of the bibliography being evaluated first.

Rather than ignoring non-scholarly sources like Wikipedia, educators can discuss the questionable reliability of the resource and re-direct students to more appropriate materials. For example, I told our students that if they were researching Grace Murray Hopper, the computer scientist, Wikipedia might be a good starting point for general information such as names, dates, and concepts. Those terms could be used in a search of scholarly databases. I emphasized that Wikipedia should *never* be used on a research paper, as Wikipedia itself has pages devoted to its own criticism and accuracy of the wiki editing model. I was pleased to find in the same seminar during the second year of the program that not a single student used Wikipedia for the bibliography assignment.

Later in the semester, the second part of the seminar focused on contemporary women in math and science. The third and final part of the seminar researched women who are Hollins alumnae of the math and science programs. I met with the students again, covering the contemporary scientists for another instruction session. We discussed using non-scholarly sources such as the individual home pages of the scientists to find forthcoming research. We looked at relevant sites such as the Noble Prize Web site, in addition to a few more of the library's subscription databases. The students completed a second bibliography as the assignment. In the third instruction session, students met with the university archivist, who instructed them on using the archives to find information on the alums and on how to develop a biography. The students researched how the women went from being curious Hollins undergraduates like themselves to successful leaders in their fields. Many of the students contacted the alums directly for additional biographical information. The final semester project was a poster session on these Hollins alumnae, to which my colleagues and I were invited. I was impressed at the professionalism and thoroughness of the posters out of the group of first-year students.

FORMAL AND INFORMAL ASSESSMENTS

While college administrators realize the value of First Year Seminar programs, not only for retention purposes, but also for how the quality of the experience enhances the education of the student, data gathering is necessary to provide support for these claims. Formal assessments are a way to accomplish this in a standardized fashion; however, I find the subjective assessments better to improve my teaching. Hollins University uses both formal and informal methods of measuring student learning.

We began the First Year Seminar program with a pre-test for all incoming first-year students, designed by project SAILS. The Standardized Assessment of Information Literacy Skills (SAILS) test, developed by the librarians at Kent State University, promises to answer the question for the library: "How information literate are our students?" (project-SAILS, 2007: 115). The SAILS test, designed in 2000, is closely based on the ACRL *Information Literacy Competency Standards* discussed earlier in this chapter. The test quantifies four of the five competency standards: "Standard 1: Determines the Nature and Extent of the Information Needed; Standard 2: Accesses Needed Information Effectively and Efficiently; Standard 3: Evaluates Information and Its Sources Critically and Incorporates Selected Information Into His or Her Knowledge Base and Value System; Standard 5: Understands Many of the Economic,Legal, and Social Issues Surrounding the Use of Information and Accesses and Uses Information Ethically and Legally" (projectSAILS, 2007: 3). The one ACRL standard unmeasured by the SAILS test is: "The information literate student, individually or as a member of a group, uses information effectively to accomplish a specific purpose" (Association of College and Research Libraries, 2000: 13). Librarians and faculty at the institution determine if the student has achieved this goal. The test measures eight specific skills: developing a research strategy; selecting finding tools; searching; using finding tool features; retrieving sources; evaluating sources; documenting sources; and understanding economic, legal, and social issues (projectSAILS, 2007).

During the fall 2007 semester, all Hollins first-year students were required to take the SAILS test twice, a pre-test at the start of the semester and a post-test at the end. What we found was not much change overall and several seminars with a slight decrease in scores in the post-test. This result is not surprising to me, as our instruction sessions are not designed to teach information literacy in one semester. We use the first-year semester instruction as a foundation and continue to build upon this knowledge as the student advances in his/her coursework.

Other aspects of student performance changed with each test as well. The first test, taken within weeks of starting college, showed that students took between a half hour and an hour to complete the test. The second test was not part of their course grade. Only 152 students took the post-test as compared to 188 who took the pre-test (projectSAILS, 2007). The length of time students used to complete the test decreased; some students only used five minutes for the forty-five question proxied exam.

We feel that can be lessons learned from this experience: the main one being that information literacy cannot be taught in a single semester with a single instruction session. Although we did have the opportunity to work multiple times with some of the seminars, most of the seminars received a one-shot instruction session. A few seminars chose not to have an instruction session at all. These showed the same decrease in scores as those with multiple instruction session. For example, in the category of "Developing a Research Strategy," one seminar scored 565 on the pre-test and 516 at the end of the semester. Another seminar in the same category scored 594 on both assessments (projectSAILS, 2007). The low scores were matched by many complaints about having to complete a similar post-test later in the semester. Naturally, we discussed the disappointing outcomes and chose to re-examine the method in which we were formally assessing our students, discontinuing the pre- and post-testing. We resolved that it would be more accurate to test this class of students again during their senior year, which will give a truer picture of the information literacy of our students, and, subsequently, we opted not to use the SAILS test during the 2008–2009 academic year.

But it is not all bad news, as in addition to the SAILS test we continued with our informal course assessments, which had been in place for years. Predominantly, we rely on a paper form, handed out at the end of each one-shot instruction session or set of sessions. It is a simple rating system of our usefulness plus room for comments and suggestions, as mentioned earlier in this chapter. This form is collected and used only for the librarians' professional improvement. I've found this form helps to modify my instruction better than the informal assessment of judging from reactions of the students in class.

To replace the SAILS test, we used a two-part bibliography assignment during the second year of the seminar program, similar to what a colleague and I had done the previous year in one seminar. As discussed earlier in this chapter, it was a bibliography designed to reveal *how* the students were researching, not *what* sources they found. This bibliography will evaluate how well the students begin to understand what information is necessary; access it effectively; and evaluate this information on our criteria of authority, objectivity, currency, and coverage. The bibliography is an essential summary of the first three Information Literacy Competency Standards.

The professor determines the second part of the assignment, which will measure the final two *Information Literacy Competency Standards* concerning students using "information effectively to accomplish a specific purpose," and "understand[ing] many of the economic, legal, and social issues surrounding the use of information and access[ing] and us[ing] information ethically and legally" (Association of College and Research Libraries, 2000: 13–14). Students use the bibliography as a foundation on which to build the rest of the task. In a few of the courses I taught, the assignment was a biography and the students produced a written report, an oral presentation, or poster session. This method would work with any subject requiring research, not just biographies.

This bibliography assignment, compared with other librarians across the disciplines, is more telling than the SAILS test for two reasons. One, we can tell what type of effort the student is putting in and where he/ she is searching, for instance, if we have ten sources from a student, all found using Google Scholar versus ten diverse sources throughout our electronic journals, print collection, government documents, and Internet sources. We had a few students note that they used WorldCat to find the book available at a nearby library and ordered it through our interlibrary loan services. I would be convinced that these students had a firm grasp on information literacy and on their way to producing high-quality documents. The second reason this method of assessment works well is that it is not anonymous. We can, and we have, asked students to re-do their bibliographies. We can suggest a diversity of resources, recommend students search for more current sources, and provide individual help outside of class time if needed. Hollins is small university with just over 200 first-year students, so this individual method may not be scaleable without an equally large library instruction staff. Combined with our post-session assessments the bibliographic assignment gives us the confidence to say the library is a benefit in the success of our First-Year Seminar program.

CONCLUSION

The First-Year Seminar is an ideal place to teach information literacy. These information skills cannot be compressed into one bibliographic session. This seminar is a "jumping-off" point for the start of the incoming student's academic career. As discussed previously, the typical Gen M student arrives at college already armed with an arsenal of computer literacy skills. The First-Year Seminar blends these technological skills with research skills. In addition, in a collaborative academic environment, the student becomes part of a learning community with the library at the heart of that campus experience. Faculty and librarian collaboration is the key to the successful teaching of information literacy. Preparing undergraduates to become lifelong learners who will go onto graduate schools or careers is a team effort that should begin with the first semester.

REFERENCES

American Library Association. 1989. *Presidential Committee on Information Literacy: Final Report.* Chicago: American Library Association. Available: www.ala.org/ala/mgrps/divs/acrl/publications/whitepapers/presidential.cfm (accessed November 15, 2008).

Association of College and Research Libraries. 2000. *Information Literacy Competency Standards for Higher Education.* Chicago: American Library Association. Available: www.ala.org/ala/mgrps/divs/acrl/standards/standards.pdf (accessed November 15, 2008).

Balkun, Mary M., Beth Bloom, and Marta Mestrovic Deyrup. 2007. "Librarians in the Wired Classroom: The Seton Hall University Experience." In *The Role of the Library in the First College Year*, edited by L. Hardesty. Columbia: University of South Carolina, National Resource Center for The First-Year Experience and Students in Transition.

Boff, Colleen, Cheryl Albrecht, and Alison Armstrong. 2007. "Librarians with a First-Year Focus: Exploring an Emerging Position." In *The Role of the Library in the First College Year*, edited by L. Hardesty. Columbia: University of South Carolina, National Resource Center for The First-Year Experience and Students in Transition.

Egger-Sider, Francine, and Jane Devine. 2005. "Google, the Invisible Web, and the Librarians: Slaying the Research Goliath." *Internet Reference Services Quarterly* 10, no. 3/4: 89–101.

Erickson, Bette L., Calvin B. Peters, and Diane Weltner Strommer. 2006. *Teaching First-Year College Students*. San Francisco: Jossey-Bass.

Jones, Steve et al. 2002. *The Internet Goes to College: How Students Are Living in the Future with Today's Technology*. Washington, DC: Pew Internet and American Life Project. Available: www.pewinternet.org/report_display.asp?r=71 (accessed November 15, 2008).

Junco, Reynol. 2005. "Technology and Today's First-Year Students." In *Challenging & Supporting the First-Year Student: A Handbook for Improving the First Year of College*, edited by M. Lee Upcraft, John N. Gardner, and Betsy O. Barefoot. San Francisco: Jossey-Bass.

Lewandowski, Dirk, and Philipp Mayr. 2006. "Exploring the Academic Invisible Web." *Library Hi Tech* 24, no. 4: 529–539.

National Resource Center for The First-Year Experience and Students in Transition. 2006. *Preliminary Summary of Results from the 2006 National Survey on First-Year Seminars*. Columbia: University of South Carolina. Available: www.sc.edu/fye/research/surveyfindings/surveys/survey06.html (accessed November 15, 2008).

Oblinger, Diana G., and James L. Oblinger. 2005. "Is It Age or IT? First Steps towards Understanding the Net Generation." In *Educating the Net Generation* (pp. 2.1–2.20), edited by Diana G. Oblinger and James L. Oblinger. Boulder, CO: EDUCAUSE.

Porter, Stephen, and Randy Swing. 2006. "Understanding How First-year Seminars Affect Persistence." *Research in Higher Education* 47, no. 1: 89–109.

projectSAILS. 2007. *Results of the Standardized Assessment of Literacy Skills (SAILS) for Hollins University Administration: 2007 Fall FYS* (December). Kent, OH: Kent State University.

Schwartz, Stephen W., and Michael J. Siegel. 2005. "The First Year at Eckerd College: Responsible Innovation." In *Achieving and Sustaining Intuitional Excellence for the First Year of College* (pp. 87–112), edited by Betsy O. Barefoot, John N. Gardner, Marc Cutright, Libby V. Morris, Charles C. Schroeder, Steven W. Schwartz, Michael J. Siegel, and Randy L. Swing. San Francisco: Jossey-Bass.

Watts, Margit M. 2005. "The Place of the Library versus the Library as a Place." In *Challenging & Supporting the First-Year Student: A Handbook for Improving the First Year of College* (pp. 339–355), edited by Lee M. Upcraft, John N. Gardner, and Betsy O. Barefoot. San Francisco: Jossey-Bass.

Conclusion

Laura B. Spencer
Vibiana Bowman Cvetkovic

O BRAVE NEW WORLD THAT HAS SUCH PEOPLE IN'T

Our world is increasingly wired and online. A recent industry report estimates that, worldwide, 694 million people aged 15-and-up are Internet
users (comScore, accessed 2008). Members of Gen M, particularly those
young adults in industrialized countries, are in online communities communicating, socializing, and engaging in creative self-expression. In this
book's Introduction, Robert J. Lackie, John W. LeMasney, and Kathleen
M. Pierce have given a detailed description of Gen M and in Chapter 12,
Stephen Abram has presented a portrait of the world that they will come
to inhabit. The main theme running through these depictions—present
and future—is that of the increasing importance of technology and connectivity in day-to-day life. The Web represents a new mass medium, one
that is global, visual, interactive, real-time, and participatory. With this
constant connectivity as part of the social fabric of modern adolescence
and young adulthood, an obvious question regarding Gen M arises: is
the impact of this technological cultural shift positive or negative?

This question, of course, is ultimately moot. For better or for worse
new technologies and new media are parts of the evolutionary process
of human development. Media scholar, Neil Postman, in the early 1980s,
expressed the concern that non-print media, particularly television, were
destroying childhood (Postman, 1982). Postman viewed children as
acutely vulnerable to television, which he characterized as an unmedi-

343

ated medium, one that gave children access to adult secrets before they had an apprenticeship to the grown-up world. Such access eroded adult authority, destroyed childhood innocence, and undermined children's creativity. One can easily trace the same line of arguments with regard to critiques about that other ubiquitous home screen, the computer, which was making in-roads at this time. If change then is unavoidable, and if our young people will be interacting with new and sophisticated media, another question waits to be asked: What, if anything, can be done about it?

Moral Panic

In the United States, from the mid-1990s onward, as the number of children using the Web grew, so did adult anxiety. One response to this was a spate of federal legislation meant to provide protections for children on the Web. These included: the Communications Decency Act (passed in 1996, overturned by the Supreme Court in 1997); the Child Online Protection Act (COPA) (passed in 1998, overturned by the Federal Third District Court in 2007); the Children's Online Privacy Protection Act (COPPA) (passed in 1998); and the Children's Internet Protection Act (CIPA) (passed in 2000, upheld in a Supreme Court decision in 2003). COPPA's intent was to create a safe harbor on the Web for children under the age of 13. It prevented the collection and use of their personal data by online commercial interests. With that exception, the rest of these acts were designed to protect children from exposure to pornography and sexual predators. CIPA (which is still active law) requires public and school libraries to install filters on computers children use in order to receive federal funds (American Library Association, accessed 2008).

In addition to legislators, researchers began to take notice of young people and the Web. One such research response was the Youth Internet Safety Survey (YISS) conducted in 1999 by lead researcher, David Finkelhor, of the University of New Hampshire Crimes and funded by the National Center for Missing & Exploited Children. To gather data regarding possible sexual victimization of children on the Web, Finkelhor and his team conducted telephone interviews of 1,501 Internet users aged 10 through 17. The children were questioned about sexual solicitations, unwanted exposure to sexual materials, and sexual harassment during their use of the Web (Finkelhor, Mitchell, and Wolak, 2000). When the results of the study were published, they created quite a stir; they were used by the popular press and by child-safety advocates as evidence of the dangers that awaited children on the Web. As a consequence, calls increased for net filtering and for stricter laws regarding Internet safety.

A finding often quoted from the study was that, of the children in the survey, "approximately one in five received a sexual solicitation over the Internet *in the last year*" [emphasis in original] (Finkelhor, Mitchell, and Wolak, 2000: ix). While selected results from the report were frequently sensationalized in popular media, the complete report presented a more nuanced picture of the Web. Over 77 percent of the youth who had received solicitations were 14 or older (Finkelhor, Mitchell, and Wolak, 2000: 2). Also, 48 percent of the solicitors were juveniles; only 4 percent were older than 25 (Finkelhor, Mitchell, and Wolak, 2000: 3). Although the specter of the Internet predator loomed largely in adults' fears Frinkelhor found that only seven children in the sample were "offered assistance to run away;" of those only one offer was reported as having potential sexual overtones (Finkelhor, Mitchell, and Wolak, 2000: 2).

Thus, the results of YISS did not validate the prevailing narrative that the Web was a space fraught with stranger danger. In the intervening years since then, several other large studies were undertaken in the United States and the United Kingdom (Finkelhor, Mitchell, and Wolak, 2000; Holloway and Valentine, 2000; Valentine and Holloway, 2002; Ybarra and Mitchell, 2004; Ybarra and Mitchell, 2005; Wolak, Mitchell, and Finkelhor, 2006; Wolak, Finkelhor, Mitchell, and Ybarra, 2008). There was also a follow-up to YISS (YISS-2) the results of which were published in 2006 (Wolak, Finkelhor, and Mitchell, 2006). All of these studies have yielded similar results. Indeed, despite nearly a decade of research, the publication of scores of scholarly journal articles and reports, and a wealth of empirical data to the contrary, the popular narrative about children, sexual predators, and the Internet persists unabated in the popular discourse about children and the Web. The "moral panic" regarding adult's fears that children will be exposed to sexually inappropriate materials or approached by pedophiles has had direct results in public policy. Legislation passed regarding children and Internet use has had very real and continuing ramifications for free speech and unfiltered access to information for all citizens of the online community.

The dark side of the Web, however, was only one of the popular perceptions of this new medium. The other prevailing narrative was that of the Web as the great democratizer and the great educator.

Using "The Force" for Good

The yin to the yang of these "moral panics" was the notion of the Internet as a force for good, a people's university, and a conduit for sharing art, music, and enlightenment. Although the Web was replete with nonsense and darkness, it could also enrich and ennoble. Historical photographs, diaries, and first-person accounts, full-text versions of literary world masterpieces, art exhibits from renowned museums, all became available with a mouse click. Projects and initiatives intended to make information freely available without censorship or intellectual restrictions, sprang-up. Two of these were Google and Wikipedia.

In the early 1990s, Web browsers and Web search engines were developed. By mid-decade, they had transformed the way that the Internet was viewed and used. It almost goes without saying that the most popular and most successful of all search engines is Google. Indeed, Google has become so popular that its very name has become a verb for searching the Web. Wikipedia, which can trace its intellectual DNA back to the open source movement, was originally envisioned by its cofounders Jimmy Wales and Larry Sanger as an encyclopedic repository of information "written by open and transparent consensus." The philosophy was that no top-down point of view would be imposed; rather all "notable views" would be heard and a neutral consensus regarding a topic would be reached (Wikipedia, accessed November 28, 2008). Google had its origins as a research project of two Stanford University graduate students, Larry Page and Sergey Brin in 1996. The project was so successful that Page and Brin registered the domain name in 1997 and incorporated in 1998.

Wikipedia and Google have been discussed in-depth elsewhere in this work (see Chapters 9 and 17 by Jeff Knapp and Mitch Fontenot, respectively). The bottom line is that despite their misuses and shortcomings, these resources are successfully delivering meaningful answers to the questions posed by the global village of the Web. They have radically and irrevocably transformed the way that research is done—at all levels. Gen M takes the existence of such tools as a given, views these tools as the paradigm of the research experience: instant search/instant result. As suggested by Knapp and Fontenot, it behooves educators and librarians to instead use these familiar Web tools as teaching opportunities for working with Gen M.

Google and Wikipedia have arguably had the largest impact on research and information delivery, but online gaming, social networking sites, and file-sharing sites have all had cultural and societal impact. You-

Tube and Napster have changed entire industries. Facebook and MySpace have reshaped notions of friendship and community. The authors who have contributed to Parts II and III of this book have discussed this Gen M culture of technology and included in their discussions suggestions for the implementation of artifacts of this culture as *meaningful* teaching tools. For example, as Anderson points out in Chapter 8, YouTube is so much more than skateboarding dogs and dramatic-looking gophers. It is a repository for virtually every important film artifact of the last century. On YouTube, you can view the 1902 Georges Melies silent movie, *A Trip to the Moon*; footage of the 1969 moon landing with Neil Armstrong; and vintage music videos of The Who drummer, Keith Moon from the 1960s and the 1970s.

Thus, it would seem then that technological advances are inevitable and technology inevitably changes society. Individuals and institutions adapt to the change. For educators, the question arises: What will the impact be on education and scholarship?

SCHOLARSHIP, TECHNOLOGY, AND WISDOM

Many years ago, a philosopher reported that an inventor had presented the head of a government with his invention, claiming that it had the power to improve the memories and increase the wisdom of the people. The head of the government was skeptical that this invention would do any such thing, and declared that this new technology would in fact do the opposite. It would be a crutch. People's memories would deteriorate, because they would outsource their memories to the invention. They would not develop wisdom, but instead a superficial, amateurish sense of things. This touted invention was not a diabolically powerful super-computer, either in reality or in science fiction. The new, transformative technology was the art of writing; the head of the government was an ancient Egyptian king; and the philosopher reporting on the story was Socrates. We know about this because, irony of ironies, Plato wrote it down in his dialogue, the *Phaedrus*.

For Socrates, literacy was no substitute for live discussion between a teacher and a carefully chosen student, who both sought the truth. Words written in "that black fluid we call ink" (Plato, 1963: 522) are a pale imitation of the truth they attempt to convey; and are deaf, dumb, and useless if approached by a reader who wishes clarification or further edification from them. Words on a page cannot teach a reader about things he does not know, but only remind him of what he knows already (Plato, 1963). As it turns out, centuries of widespread literacy and cultural advancements that have been built upon that widespread literacy suggest that reading and writing were an excellent idea after all. Yet, Socrates had a point. One can become neither a board-certified physician nor a licensed motorist merely by reading a few books about anatomy or driving. A fourth-grade schoolteacher has considerably more than a fifth-grade education. In our age of mass literacy, reading is still fundamentally necessary, although one could argue about how long that may be true in the future.

A modern observer of digital developments could take a page from Socrates and inquire if Gen M "will fail to probe beyond the information given" in the digital environment "to the deeper layers of insight, imagination, and knowledge" (Wolf, 2007: A15). That observer might also ask if a "surfeit of information is at the expense of creative and independent thinking" (CIBER, 2008: 7) and agree with cognitive neuroscientist Maryanne Wolf that the "immediacy and volume of information should not be confused with true knowledge" (Wolf, 2007: A15). Socrates saw the limitations of the new technology of writing, but he did not see the possibilities. His inability to see the future does not, however, undermine the validity of his criticism—or its applicability to the new technologies of today. What Socrates' parable suggests is that technological advances could provide the intellectual equivalent of the dessert course before the main meal of bread and meat (or the vegetarian equivalent) is served. Thus, while he may have been wrong about the invention of writing, his warnings about the limits of new technologies and their unintended consequences are still pertinent.

But Gen M Is Different, Correct?

The answer is, of course, yes and no. Surely members of Gen M's lifelong familiarity with digital technologies will enable them to navigate those technologies with ease. Surely over time, careful reading, reflective thinking, and clear writing will be conducted in their digital worlds, without their needing to resort to older, quaint, space-consuming technologies such as print on paper. Perhaps that will be so. It is too soon to tell, but some evidence suggests that the digital world encourages searching and viewing habits that do not combine well with or support careful, thorough reading and deep, reflective thinking.

In an online environment, searchers skim, bounce around, click through to other pages, and rarely spend much time looking at any one given page. This behavior is well suited to picking up the gist of an argument or a superficial overview of a topic; but poorly suited to picking up on nuance or comprehending a complex, lengthy argument. To do the latter, one must read more than a few paragraphs on a few pages. According to the Centre for Information Behaviour and the Evaluation of Research (CIBER), many users are not doing the latter. Viewers of e-journals spend, on average, about eight minutes viewing about three pages of a given article (CIBER, 2008). Significantly, skimming habits are not unique to the young. "Everyone exhibits a bouncing/flicking behaviour, which sees them searching horizontally rather than vertically. Power browsing and viewing is the norm for all" (CIBER, 2008: 8). This suggests that the technology, rather than an age cohort's preferences, is shaping searching behavior. There is nothing inherently wrong with power browsing; it is an excellent technique for assessing whether an item is worth closer examination. It is no substitute, however, for that closer examination, also known as carefully reading—and often re-reading—the whole document. Digital technology does not appear to be as conducive to this kind of reading as paper-based reading.

Scholarly best practices include thoroughness, and leaving no stone unturned. For humanities scholars, for example, that means conducting exhaustive searches of the literature in the field, to make certain that all pertinent data and all interpretations of that data have been duly considered and weighed. Even if the thoroughness is more an ideal than a reality, it is a worthy one to strive toward. It is also a worthy endeavor to inculcate such scholarly best practices with the undergraduates that one teaches, whether or not they take heed and adopt the practices themselves. Students who get by or make do with the first ten articles that look good enough are not adopting their professor's culture of scholarly thoroughness. What if digital technologies are exacerbating the difference between scholarly thoroughness and student survival techniques? If the online environment is making it easier for faculty to be thorough, yet simultaneously making it easier for students to be superficial, then the pedagogical problems at hand are more serious than discovering how best to adopt and adapt new media into the classroom for the sake of reaching students who are familiar with those new media.

The culture of Gen M is a culture where data are constantly pushed. Unlike previous generations, the task is not finding information but finding out what, in the sea of available information, is useful, reliable, and pertinent. Information literacy skills, along with computer literacy skills are the key components for success in the data-driven and media-soaked ecology of the twenty-first century. So, rather than adopting a Dylan Thomas-esque posture of raging against the dying of the light of good scholarship, the contributors to *Teaching Generation M: A Handbook for Librarians and Educators* have argued that the better stance is for educators to utilize technology based on solid pedagogy to prepare the next generation of world leaders for how to navigate these troubled seas.

The problems at hand become the limits of the new media, working around those limits, and crossing a widening gap between faculty and students in order to fulfill the mission of higher education.

But what indeed is this mission?

In this work the authors have poked, prodded, and troubled the notion of "Gen M" as a valid construct for discussing the current crop of undergraduates. The conclusion reached is that this *is* a valid construct; that Gen M represents a unique generational cohort with distinct characteristics and a distinct culture. Next the contributors troubled and validated the use of technology and technological advances in teaching and its underlying pedagogical planning. This one final notion that underlies this entire discussion remains unexamined. Educators and librarians who read this work are either preparing members of Gen M for higher education or are actively engaged in enabling them in its pursuit. Why?

WHAT GOOD *IS* A COLLEGE EDUCATION ANYWAY?

Educators know all too well that the short, simple questions are often the most difficult to answer, because their brevity obscures complexity. But the above short, simple question seems apt, particularly because this book advocates that information literacy skills are imperative for academic success. What is a college education for?

The universities of the ancient world were scholastics guilds of teachers and scholars who met informally and spontaneously. As the great cities developed so did great centers of learning—the world's colleges and universities. In the New World, the first American university was Harvard, established by the Massachusetts legislature in 1636 (Rudolph, 1962) The New England Puritans, founders of Harvard, had a sense of high purpose in this endeavor. The mission of this university was to ensure the colonies would prosper by creating leaders with education and vision. In an address to Harvard's Board of Overseers, Henry

Dunster, the University's first president, stated, "You shall take care to advance in all learning, divine and humane, each and every student who is or will be entrusted to your tutelage" (Rudolph, 1962: 6). For a contemporary sense of mission from institutions of higher learning one can turn to the Web.

A survey of mission statements from college and university yields an interesting array. The aforementioned Harvard, for instance, wants its students "to rejoice in discovery and in critical thought" (Harvard College [sic], accessed 2008). Brown seeks to prepare its students "to discharge the offices of life with usefulness and reputation" (Brown University, accessed 2008). A liberal education at St. John's College "seeks to free men and women from the tyrannies of unexamined opinions and inherited prejudices" (St. John's College, accessed 2008). Cheyney University of Pennsylvania's stated purpose is "to prepare confident, competent, reflective, visionary leaders and responsible citizens" (Cheney University of Pennsylvania, accessed 2008). Ferris State University, like many other institutions of higher education, seeks to prepare its "students for successful careers, responsible citizenship, and lifelong learning" (Ferris State University, accessed 2008). Many universities speak of "global citizenship," while others acknowledge that they exist in part to serve the needs of the community and state or commonwealth in which their campuses reside. Service to others, whether in this nation or abroad, is a common theme.

Another common theme, from small, private liberal arts colleges to large, public research universities, is a mission to teach students to think critically and communicate effectively. Bates College expects "students to appreciate the discoveries and insights of established traditions of learners, as well as to participate in the resolution of what is unknown" (Bates College, accessed 2008). Grinnell believes that "knowledge is a good to be pursued both for its own sake," as well as for a larger societal good, and their graduates are ones "who can think clearly, who can speak and write persuasively and even eloquently" (Grinnell College, accessed 2008). This Web survey demonstrates a proclivity for philosophical declarations in college and university official missions statements, particularly betterment of oneself, and one's society. A search of business literature yields a more prosaic rationale for attending college—a college degree is a prerequisite for a good paying job.

According to the *Chronicle of Higher Education*, by the year 2028 (when Gen M will be at its peak earning years) American manufacturing jobs will be hovering around zero percent. "The employment that is expanding in America is in service-providing industries . . . The better paying jobs in those service industries require a great deal of education beyond high school" (Mortenson, 2008: 31). The most frequently cited skill set that potential employers state that they are looking for is good communications skills. Employers specifically want employees who can write well and prepare coherent, well-researched presentations (*Career World,* 2007; Farquharson, 2008: 12; Stevens, 2005, Wilson, 2006). It becomes apparent, from the literature, that the information literacy skills that underlie good scholarship and good communication skills have verifiable, real-world value.

This contemporary expression of the duality of the nature and the benefit of a college education—between the lofty and the lucrative—is neither irreconcilable nor without precedent. Education scholar, Philip G. Altbach writes:

> Universities are not ivory towers and never have been. They are subject to pressures and influences from external forces of many kinds . . . In the twenty-first century, universities are subject to the pressures of society more than ever, largely because of their impor-tance to knowledge-based economies, and because more than half of the college-age population attends post-secondary institutions. (Altbach, 2002: 1023)

A FINAL THOUGHT: "YOU KNOW, WE'VE REALLY LEARNED SOMETHING TODAY"

With a nod to this signature line from Comedy Central's *South Park* (a Gen M favorite), this book closes with a true story. Many years ago, one of the authors was tutoring a high school sophomore in algebra. After a grueling session of solving for "x," the student exclaimed, "I don't mind working, but I sure hate thinking." The young man had a point. Serious thinking is serious work. It requires an expenditure of effort and guid-ance and that guidance comes from librarians and educators.

In *Teaching Generation M: A Handbook for Librarians and Educators*, the contributors have provided insights and strategies for understanding and interacting with a new generation of high school and college students. We trust that this information will support those charged with guiding the next generation of scholars, artists, and leaders through the important endeavor of serious thinking.

REFERENCES

Altbach, Philip G. 2002. "Higher Education in Context." In *Encyclopedia of Education* (pp. 1023–1027), edited by James W. Guthrie. New York: Macmillan Reference Library.

American Library Association. "CPPA, COPA, CIPA: Which Is Which." American Library Association. Available: www.ala.org/ala/oif/ifissues/issuesrelatedlinks/cppacopacipa.cfm (accessed November 28, 2008).

Bates College. "Mission Statement." Available: www.bates.edu/ip-bates-mission-statement.xml (accessed December 2, 2008).

Brown University. "Brown's Mission." Available: www.brown.edu/web/about/facts/ (accessed December 2, 2008).

Career World (Job Watch). 2007. "Lights! Camera! Action." *Career World* 26, no. 2 (October 1): 5.

Cheney University of Pennsylvania. "Mission and Vision." Available: www.cheyney.edu/pages/index.asp?p=277 (accessed December 2, 2008).

CIBER (Centre for Information Behaviour and the Evaluation of Research). 2008.*Information Behaviour of the Researcher of the Future: A CIBER Briefing Paper* (January 11). London: University College London (UCL). Available: www.jisc.ac.uk/media/documents/programmes/reppres/gg_final_keynote_11012008.pdf (accessed December 3, 2008).

ComScore Press Center. 2008. "694 Million People Currently Use the Internet Worldwide." ComScore. Available: www.comscore.com/press/release.asp?/press=849 (accessed November 28, 2008).

Farquharson, Bill. 2008. "That Was Then. This Is Now." *Graphic Arts Monthly* 80, no. 2 (February): 53.

Ferris State Univeristy. "Mission." Available: www.ferris.edu/htmls/ferrisfaq/mission.htm (accessed December 2, 2008).

Finkelhor, David, Kimberly J. Mitchell, and Jane Wolak. 2000. *Online Victimization: A Report on the Nation's Youth.* Alexandria, VA: National Center for Missing and Exploited Children.

Grinnell College. "Mission Statement." (February 2002). Available: www.grinnell.edu/offices/president/missionstatement/ (accessed December 2, 2008).

Harvard University. "The Mission of Harvard College." Available: http://webdocs.registrar.fas.harvard.edu/ugrad_handbook/current/mission.html (accessed December 2, 2008).

Holloway, Sarah L., and Gill Valentine. 2000. "Spatiality and the New Social Studies of Childhood." *Sociology* 34, no. 4 (November): 763–783.

Juliussen, Egil. 2004. *Internet User Forecast by Country.* Arlington Heights, IL: Computer Industry Almanac.

Mortenson, Thomas G. 2008. "Where the Boys Are." *Chronicle of Higher Education* 45, no. 39 (June 6): A31.

National Conference of State Legislatures. "Children and the Internet: Laws Relating to Filtering, Blocking and Usage Policies in Schools and Libraries." Available: www.ncsl.org/programs/lis/cip/filterlaws.htm (accessed November 28, 2008).

Plato. 1963. *The Collected Dialogues of Plato: Including the Letters*. Princeton: Princeton University Press.

Postman, Neil. 1982. *The Disappearance of Childhood*. New York: Delacorte.

Rudolph, Frederick. 1962. *The American College and University: A History*. New York: Alfred A. Knopf.

Stevens, Betsy. 2005. "What Communication Skills Do Employers Want? SiliconValley Recruiters Respond." *Journal of Employment Counseling* 42, no. 1 (March): 2–9.

St. John's College. "About St. John's College." Annapolis, MD. Available: www.stjohnscollege.edu/about/main.shtml (accessed March 30, 2009).

Valentine, Gill, and Sarah L. Holloway. 2002. "Cyberkids? Exploring Children's Identities and Social Networks in On-Line and Off-Line Worlds." *Annals of the Association of American Geographers* 92, no. 2 (June): 302–319.

Wikipedia. 2008. "About Wikipedia." Available: http://en.wikipedia.org/wiki/Wikipedia:About (accessed November 28, 2008).

Wilson, Mike. 2006. "What Recruiters Look for in On-Campus Interviews." *The Black Collegian* 37, no. 1 (October): 33–36.

Wolak, Janis, David Finkelhor, and Kimberly Mitchell. 2006. *Online Victimization: Five Years Later*. Alexandria, VA: National Center for Missing and Exploited Children.

Wolak, Janis, David Finkelhor, Kimberly J. Mitchell, and Michele L. Ybarra. 2008. "'Online Predators' and their Victims: Myths, Realities, and Implications for Prevention Treatment." *American Psychologist* 63, no. 2 (February-March): 111–128.

Wolf, Maryanne 2007. "Learning to Think in a Digital World" *Boston Globe* (September 5): A15.

Ybarra, Michele L., and Kimberly J. Mitchell. 2004. "Online Aggressor/Targets, Aggressors, and Targets: A Comparison of Associated Youth Characteristics." *Journal of Child Psychology & Psychiatry* 45, no. 7 (October): 1308–1316.

Ybarra, Michele L., and Kimberly J. Mitchell. 2005. "Exposure to Internet Pornography among Children and Adolescents: A National Survey." *CyberPsychology and Behavior* 8, no. 5 (October): 473–486.

About the Editors
and Contributors

Vibiana Bowman Cvetkovic is Reference Librarian and Web Administrator at the Paul Robeson Library, Rutgers University, Camden, New Jersey. Her books include *The Plagiarism Plague: A Resource Guide and CD-ROM Tutorial for Educators and Librarians* (Neal-Schuman, 2004) and *Scholarly Resources for Children and Childhood Studies: A Research Guide and Annotated Bibliography* (Scarecrow Press, 2007). She has also published in various refereed journals and library and information science publications. At present, Vibiana is Chair of the Children and Childhood Studies Section of the Mid-Atlantic Popular/American Culture Association. She was named one of the "Library Movers and Shakers for 2005," an annual feature of *Library Journal* that profiles "emerging leaders in the library world . . . who are innovative, creative, and making a difference."

Robert J. Lackie is Associate Professor-Librarian at Rider University, Lawrenceville, New Jersey, where he co-leads the Library Instruction Program and serves as Reference Collection Development Librarian. Since 1998, Robert has provided hundreds of teacher-librarian seminars, presented frequently at conferences, and published in various professional books and periodicals, in addition to serving for four years as Rider University's first Faculty-in-Residence. For his teaching, writing, and service to the profession, he was chosen as "2004 New Jersey Librarian of the Year," was a recipient of the "2004 Rider University Award for Distinguished Teaching," granted the 2006 ALA "Ken Haycock Award for Promoting Librarianship," and was selected for inclusion within recent editions of *Who's Who in America, Who's Who in American Education*, and *Who's Who in the World*.

* * *

Stephen Abram, MLS, is Vice President of Innovation for SirsiDynix and Chief Strategist for the SirsiDynix Institute. He was 2008 President of SLA and Past President of the Canadian and Ontario Library Associations. He was Publisher Electronic Information at Thomson after managing several libraries. Stephen was listed by *Library Journal* as one of the top 50 people influencing the future of libraries. He has received numerous honors and speaks internationally on a regular basis. His columns appear in *Information Outlook* and *Multimedia and Internet@Schools, OneSource, Feliciter, Access,* as well writing for *Library Journal.* He is the author of ALA Editions' bestselling *Out Front with Stephen Abram.* His blog, *Stephen's Lighthouse,* is a popular blog in the library sector.

Katie Elson Anderson is Supervisor of Access and Collection Services at the Paul Robeson Library, Rutgers University, Camden, New Jersey. She holds an MLIS (2007) from Rutgers University and BA degrees in Anthropology and German from Washington University, St. Louis, Missouri.

Susan Avery is Coordinator of Instructional Services at the Undergraduate Library of the University of Illinois at Urbana-Champaign. She received a Master of Information and Library Studies from the University of Michigan, a Master of Music from the University of Minnesota, and a BS in Music Education from St. Cloud (MN) State University. Her research interests focus on creating meaningful instruction for first-year students, faculty/librarian collaboration, and training of those participating in library instruction. She has presented at LOEX, ACRL, ALA, and regional conferences and published in various conference proceedings and book chapters, andis also an active member of the ACRL Instruction Section and LIRT.

Laurie M. Bridges is Business and Economics Librarian and Assistant Professor at Oregon State University. She has a MLIS from the University of Washington and MS in College Student Services Administration from Oregon State University. She has delivered numerous national presentations about the use of Facebook by educators and librarians.

Diane K. Campbell, Assistant Professor I-Librarian, is the Moore Library liaison to the Departments of Business Policy and Environment, Economics, Finance, Management and Human Resources, and Marketing. She has a BA in History from the University of North Carolina at Chapel

Hill and a MLIS from the School of Communication, Information and Library Studies at Rutgers University. Diane received her MLIS in 2004 and began her career with an academic year appointment to the Social Science Reference Center of Princeton University. Diane is in the process of completing her MBA at Rider University.

Michele Kathleen D'Angelo, MAT, EdS, is a School Psychologist and Adjunct Assistant Professor of English at Rider University. She has previously published two chapters in The Plagiarism Plague: A Resource Guide and CD-ROM Tutorial for Educators and Librarians and has presented papers at international conferences in Ireland, Norway, Scotland, Spain, and Wales. Currently, she teaches in the Gender and Sexuality Studies Program and the Multicultural Studies Program at Rider University.

Patricia H. Dawson, Assistant Professor I-Librarian, is the Moore Library liaison to the Environmental Sciences, Geological Sciences, Marine Sciences, Biology, Chemistry, Physics, Mathematics, and Psychology departments at Rider University. She has a BA in Biology, a MS in Microbiology, and a MLS from the School of Communication, Information and Library Studies at Rutgers University. Prior to her academic appointment to Rider University in 2006, she was Reference Information Specialist at Burlington County College, Pemberton, New Jersey, and worked as a Reference Analyst at Merck after graduating from the Rutgers MLS program.

Mitch Fontenot is Information Literacy and Outreach Services Librarian at Louisiana State University Middleton Library. He is a former law librarian with 15 years experience at the Universities of Nebraska and Colorado, and sailed around the world as an assistant librarian on the Semester at Sea program (www.semesteratsea.com) in 2001. He graduated from Louisiana State University with a BA in English Literature, and from the University of Texas with a MLIS, and currently teaches LIS (Library and Information Science) 1001 to pie-eyed undergraduates at LSU.

Steve Garwood is Staff Training and Development Coordinator for the Princeton University Library System. He is a former full-time lecturer at the School of Communication, Information, and Library Studies (SCILS), Rutgers University, where he taught in the graduate Library and Information Science program and the undergraduate Information Technology and Informatics program. Steve taught courses on Information Technology, Web and Multimedia Design, Social Software Integration, and Research and Reference Skills. Before working at SCILS, he was Program and Services Coordinator at INFOLINK Regional Library Cooperative, Customer Education/Reference Librarian at the Camden County Library and the New Jersey Statewide Reference Center, and was Technology Center Training Coordinator at Burlington County Library.

Colleen S. Harris is Associate Head of Access and Delivery Services at North Carolina State University. A former reference and instruction librarian, she holds a MLS (2006) from the University of Kentucky and bachelor's degrees in International Relations and Economics from Centre College. Her professional interests include information literacy and research training for undergraduate and graduate students, library involvement in student retention, and human resources issues related to academic librarianship. In her free time, she pursues additional graduate degrees, and expects her MFA in Creative Writing from Spalding University in 2009.

Joseph F. Joiner received a BA in Psychology from Rutgers University-Camden Campus, MA from La Salle University, and a PhD in Marriage and Family Therapy. He is Adjunct Psychology Instructor at Rutgers University-Camden Campus. His current research interests are intergenerational qualitative narratives.

Amy J. Kearns is Program Coordinator for the Central Jersey Regional Library Cooperative (CJRLC) and a part-time lecturer at the School of Communication, Information and Library Studies (SCILS), at Rutgers in New Brunswick, New Jersey. She received her MLIS from Rutgers and previously worked in public libraries, first as a Librarian and then as Head of Reference, before joining CJRLC. Currently President of the New Jersey Library Association (NJLA) Information Technology Section, she conducts in-service programs for teachers and librarians, as well as one-on-one and group training on CJRLC databases and services. She also does technology training on tools such as blogs, wikis, and social networking software and their uses in libraries and classrooms. She blogs at www.librarygarden.blogspot.com.

Karen J. Klapperstuck, MSLS, is Director of the Bradley Beach Public Library. She is actively involved in local, state, and national organizations. Along with her other NJLA executive board and committee work, she currently chairs the NJLA's Leadership and Education subcommittee, which is responsible for the successful statewide Emerging Leaders program. Karen presently serves on the ALA Council Committee on Education and the YA Galley Committee. She has presented at the PLA Conference, as well as numerous times at the NJLA Annual Conference and the NJ Library Trustee Association Institute. A self-confessed "leadership training junkie," Karen is a graduate of NJLA's Emerging Leaders, NJ Academy of Library Leadership, and ALA Emerging Leaders. Her interests include leadership and professional development, in addition to service to teens and young adults, as well as technology integration into staff development programs and services to the public.

Jeffrey Knapp is Reference and Instruction Librarian at Penn State Altoona. He became a librarian chiefly because of his interest in everything—his favorite book as a child was the *World Book Encyclopedia*. He holds a BA in International Politics from Penn State University and a MSLS from Clarion University of Pennsylvania. He teaches a Library Studies course in legal research skills online for Penn State's World Campus and can be reached at knapp@psu.edu.

Beth Larkee is Information Technology Librarian at Hollins University in Roanoke, Virginia. She is also the liaison for Math, Computer Science, Psychology, and the Sciences. She can be reached at blarkee@hollins.edu.

John W. LeMasney is Manager of Technology Training at Rider University, where he helps faculty, staff, and students to integrate technology effectively into work, play, teaching, and learning. He also is Instructional Technology Coordinator for the Center for Innovative Instruction at Rider, the dissemination arm of the Teaching and Learning Center. John completed his BFA in Sculpture at the University of the Arts in Philadelphia, and enjoys the creative aspects of any project in which he is involved. He has recently served as Chair for the Ewing (NJ) Township Website Committee, Captain of the Hillwood Manor Community Group, and as Marketing Mentor for the Ewing High School Team 2016 Robotics Team. He enjoys speaking about Open Source Software and Web 2.0 technologies at every opportunity. He is currently pursuing a Master of Arts in Organizational Leadership with a concentration in Communication at Rider University.

Sharon L. Morrison is Library Director at the Henry G. Bennett Memorial Library, Southeastern Oklahoma State University, in Durant, Oklahoma. Since earning a degree in History and Political Science and a MLS, she has been active in the Texas Library Association, the Oklahoma Library Association, the American Library Association, and the Oklahoma Division of the Association of College and Research Libraries. Her professional interests are in library administration, library assessment, and distant education.

Kathleen M. Pierce, PhD, is Associate Professor and Chairperson in the Graduate Education, Leadership, and Counseling Department at Rider University. Having taught high school English for more than 20 years before joining Rider's faculty, she currently teaches courses in English Education and literacy, teaching, and curriculum across subject areas in middle/secondary schools. She also works with student teachers in campus-based seminars and supervises English Language Arts student teachers in the field. Interested in the professional, interpersonal, and institutional dimensions of new teacher induction and mentoring in P-12 and university settings, she has worked through the Center for Innovative Instruction at Rider's Teaching and Learning Center with new and experienced instructors and faculty to create more student-centered classroom engagement.

Lauren Pressley is Instructional Design Librarian at Wake Forest University. She holds a MLIS degree from the University of North Carolina at Greensboro and BA degrees from North Carolina State University in Communication and Philosophy. Her primary professional interests include pedagogy, incorporating instructional design principles in librarianship, the appropriate use of technology, digital literacy, and the future of libraries. She writes about these topics at www.laurenpressley.com.

Tyler Rousseau is Vice President of the Information Technologies section of the New Jersey Library Association. He is particularly interested in examining the use of 2.0 technologies among youth and how this potentially changes the structure in which communications and information are gathered. An avid gamer and graphic novel enthusiast, Tyler enjoys researching the various issues concerning these formats, particularly learning and literacy. He strongly advocates for including these in public libraries and academic settings and regularly speaks on both topics to various organizations and has presented at the NJLA and PaLA annual conferences. Tyler also offers his expertise for consultation to various companies and organizations. When he is not pursuing his dream of being a comic writer, he is Reference Librarian for the Ocean County Library System and writes for the professional blog, Library Garden.

Nicholas Schiller is Library Instruction Coordinator at Washington State University Vancouver and an avid gamer. He presented a paper on instruction design in the game Portal at the 2008 LOEX of the West conference. Together with Carole Svensson he has also taught workshops on providing library instruction to a generation of gamers.

Laura B. Spencer is Reference Librarian at Rutgers University, Camden, New Jersey. A late Boomer with Gen X sympathies, she is neither Luddite nor geek. In her frequent quests for the hardy perennials of human society and culture, she is pleased to employ both old-fashioned and new-fangled methods as needed. She has previously written about end-user searching behavior, interdisciplinarity, and student plagiarism practices.

Carole Svensson is Assistant Director of the Library at the University of Washington, Tacoma.

Art Taylor is a professor in the Computer Information Systems department at Rider University. Prior to this position, he worked in a variety of technical and managerial jobs in the computer industry. Throughout his computer career, he has worked to help businesses find useful information in an ever- increasing sea of data. His personal experience with Gen M includes teaching a variety of students from this generation at the college level for the past six years.

Boris Vilic, Dean of the College of Continuing Studies at Rider University, won the Creative Uses of Technology Award from the Association for Continuing Higher Education in two consecutive years for his projects involving m-Learning. He was also honored with the 2005 Nofflet Williams Up and Coming Leadership Award from the University Continuing Education Association, and the Distinguished Faculty Award from Duquesne University's School of Leadership and Professional Advancement.

Susan L. Webb is Collection Development Librarian at the Henry G. Bennett Memorial Library, Southeastern Oklahoma State University in Durant, Oklahoma. Since earning a BA in Education–Social Science and a Master of Library and Information Science from the University of Oklahoma, she has received certification of Library Media Specialist from the State of Oklahoma Department of Education for Grades K-12, and a Level VII Public Librarian Certification from the State of Oklahoma. She is active in the Oklahoma Library Association, the American Library Association, and the Oklahoma Division of the Association of College and Research Libraries. Her professional interests are in children's and young adult literature, Native American Studies, collection development, information literacy, and lifelong learning.

Index